*The Author*

**ARVIND VIRMANI**, b. June 22, 1949, is Ph.D. in Economics from Harvard University, USA (1975). His thesis supervisor was Nobel Laureate Prof. Kenneth Arrow.

Dr. Virmani is currently Principal Advisor, Planning Commission. He also serves as Chairman, Board of Trustees of SBI Mutual Fund, Member of the Board of Life Insurance Corporation of India and Member, Telecom Regulatory Authority of India (TRAI). He is a Member of the Task Force on "Global Strategic Developments: Implications and Suggested Response" set up by National Security Council Secretariat. He is a Member of the Technical Advisory Committee (TAC) on Money, Foreign Exchange and Government Securities Markets, Reserve Bank of India, February 2004. He was Director and Chief Executive, Indian Council for Research on International Economic Relations (ICRIER), New Delhi. He has served as Senior Economic Advisor in the Department of Economic Affairs, Ministry of Finance. He was Advisor (Policy Planning) to Finance Minister in 1991-92 and 1992-93. Before joining the government he was Senior Economist at the World Bank and was acting chief of the Public Economics Division for a part of this tenure.

He chaired the Working Group on Public Debt Management (middle office) and Inter-Ministerial Group on Customs Duty Reform and was Member- Secretary of the Steering Group on Foreign Investment. He was a Member of the Joint Study Group (JSG) on India-China (and India-Korea) trade and economic cooperation. He served as member of the Appellate Tribunal for the Securities and Exchange Board of India (SEBI) and the Depositories Act. He has served as Director of Punjab National Bank and Allahabad Bank and as Trustee of the Unit Trust of India (UTI). Dr. Virmani was Member of the RBI Technical Advisory Group on Money and Government Security markets, the Steering Group on International Financial Standards and Codes and the UTI committee on reform and stabilisation of the US-64 scheme.

He has researched on Macroeconomics and Growth, International Trade and Tariffs and Credit Markets. He has advised and written extensively on all aspects of economic reforms including the book, *Accelerating Growth and Poverty Reduction: A Policy Framework for India's Development* (Academic Foundation, 2004).

*Propelling India from Socialist Stagnation to Global Power*

***Volume One***

# *Propelling India* from **Socialist Stagnation** to ***Global Power***

**VOLUME 1 : GROWTH PROCESS**

ARVIND VIRMANI

***Academic Foundation***
NEW DELHI

ACADEMIC FOUNDATION

Published in 2006 by
**ACADEMIC FOUNDATION**
4772-73 / 23 Bharat Ram Road, (23 Ansari Road),
Darya Ganj, New Delhi - 110 002 (India).
Phones : 23245001 / 02 / 03 / 04.
Fax : +91-11-23245005.
E-mail : academic@vsnl.com
www.academicfoundation.com



*Propelling India from Socialist Stagnation to Global Power:*
*Volume One: Growth Process*
by Arvind Virmani

**ISBN 81-7188-530-6**

Printed and bound in India

# CONTENTS

## *Volume 1 (the present volume)*



### *Section I*

### Economic Growth: History and Lessons

## *Section II*

## Global Growth, Power and International Relations



## *Section III*

## Political Economy: Social Welfare and Voting

# Contents

## *Volume 2 (the companion volume)*

...CONTD. ...

# List of Figures, Tables, and Appendices

## FIGURES

## TABLES

**APPENDICES**

## Acknowledgements

I am grateful to the late Dr. I.G. Patel for providing me an opportunity to both direct and carry out policy research and to benefit from his great wisdom and intellectual integrity.

I would like to thank Prof. Bishwanath Goldar, Dr. Amita Batra, Dr. Chooriked Veeramani, Dr. Sanghamitra Sahu and Vipul Bhatt the co-authors of some of the chapters in this book.

I would also like to thank my wife Manju who has always provided unstinted support for my research activities.

My thanks also to Manmeet Ahuja for his secretarial assistance.

# Introduction

While serving as Senior Economic Advisor in the Finance Ministry eight years ago, one had been struck by the lack of Indian empirical research in the diverse subjects and topics where advice was needed. On several policy issues one had to depend on an application of theory to the Indian situation, with the only empirical support coming from quantitative studies of other developing countries/ emerging markets. The alternative was to either be swamped by the diverse, micro personal experience based wisdom of administrators or depend on the accumulated transnational wisdom of prominent non-resident Indians. When Dr. I.G. Patel, Chairman of ICRIER raised the possibility of my coming to ICRIER as its Director and Chief Executive in August 2002, it was a welcome opportunity to do something about a situation that one had occasion to lament earlier. The present book is the outcome of three years of policy research at ICRIER.

The book is divided into two volumes: Volume I covers the growth process in India and the role of India in the global economy and polity. Volume II delves in depth into a number of policy issues. The present Volume I is divided into three sections. Section I, has three chapters dealing with different aspects of the Indian economy and a fourth that compares and contrasts the growth experience of China with a view to drawing lessons for India and other countries.

How has the Indian economy performed since Independence? Prof. Raj Krishna popularised the phrase "Hindu rate of growth" in the seventies, during the period of increasing controls and slowing growth rate. K.N. Raj, however, questioned this "so-called 'Hindu' rate of growth," as did other scholars. Nevertheless, there was a widespread belief in the general public, among non-resident Indians and foreigners that the Indian economy was stuck since Independence to the 'Hindu rate of growth', of about 3.5 per cent per annum. This conventional wisdom prevailed throughout the eighties and perhaps into the nineties.

The conventional wisdom changed again around the mid-nineties. The new conventional wisdom was that the 'new economic policy' introduced in 1991-92 had transformed the Indian economy and pushed it from the 'Hindu rate of growth' of 3.5 per cent to a new higher rate that was variously estimated to lie between 5 per cent and 6 per cent. The latter has sometimes been referred to as the 'new Hindu rate of growth'. This new conventional wisdom was also immune to papers such as by the author that demonstrated that the growth acceleration preceded the new economic policy. The paper confirms that, what the author has earlier dubbed, the "Bharatiya Rate of Growth" phase, began around 1980-81.

The most important innovation of the research presented in Section I of this book (chapters 1 and 2) is the use of a rainfall index to remove the confounding effect of large droughts. We use a consistent and better rainfall index than the indices used by the author in previous papers. The second difference from other studies is the use of growth rates (as in author's earlier papers) rather than logs or log differences.

Chapter 1 starts with a macro analysis and overview that sets forth the basic unvarnished facts and sets the record straight. The chapter shows that Indian economic history can be divided into two phases, the first of Socialist stagnation from Independence till the end of 1970s and the second of market reform driven growth acceleration from 1980 to the present. The chapter also confirms that there was a new phase of growth, measured by the rate of growth of the GDP (gross domestic product) at factor cost (GDPfc), starting in 1980-81 which we call the 'Bharatiya rate of growth (BRG)'.

Chapter 2 analyses the data at a greater level of dis-aggregation (sectors, public-private sector and sub-phases). This chapter also explores at a macro level some of the causes of changes in growth trends and variations in performance. We also find that each phase can be further sub-divided into two sub-phases characterised by differences in policy approach and growth performance. One sub-phase of economic growth, dubbed the "Socialist Rate of Growth (SRG)," showed the worst economic performance in India's post-independence history. The two sub-phases of BRG throw up important puzzles regarding the impact of policy changes and economic reforms on growth performance. It attempts to unravel these puzzles, as they need to be resolved for informing the debate on future Indian growth. The chapter also puts the Indian growth performance in an international perspective, to assess how India's growth rate during the different sub-phases compared with that of other countries.

Chapter 3 uses the sources of growth methodology to estimate and evaluate Total Factor Productivity Growth and its links to economic policy. This chapter reviews India's productivity performance that underlines the growth performance since Independence. The primary focus is on estimation of trends in total factor productivity (TFP) for the economy. This information is also used to derive average TFPG for the periods and sub-periods identified in chapter 1 as constituting significant growth episodes in India's economic history. It links changes in TFPG growth to the changes in economic growth analysed in the previous chapter. Subject to the limitations of data availability, an effort is also made to estimate TFPG for all (NAS) sectors of the economy. These are used to estimate their relative contribution to overall productivity growth. Some light is also shed on the contribution of inter-sectoral shifts in factors on TFPG. The analysis deepens our understanding of the collapse of growth during 1965-66 to 1979-80 and its revival from 1980-81.

China is widely and often held up as a paragon of economic policy reform driven growth and an example for others to follow. We, in India, have not been immune to the temptation to do the same. There is no doubt that China has lessons that India and many other countries can learn, lessons that will help improve their growth rate. Some of these lessons have been correctly learned, for instance, those related to the export led growth model adopted by many S.E. Asian and E. Asian countries. On the other hand, China's high investment rate can lead to wrong conclusions if the socialist ownership of assets is ignored. Chapter 4 derives a more balanced picture of China's past success so that better and more fruitful lessons can be drawn for the use of other non-communist countries. In this context, the economic history of India, characterised as it is by 30 years of Indian Socialism, can be quite beneficial as it comes closest to the market based 'Socialism with Chinese characteristics'.

Section II, situates India in the global economy and investigates how the role of India in the world has changed and will change even more dramatically in the next 25 to 50 years. The fast growth of Japan till the seventies, led scholars to predict a "Pacific Century." This talk gradually faded with the bursting of the 'Japanese Bubble', but was revived with the rise of the Asian Tigers. Some called it the, "Asia-Pacific century" while others predicted an "Asian century." Such talk reached its peak before the Asian crisis of 1997-98. In parallel, the world became recognisably unipolar with the collapse of the USSR. Since then talk of multi-polarity has been in the air, joined more recently by sounds of China's challenge to US uni-polarity. This section presents a more radical thesis, i.e. that the world will be transformed into a tripolar one by the middle of this century. It asserts that there is little possibility of the world becoming multi-polar.

One must recognise that long term forecasts have a very high degree of uncertainty. These risks do not, however, disappear if we assume that the future will be like the present (as most people tacitly do). Forecasts are essential for effective planning of national and international security policies. If the projections of the global economy given in this section approximate reality, they will have profound implications for the USA, India, European Union (EU) and Japan and the emergence of a new international order.

Though economic relations have to be grounded in economic facts, economic laws and economic impact, international relations go beyond these to incorporate geopolitical and other issues. This section draws inspiration from this literature, and attempts to link and ground geopolitical interactions in economic reality. The starting point of the analysis is the economic size of the nation states and their relative economic power. The section starts by analysing past trends and ends by projecting them into the future to define a global economic scenario for the next 30 years. Implications are then drawn for geo-political evolution.

State power is the "extent that [one] affects others more than they affect [one]" (Waltz, 1979). It is, therefore, a "combination of its capacity to resist the unwelcome influence of others and conversely to influence others to behave as it wants them to." International relations experts have been divided on the relative importance of economic strength and military might in the global power of a nation. Levy (1983), Mearshiemer (2001) and others have emphasised the importance of military power. Kennedy (1988) and others have emphasised the importance of economic factors. We resolve this conflict by decomposing national power into two elements: (a) The 'power potential' of a country, which depends on economic strength and general technological capability, and (b) military/strategic capability. This includes defence and strategic equipment and specific technologies needed for attaining military superiority. Together, these define the actual power of a country. International ambition and determination, the 'will to power', play a role in transforming the 'power potential' into 'actual power'.

The first chapter in this section (chapter 5) gives a simple overview of the past and future world economy and the emerging global power structure based on the other three chapters, which cover the issues in greater detail.

Chapter 6 proposes a definition of economic power that can be widely applied using easily available published data. A simple index of 'power potential' is presented based on concepts from growth theory that are familiar to economists but not previously applied to the strategic arena. It calculates the value of this index for all the medium and large countries in the world (over 100) and uses it to show which countries have the potential to be regional and global powers. Using economic forecasts made in subsequent chapters, it also shows, which countries are likely to have the potential over the next 20 years to emerge as global powers, and how the balance of power will change during this period. The chapter also defines an index of actual power (VIP) based on $VIP^2$, which requires a separate measure of military/strategic capability.

Chapter 7 defines and discusses the principles on which a fair and just global governance structure must be based. It argues that the relative power potential defined in the previous chapter, represents the 'natural power potential' of a nation. It is argued that the system of global governance must be based on a fair sharing of the rights and responsibilities and that the 'natural power potential' represents such a fair metric. If global power is shared in proportion to this power potential, not only will it be fair, it will also give the right incentive to nation states to compete in terms of economic advancement rather than in terms of military might. As many have written before, the current UN system reflects neither the current economic realities nor the democratic impulse that has characterised the 20th century. It goes on to define certain principles and then applies them to show what a reformed system of global governance, including UN General Assembly and the UN Security Council, would look like, based on the relative position in 2002.

Chapter 8 focuses on the emerging global power structures and forecasts that the current unipolar world will become bipolar by 2025 and tripolar by 2050, with India becoming the third most powerful country in the world. The chapter revises and extends the projections of chapter 7 to 2050. It explores the implications of the developments in the global economy and in national power potential during the first half of the 21st century. It concludes that the current unipolar world will be transformed into a bipolar world during the first quarter of this century and into a tripolar one (China, USA, India) during the second quarter of the century. If these projections come true, such a development will have implications for the USA, India, EU and Japan.

The projections of economic size and power potential show that tectonic shifts are under way and will occur over the first half of the 21st century. These will result in a shift in global economic and political power. Asia, in particular China, followed a decade later by India, will become an important driver of world economic growth. The weight of the world economy will gradually shift from the Atlantic to the Pacific and from Europe to Asia. Within Asia, the relative weight of China and India will rise and that of Japan will decline. This will mean a dilution of the super-power status of the USA and possibly a move to a bipolar world (China) followed gradually by the emergence of tripolarity as India begins to catch up with China. Eventual multi-polarity would depend on the emergence of the EU as a virtual Nation State with independent defence forces and taxation power. Because of the very sharp ascent of China, the relative decline of the USA and a large gap between China and the rest of Asia, the second quarter of the 21st century will be a period of heightened risk to peace in Asia. Use of an alternative parameter to represent power potential, however, yields a different sub-scenario in which the world will remain unipolar for at least 25 years.

The USA, EU and India are democratic, free and culturally open societies that share fundamental human values. It will be in the interests of the USA and EU to strengthen India's economic and technological capability over the next two decades for mutual benefit, peace and stability in Asia. The scenarios presented in this chapter are merely one among many possibilities that so often surprise forecasters. The USA, EU, Japan, India and other democratic countries can by their enlightened and determined actions help bring about a world that is much more beneficial to all its citizens than is suggested by some of these scenarios.

The chapters of this section recommended the formation of an Asian Economic Community, patterned on the (former) European Economic Community, with China, India and Japan at its core and including other countries of Asia. Such an inclusive and co-operative venture would draw upon the experience of European history and of the EU to minimise the risk of conflict in Asia. Improved bilateral relations between India and China, which hold great importance for peace and stability in Asia, would facilitate the building of such a regional organisation.

The section also recommends the formation of an Indo-US partnership for peace. One element of this partnership would be a comprehensive economic co-operation agreement. Such a partnership would require a change in the attitude of the governing elite in both countries and a mutual recognition of each other's fundamental national interest. To become effective and mutually beneficial, it also requires changes in laws, rules and bureaucratic procedures that affect the other country. Till such a genuine and balanced (broadly equal) partnership emerges, intensified technological collaboration between Russia, UK, Germany, France and Japan (on one hand) and India (on the other) will remain important.

The research papers on which this section was based presaged a historic transformation of the Indo-US relationship. If the framework agreements reached so far are implemented in their entirety, they will transform the role of India in Asia and the globe over the next 20 years or so and mark President Bush and Prime Minister Dr. Manmohan Singh in the history books.

The last two chapters 9 and 10 in this section, written with Dr. Amita Batra, explore the potential of India's relations with ASEAN and China respectively.

Section III concludes the book with a chapter that develops a model of voting behaviour based on the economic concepts of social behaviour. After every election there is a spate of articles on whether economic reforms were or were not responsible for the fall of the incumbent government. Many theories are floated to explain the voting behaviour of the public. The recent general election was no exception. Though we are not in the business of forecasting elections, we do believe that good theoretical and empirical analysis can and should be brought to bear on all issues that may affect economic reform and policy change, in the interests of the nation.

This chapter attempts to relate standard economic analysis of consumer utility to voting behaviour. It then goes on to authenticate (not test) the model against the results of the 2004 elections. At this stage, the model remains a hypothesis. It would have to be subjected to much more thorough testing before we can give it the status of a theory. Nevertheless, given the publicly available data it provides an interesting explanation of the 2004 election results in India and a useful starting point for more refined and perhaps even much better models of voter behaviour.

The overall message of the book is that we have shed some of the legacy of the socialist past and have been moving forward at a faster clip with market reforms. The role of government and its method of functioning needs to be changed for a new phase to begin. Some of the required reforms are spelt out in Volume II. With continuing reforms, India is well on the way to becoming a global power in the next 25 years.

# Section I

## Economic Growth:
## History and Lessons

# 1

# India's Economic Growth

## *Fluctuations Trends, Break Points and Phases*

## 1. INTRODUCTION

How has the Indian economy performed since Independence? Prof. Raj Krishna popularised the phrase "Hindu rate of growth" in the seventies, during the period of increasing controls and slowing growth rate.[1] K.N. Raj (1984) however questioned this "so-called 'Hindu' rate of growth," hypothesis. Patnaik (1987) and Dhar (1988) discerned some acceleration of growth in the eighties, while Virmani (1989a) asserted a break in the GDP growth rate from 1980–81. Nagaraj (1990) and Bhargava and Joshi (1990) did not find the break statistically significant. Dandekar (1992) concluded that the evidence of a break 'can not be rejected'. Ahluwalia (1995) also noted the increase in growth rate during the eighties.[2] Nevertheless, there was a widespread belief in the general public, among non-resident Indians and foreigners that the Indian economy was stuck since Independence in the 'Hindu rate of growth', of about 3.5 per cent per annum. This conventional wisdom prevailed throughout the eighties and perhaps into the nineties.[3]

The conventional wisdom changed again around the mid-nineties. The new conventional wisdom was that the 'new economic policy' introduced in 1991–92 had transformed the Indian economy and pushed it from the 'Hindu rate of growth' of 3.5 per cent to a new higher rate that was variously estimated to lie between 5 per cent and

1. B.P.R. Vithal was perhaps the first to refer to Hindu culture as in some way affecting economic development. My thanks to Y.V. Reddy and Sanjaya Baru for this information.
2. But did not try to prove it statistically.
3. This was reflected in domestic and foreign newspapers and magazine articles.

6 per cent. The latter has sometimes been referred to as the 'new Hindu rate of growth.' This new conventional wisdom was also immune to papers such as Virmani (1997b and 1997c) that demonstrated that the growth acceleration preceded the new economic policy. While Bhagwati (1998) acknowledges the higher growth rate of the eighties, he does not consider the 1980s as a new phase in Indian development because he believes that the unsustainable policies of the eighties led to the 1990-91 BoP crisis. Only recently has this been explicitly recognised (DeLong, 2001; Williamson and Zagha, 2002 and Acharya, 2002).[4] The chapter confirms that, what the author has earlier dubbed, the "Bharatiya Rate of Growth" phase, began around 1980-81.[5]

The most important innovation of this chapter is the use of a rainfall index to remove the confounding effect of large droughts. A consistent and better rainfall index has been used than the indices used by the author in previous papers.[6] The second difference from other studies is the use of growth rates (as in the author's earlier papers) rather than logs or log differences. We have examined the growth of total GDP as well as its major sub-aggregates (Agriculture, Manufacturing, Services) from 1950-51 onwards (growth rates from 1951-52), using the consistent GDP data from the new series of national accounts statistics.

The chapter is structured as follows. Section 2 outlines the simple methodology used in the chapter. Section 3 analyses the historical growth experience of the Indian economy in terms of fluctuations and trends. Further, it examines structural breaks in growth trends. These breaks define the border between different phases of growth. A new phase of growth, the Market Reform phase, started in 1980-81. Section 4 outlines the policy changes that characterise the two phases of economic growth. Section 5 concludes the chapter.

---

4. Virmani (2004b) and Wallack (2003) also formally showed the break in GDP and NNP series respectively.
5. The word 'Bharatiya' was used as a counterpoise to 'Hindu' and has no other significance. An alternative term could be the 'Indian' rate of growth, though personally, the author would like to reserve that term for a future third phase in which India's growth rate is 7% + on a sustained basis.
6. Virmani (1989a), Virmani (1997a) and Virmani (1997b).

## 2. METHODOLOGY

The analysis throughout the volume is based on rates of growth. The annual rate of growth (GrY) is defined for any variable Y as, GrY(t) = Y(t)/Y(t-1) – 1. Trend growth rates are defined in three ways:

(a) By taking a moving average. Thus, a five year moving average can be defined as MA5Y(t) = [Y(t)+Y(t-1)+Y(t-2)+Y(t-3) +Y(t-4)]/5. This moving average is centred on year t-2.

(b) By applying the Hoderick-Prescott filter to the basic series Y to get the filtered series Xhp and then determining its growth rate i.e. GrYhp(t) = Yhp(t)/Yhp(-1) –1. GrYhp(t) then shows the trend rate of growth as against the actual annual growth rate GrY(t).

(c) By fitting a polynomial of order 2 or 3 or more to the actual growth rate GrY(t) i.e. estimating the coefficients a, b, c (d etc.) in the equation $GrY(t) = a + bt + ct^2 (+ dt^3) + ut$, where t is time or year and ut is a random error term.

We also use growth regressions to search for breaks in the growth performance of the economy. Conceptually, the evolution of the economy can be defined by a set of (endogenous) variables such as GDP, current account deficit, foreign exchange reserves, fiscal deficit, exports, imports, prices, money supply, employment etc. Each of the endogenous variables (vector Y) are functions of each other and of exogenous variables. The latter consist of policy variables P (e.g. tariff rates) and external environment Z (e.g. rainfall, world oil prices, world GDP growth). In reduced form we can write the endogenous variables as functions of the exogenous variables, Y = F (P, Z).

In the Indian context, the most important exogenous variable Z is rainfall variation and we take account of this variable in examining GDP growth and growth of GDP from different sectors. Other exogenous variables, such as oil price shocks have been thought to affect the growth of the economy, but the rate of growth of oil prices is found to be statistically insignificant in the GDP growth regressions.[7] Therefore Y = F (P, rainfall). There are two difficulties

7. When growth rate of world oil prices is added to equation (1) of text, its t statistic is -1.4 and Probability 0.167, *i.e.* it is not significant at the 10 per cent level of confidence.

that arise in directly introducing policy variables into the estimating equation. Firstly, continuous series are not available from 1950 to the current time. For instance, the average tariff rate is available from 1980 onwards, but not before. The second problem is that some variables may be either exogenous policy variables (P) or endogenous outcomes (Y), depending on the policy regime. Thus, for instance, in a controlled system the exchange rate and many interest rates are directly controlled policy variables set by the government while in a market system they are outcomes of market supply and demand. The difficulty is compounded if they are target variables even in the market situation. These technical problems can be dealt with by appropriate econometric techniques. In this chapter, however, we take an alternative simpler route.

We assume that different periods (i) in India's history were characterised by different sets of policies Pi. For instance, if there were four periods, then i= 1, 2, 3, 4. To find out whether any set of policies Pi had an effect on the growth rate, we introduce a dummy variable Di into the equation to represent the policies during the period (the time subscript t is dropped):

$$GrY = A + B^*Drainm + Di + U$$

Where Drainm is the per cent deviation of rainfall from mean and U is the error term.[8] We use the Parthasarthy *et al.* (1995) all India rainfall index to take account of rainfall fluctuations. This is an area-weighted index of average rain during the monsoon months of June to September.

If Di for period i is statistically significant, we take this as a demonstration of a significant effect of the complex of policies Pi pursued on the growth of Y during the period. The policies Pi are then analysed in a qualitative way. Formal modelling of the effect of policies on endogenous variables and its econometric estimation is pursued in subsequent chapters.

As far as Y is concerned, it should be kept in mind that total GDP is by definition the sum of the GDP from different sectors (e.g. agriculture, manufacturing and services). Thus, a policy that affects even one sector will affect the overall GDP growth through this sector.

---

8. i.e. (current-average)/average.

Some polices may affect more than one sector, with the relative effect on these sectors varying over time. A given policy may also affect one sector positively and another negatively. In this case, the effect on overall GDP growth may be either positive or negative. A set of policies will, in general, have positive and negative effects on different sectors, with the net effect on overall GDP being an aggregation of these sectoral impacts. The dummy variable method will only indicate the net affect of all these policies and will not help us in identifying which policy has a positive and which a negative effect on a specific sector (or on aggregate GDP).

Though the GDP series is far from perfect, its construction involves fewer *ad hoc* assumptions (of questionable economic validity) than other series such as NDP, GNP and NNP. In our analysis, therefore, Y is Gross Domestic Product at factor cost.

## 3. GDP GROWTH TRENDS

The section starts by showing the rainfall driven fluctuations in GDP growth. It then examines the growth trends in the Indian economy since Independence to determine what, if any, breaks there have been in growth performance. It then goes on to statistically determine the break points, which form the dividing line between different phases of economic growth. Subsequent sub-sections investigate as to what extent the break in overall growth trends was due to a break in the growth trend of agriculture, manufacturing and services.

### 3.1 Rainfall Fluctuations and Growth Trends

Figure 1.1 shows the links between rainfall fluctuation and fluctuations in GDP growth. It is clear that the latter cannot be explained without taking account of the former. It also shows that in the first 30 years there were four years in which the annual rate of growth was negative, and another four in which it was between 0 per cent and 2 per cent. In the subsequent 22 years, there was no year of negative growth and only one year in which economic growth was between 0 per cent and 2 per cent. The average growth rate was, therefore, higher during this second phase.

Figure 1.2 show the annual growth rate of the economy, the growth trend in the HP (Hodrick-Prescott) filtered GDP series and the moving average of the growth rates over half the century. Two phases are clearly discernible, with the second phase having a significantly higher rate of economic growth than the first. The five-year moving average is centred on the given year, while the 10-year moving average has five earlier and four later years. The growth trend as measured by the HP-filtered series reached a low point of 3.3 per cent per annum during the first phase (1971–72 to 1973–74) and a high point of 6.1 per cent per annum during the second phase (1994–95 to 1995–96). Thereafter, the trend growth rate has declined continuously (see HP filtered series). The 10-year moving average fluctuated between 3 per cent and 4 per cent during the first 30 years with occasional forays below (twice) and above (thrice) this band. Starting from 1978–79 there was a clear and unambiguous up trend in the 10-year moving average and it never fell below 4 per cent. On the contrary it exceeded 5 per cent from 1985–86 onwards (Figure 1.2).

## FIGURE 1.1

*Rainfall Variation and Annual GDP Growth Rate Fluctuation*

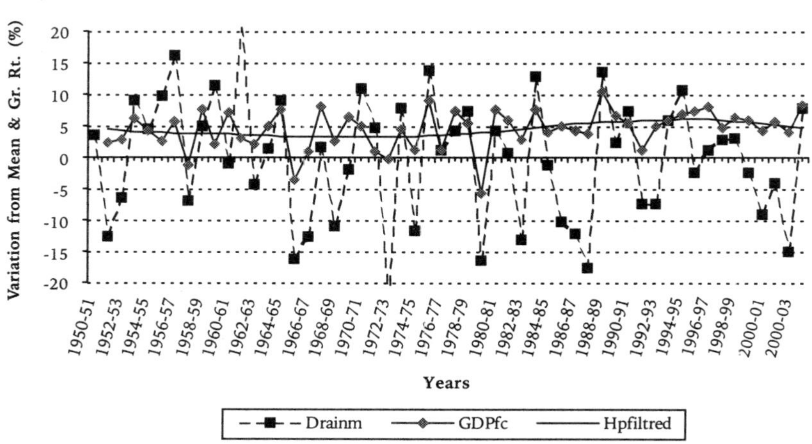

## FIGURE 1.2

*GDP Growth Rates:*
*Moving Average and Hodrick-Prescott Filtered Series*

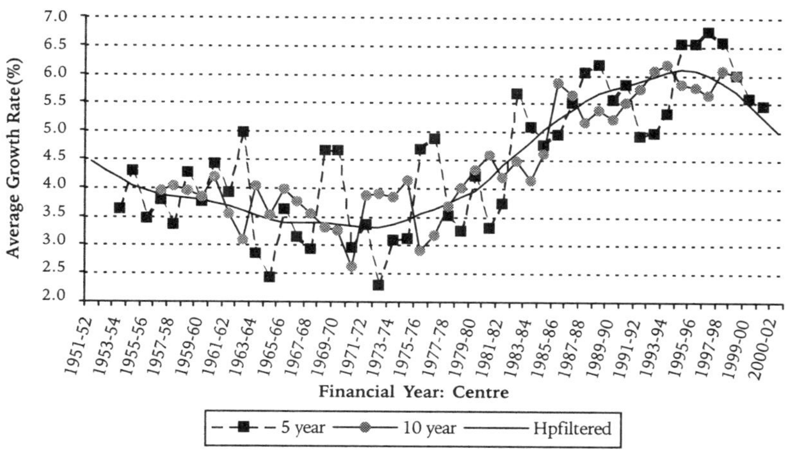


To find the precise dividing line between these two phases (the year T in which the first phase ended) one can look at the nature of the prevailing development regime or the nature of the growth experience or a combination of both. First, consider what happens to the average growth rate and the co-efficient of variation (CV) of the growth rates of phase I (1950-51 to T) relative to phase II (T to 2002-03) as we change the year T (Figure 1.3).[9] There is a clear break in both the mean and CV if phase I ends in 1978-79. The relative CV falls sharply from 0.7 if T = 1978-79 to 0.3 if T = 1979-80. The relative mean correspondingly rises from 1.4 to 1.65. This is the lowest relative CV and the highest relative mean seen in Figure 1.3, suggesting that phase I ends in 1978-79.

---

9. CV = Standard deviation/Mean.

## FIGURE 1.3

*GDP Growth Rates:*
*Moving Average and Hodrick-Prescott Filtered Series*

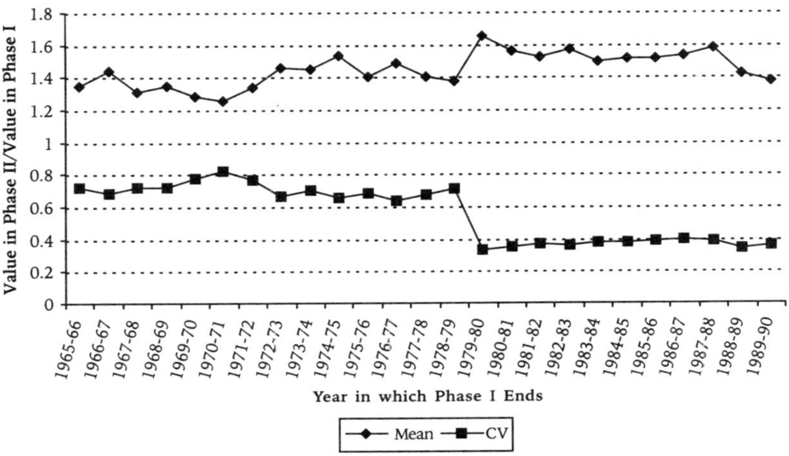


### 3.2 Break Points in GDP Growth

Given this picture of fluctuations and trends, the most important requirement is to purge the growth data of the effects of rainfall fluctuations. In this chapter, we do this by running growth regressions and testing for changes in growth rate. The chow test can also be applied to the coefficients obtained in these regressions.

Equation (1) presents the results for a standard regression for the period 1950-2002, with the growth rate of the GDP at factor cost (GrGDPfc) on the left-hand side. The severe droughts of 1965-66 and 1966-67 and 1979-80 can lead to misleading results if the rainfall is not accounted for. We, therefore, introduce the deviation of current rainfall from the mean for the entire period, Drainm as an exogenous variable on the right hand side of the growth regression.

Separating the effect of trends in rainfall allows a more accurate determination of underlying growth trends, particularly if the end point is a drought year.

$$\text{GrGDPfc} = \underset{(13.8)}{0.045} + \underset{(5.0)}{0.161}*\text{DrainM} - \underset{(-3.5)}{0.117}*\text{DrainM}(-1) \qquad (1)$$

$R^2 = 0.447$, $R^2$ (adjusted) $= 0.425$, DW $= 2.029$, and the numbers in parentheses are t-statistics. This is a rather remarkable result. It says that about 45 per cent of the variation in India's GDP growth is explained by the fluctuations in rainfall. Only 55 per cent of the growth fluctuation remains to be explained by the conventional set of exogenous shocks and policy variables.

The Chow test on this equation clearly reveals a break in the growth rate in 1980-81 with the null hypothesis rejected at an F value of 5.562 (probability 0.0024). 1981-82 is however a close second with an F of 5.347 (Pr=0.003). The log likelihood ratio is 16.1 and 15.6 for 1980-81 and 1981-82 break respectively. A 1979-80 break is much less plausible as the F value is much lower at 2.88 (Pr=0.045) for 1979-80.

We now add a dummy for 1980-81 onwards (D80+) on the right-hand side to get

$$\begin{aligned}\text{GrGDPfc} = {} & \underset{(12.0)}{0.0345} + \underset{(5.2)}{0.023}*(\text{D80+}) + \underset{(6.7)}{0.190}*\text{DrainM} \\ & - \underset{(-3.6)}{0.104}*\text{DrainM}(-1) - \underset{(2.1)}{0.303}*\text{AR}(1)\end{aligned} \qquad (2)$$

$R^2 = 0.623$, $R^2$ (adjusted) $= 0.590$, DW $=2.054$.

Regression (2) confirms that the growth rate increased from 1980–81. We also define Drainm80 = Drainm*D80+ and estimate the following equation to test for changes in the coefficients from 1980-81 onwards.

$$\begin{aligned}\text{GrGDPfc} = {} & \underset{(12.2)}{0.0349} + \underset{(5.2)}{0.023}*(\text{D80+}) + \underset{(5.9)}{0.218}*\text{DrainM} \\ & - \underset{(-3.5)}{0.124}*\text{DrainM}(-1) - \underset{(-2.3)}{0.339}*\text{AR}(1) \\ & - \underset{(-1.23)}{0.072}*\text{Drainm80} + \underset{(+0.98)}{0.060}*\text{Drainm80}(-1)\end{aligned} \qquad (3)$$

$R^2 = 0.638$, $R^2$ (adjusted) $= 0.589$, DW $=2.044$.

The two new variables are found to be insignificant, while all variables present in equation (2) remain significant with their coefficients virtually unchanged. Thus, we conclude that there is no break in the effect of rainfall on the growth rate from 1980-81 onwards and we can use equation (2) for further analysis. Before doing so however, let us consider one puzzle that this gives rise to.

We know that the share of GDP from agriculture has been declining continuously since Independence. Then how is it possible that the effect of rainfall on GDP has remained unchanged for over five decades. We confront this question directly by taking agriculture's share of GDP and regressing it on time to determine the time trend of the decline. We then multiply Drainm by this forecast share of agriculture (Sagf say) to get Drainm(adj) = Sagf*Drainm. If equation 1, 2 and 3 are re-estimated using this variable instead of Drainm (4, 5 and 2'a say) the $R^2$ is marginally lower in every case but the results are virtually identical.[10] It is, therefore, clear that (from 3 and 2'a) that there is no break in the impact of rainfall variation on the growth of GDP. The equations 4 and 5, in contrast to 1 and 2, however, show that the impact of rainfall variation has been declining with the share of agriculture in GDP.

$$\text{GrGDPfc} = \underset{(13.6)}{0.0449} + \underset{(4.8)}{0.4137}\text{*Drainm(adj)} - \underset{(-3.4)}{0.294}\text{*Drainm(adj)(-1)} \quad (4)$$

$R^2$ = 0.436, $R^2$ (adjusted) = 0.412, DW = 2.09.

$$\text{GrGDPfc} = \underset{(11.7)}{0.0345} + \underset{(5.1)}{0.0227}\text{*D80} + \underset{(6.5)}{0.50}\text{*Drainm(adj)} \quad (5)$$
$$- \underset{(-3.6)}{0.28}\text{*Drainm(adj)(-1)} - \underset{(2.24)}{0.316}\text{*AR(1)}$$

$R^2$ = 0.61, $R^2$ (adjusted) = 0.58, DW =2.07.

Though statistically we cannot distinguish between 1 and 4 or 2 and 5, if rainfall was affecting aggregate GDP only through the agriculture supply channel we would have expected the $R^2$ and fit to be better for 4 and 5 than for 1 and 2 respectively. The result suggests that while the supply (production) side impact is declining, the demand side effects are increasing and offsetting this factor. As

10. As Sag averaged 0.366 from 1950 to 2003, we expect the co-efficients on Drainm*Sag to be 2.7 times those on Drainm. As 2'a is identical to the others, it is not printed (to save space).

agricultural income rises above subsistence we expect the demand for non-agricultural goods by those whose primary income source is agriculture, to rise sharply. This is reflected in the rising share of manufactured goods and services in the consumption basket. Another channel through which rainfall affects GDP is through other sectors such as electricity (hydro) and this could also be a contributory factor.

A significant experiment with a coalition government ended in 1979–80 and the Congress(I) party returned to power in 1980–81. The recognition that the controls and subsidies introduced by the Congress governments during the earlier phase were not serving their intended purpose, had gradually dawned on the establishment during the late seventies.[11] The new government gradually initiated a new approach to economic management. We, therefore, take 1979-80 as the end of the first development phase and 1980-81 as the start of the next.

The issue of stagnation or deceleration in Indian growth after 1965–66 has been the subject of much debate and analysis. According to Bhagwati and Srinivasan (1984), Srinivasan and Narayana (1977), was the first paper "to analyse the growth stagnation of the Indian economy since the mid-sixties". Other papers to discuss these issues were Bhagwati and Srinivasan (1984), Chakravarty (1984), Raj (1984), Dhar (1988), Nagaraj (1990), Bhargava and Joshi (1990). We, therefore, investigate the possibility of a break in the sixties. Chow stability tests on equation (1) show a possible break point around 1963-64 with an F value of 2.09 (prob=0.11) and a log likelihood ratio of 6.64 (probability 0.084) with marginally lower values of F and log likely hood in 1962-63 and 1964-65. These values are however much lower than for the breakpoint at 1980-81(above). A joint Chow test for 1980-81 and 1963-64 (etc.) yields a singular matrix.

We, therefore, use growth regression analyses equation (2) and introduce another dummy for 1965-66 to 1979-80.[12] Dummies with a starting year of 1963-64 etc. were also tried. All these dummies turn out to be non-significant. Other papers have suggested breaks in the

---

11. The Dagli Committee on Controls and Subsidies, set up by the coalition government which was aware of the problem, submitted its Report in 1979-80.

12. We continue to use equation (2) as a base equation in preference to 2a because it is the simpler and straight-forward one and has a marginally better fit. Introduction of dummy for 1965-1979 into 2a gives identical results.

seventies. Dummy variables for potential breaks in 1971–72 and 1975–76 are however, found to be even less significant. To summarise, there are no statistically significant breaks in GDP growth from 1951-52 to 1979-80 once the 1980-81 break is accounted for. This result implies that any policy conclusions drawn on the basis of a presumed slowdown in the sixties and/or seventies are likely to be wrong! Further, studies on the determinants of India's growth based on old data could be highly misleading from the current perspective. Only policy analysis for this period that takes account of the rainfall fluctuations and reduced rainfall during 1965-66 to 1979-80 will be credible.

Figure 1.4 indicates why this may be so. If we divide the entire period of phase I into two sub-phases ending in different years, and measure the relative CV of the two sub-phases we find a sharp change in 1965-66. The CV of sub-phase IB relative to that of sub-phase IA falls from 2.3, if the end-year for sub-phase IA is 1964-65, to 1.3 if the end-year is 1965-66. The relative mean, however, changes by a very small amount. Thus, the break is more in terms of the degree of variability of growth rather than in terms of the mean growth rate (Figure 1.4).

**FIGURE 1.4**

*Pattern of Change of Relative Mean and CV (Sub-phases) with Dividing Year T*

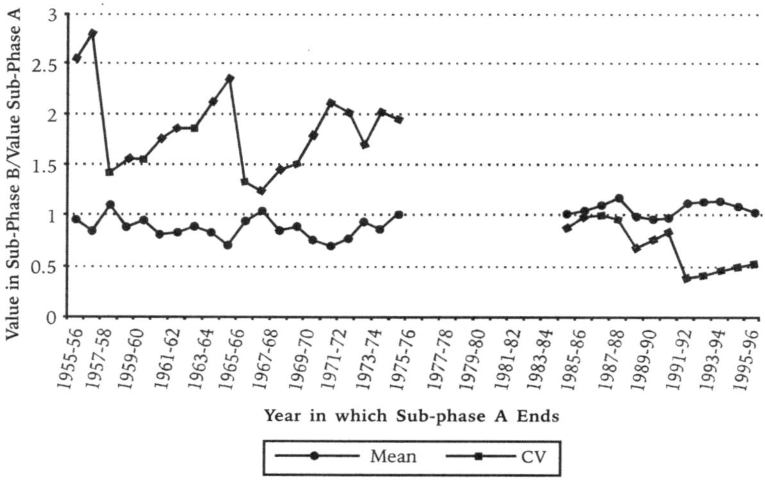

The economic reforms in 1991-1992, and the high growth rates that followed thereafter, led to widespread speculation and assertion that India had entered a new phase of growth and development with the enactment of radical new economic policy framework in 1991-92.[13] It is, therefore, important to determine whether a new phase started in 1991 or 1992 or whether the phase that started in 1980–81 continues till today. We, therefore, investigate for a possible break at the end of the eighties/beginning of the nineties using equation (1). The Chow test shows a significant value for F and Log likelihood ratio in 1989-90 and 1992-93 but these values are lower than for the 1980-81 break. Thus, for the potential 1989-90 breakpoint the F value is 3.22 (probability 0.031) and likelihood 9.934 (probability 0.019). Both these fall sharply in 1990-91 and 1991-92 and then rise in 1992-93 to 3.37 (prob=0.026) and 10.3 (prob=0.015). When, however, the Chow test is used on equation (2) i.e. along with the 1980-81 dummy, it yields a singularity (near singular matrix).

We, therefore, have to test for breaks using equation (2) with an additional dummy for the period 1991-92 to 2002-03 (D91+) or for the period 1992-93 to 2002-03 (D92+). In each case the additional dummy is found to be non-significant while D80 (1980-81 to 2002-03) remains strongly significant (as are others starting in 1990-91). An alternative formulation with D80 replaced by two dummies for 1980-81 to 1991-92 and 1992-93 to 2002-03 shows that the coefficients on these are virtually identical. Therefore, we find no additional breakpoint in the nineties, once the breakpoint in 1980-81 is accounted for.

## 3.3 Agricultural Slowdown or Green Revolution?

There has been a suspicion that the drop in GDP growth from 1965-66 is due to the fall in agricultural growth from the mid-sixties. Further, it was felt that the introduction of the Green Revolution thereafter (around the early seventies) led to a fundamental change in the growth potential of agriculture. We, therefore, test statistically for break points using the following equation for the growth rate of GDP from agriculture (GrGDPag):

---

13. For instance, in Investment Bank research reports and economic newspapers and magazines.

$$\text{GrGDPag} = \underset{(4.8)}{0.03} + \underset{(5.9)}{0.36}\text{*Drainm} - \underset{(-5.3)}{0.34}\text{*Drainm(-1)} \quad (6)$$

$R^2$ = 0.58, $R^2$ (adjusted) = 0.56, DW = 2.93.

The Chow test using this equation reveals a potential breakpoint at 1964-65, with an F = 3.583 (probability 0.0207) and Log likelihood ratio = 10.921 (probability (0.031). The F is also above 3 for 1963-64 and 1962-63, while the Log likelihood ratio is above 10 for 1963-64. These values are much higher than found for a breakpoint for GDP around these years. However, when we introduce a dummy for 1964-65 onwards (or for 1950-51 to 1963-64), we find that it is insignificant.

Because of the significant auto-correlation in equation (6), we also estimate an alternative specification as follows:

$$\text{GrGDPag} = \underset{(8.0)}{0.029} + \underset{(7.26)}{0.3885}\text{*Drainm} - \underset{(-6.67)}{0.372}\text{*Drainm(-1)} \underset{(-3.93)}{-0.492}\text{ AR(1)} \quad (7)$$

$R^2$ = 0.686, $R^2$ (adjusted) = 0.666, DW = 2.27

The Chow test using this equation reveals a potential break point at 1962-63, with an F = 3.31 (probability 0.0189) and Log likelihood ratio = 11.59 (probability (0.021). The F is 1.47 for 1961-62 while the Log likelihood ratio is above 6.55. The value for 1962-63 is much higher than found for a break point for GDP in the mid-sixties. However, when we introduce a dummy for 1962-63 onwards (or for 1950-51 to 1961-62), we find that it is insignificant. Alternative dummies for 1963-64, 1964-65 etc. are also insignificant. If we apply the Chow test for these years, we find that the F value falls to about 1 for 1967-68 to 1980-81 and is lower than one for any potential break points thereafter (up to the 1990s).[14] Thus, we do not find any statistical break in the growth of GDP from agriculture during the 53-year period, once the variations in rainfall are accounted for.

When Drainm80 and its lagged value are introduced into the right hand side of equation (7) their coefficients are found to be

14. A similar equation is also estimated for manufacturing growth: Using this equation Chow tests for growth break for 1980-81 shows an F = 1.653 (0191) and LLR = 5.33 (0.149). The values become even less significant for 1979-80 and 1981-82.

insignificant. This confirms that there is no statistically significant change in the effect of rainfall variations on GDP from agriculture even after 1980-81.

### 3.4 Manufacturing

The same exercise was repeated for the manufacturing sector with similar results. The basic equation with GrGman as the rate of growth of GDP from manufacturing, is as follows:

$$GrGman = \underset{(12.2)}{0.059} + \underset{(2.68)}{0.127}{*}Drainm \qquad (8)$$

$R^2$ = 0.126, $R^2$ (adjusted) = 0.108, DW = 1.63.

This is tested using the Chow test for the years from 1979 to 1987. We find a potential break point at 1981 [F=2.02 (Pr=0.14)]. To confirm this we introduce D81 the dummy for 1981-82 to 2002-03 into this equation:

$$GrGman = \underset{(8.3)}{0.051} + \underset{(2.03)}{0.019}{*}D81 + \underset{(3.03)}{0.14}{*}Drainm \qquad (9)$$

$R^2$ = 0.194, $R^2$ (adjusted) = 0.181, DW = 1.75.

This shows that the growth rate of manufacturing accelerated after 1980-81. This contributed to the acceleration of the rate of growth of GDP from 1981-82.

Ahluwalia (1985, 1991) has analysed the stagnation in growth of value added in the registered manufacturing sector (ASI & IIP) since the mid-sixties and the turnaround in growth in early eighties in terms of trends in TFPG growth in this sector. In the current context we can therefore find out whether there was a statistically significant decline in the growth of (total) GDP from manufacturing between the mid-sixties and the end-seventies. A dummy for the period 1965-66 to 1979-80 (D6579) is introduced into equation (8). Its co-efficient is found to be significant at the 10 per cent level. The best fit is however found with the dummy for 1965-66 to 1980-81 (D6580) whose co-efficient is highly significant:

$$GrGman = \underset{(12.1)}{0.066} + \underset{(-2.54)}{-0.0252}{*}D6580 + \underset{(2.53)}{0.114}{*}Drainm \qquad (10)$$

$R^2$ = 0.228, $R^2$ (adjusted) = 0.196, DW = 1.74.

This equation establishes that there was a reduction of 2.5 per cent per annum in the growth rate of manufacturing during 1965-66 to 1980-81. In general this could have been due either to the policies we followed or to external/exogenous factors. In our view, the policies followed during 1965-66 to 1979-80 (combined with the accumulating costs of policies followed earlier), reduced the rate of growth of manufacturing by 2.5 per cent points during the period 1965-66 to 1980-81.

If we compare this equation with (9) containing the dummy D81 (1981-82 to 2002-03) we find that the (10) has greater explanatory power. Further, when both dummies are included simultaneously D6580 has greater significance than D81.[15] This suggests that the removal of some of the constraints/barriers to growth imposed during 1965-66 to 1979-80 had a greater role in the acceleration of manufacturing growth from 1981-82 than the stimulation of new growth impulses from 1981-82 onwards. We will examine this issue below, in greater detail.

### 3.5 Services

Virmani (2002c) showed that non-tradable services have played an important role in the growth of the Indian economy since 1950. It is useful to investigate a potential break out in the growth of non-tradable services (GrGntrdbl). To ensure that the changes are not due to government administration or the way these are measured we also use non-tradable services excluding GDP from government administration (GrGserv). The basic equation is:

$$\text{GrGntrdbl} = \underset{(11.8)}{0.058} + \underset{(1.82)}{0.039}\text{*Drainm} + \underset{(4.00)}{0.501}\ \text{AR}(1) \qquad (11)$$

$$R^2 = 0.287,\ R^2\ \text{(adjusted)} = 0.257,\ DW = 2.10.$$

The Chow test using equation (11) reveals potential breakpoints in every year from 1980-81 to 1985-86. The highest probability of a break is however found for 1985-86 with an F = 5.28 (probability 0.003) and Log likelihood ratio = 15.37 (probability 0.0015). These values and probabilities are similar to those found for the GDP growth break point in 1980-81. In this case, however, the F value is higher

15. T = 1.57 (prob = 12.3%) *versus* t = 0.67 (prob = 50%).

than 4 and log likelihood ratio higher than 12 for all years from 1980-81 to 1985-86. To confirm the break point for non-tradable services in 1985-86 we add a dummy for 1985-86 onwards into (5a);

$$GrGntrdbl = \underset{(18.3)}{0.0475} + \underset{(6.1)}{0.027^{*}D85} + \underset{(3.26)}{0.068^{*}Drainm} \qquad (12)$$

$R^2 = 0.465$, $R^2$ (adjusted) $= 0.443$, DW $= 1.67$.

This confirms that there is a breakout in the rate of growth of non-tradable services in 1985-86. Alternative equations with D80, D81 etc, still show high (but lower) statistical significance but have lower explanatory power ($R^2$).

The equation for GrGerv is very similar but has an even higher explanatory power because of stronger effect of variations in rainfall. The Chow tests on this equation also show the same pattern with 1985-86 as the most probable breakpoint [F=5.15(Pr=0.003), LLR=15.06 (Pr 0.0018)] and 1984-85 a very close second [F=5.14 (Pr=0.003), LLR=15.06(Pr=0.002)]. The final equation corresponding to (12) is,

$$GrGserv = \underset{(17.5)}{0.0463} + \underset{(6.16)}{0.028^{*}D85} + \underset{(3.78)}{0.083^{*}Drainm} \qquad (13)$$

$R^2 = 0.498$, $R^2$ (adjusted) $= 0.477$, DW $= 1.82$.

The analysis of this section suggests that the acceleration in the growth of GDP from services was a gradual process from 1980-81 to 1985-86, and it became firmly established in 1985-86.

## 3.6 Conclusions

The rate of growth of agriculture as well as the effect of rainfall on it remained unchanged during the entire period of over 50 years. Though the effect of rainfall variation on GDP supply (agriculture GDP) declined with the share of GDP in agriculture, demand side effects (demand for non-agricultural goods from agriculture income) seems to have grown. Thus, there was little change in the marginal impact of rainfall variation on economic growth. Manufacturing growth, however, started reviving in 1980-81 and was soon joined by services. This led to a significant acceleration in overall growth starting 1980-81. Subsequently, around 1984-85 or 1985-86 there was an additional (sustained) growth impulse arising from the service sector.

This section also shows that there were only two statistically significant phases in independent India's growth history. The first phase was from independence to 1979-80 and the second was from 1980-81 to the current time. As we show in the next section, these two phases can be identified with two different policy regimes, that may be termed as, 'The Indian Version of Socialism,' and 'Experiments with Market Reform' respectively. Previous authors have referred to the average GDP growth rate that prevailed during these two phases as the "Hindu Rate of Growth," and the "Bharatiya Rate of Growth."

## 4. FROM HINDU TO BHARATIYA RATE OF GROWTH

The purpose of this section is to briefly flesh out the policy regimes that underlay the two phases of growth identified in the previous section.

### 4.1 Phase I: Indian Version of Socialism

The period of 30 years from 1950–51 to 1979–80 was the phase of socialist experimentation, in which the Indian version of socialism was developed. Chakravarty (1987) presents a detailed exposition of the underlying economic rationale and documents some of the ideological and political factors. In this phase, the economy averaged a rate of growth of 3.5 per cent per annum (Table 1.1) and average income, measured by per capita GDP, grew at 1.3 per cent per annum. Growth during this period was fairly volatile, with a co-efficient of variation of 1.

Though our focus is on the post-colonial period it should be noted that this GDP growth rate was five times the average rate of growth of 0.7 per cent per annum during the 30 year period from 1917 to 1946. It also represented a major jump from the –0.3 per cent growth of per capita GDP during these 30 years.[16] This was, however, a very difficult period in world history, with the two World Wars bracketing it and the Great Depression in between. The Indian economy grew at 1.5 per cent per annum during 1900 to 1913, which was less than half the rate during phase I of the post-independence period.

---

16. Based on data in Sivasubramonian (2000).

## Table 1.1

*Macro-Economic Growth Parameters during Different Phases*

*(Per Cent)*

| | *Phase I (1951-52 to 1979-80)* | | | *Phase II (1980-81 to 2001-02)* | | |
|---|---|---|---|---|---|---|
| | | *Sub-phase* | | | *Sub-phase* | |
| | *Phase I* | *I A (1951-64)* | *I B (1965-79)* | *Phase II* | *II A (1980-91)* | *II B (1992-2001)* |
| Growth Rate (%) | | | | | | |
| *GDP (Market Prices)* | 3.6 | 4.4 | 2.9 | 5.7 | 5.5 | 6.0 |
| *GDP (Factor Cost)* | 3.5 | 4.1 | 2.9 | 5.2 | 5.5 | 6.1 |
| *GDP at Factor Cost (HP Filtered)* | 3.7 | 3.9 | 3.5 | 5.5 | 5.2 | 5.8 |
| *Per Capita GDP at Market Prices* | 1.4 | 2.3 | 0.6 | 3.6 | 3.3 | 3.9 |
| *Per Capita GDP at Factor Cost* | 1.3 | 2.0 | 0.6 | 3.6 | 3.2 | 4.1 |
| Private Consumption (PFCE) | 3.2 | 3.7 | 2.8 | 4.7 | 4.5 | 4.9 |
| Government Consumption (GFCE) | 5.8 | 6.6 | 5.1 | 6.3 | 6.0 | 6.6 |
| Investment (GDCF) | 6.1 | 7.9 | 4.5 | 6.3 | 5.0 | 7.8 |
| *Machinery & Equipment* | 6.6 | 9.7 | 3.7 | 8.9 | 9.9 | 7.9 |
| *Private GFCF* | 3.6 | 3.5 | 3.8 | 8.5 | 8.4 | 8.6 |
| *Goods & Services Export* | 3.8 | 0 | 10.2 | 9.5 | 8.4 | 10.8 |
| *Oil Import* | | | 37.1 | 9.8 | 6.9 | 13.2 |
| Coefficient of Variation (Std/Mean) | | | | | | |
| *GDP at Market Prices* | 0.9 | 0.5 | 1.4 | 0.3 | 0.4 | 0.2 |
| *GDP at Factor Cost* | 1.0 | 0.6 | 1.5 | 0.3 | 0.5 | 0.2 |

*Sources:* CSO (Series at 1993-94 prices); RBI (Series converted using implicit price deflator for GDP).

*Notes* : Data on the GDP is till 2002-03 and on other aggregates it is till 2001-02.

This phase was characterised by a conscious effort to increase the role of the state in the economy. This was perhaps a reflection of what Chakravarty (1987) calls a "profoundly interventionist economic philosophy" prevailing at the time among Nehru and other intellectuals. He states that given similar perceptions of the reasons for India's "structural backwardness," which he presents, "even a more pragmatically inclined politician than Nehru could well have opted for the same set of arrangements for promoting economic development." There was an inherent assumption that market failure was a serious underlying problem, that the private sector could not be trusted and that the public sector would produce economic and socially superior outcomes. The expansion of the State's role took place through multiple channels including nationalisation of selected production activities, increased public investment in infrastructure and other production activities, and legislative measures to control and direct private activity and economic agents. Though the mix of measures used varied over the phase, the concept of modern regulation as against bureaucratic control was sorely missing throughout the first phase of economic growth.

In this phase, investments grew strongly at 6.1 per cent per annum led by the growth of government fixed investment at 7.2 per cent per annum. Rapid growth of government consumption at 5.8 per cent also far exceeded economic growth. In contrast, the growth rate of private consumption was a very modest 3.2 per cent per annum, a rate slower than that of GDP. Though initially government investment and consumption may have led private consumption at some point during this phase, it started substituting for and crowding out private investment and consumption.

From the supply side, a noticeable feature of this growth was the fact that the tradable goods sector—manufacturing, mining, and agriculture—grew at about half the rate (2.8 per cent per annum) of the non-tradable services sector (Table 2.2, chapter 2).[17] Electricity production was the leading sector in this growth (9.6 per cent per annum)). Other sectors with relatively robust growth were banking and insurance (6.7 per cent per annum), communication (6.7 per cent), other transport (6.3 per cent) and registered/modern manufacturing (6.1 per cent per annum).

The share of production (GDP) originating in the public sector increased rapidly over most of this phase. The share of public investment, on the other hand, initially increased rapidly but then fell. Despite the fall in investment during the latter years of this phase, the government's share of production continued to increase fairly rapidly because of nationalisation of certain sectors. In addition, the pace of

17. Virmani (2004c).

the control of activities accelerated through the passage of new legislation and the introduction of more stringent rules and more elaborate procedures.

During this 30-year period of 'socialism with an Indian face', we can discern some change in emphasis between two sub-phases. Till about 1964-65, the leadership was infused with moral righteousness and developmental enthusiasm based on the philosophical background of Fabian socialism and the experience of Soviet state socialism. The best and brightest development economists in the world journeyed to India to advise on how to accelerate development and growth and some of them even worked with the Indian government or the Planning Commission to convert ideas into practical policy.[18] Starting from 1965–66 and ending in 1979–80, both the moral fervour and the academic certainties gradually seeped away. The policies were driven more by immediate crisis and political expediency than by economic logic. A less secure leadership struggling to establish itself was much more inclined to use economic policy as a political tool for besting its rivals.[19] As Dhar (1990) points out, this period saw "incoherence in the policies of the government." Socialistic legislation was presented as a policy for improving the lot of the poor while its main outcome was the suppression of market responses through quantitative controls implemented by an increasingly self-serving politico-bureaucratic system. Bhagwati (1993) analysed the failure of strategies adopted for Indian development prior to the nineties' reforms. He argued that the extensive controls and the inward-looking policies, which hobbled private sector efficiency, along with the substantial and inefficient public sector, were the three broad factors that stifled Indian growth in the seventies and, to a lesser extent, in the eighties. He states that, "the weak growth performance reflects, not a disappointing savings performance, but rather a disappointing productivity performance." [20]

---

18. See Bhagwati and Chakravarty (1969) for a survey of some of the technical literature and Chakravarty (1987) and the first chapter in Bhagwati (1993) for general expositions
19. Patel (2002), in his fifth chapter, describes a failed attempt by economists to ensure political stability and a strong and united leadership for the troubled period after 1965.
20. The fact that India's growth rate did not rise significantly, despite an impressive savings performance, and the implications thereof for future growth strategies has been much analysed and debated, for instance, by Chakravarty (1984) and Bhagwati and Srinivasan (1984).

## 4.2 Phase II: Experiments in Market Reform

This was the phase of market experimentation. The second phase of economic growth started at the beginning of the eighties. The high growth rates during 1994-95 to 1996-97 led to widespread speculation and assertion that India had entered a new phase of growth and development with the enactment of a radical new economic policy framework in 1991-92. We have earlier shown that there was no break-point in 1991 or 1992 and therefore, the phase that started in 1980–81 continues till today. The 1994-1996 period is, however, found to be a growth spurt that could not be sustained.

During the period 1980–81 to 2002–03 economic growth averaged 5.7 per cent per annum (Table 1.1). This rate is 2.1 percentage point higher than that during the first phase of development. It is 2.8 percentage points higher than that in the sub-phase IB. Economic growth during this phase has been remarkably stable with a CV of only 0.3, one-third of the CV during the first phase of development (Table 1.1). We call this the 'Bharatiya rate of growth,' to distinguish it from the 3.5 per cent average rate of growth during the first phase of development, a rate that has come to be associated in most people's minds as the 'Hindu rate of growth', but is more accurately called the "Indian-socialist" phase. Per capita income has been growing at 3.6 per cent per annum during the Bharatiya rate of growth phase, more than double the per capita income growth of 1.3 per cent per annum during the Hindu-socialist rate of growth phase.

The market reform phase has been characterised by recognition of the harmful effects of industrial and other controls on distribution, production, and investment and the need to remove the distortions created by government policy on the industry and exports. There was a much more gradual and hesitating recognition of the problem of government and public sector failure. This was reflected in the 0.5 per cent point step-up in the rate of growth of government consumption to 6.3 per cent (from 5.8 per cent).

The step-up in the growth rate during the market reform phase has been led, on the demand side, by an increase in private consumption, whose growth accelerated to 4.7 per cent per annum from 3.2 per cent per annum in the Indian socialist phase. The acceleration of export growth to 9.5 per cent per annum, over 2½ times the earlier growth rate of 3.8 per cent per annum, in the Indian socialist phase contributed to the acceleration, even though part of this may have been offset by higher oil import bill due to rising prices. Investment growth remained virtually unchanged at 6.3 per cent per annum relative to 6.1 per cent earlier. The fact that growth accelerated despite this small change implies that the efficiency of investment must have improved during the market reform phase. This is supported by a change in the structure of investment towards machinery and investment, whose growth accelerated to 8.9 per cent per annum during the market reform phase from 6.6 per cent per annum during the Indian socialist phase. The rate of growth of private fixed investment more than doubled from 3.6 per cent in the Indian socialist phase to 8.5 per cent per annum in the market reform phase. With completely different objective function of profit maximisation (*versus* political support maximisation in public sector), this would have contributed to the efficiency of capital use.

### *4.2.1 Growth Impulse*

To test the statistical significance of the (temporary) growth boom during the mid-nineties, we estimate equation (2) for the period 1980-81 to 2002-03 (phase II) by dropping the dummy for 1980-81+ and inserting a dummy for 1994-95 to 1996-97:

$$\begin{aligned} GrGDPfc = \; & \underset{(19.9)}{0.0559} + \underset{(2.1)}{0.016}{*}D9496 + \underset{(5.1)}{0.139}{*}DrainM \\ & - \underset{(-2.9)}{0.083}{*}DrainM(-1) \end{aligned} \quad (14)$$

$R^2 = 0.892$, $R^2$ (adjusted) $= 0.644$, DW $=1.68$.

The dummy is found to be significant at the 5 per cent level of confidence. The confidence level falls to 10 per cent if D9496 is replaced by a dummy for 1994-95 to 1999-2000 (or 1998-99).[21] Alternative dummy variables starting from 1993-94 are not found to be significant at the 10 per cent level. Interestingly the dummy D9497 for 1994-95 to 1997-98 is insignificant, indicating that something happened during 1997-98 to bring the boom to a halt. One possibility is that the change of government during the year undermined the credibility of reforms.[22] This is not surprising given the fall of a

21. These variables when introduced into equation (2) and estimated for the full 52 year period are not, however, statistically significant at the 10 per cent level.
22. United Front coalition government.

government widely perceived as reform oriented and its replacement with one in which many members still used the rhetoric of phase IB socialism. There was apparently some recovery, thereafter, as another government that was traditionally perceived as relatively pro-market/ anti-Statist came to power.[23]

We also estimate equation (2) for the entire period with a dummy for 1994-95 to 1996-97:

$$\begin{aligned} GrGDPfc = {} & \underset{(12.6)^{***}}{0.035} + \underset{(4.5)^{***}}{0.02^{*}D80} + \underset{(1.8)^{*}}{0.018^{*}D9496} + \\ & \underset{(6.7)^{***}}{0.185^{*}Drainm} - \underset{(-4.1)^{***}}{0.083^{*}Drainm(-1)} \end{aligned} \quad (15)$$

$R^2 = 0.65$, $R^2$ (adjusted) $= 0.62$, DW $=2.08$

The confidence level on the coefficient for D9496 drops to 10 per cent.

We repeat this exercise by inserting the same dummy(s) into the growth equation (9) for manufacturing.

$$\begin{aligned} GrGman = {} & \underset{(11.5)}{0.063} - \underset{(-2.25)}{0.0216^{*}D6580} + \underset{(2.41)}{0.046^{*}D9496} \\ & + \underset{(2.46)}{0.106^{*}Drainm} \end{aligned} \quad (16)$$

$R^2 = 0.31$, $R^2$ (adjusted) $= 0.268$, DW $= 1.92$.

D9496 the dummy for the period 1994-95 to 1996-97 is very significant but D9497, D9498 and D9499 are not.

Similarly in the equation for non-tradable service growth, equation (12), D9496 is not significant but the dummy D9599 for the period 1995-96 to 1999-2000 is highly significant.

$$\begin{aligned} GrGntrdbl = {} & \underset{(19.1)}{0.0475} + \underset{(4.6)}{0.022^{*}D85} + \underset{(2.25)}{0.017^{*}D9599} \\ & + \underset{(3.09)}{0.063^{*}Drainm} \end{aligned} \quad (17)$$

$R^2 = 0.516$, $R^2$ (adjusted) $= 0.486$, DW $= 1.67$.

This is, however, no longer true if we use the equation (13) for government administration (GrGerv). None of these dummies are found to be significant.

---

23. National Democratic Alliance (NDA) led by the Bharatiya Janta Party (BJP).

These results suggest that the economic reforms of the early-nineties imparted an additional growth impulse to the manufacturing sector. This led the growth boom of the Indian economy during 1994-95 to 1996-97. The boom, however, petered out in 1997-98. The reasons for this are explored in chapter 2 (Virmani, 2004c).

## 5. CONCLUSIONS

This chapter has reviewed the growth performance of India since 1950-51. It is widely believed that the Indian economy has become less dependent on the weather over the last half century of independence. This chapter shows that there is a statistically insignificant reduction of the impact of rainfall on Indian agriculture and of rainfall on the Indian economy (as a whole). In other words, agriculture is as dependent on rainfall in the fourth quarter of the century as it was in the third. On the overall impact of rainfall on GDP, the expected decline in the supply side effect (share of agriculture in GDP), seems to have been offset by demand side effects.

The chapter also shows that Indian economic growth has been remarkably stable. We are statistically able to distinguish only two phases of growth during its post-colonial history. The first phase characterised as the 'Indian Version of Socialism' starts after Independence and lasts to the end of the seventies. The second phase, which starts thereafter (1980-81), is still going on and is characterised by 'Experiments in Market Reform'. There was a sharp and statistically significant acceleration in the growth rate during the market reform phase. During the first socialist phase the economy averaged a growth of 3.5 per cent per annum with per capita growth averaging 1.3 per cent per annum. Growth accelerated to an average of 5.7 per cent per annum during the market reform phase with per capita income growing at an average rate of 3.6 per cent per annum.

We also find a (statistically) significant acceleration in the rate of growth of services during the market reform phase. In the case of manufacturing, the higher growth rate during the eighties was more in the nature of a recovery from the oppressive hand of socialist controls and public monopolies and a closing of the gap between actual and potential output that had opened as a consequence. As a consequence the share of GDP from services does not show any abrupt change (discontinuity) and has been rising slowly but steadily over the past half century.

With a change in orientation of the government from socialism to market there was a change in the rhetoric of the government and of intellectuals and consequently in the atmosphere/environment in which private agents and investors operate. This change in orientation started in the late-seventies when the still 'socialist' oriented Mrs Gandhi broke the railway strike in 1976. The change continued with the coming to power of the so-called 'right-wing' political parties such as the Congress (O) and the BJP (though some of the coalition partners were Indian socialists). There was consequently an acceleration of GDP growth from 2.6 per cent per annum during 1965-66 to 1979-80 to 5.6 per cent annum during 1980-81 to 1991-92.

One 'puzzle' is how such a significant growth impulse resulted from what appear *prima facie* to be modest changes in the control regime relative to what happened in 1991-92. The chapter has argued that the economic reforms introduced during the 1980s had a great deal of credibility. As a result, the rate of growth of private investment accelerated and the structure of investment moved towards machinery and equipment and the quality of machinery and equipment improved because of greater access to imported capital goods. This played an important role in the acceleration of growth. In addition, the output gap which had opened up during the socialist growth sub-phase due to the (policy resultant) suppression of economic growth below its potential, was closed during the 'modest reform' sub-phase. This gap was eliminated during the first half of the market reform phase, partly because of the supply side stimulus provided by the slower growth of oil prices and the demand side stimulus provided by the rising fiscal deficit. Thus, the acceleration of growth in the market reform phase had a substantial element of temporary acceleration above its potential, a catch-up process that bridged the output gap by around 1990-91.

There was also a small increase in the growth rate during 1992-93 to 2003-04 (over and above this 'gap closing' acceleration) following the introduction of broader reforms. The chapter showed that these reforms gave rise to a statistically significant spurt in the growth rate of manufacturing, which was reflected in a spurt in overall growth. Among the likely reasons are: (a) The economy's inability to

# 2

# From Socialist Rate of Growth to Bharatiya Rate of Growth

## 1. INTRODUCTION

As already discussed in chapter 1, there was a widespread belief in the general public that the Indian economy was stuck since Independence in the 'Hindu rate of growth', of about 3.5 per cent per annum. This conventional wisdom prevailed throughout the eighties and perhaps into the nineties. The conventional wisdom changed around the mid-nineties. The new conventional wisdom was that the 'new economic policy' introduced in 1991-92 had transformed the Indian economy and pushed it from the 'Hindu rate of growth' of 3.5 per cent to a new higher rate that was variously estimated to lie between 5 per cent and 6 per cent referred to as the 'new Hindu rate of growth'.

A new series of national accounts statistics was introduced by the Central Statistical Organisation (CSO) based on 1993-94 prices. Over the last few years the series has been extended backwards and is now available from 1950 onwards. We use this data to revisit the issue of growth phases in Indian economic development.

The chapter is structured as follows. Section 2 analyses the historical growth experience of the Indian economy in terms of phases. The chapter finds a sub-phase of economic growth, dubbed the 'Socialist Rate of Growth (SRG)' in which the Indian economy had the worst performance in its post-independence history. The chapter also confirms that there was a new phase of growth, measured by the

---

I would like to thank Roberto Zagha, Bishwanath Goldar, K.L. Krishna, Surjit S. Bhalla, Montek S. Ahluwalia and Wilima Wadhwa for comments on earlier versions (starting with June 2003 version) of the chapter. My thanks to Jayant V. Ganguli for excellent research assistance.

rate of growth of the GDP (gross domestic product) at factor cost (GDPfc), starting in 1980-81, that we call the 'Bharatiya rate of growth (BRG)'. We also find that each phase can be further sub-divided into two sub-phases characterised by differences in policy approach and growth performance. The two sub-phases of BRG throw up important puzzles regarding the impact of policy changes and economic reforms on growth performance. Section 2 attempts also to unravel these puzzles, as they need to be resolved for informing the debate on future Indian growth.

Section 3 puts the Indian growth performance in an international perspective, to assess how India's growth rate during the different sub-phases compared with that of other countries. Section 4 concludes the chapter.

## 2. PHASES OF INDEPENDENT DEVELOPMENT

The focus of our analysis is on the post-colonial period after India attained independence in 1947. The term "independent development" is therefore merely a short form for 'development of Independent India'. This chapter covers the period from 1950-51 onwards, for which consistent data series are available. This means that growth rates are available from 1951-52 onwards. Though we use a fairly simple methodology, a brief overview of which is given in chapter 1.

### A. Phase I: Indian Version of Socialism

The overall macro perspective on this phase was covered in chapter 1. In this chapter, we go into greater detail in the context of the sub-phases of each phase.

#### *1. Phase I A: Quest for Commanding Heights*

#### a) Overview of Phase I A

The first sub-phase of economic growth stretched 15 years from 1950-51 to 1964-65. On an average, 52.5 per cent of the population was poor during this phase. In this post-colonial period economic growth accelerated sharply to an average of 4.1 per cent per annum and average income grew by 2 per cent per year (Table 1.1, chapter

1).[1] This growth was led by the modern manufacturing sector and supported by modern services such as electricity, communications, banking and insurance and 'other transport'. Modern manufacturing was the leading sector in economic growth, growing at an unprecedented annual average rate of 7.9 per cent and contributing 17.3 per cent to overall growth (Table 2.1 and Table 2.2).[2] Two critical infrastructure services essential for this sector kept pace with this growth. The electricity, gas, and water sector grew at an even faster 11.2 per cent per annum while the communication sector grew at 7.4 per cent per annum (Table 2.1), all from a small base.[3]

The financial sector (6.6 per cent) and 'other transport' which grew at 6.4 per cent (Table 2.1), complemented the development of the modern manufacturing sector. Manufacturing, finance, and 'other transport' were largely private during this phase and driven by market forces and the last partly substituted for the inadequacy of the monopoly railway sector.

**b) Sector Growth**

The communication and electricity sectors needed public investment to grow and this was apparently forthcoming. The railway and communication sectors were monopolised by the government with 100 per cent of the GDP from these sectors as well as 100 per cent of the investment coming from the government in 1960-61 (Table 2.3). The existing companies in the electricity, gas and water sector were allowed to continue to operate, but all green-field investment came under the government with 87 per cent of the GDP from this sector and 92 per cent of the investment in this sector coming from the government in 1960-61 (Table 2.3). These three sectors—electricity, communication, and railways—accounted for 40.5 per cent of government investment in 1964-65, the end of the first sub-phase.

---

1. As measured by the rate of growth of the GDP at factor cost at 1993-94 prices. The rate of growth using the GDP-at-market-price series is 4.4 per cent per annum.
2. Much of traditional manufacturing is in the unregistered household sector. For expositional simplicity we are assuming that the registered manufacturing sector is 'modern'.
3. The former is an abbreviation for the 'electricity, gas, and water supply' sector as electricity is the overwhelming component of this composite.

## Table 2.1

*Sector Growth Rates during Different Phases*

*(Per Cent)*

| Sector | Phase I (1951-52 to 1979-80) | Sub-phase I A (1951-64) | Sub-phase I B (1965-79) | Phase II (1980-81 to 2001-02) | Sub-phase II A (1980-91) | Sub-phase II B (1992-2001) |
|---|---|---|---|---|---|---|
| 1 Agriculture & Allied | 2.1 | 2.9 | 1.4 | 3.6 | 3.9 | 3.3 |
| *1.1 Agriculture* | 2.3 | 3.1 | 1.5 | 3.8 | 4.2 | 3.3 |
| 2 Mining | 4.6 | 5.6 | 3.7 | 6.3 | 8.4 | 3.8 |
| 3 Manufacturing | 5.3 | 6.6 | 4.1 | 6.4 | 6.1 | 6.8 |
| *3.1 Registered (Modern)* | 6.1 | 7.9 | 4.4 | 6.9 | 6.8 | 7.1 |
| *3.2 Unregistered* | 4.5 | 5.4 | 3.7 | 5.6 | 5.0 | 6.3 |
| 4 Electricity, Gas, & Water | 9.6 | 11.2 | 8.1 | 7.5 | 9.0 | 5.7 |
| 5 Construction | 4.9 | 6.8 | 3.2 | 5.2 | 5.2 | 5.3 |
| 6 Trade, Hotels & Restaurants | 4.8 | 5.6 | 4.0 | 6.7 | 5.4 | 8.1 |
| *6.1 Trade* | 4.8 | 5.6 | 4.0 | 6.6 | 5.4 | 8.0 |
| *6.2 Hotels & Restaurants* | 4.8 | 5.6 | 4.0 | 8.0 | 6.1 | 10.3 |
| 7 Storage, Transport & Communication | 5.7 | 5.9 | 5.6 | 7.2 | 5.7 | 8.9 |
| *7.1 Railway* | 4.2 | 4.8 | 3.6 | 4.2 | 4.9 | 3.3 |
| *7.2 Other Transport* | 6.3 | 6.4 | 6.3 | 6.5 | 6.0 | 7.0 |
| *7.3 Storage* | 5.5 | 2.3 | 8.5 | 2.3 | 2.5 | 2.0 |
| *7.4 Communication* | 6.7 | 7.4 | 6.1 | 11.6 | 6.3 | 18.0 |
| 8 FIREBHS | 3.5 | 3.1 | 4.0 | 8.6 | 9.4 | 7.7 |
| *8.1 Banking & Insurance* | 6.7 | 6.6 | 6.9 | 10.6 | 11.6 | 9.4 |
| *8.2 Real Estate, Housing & Business Services* | 2.6 | 2.1 | 3.0 | 7.2 | 8.0 | 6.3 |
| 9 Community, Social & Personal Services | 4.3 | 4.4 | 4.2 | 6.3 | 5.6 | 7.1 |
| *9.1 Public Administration & Defence* | 6.1 | 6.6 | 5.7 | 6.2 | 6.2 | 6.3 |
| *9.2 Other Services* | 3.3 | 3.3 | 3.3 | 6.4 | 5.2 | 7.7 |
| Sub-aggregates | | | | | | |
| A *Tradable Goods* | 2.8 | 3.6 | 2.0 | 4.6 | 4.7 | 4.5 |
| B *Non-tradable Services* | 4.7 | 5.2 | 4.2 | 6.9 | 6.3 | 7.5 |
| *B.1 Services, Excluding FIREHBS* | 4.9 | 5.6 | 4.3 | 6.5 | 5.7 | 7.4 |
| C *GDP, Excluding GDP Administration* | 3.4 | 4.0 | 2.8 | 5.7 | 5.4 | 6.1 |
| D *Services Excluding GDP Administration* | 4.5 | 5.0 | 4.1 | 6.9 | 6.4 | 7.6 |

*Source* : CSO (all series at 1993-94 prices).

*Notes* : Data on growth by sector is available only until 2001-02.

## Table 2.2

*Sector Contribution to Overall Growth by Phase*

*(Per Cent)*

| Sector | *Phase I (1950-51 to 1979-80)* | | | *Phase II (1980-81 to 2001-02)* | | |
|---|---|---|---|---|---|---|
| | | *Sub-phase* | | | *Sub-phase* | |
| | *Phase I* | *I A (1951-64)* | *I B (1965-79)* | *Phase II* | *II A (1980-91)* | *II B (1992-99)* |
| (Contributions Calculated as Proportion of GDP at Factor Cost) | | | | | | |
| 1 Agriculture & Allied | 23.0 | 36.9 | 16.8 | 18.0 | 21.9 | 13.8 |
| *1.1 Agriculture* | 21.0 | 34.7 | 14.6 | 16.9 | 20.9 | 12.6 |
| 2 Mining & Quarrying | 2.1 | 2.2 | 2.5 | 2.3 | 3.6 | 1.6 |
| 3 Manufacturing | 16.4 | 17.3 | 19.4 | 17.7 | 20.5 | 17.1 |
| *3.1 Registered (Modern)* | 10.2 | 10.8 | 12.1 | 12.0 | 13.9 | 11.7 |
| *3.2 Unregistered* | 6.2 | 6.5 | 7.3 | 5.7 | 6.6 | 5.3 |
| 4 Electricity, Gas & Water Supply | 2.3 | 1.5 | 3.4 | 2.8 | 3.2 | 2.6 |
| 5 Construction | 6.1 | 7.7 | 6.1 | 4.9 | 4.7 | 4.7 |
| 6 Trade, Hotels & Restaurants | 13.1 | 13.3 | 16.0 | 16.1 | 13.0 | 18.1 |
| 7 Transport, Storage & Communication | 7.2 | 5.5 | 10.2 | 9.3 | 6.1 | 11.1 |
| *7.1 Railways* | 1.5 | 1.6 | 1.8 | 0.9 | 1.2 | 0.8 |
| *7.2 Other Transport* | 4.3 | 3.0 | 6.4 | 4.5 | 3.9 | 4.9 |
| *7.3 Storage* | 0.1 | 0.0 | 0.2 | 0.0 | 0.1 | 0.0 |
| *7.4 Communication* | 1.2 | 0.9 | 1.7 | 3.9 | 1.1 | 5.5 |
| 8 FIREHBS | 6.2 | 4.7 | 8.9 | 14.8 | 14.0 | 15.8 |
| *8.1 Banking & Insurance (Finance)* | 3.0 | 2.0 | 4.5 | 8.1 | 6.7 | 9.2 |
| *8.2 Real Estate, Housing, Business Services* | 3.3 | 2.6 | 4.6 | 6.7 | 7.3 | 6.6 |
| 9 Community, Social, Personal Services | 12.1 | 10.4 | 16.4 | 14.1 | 12.9 | 15.1 |
| *9.1 Public Administration & Defence* | 6.3 | 4.9 | 8.8 | 6.1 | 6.3 | 6.0 |
| *9.2 Other Services* | 5.8 | 5.3 | 7.6 | 8.0 | 6.6 | 9.1 |
| (Contributions Calculated as a Proportion of GDP at Market Prices) | | | | | | |
| *Tradable Goods* | 41.5 | 49.2 | 34.9 | 34.7 | 40.4 | 30.2 |
| *Non-Tradable Services* | 47.3 | 37.9 | 55.3 | 56.6 | 47.5 | 62.6 |
| *FIREHBS* | 6.2 | 4.7 | 8.9 | 14.8 | 14.0 | 15.8 |
| *Services Excluding FIREHBS* | 41.1 | 33.8 | 47.3 | 43.1 | 35.2 | 48.0 |

*Source* : CSO (all series at 1993-94 prices).

*Notes* : Data on shares of each sector in the GDP is available only until 1999-2000. Contributions are period averages.

## Table 2.3

*Public Sector Share in GDP and GCF by Economic Sector*

(Per Cent)

| Sector | Share in Total Sector GDP (Factor Cost) | | | | | Share in Total Sector GCF | | | | |
|---|---|---|---|---|---|---|---|---|---|---|
| | Earliest Year of Data (1960-61) | End of Sub-phase I A (1964-65) | End of Sub-phase I B (1979-80) | End of Sub-phase II A (1991-92) | Last Year of Data for sub-phase II B (2000-1) | Earliest Year of Data (1960-61) | End of Sub-phase I A (1964-65) | End of Sub-phase I B (1979-80) | End of Sub-phase II A (1991-92) | Last Year of Data for Sub-phase II B (2000-1) |
| Agriculture & Allied | 1.6 | 2.1 | 3.8 | 3.1 | 2.7 | 38.2 | 45.0 | 40.5 | 29.2 | 22.6 |
| *Agriculture* | 0.7 | 1.3 | 3.0 | 2.7 | 2.4 | 38.5 | 45.6 | 40.4 | 28.9 | 23.5 |
| Mining & Quarrying | 19.1 | 26 | 97.2 | 90.3 | 86.7 | 53.8 | 77.2 | 70.3 | 95.8 | 86.1 |
| Manufacturing | 7.0 | 13 | 15.4 | 19.7 | 12.1 | 31.6 | 28.6 | 38.5 | 16.1 | 5.9 |
| Electricity, Gas & Water Supply | 86.9 | 92 | 102 | 100 | 100 | 91.8 | 89.4 | 87.3 | 89.6 | 81.0 |
| Construction | 4.6 | 4.7 | 13.6 | 14.4 | 16.4 | 6.2 | 13.3 | 24.5 | 21.8 | 10.6 |
| Trade, Hotels & Restaurants | 1.4 | 2.4 | 7.5 | 4.8 | 2.9 | 2.5 | 3.4 | 6.5 | -48 | 38.9 |
| Transport, Storage & Comm. | 61.8 | 61 | 58.9 | 52.4 | 54.9 | 57.8 | 66.4 | 45.8 | 45.7 | 56.9 |
| *Railways* | 100 | 100 | 100 | 97 | 100 | 100 | 100 | 100 | 100 | 100.0 |
| *Communication* | 100 | 100 | 100 | 96.2 | 89.7 | 100 | 100 | 100 | 100 | 100.0 |
| FIREHBS | 6.5 | 8.4 | 26.0 | 35.5 | 30.9 | 8.8 | 8.3 | 10.5 | 15.5 | 12.4 |
| *Banking & Insurance* | 29.2 | 34 | 72.5 | 78.3 | 58.4 | 46.2 | 51.3 | 59.8 | 46.8 | 62.8 |
| Community, Social & Personal Services | 39.8 | 46 | 61.3 | 66.6 | 66.5 | 85.2 | 86.2 | 91.5 | 81.2 | 72.5 |
| *Public Administration & Defence* | 100 | 100 | 100 | 97.8 | 100 | 100 | 100 | 100 | 100 | 100 |
| *Other Services* | 12.3 | 15.8 | 30.4 | 39.0 | 39.5 | 25.1 | 23.9 | 54.6 | 36.0 | 21.8 |
| All Sectors | 9.0 | 11.8 | 22.1 | 25.9 | 25.8 | 44.6 | 50.1 | 47.3 | 38.4 | 32.8 |
| | | | | | | *1950-01* | | | | |
| *Total GDP from Public Sector* (Alternative Source) | | | | | | 26.7 | 52.4 | 49.2 | 38.8 | 25.8 |

*Source* : CSO (all series in 1993-94 prices).
*Note* : Data on the public sector share in output and investment by sector is available only between 1960-61 and 2000-01.

Agriculture (and allied sector) growth was a modest 2.9 per cent per annum given the low priority accorded to it in the Mahalanobis model of development (Table 2.1). As a result, the tradable goods sector grew at only 3.6 per cent per annum, half the rate of the non-tradable sector (5.2 per cent). The share of both manufacturing and mining increased. In this initial phase of development, government administration grew rapidly at 6.6 per cent per annum. This pulled up the non-tradable sector's growth by 0.2 percentage points per annum from the service sector (excluding administration) growth of 5 per cent per annum. Telecommunications, in contrast, became a public sector company with an independent set of accounts and the potential of putting some distance between the governments functioning and the commercial objective of providing telephone services (Table 2.1).

### c) Role of the State

The role of the State in production increased inexorably through the first sub-phase. The share of the government in gross capital formation (GCF) doubled from 26.7 per cent in 1950-51 to a peak of 53.6 per cent in 1963-64.[4] Public share of gross fixed capital formation (GFCF) also doubled from 27.2 per cent of the total in 1950-51 to 54.4 per cent in 1963-64. Government investment was not, however, limited to public goods and infrastructure, as manufacturing, and mining received 16.6 per cent of the total gross investment by the government in 1964-65 with another 11.5 per cent going to agriculture.[5] The government built not only large irrigation dams and canal systems but also large capital-intensive factories; both termed as the 'temples of modern India'. Though at the end of phase IA, the public sector's share in GDP from mining and manufacturing was 26 per cent and 13 per cent respectively, the jump in public share in GCF to 77.2 per cent and 32.1 per cent (1963-64) respectively were initial

---

4. These figures are from the CSO statement on capital formation by type of asset and institution, which provide data from 1950-51 onwards. These differ from the figures provided in the CSO statement on capital formation by sector, which are used for constructing Tables 2.4 and 2.6 and provide data only from 1960-61 onwards. Therefore, there may be discrepancies in the numbers cited here and in Tables 2.4 and 2.6 for comparable years.

5. The division between private goods and public infrastructure (dams and canals) is not available in the National Accounts Statistics.

steps on the road to fiscal and financial crowding out.[6] Public investment in sectors like trade, hotels and restaurants, storage and real estate, housing and business services compounded the problem in subsequent years.

The monopolisation of the infrastructure sectors and the complete removal of the threat of competition[7] from these critical infrastructure sectors laid the foundation for future increases in X-inefficiency. The merger of regulatory functions in the administrative ministries (telecom), or worse, in the organisations that were operationally responsible for service delivery (railways, electricity), laid the basis for progressive neglect of user interests and deterioration in the quality of service. The institutional structure of railways and electricity also affected the speed of deterioration. Both were departmental undertakings whose financial accounts was part of the government budget. Thus, the ills of bureaucratic red tape and political interference were multiplied for organisations whose ostensible objective was to supply commercial services.

The monopolisation of these sectors by the government also had the unfortunate effect of converting a technical issue into an ideological one. The technical issue was one of the degree of complementarity between production of and investment in infrastructure (or utility) services and the other sectors of the economy. This was converted into an ideological issue of the complementarity between public investment and 'private' investment. *A priori* one would expect that electricity and to a lesser extent, modern communications and transport are complements to modern industrial production and market systems. The technical possibility of complementarity or substitutability does not, depend on whether one or other or both are private or government owned.[8] The fact that these sectors were under government monopoly misled many economists into thinking and arguing as if the issue was one of complementarity between private and government investment in all sectors (i.e. including manufacturing, mining, agriculture and other services).

6. By fiscal crowding out we mean the crowding out of government expenditure on public and quasi-public goods. Financial crowding out refers to the effects of government borrowing on private credit and interest rates.
7. By reserving them for the public sector.
8. The best way to estimate substitutability can, however, depend critically on the ownership pattern and consequently the incentives and behaviour of the managers.

## 2. *Phase I B: Socialist Rate of Growth*

### a) Overview of Outcomes

The second sub-phase started with a severe drought in 1965-66 and was followed five years later by the first oil shock. The sub-phase ended in 1979-80 with one of the worst droughts since Independence coupled with the second (smaller) oil shock. Economic growth collapsed to 2.9 per cent per annum during this sub-phase, with per capita income growing at a minuscule 0.6 per cent per annum (Table 1.1). Agriculture led the downward spiral with an average growth of 1.4 per cent per annum, half of its growth rate in sub-phase IA (Table 2.1). Given the bad monsoons and the consequent decline in agriculture growth this is perhaps not surprising, except when one recalls that this was also the period during which the relative neglect of agriculture ended and the Green Revolution was introduced in India. The reason for calling it a sub-phase rather than the second growth phase is because the decline of 0.6 per cent points below the average of 3.5 for the entire period is not statistically significant.[9] The contribution of agriculture to overall growth fell dramatically from about 35 per cent of the total growth in the first sub-phase, to less than 15 per cent in the second (Table 2.2).

The growth rate of modern manufacturing decelerated only a little less sharply than agriculture to 4.4 per cent or 0.56 of IA growth (Table 2.1).[10] As unregistered manufacturing decelerated less, total manufacturing contributed 19.4 per cent of the total growth during this sub-phase, a higher contribution than during the previous sub-phase (Table 2.2). The rising share of manufacturing and declining share of agriculture was also responsible for the former's contribution exceeding the latter during this sub-phase.

Somewhat surprisingly, the three service sectors that had shared the high growth of the previous period, did not decelerate as rapidly as can be seen from Table 2.1. The electricity sector remained the top performer at 8.1 per cent per annum—0.72 of its sub-phase IA growth—while communication growth decelerated even less to 0.82 of

9. In other words, there is no statistical difference in growth during this period once monsoon fluctuations are accounted for by using a rainfall index in the growth regression as in Equation 1 (Ch. 1).

10. See Krishna (2002) or Goldar and Mitra (2002) for a review of the extensive literature on the deceleration in registered manufacturing growth.

previous levels—6.1 per cent per annum. The banking and insurance sector was one of the few sectors that grew faster than in the first sub-phase at 6.9 per cent per annum, because of policy decisions by the government with respect to the banking sub-sector after nationalisation.[11] The non-tradable services sector, as well as the service sector excluding public administration, continued to grow at about twice the rate of the tradable goods sector.

**b) Policy Change and Effect**

Overall, this was an extremely volatile period of economic history.[12] The severe droughts in 1965 and 1966 followed by the devaluation of the rupee, the oil crisis of 1971, and a number of other exogenous shocks led to a re-evaluation of existing policies and a re-orientation of development policies. There were both positive and negative features of this re-orientation. The former included a renewed recognition of the importance of agriculture and the initiation of the 'Green Revolution' and conservative and successful management of the macroeconomic imbalances created by the oil shock. There was, however, increasing resort to the rhetoric and methods of 'State socialism' during this phase of development. In a country in which fairly sophisticated markets for commodities and finance (the 'Hundi' system) had existed for centuries, in which there were well developed traditional stock exchanges and forward markets for commodities at the turn of the century, this represented something of a contradiction. The negative features included the following:

(a) A number of laws, such as the Monopolies and Restrictive Trade Practices (MRTP) Act and the Foreign Exchange Regulation Act (FERA) designed to control the private sector and private economic activity.

(b) The nationalisation of banks[13] and general insurance designed to supplant the private sector by the public sector.

---

11. Storage sector growth more than tripled during this phase. The public sector's share of the total GDP from this sector was 23.3 per cent in 1980-81, the first year for which data is available in the national account statistics.

12. The standard deviation in growth was 4.2 per cent, implying a CV of 1.5. This CV is 2.5 times the CV of 0.62 in sub-phase IA (Table 2.1).

13. See Patel (2002), chapter 5, for a description of how the nationalisation happened and the subsequent public reaction.

(c) An increasing resort to licensing and controls to direct industrial investment, imports, and agricultural exports.

(d) The spread of the public sector into a variety of areas such as consulting and consumer goods.

(e) Tightening of labour laws and procedures, such as requiring prior permission from the state government for retrenchment in firms with 300 or more employees.[14]

The inefficiency arising from this legislative-bureaucratic socialism was reflected in the near doubling of the real ICOR (incremental capital-output ratio) for the economy from 3.9 in the first sub-phase to 6.7 in the second sub-phase (Table 2.4).[15] The ICOR for mining more than tripled from 2.1 in sub-phase IA to 6.3 in sub-phase IB, while the ICOR for agriculture almost tripled to 5 from 1.8 in sub-phase IA (Table 2.4). The ICOR for manufacturing almost doubled to 7.9 during this sub-phase from an average of 4.2 in the first sub-phase (Table 2.4).

The issue of inefficient resource use or stagnation, also finds support in figures on decadal total factor productivity growth (TFPG) and capital stock growth.[16] Using data from Nehru and Dhareshwar (1993) and Barro and Lee (1994), Guha-Khasnobis and Bari (2003) find that for India, TFPG for the economy turned negative in the seventies from a positive value in the sixties. The largest change is of 1.60 percentage points, from 1.20 per cent in the sixties to –0.40 per cent in the seventies. In contrast, the growth rate of capital stock in India remained positive and decelerated only marginally in the seventies.[17] In our view, negative TFPG growth is inconsistent with the concept of technical change that TFPG was initially constructed to measure and (most likely) indicates declining capacity utilisation of capital and other fixed factors.[18]

---

14. Earlier, they were only required to report to the government their intent to retrench (on a 'last come first go' rule). The number of employees for this rule to apply was changed to 100 in 1982.

15. See the caveats in Srinivasan and Narayana (1977) and Raj (1984) on using the ICOR.

16. It is not commonly recognised, however, that variation in capacity utilisation will affect estimates of both ICOR and TFPG. Ignoring capacity utilisation is likely to yield biased estimates of TFPG as a measure of productivity.

17. The change in the capital-stock growth estimate of Table 1.4 (corresponding to the TFPG figures in footnote 14) is of 0.21 percentage points, from 1.70 per cent to 1.49 per cent.

18. When labour laws make it difficult to fire workers and/or exit is difficult, regular blue-collar workers may also be a quasi-fixed factor and would also be affected in the same way.

## Table 2.4

*Incremental Capital-Output Ratio: Period Averages at 1993-94 Prices*

| Sector | Economy-wide | | | | | | Public Sector | | | | | |
|---|---|---|---|---|---|---|---|---|---|---|---|---|
| | Phase I (1951-52 to 1979-80) | | | Phase II (1980-81 to 2002-03) | | | Phase I (1951-52 to 1979-80) | | | Phase II (1980-81 to 2002-03) | | |
| | | Sub-phase | | | Sub-phase | | | Sub-phase | | | Sub-phase | |
| | Phase I | I A 1951-64 | I B 1965-79 | Phase II | II A 1980-91 | II B 1992-99 | Phase I | I A 1960-64 | I B 1965-79 | Phase II | II A 1980-91 | II B 1992-99 |
| Agriculture & Allied | 2.9 | 1.9 | 4.9 | 1.8 | 1.9 | 1.8 | 16.3 | 13.5 | 17.3 | 40.0 | 50.2 | 25.7 |
| *Agriculture* | 2.9 | 1.8 | 5.0 | 1.7 | 1.8 | 1.6 | 17.8 | 13.5 | 20.2 | 42.5 | 40.3 | 50.0 |
| Mining & Quarrying | 3.8 | 2.1 | 6.3 | 6.6 | 6.1 | 8.2 | 2.9 | 3.2 | 2.7 | 8.4 | 7.2 | 14.6 |
| Manufacturing | 5.7 | 4.2 | 7.9 | 8.0 | 8.0 | 8.0 | 9.8 | 4.1 | 17.4 | 6.1 | 7.4 | 3.7 |
| *Registered (Modern)* | 7.7 | 6.5 | 9.6 | 7.5 | 6.9 | 8.3 | — | — | — | — | — | — |
| *Unregistered* | 2.4 | 0.7 | 4.8 | 8.3 | 10.4 | 5.9 | — | — | — | — | — | — |
| Electricity, Gas & Water Supply | 17.2 | 16.2 | 18.4 | 15.8 | 15.7 | 16.0 | 15.0 | 13.4 | 15.3 | 11.8 | 15.1 | 6.9 |
| Construction | 1.0 | 0.7 | 1.5 | 1.4 | 1.3 | 1.5 | 2.0 | 2.6 | 1.9 | 1.6 | 1.8 | 1.3 |
| Trade, Hotels & Restaurants | 1.6 | 0.8 | 2.7 | 1.1 | 1.5 | 0.7 | 2.0 | 0.5 | 2.7 | 4.5 | 3.5 | 5.9 |
| Transport, Storage & Communication | 12.8 | 14.3 | 11.4 | 6.3 | 7.6 | 5.0 | 11.7 | 16.2 | 9.9 | 7.1 | 8.8 | 5.4 |
| *Railways* | 23.1 | 27.9 | 17.1 | 10.6 | 8.9 | 15.0 | 21.9 | 30.8 | 17.3 | 11.5 | 9.4 | 18.4 |
| *Other Transport* | 10.9 | 10.0 | 11.8 | 6.2 | 7.3 | 4.9 | 6.4 | 6.3 | 6.6 | 7.8 | 10.2 | 5.5 |
| *Communication* | 4.4 | 3.9 | 5.0 | 4.6 | 6.8 | 3.3 | 4.7 | 3.6 | 5.1 | 5.0 | 7.4 | 3.4 |

*Contd. ...*

*Contd. ...*

| Sector | *Economy-wide* | | | | | | *Public Sector* | | | | | |
|---|---|---|---|---|---|---|---|---|---|---|---|---|
| | *Phase I (1951-52 to 1979-80)* | | | *Phase II (1980-81 to 2002-03)* | | | *Phase I (1951-52 to 1979-80)* | | | *Phase II (1980-81 to 2002-03)* | | |
| | | *Sub-phase* | | | *Sub-phase* | | | *Sub-phase* | | | *Sub-phase* | |
| | *Phase I* | *I A 1951-64* | *I B 1965-79* | *Phase II* | *II A 1980-91* | *II B 1992-99* | *Phase I* | *I A 1960-64* | *I B 1965-79* | *Phase II* | *II A 1980-91* | *II B 1992-99* |
| FIREHBS | 11.3 | 13.8 | 9.5 | 3.5 | 3.5 | 3.4 | 2.1 | 4.4 | 1.5 | 1.2 | 1.1 | 1.3 |
| *Banking & Insurance* | 0.7 | 0.6 | 0.8 | 1.1 | 0.8 | 1.5 | 0.4 | 0.6 | 0.4 | 0.7 | 0.6 | 0.9 |
| *Real Estate, Housing & Business Services* | 20.3 | 25.0 | 17.2 | 6.3 | 5.9 | 7.0 | | | | 77.1 | 77.6 | 75.3 |
| Community, Social & Personal Services | 5.8 | 6.0 | 5.6 | 3.2 | 3.9 | 2.5 | 6.3 | 6.1 | 6.2 | 4.1 | 4.6 | 3.3 |
| *Public Administration & Defence* | 9.5 | 10.3 | 8.6 | 4.9 | 5.8 | 3.8 | 8.3 | 7.5 | 8.4 | 5.3 | 6.1 | 4.1 |
| *Other Services* | 2.3 | 2.4 | 2.2 | 1.6 | 1.8 | 1.4 | 1.5 | 1.3 | 1.5 | 1.5 | 1.6 | 1.3 |
| **Total** | 5.1 | 3.9 | 6.7 | 4.1 | 4.3 | 3.9 | 8.1 | 7.7 | 8.0 | 6.1 | 7.0 | 4.6 |

*Source* : CSO

*Notes* : 1. Data on investment by sector is available only until 1999-2000.

2. Data for the public sector's investment by sector is available only from 1960 onwards.

### c) Impact of Expanding Public Sector

Though the public share of investment stabilised during this sub-phase, its share of the GDP, however, continued to grow, thus increasing the direct role of the government in the economy and the crowding out of private activity and initiative. The allocation of public investment worsened. The ratio of government investment to total investment in the economy declined from 52 per cent in 1964-65 to 49 per cent in 1979-80.[19] This was partly because the administrative infrastructure had been largely completed, allowing the share of public investment allotted for this purpose to decline by six percentage points (Table 2.5). The share of public investment going to mining and manufacturing increased from 16.7 per cent to 27 per cent, an indication of distorted priorities in public investment towards private goods and away from public goods. Agriculture's share of public investment also increased by about 4 percentage points. There were contrary developments with respect to the monopolised infrastructure or utility sector—the share of public investment allocated to electricity increased to 20 per cent while that going to railways plummeted to 6 per cent from 23.1 per cent at the end of sub-phase IA (Table 2.5). Though, this appears to be a rather drastic cut, one positive result was to cut wasteful expenditure in the railways, a fact reflected in the dramatic decline in the ICOR for the sector to 17 from about 28 in the previous sub-phase (Table 2.4).[20] In contrast, the ICOR in the fast growing utility and infrastructure sectors, communication and electricity increased by 1.1 points (to 5.0) and 2.2 points (to 18.4), respectively (Table 2.4).

Srinivasan and Narayana (1977) had a somewhat different view of government investment, stating that, "if the Indian economy is to break away from its recent stagnation, a return to vigorous growth in public sector investment as a part of a return to planned development is essential." They attribute the growth stagnation since the mid-sixties to the downturn in public sector real GFCF after 1965-66, on the grounds of public investment driving private investment

---

19. These figures used in this paragraph are again from the CSO statement on capital formation by the type of asset and institution.

20. The high ICOR in phase IA was probably due to over ambitious extension of new railway lines ignoring long gestation lags and low traffic projections.

profitability, employment, and poverty reduction.[21] They also point to the exhaustion of possibilities from import-substituting industrialisation, low agricultural growth, problems in public-sector management and operation, non-growing public saving and declining aid, and state that the 1966 devaluation and other liberalisation measures were not taken far enough.

## Table 2.5

*Distribution of Public Gross Capital Formation (GCF) by Sector*

*(Per Cent)*

| Sector | Earliest Year of Data (1960-61) | End of Sub-phase I A (1964-65) | End of Sub-phase I B (1979-80) | End of Sub-phase II A (1991-92) | Last Year of Data for Sub-phase II B (2000-01) |
|---|---|---|---|---|---|
| Agriculture & Allied | 13.1 | 12.1 | 15.9 | 6.6 | 5.3 |
| *Agriculture* | 12.4 | 11.5 | 15.2 | 5.8 | 4.7 |
| Mining & Quarrying | 2.4 | 3.4 | 6.1 | 10.8 | 3.7 |
| Manufacturing | 18.0 | 13.3 | 20.7 | 14.5 | 6.4 |
| Electricity, Gas & Water Supply | 8.6 | 14.6 | 19.8 | 30.3 | 23.4 |
| Construction | 0.4 | 0.6 | 1.0 | 0.7 | 0.7 |
| Trade, Hotels & Restaurants | 0.1 | 0.2 | 0.7 | -3.0 | 6.0 |
| Transport, Storage & Communication | 22.9 | 27.6 | 12.5 | 16.0 | 24.6 |
| *Railways* | 19.1 | 23.1 | 5.8 | 5.8 | 4.7 |
| *Other Transport* | 2.3 | 2.0 | 4.2 | 4.5 | 3.2 |
| *Storage* | | | | 0.0 | 1.0 |
| *Communication* | 1.5 | 2.5 | 2.5 | 5.6 | 15.8 |
| FIREHBS | 2.6 | 1.9 | 2.2 | 5.5 | 4.9 |
| *Banking & Insurance* | 0.4 | 0.3 | 0.5 | 4.0 | 3.3 |
| *Real Estate, Housing & Business Services* | 2.2 | 1.6 | 1.7 | 1.5 | 1.6 |
| Community, Social & Personal Services | 31.9 | 26.3 | 21.0 | 18.7 | 25.0 |
| *Public Administration & Defence* | 30.0 | 25.0 | 18.7 | 16.3 | 22.4 |
| *Other Services* | 1.9 | 1.3 | 2.3 | 2.4 | 2.6 |
| **Total** | 100 | 100 | 100 | 100 | 100.0 |

*Source* : CSO (all series in 1993-94 prices).

*Notes* : Data on sector shares in public sector investment is available only between 1960-61 and 2000-01.

21. The authors note that the trends established before 1965 could not have been carried forward without major changes in policies and acknowledge that efficiency issues are important [as in Bhagwati and Desai (1970) and Bhagwati and Srinivasan (1974)].

The share of the public sector in total GDP almost doubled during sub-phase IB to 22.1 per cent from 11.8 per cent at the end of the previous sub-phase (Table 2.3). This was due to a tripling of the share in mining to 97 per cent and in trade hotels and restaurants to 7.3 per cent, and a more than doubling in agriculture (to 3 per cent), construction (to 13.6 per cent) and banking and insurance (to 72.5 per cent). In other community, social and personal services it almost doubled to 30.4 per cent. Thus, the direct role of the government in production of goods and services expanded vigorously during this sub-phase, and along with the legislative and procedural control stifled private initiative, entrepreneurship and innovation.

**d) Throttling Manufacturing**

As discussed earlier (chapter 1), Ahluwalia (1985, 1991) has analysed the stagnation in the growth of value added in the registered manufacturing sector (ASI & IIP) since the mid-sixties and the turnaround in growth in the early-eighties in terms of trends in TFPG growth in this sector. We analysed in a qualitative way the effect of the 'socialist' policies introduced during phase IB on the manufacturing and other sectors of the economy. The question that we address here is the quantitative impact of the 'socialist' policies, as well as the lagged effect of similar policies introduced in the previous phase, on the growth of GDP from manufacturing. A dummy for the period 1965-66 to 1979-80 (D6579) is introduced into equation (4a). Its co-efficient is found to be significant at the 10 per cent level. The best fit is however found with the dummy for 1965-66 to 1980-81 (D6580) whose co-efficient is highly significant:

$$\text{(4c) GrGman} = \underset{(12.1)}{0.066} + \underset{(-2.54)}{-0.0252^{*}\text{D6580}} + \underset{(2.53)}{0.114^{*}\text{DrainMean}}$$

$R^2 = 0.228$, $R^2$ (adjusted) $= 0.196$, DW $= 1.74$.

This equation establishes that there was a reduction of 2.5 per cent per annum in the growth rate of manufacturing during 1965-66 to 1980-81. In general, this could have been due either to the policies we followed or to external/exogenous factors. In our view, the policies followed during sub-phase IB (1965-66 to 1979-80) reduced the rate of growth of manufacturing by 2.5 per cent points during the period 1965-66 to 1980-81. If we compare this equation with (4b), containing the dummy D81 (1981-82 to 2002-03), we find that the equation (4c) has greater explanatory power. Further, when both dummies are included simultaneously D6580 has greater significance than D81.[22] This suggests that the removal of some of the constraints/barriers to growth imposed during 1965-66 to 1979-80 had a greater role in the acceleration of manufacturing growth from 1981-82 than the stimulation of new growth impulses from 1981-82 onwards. We will examine this issue below in greater detail.

### e) Governance Impact

This sub-phase of legislative-bureaucratic socialism and the political and other developments that took place during this period, set in motion a gradual deterioration in formal government institutions. The effect of this deterioration in governance is with us to this day.

## B. Phase II: Bharatiya Rate of Growth

The macro aspects of this phase were analysed in chapter 1. In this chapter, we analyse the two sub-phases of the phase and go in greater detail into sector evolution.

The second phase of development can be divided into two sub-phases. In the first sub-phase (IIA), exchange management, tax, and tariff policies continued their earlier trajectories. It was only during the second sub-phase (IIB) that there was a quantum change in approach, with a much clearer articulation of the reform philosophy and acceleration in actual economic reform measures. The relative CV falls sharply after 1990-91, while the relative mean rose, a phenomenon also observed in between sub-phases IA and IB (Figure 1.4). From this perspective, the first sub-phase ended in 1990-91 and the new one began in 1991-92.

There is, however an alternative dividing line based on growth. From this perspective, the low growth rate in 1991-92 is linked to the policy mistakes during earlier years and the problems accumulated as a result of such policies. These mistakes and problems cannot be corrected instantaneously; there is a lag of about a year for any new

---

22. T = 1.57 (prob=12.3%) *versus* t=0.67 (prob=50%).

policy to take effect. Thus, any change in policy during 1991-92 would only affect growth in 1992-93.[23] From this perspective the new growth phase would begin in 1992-93, after the old growth phase ended in 1991-92. We replace D80+ in equation (1) by two dummies, D8091 for the period 1980-91 and D92+ for the period after 1992-2002 and find both significant. This has slightly greater explanatory power[24] than if D80+ is replaced by the dummies D8090 for the period 1980-90 and D91+ for the period after 1991-2002. In our view this division into sub-periods is more appropriate for evaluating the effect of policies—good and bad—on the economy. For the moment we adopt this division into sub-phases, and will return to the first approach subsequently.

A third commonly used approach to study crises is to leave out the main crisis year along with the year in which reforms are initiated, and lump these together as the crisis years. Comparisons are then made between the pre-crisis and post-crisis years. As our objective is to study the growth trends over fifty years and not to study the crisis *per se*, we do not pursue this approach.[25]

### *C. Phase II A: Modest Reform*

The first sub-phase of the second (BRG) phase of development started after one of the worst droughts and ended after the BoP crisis of 1990-91. During this phase, the process of reform was very selective and case by case. As K.N. Raj (1986), pointed out there was no official resolution or statement about the 'new economic policy', which saw "certain changes in policy initiated in stages over the last several months". The pace of reform was quite slow, held back by severe bureaucratic and political inertia. This inertia was certainly linked to and perhaps caused by the democratic system prevailing in

---

23. In fact in most countries across the world in which such balance of payments (BoP) crises have occurred, the recovery has taken at least two years.

24. The R-square and adjusted R-square values are higher.

25. Acharya (2001), in comparing the period from1950-51 to 1980-81 with the eighties and nineties, states that, "Some commentators believe that the growth in the crisis year of 1991-92 should be included in the earlier, 'pre-crisis' period (which would pull down that average to 5.3 per cent) on the grounds that the crisis was a direct result of the policies and trends in the eighties. Others, such as Williamson, feel that 1991-92 growth belongs in the latter period because of 'slack built up during the crisis'. My preferred option of omitting 1991-92 from both periods would seem to be a reasonable compromise."

India. Williamson and Zagha (2002) used the term 'Hindu rate of reform' to describe the entire process of reform including that in the nineties. In our view, this term is more appropriate for the reform undertaken during the eighties, when only the most glaring and obvious distortions introduced by government intervention, on which there was broad consensus among economic analysts, were corrected.

**1. Policy Reform**

Industrial de-licensing measures included automatic endorsement of capacity expansion up to 25 per cent of licensed capacity, broad banding of industrial licenses,[26] de-reservation of 40 industries, and rise in the size limit (value of output/sales) defining small-scale industry (SSI). The cement and aluminium industries, which were subject to price, distribution, and investment control, were de-licensed. In 1985, firms with assets below Rs. 5 crore were de-licensed subject to certain conditions. This limit was raised to Rs. 15 crore in 1988. The scope for large industrial groups was expanded over time by a gradual rise in the limit below which MRTP clearance was not required for investment (Rs. 100 crore). This was sorely needed to increase competition in the economy, which was being stifled by vested interests to increase their monopolistic power, with the MRTP being "reduced to the proverbial 'grin without a cat' in Alice in Wonderland", as K.N. Raj (1986) put it. The scope for diversification and expansion of capacity for the industries under investment licensing was gradually expanded.[27] There was virtually no reform in other production sectors such as mining and agriculture.

Imports of capital goods were made procedurally easier through licensing of imports for modernisation and export industries. Intermediate imports were gradually moved from licensing to tariff protection and made available for export production at lower or zero duty.[28] Tax rates declined slowly from the absurd highs they had reached in the seventies (such as an over-100 per cent marginal rate on income from assets, inclusive of wealth tax) and modified value-

---

26. This was done in stages to include 28 industry groups by 1986.
27. According to Raj (1986), the main thrust of the mid-eighties policy changes was the greater scope for expansion it offered the private sector and the opportunities opened up, thereby, for multinationals.
28. Tariff rates on manufactured goods increased during the first half of the eighties.

added tax (MODVAT) credit was introduced into the excise tax. The control regime, however, continued to be extended in areas such as exchange management and import tariffs continued to rise.

**2. Outcome: Macro Perspective**

Sub-phase IIA covered the period from 1980-81 to 1991-92. During this sub-phase, economic growth has averaged 5.5 per cent per annum, only 0.2 percentage points different from the 5.7 per cent rate for the full second growth phase (Table 1.1). As a result of the policy reforms, investment (gross capital formation) growth accelerated marginally from 4.5 per cent per annum in sub-phase IB to 5 per cent in sub-phase IIA. More important than the size of the increase, was the change in the structure of investment. The rate of growth of investment in machinery and equipment more than doubled from 3.7 per cent per annum during sub-phase IB to 9.9 per cent per annum during sub-phase IIA. This raised the average share of machinery in gross fixed capital formation by 15.4 per cent points between the two phases. As shown by De Long and Summers (1993), equipment investment is strongly co-related with long run growth. Hendricks (2000) models the effect of equipment prices and equipment investment. We find that the relative price of machinery declined by 0.8 per cent per annum during sub-phase IIA after rising by 2.2 per cent per annum during IB. The opening of capital good imports likely improved the quality (in terms of embodied technology) of capital goods and put some competitive pressure on domestic capital goods producers. Though the nominal price of imported capital goods may have been higher (thus moderating the decline) the quality-adjusted price of capital goods may have fallen even more. Thus, the increase in investment in machinery and the greater availability and use of higher quality equipment imports were important factors in the acceleration in growth during this phase.[29]

There was also a sharp acceleration in the rate of growth of private investment from 3.5 per cent per annum during sub-phase IB to 8.4 per cent per annum during sub-phase IIA. The share of private investment consequently increased by 10.9 per cent points between 1964-65 and 1979-80 (i.e. over IIA).[30] The increased role of the

29. As shown by Delong and Summers (1991) machinery investment is an important driver of economic growth.

private sector also contributed to the acceleration in the growth rate. For the entire economy, the TFPG figures given in Guha-Khasnobis and Bari (2003) turned positive in the eighties, with the largest change being of 2.90 percentage points, from (–)0.40 per cent in the seventies to 2.50 per cent in the eighties.

### 3. Sector Growth and the Public Sector

The growth of the banking and insurance sector accelerated even further to 11.6 per cent, resulting in its becoming the fastest growing sector (Table 2.1).[31] Its contribution to overall growth increased to 7 per cent from 4 per cent in sub-phase IB (Table 2.2) and it attracted much more public investment during this phase reaching 4.0 per cent of total public GCF in 1991-92, up from 0.5 per cent in 1979-80 (Table 2.3). The decline in the share of public investment in the banking and insurance sector, from 60 per cent in 1979-80 to 47 per cent in 1991-92, suggests that the role of the private sector also started expanding (Table 2.3). The share of the public sector in the GDP from banking and insurance lagged this decline in investment. It rose to a peak of 81.5 per cent in 1988-89 before starting to decline.

The decision of the government to allocate more of its investment budget to the banking and insurance sector is, however, questionable, as the ICOR and non-performing assets (NPAs) increased during this sub-phase. The ICOR increased by 50 per cent during this sub-phase to 0.6 (from 0.4 in previous sub-phase). The NPAs of the banking sector also expanded during this period. With the introduction of income and capital adequacy norms in 1992, the regulators found that banks had accumulated a large stock of NPAs. Given the political interference, 'loan melas', etc. during sub-phase IIA, it is likely that a substantial part of the outstanding NPAs on March 31, 1992 were generated during this phase. Thus, the expansion of public banking as measured by the GDP from the public sector, overstates the net benefits of public banking, as the cost of the NPAs generated in sub-phase IIA were paid in sub-phase IIB.

---

30. The average share of the private sector in gross fixed capital formation however decreased by 2.8 per cent points between these two periods because of several trend reversals over 1964-65 to 1980-81.

31. See Gordon and Gupta (2003) for an analysis of the service sector.

Electricity sector growth accelerated to 9 per cent per annum based on a substantial increase in the share of public investment going to this sector, from 20 per cent in 1979–80 to 30 per cent in 1991–92 (Table 2.1 and Table 2.4). The ICOR for electricity declined to 15.7 during this sub-phase, close to the sub-phase IA level of 16.2 and sharply down from the excessive levels reached in sub phase IB (Table 2.4).

Mining sector growth also accelerated to 8.4 per cent, the third highest sector growth rate (Table 2.1). Mining presented a mixed picture during this sub-phase. The government or public share of the GDP in mining declined to about 90 per cent in 1991–92 (from 96 per cent in 1979-80) while its share in the GCF increased to about 96 per cent from 70 per cent in 1979–80 (Table 2.3). Thus, the ICOR for public sector mining more than doubled during this sub-phase to 7.2 from 2.7 in sub-phase IB, even though the overall ICOR declined marginally because of the improved performance of the private sector (Table 2.4). Thus, the government's virtual monopoly of the mining sector continued to be a burden on the economy during sub-phase IIA.

Agricultural growth recovered to 4.2 per cent per annum and contributed 21 per cent to total economic growth even with a reduced share of agriculture (Tables 2.2 and 2.3). The improved growth rate probably resulted from the lagged effect of the Green Revolution, the steady spread of high-yielding varieties across the country complemented by better monsoons. Overall utilisation in agriculture improved dramatically, as reflected in the return of the ICOR for the sector to a normal level of 1.8 in this sub-phase, from 5 in sub-phase IB (Table 2.4). However, the public sector's ICOR in agriculture doubled to 40, from 20 in sub-phase IB, highlighting the increasing inefficiency of the public production system (Table 2.4).

### 4. Role of Demand and Supply Factors

Registered manufacturing growth picked up substantially to 6.8 per cent per annum with a sharp reduction in the ICOR to 6.9 from the previous sub-period's 9.6 (Tables 2.2 and 2.6). The ICOR in public sector manufacturing also declined to 7.4, from over 17 (Table 2.4). Consequently, the contribution of manufacturing to economic growth equalled that of agriculture during this period (21 per cent) (Table 2.2). Such a sharp reduction in the ICOR suggests that demand constraints played a role in pushing up the ICOR in sub-phase IB and these constraints were reduced or removed in sub-phase IIA.[32] Part of this stimulus could have come from the acceleration of real government consumption expenditure to 6 per cent per annum during sub-phase IIA from 5.1 per cent per annum during sub-phase IB (Table 1.1). The conventional wisdom is that it indeed came from the increase in the fiscal deficit, which for the central government grew from an average of 4.1 per cent of GDP in sub-phase IB to 7.7 per cent of GDP in sub-phase IIA.[33] Half to two-third of this, however, spilled over into the external account (Virmani, 2001b), with the current account deficit more than doubling from 0.7 per cent of GDP in IB to 1.8 per cent of GDP in sub-phase IIA (Table 2.6). To the extent that this spill over was directly linked with debt financed import of defence equipment, it constituted a future burden on the economy. On the domestic side, inflation (WPI) declined from 10.7 per cent per annum in IB to 8.6 per cent per annum in IIA. It is, therefore, possible that the (domestic component of the) fiscal deficit, in the presence of excess capacity, could have (temporarily) increased the growth rate through better capacity utilisation.

Another more important factor in our view was a supply-side stimulus. The sharp increase in oil prices and the consequent increase in the oil bill since the early-seventies, acted like a tax on the Indian economy. The real oil import bill paid by the citizens of India increased by an average of 37 per cent per annum during sub-phase IB, while it increased by only 6.9 per cent per annum during sub-phase IIA (Table 1.1, chapter 1). Thus, the huge transfer of resources to the Organisation of Petroleum Exporting Countries (OPEC) during sub-phase IB was reduced to a fraction during sub-phase IIA. This would, in principle, leave more purchasing power in the hands of Indians during the latter sub-phase, relative to that in the former, and

32. Whether these are 'structural domestic demand constraints' as emphasised by Chakravarty (1984) or those induced by 'lack of policy or failure of policy' and 'export demand constraints' as emphasised by Bhagwati and Srinivasan (1984), Srinivasan and Narayana (1977), and Bhagwati and Srinivasan (1974) is a question that needs to be answered.

33. As represented by the World Bank country reports on India. See also Joshi and Little (1994).

provide a supply-side stimulus equivalent to a tax reduction.[34] This is confirmed by the acceleration in the growth of real private consumption expenditure to 4.5 per cent per annum during sub-phase IIA, from 2.8 per cent per annum during sub-phase IB and 3.7 per cent in sub-phase IA (Table 1.1). A decline in the relative price of imported oil reduced the implicit (foreign) tax on the private sector stimulating private consumption. As a consequence, inflation declined and capacity utilisation probably increased during this sub-phase.

Another consequence of the growth recovery in agriculture, manufacturing, and mining was the narrowing of the growth differential between tradable and non-tradable goods. During this sub-phase, tradable goods production grew by 4.7 per cent per annum while non-tradable services grew by 6.3 per cent per annum (Table 2.1). This gap was narrower than that during any previous sub-phase.

### 5. Acceleration Puzzle and Solutions

A question that analysts have started raising over the last few years (without providing an answer) is, how what appears to outside observers to be limited reforms in the eighties, could produce such dramatic changes in the growth rate. One factor identified earlier is the ostensibly export-linked liberalisation of capital goods imports, under the Export Promotion Guarantee Scheme, which resulted in a dramatic increase in the import of capital goods generally (Virmani, 2001b). Such imports of embodied technology played a role in the enhanced growth rate. Another factor that has been identified in this chapter is the change in the structure of investment from structures to machinery and equipment. The third factor in our view was the credibility of the reforms that were introduced. The fourth factor (discussed below) is the under-performance of the economy during sub-phase IB, which increased the gap between the potential and actual GDP. [35] This combined with the fiscal stimulus and the supply side impact of the slower rise in oil prices to increase capacity utilisation.

---

34. Conventional wisdom has focussed on the stimulus provided by the rising fiscal deficit during the eighties as an explanation for the rise in the growth rate, but a growth rate that high could not be sustained for this very reason.

35. A third, not mutually exclusive possibility is that production from non-licensed capacity that had been built up 'illegally', gradually started to be declared officially as it began to be allowed officially.

The growth gap can be very crudely estimated as follows: Let us assume that the 4.1 per cent average growth rate of the economy during sub-phase IA represented the underlying growth potential of the economy during this period.[36] Thus, because of various reasons including bad policies, the economy under-performed by 1.2 per cent per year during sub-phase IB. At the end of the 15 years of this sub-phase, the economy had an output gap, which could potentially add 18 percentage points or about 1.5 per cent per annum to the growth rate over the next 12 years, if these wrong policies could be reversed. This would have resulted in a growth rate that was almost identical to that actually seen in sub-phase IIA.

Alternatively, we can focus on the tradable goods sector where the output gap was present and the growth potential concentrated. This result is replicated in the tradable goods sector, which under-performed by 1.6 per cent per annum during sub-phase IB relative to sub-phase IA, i.e., by 24 percentage points cumulative (Table 2.1). Thus, the output gap in this sector had the potential to raise the growth rate of the GDP from tradable goods to 4.6 per cent per annum during the next 12 years, which is exactly what happened during sub-phase IIA—the actual growth rate was 4.7 per cent per annum. The limited liberalisation that took place in the eighties was directed at the tradable goods sector, particularly manufacturing. To this extent, the above explanation is linked to the one in Virmani (2001b). The statistical analysis in equation 4b confirms that the change in the policy regime starting in 1980-81 had lifted the depressing effect of the 'socialist' policy rhetoric on manufacturing growth. Thus, the growth of manufacturing was by 1981-82 back on the track established during 1950-51 to 1964-65.

The story is similar, but not identical in the non-tradable services sector, whose growth rate increased by 2.1 percentage points between sub-phase IB and sub-phase IIA (Table 2.1). The acceleration was even higher at 2.3 percentage points if we exclude the GDP from public administration from this sector (Table 2.1). A deeper examination of the service sectors shows that only one sub-sector—'banking, insurance, real estate and housing, and business services'

36. The alternative would be to assume that the average growth rate during phase I of 3.5 per cent represented the potential. In this case 4.85 per cent per annum would result from catch-up and only 0.65 per cent from new measures.

(FIREHBS)—shows a different pattern. The growth rate of all the other services taken together declined from 5.6 per cent per annum in sub-phase IA to 4.3 per cent in sub-phase IB and then recovered to 5.7 per cent per annum in sub-phase IIA (Table 2.1). In contrast the FIREHBS sub-sector accelerated from 3.5 per cent per annum in phase I to 8.6 per cent in phase II (Table 2.1). Its growth rate was faster in sub-phase IB (4 per cent) than in sub-phase IA (3.1 per cent) followed by an unprecedented 9.4 per cent per annum during sub-phase IIA (Table 2.1). Within the FIREHBS sub-sector, the growth rate of banking (finance) and insurance (FI) as well as of real estate, personal housing, and business services (REHBS) accelerated between sub-phases IB and IIA (Table 2.1). This provided the new growth impulse to the service sector that we have statistically identified as having started from 1984-85 or 1985-86.

The credibility of the reforms instituted during the 1980s was very high for several reasons. The same leader, who had instituted the earlier control policies that slowed the economy, was changing the direction of economic policy. As she was perceived to have learnt from her own experience, the changes were more credible to both potential beneficiaries and losers. To the latter she could say, "I introduced the policies that you wanted but they need to be changed now." Her surprising come back after a period in the wilderness made her unchallenged in her own party, virtually silencing any internal critics till her death.[37] Her victory also shocked the opposition into silence, as it was so unexpected. In any case, many in the opposition had been critics of her earlier policies and could not reverse their position without losing their own credibility. Whatever reforms were introduced, were seen as examples of the new direction she was setting. These would determine the future economic environment so critical for investment decisions. Economic agents could see the economic policy clearly beginning to turn around and realised that it would like a large oil tanker changing direction, take time to face in the opposite direction. This view was further strengthened by a much younger man taking over the reigns of the government on her death as it was widely hoped that he would make the transformation to a modern market economy even faster. This hope was reflected in the

37. The importance of this factor will become apparent when we analyse phase IIB.

fact that despite limited experience of governance he received, an unprecedented and overwhelming majority in parliament.[38]

In the discussion of sub-phase IB, it was noted that government institutions started to deteriorate during this sub-phase. According to the institutional literature, this would tend to reduce the rate of growth. Virmani (2004b) has shown that, paradoxically, a deterioration in the quality of institutions may increase the rate of growth-termed the 'governance paradox' (see chapter 1 Vol. II). The chapter categorises government institutions into three types and shows that a deterioration in the quality and efficiency of one type (market substituting institutions implementing market distorting policies), will have a positive effect on growth. Anecdotal evidence suggests that this is indeed what happened during sub-phase IIA as firms started to evade the control regime and the market substituting institutions started to collude with them.[39]

To summarise, the policy framework that was responsible for the slowdown of growth started to change during the eighties and its enforcement also slackened due to deterioration in governance. Even though individual policy reforms were incremental ('tinkerisation') rather than revolutionary, remaining controls and restrictions also started to be evaded, thus, resulting in greater *de-facto* (as against de-jure) de-control. They were also politically credible signals of the intent to reform failed policies. This had an impact on the investment environment leading to more private investment and a shift from building of structures towards machinery and equipment. The opening of the economy to capital goods imports magnified the impact that they had on the efficiency of investment. In addition, the output gap that had opened up during the previous sub-phase, provided an opportunity for catch-up growth or an upturn in the growth cycle. An increase in the fiscal deficit, which stimulated government consumption and a deceleration of growth in oil prices, which stimulated private consumption, in the presence of unused capacity put the economy on the recovery leg of the growth cycle and (at least temporarily) accelerated growth.

---

38. Some observers attribute this primarily to the sympathy vote.

39. The most prominent (alleged) case was of a company that imported and built a petrochemical plant of twice the size given in the import license and the investment/production license.

### *D. Phase II B: Broader Reform*

The second sub-phase (IIB) began in 1992-93 with external reforms coupled with the macroeconomic response to the BoP crisis.[40] These reforms led to a quick recovery and an investment and manufacturing boom not seen in India's economic history. After the initiation of the nineties reforms, the trend rate of growth as measured by the HP-filtered series exceeded 6 per cent for five years, which was unprecedented, and there were four years in which the five-year moving average of the growth rate exceeded 6.5 per cent, which was again unprecedented. The boom was however short-lived and growth soon reverted back to the 'Bharatiya rate of growth'. Nevertheless, growth during this sub-phase has averaged about 6.1 per cent per annum—0.6 percentage point higher than during sub-phase IIA. The co-efficient of variation of growth also halved during this sub-phase compared to IIA, thus, showing an improvement in what has been termed as the "Quality of growth" (Table 1.1).

#### 1. Macro Overview

The rate of growth of both private and government consumption increased only marginally during this sub-phase. Growth of export of goods and services accelerated to 10.8 per cent from 8.4 per cent per annum in the previous sub-phase. The small increase in the growth stimulus provided by the faster export growth was however countered by a doubling of the rate of growth of the oil import bill to 15.7 per cent per annum, from 6.9 per cent (Table 1.1, chapter 1).[41]

The rate of growth of investment accelerated by 3.8 per cent points to 7.8 per cent per annum. Though, fixed investment in machinery continued to grow at a fast clip of 7.9 per cent, this was 2 per cent points lower than in sub-phase IIA (Table 1.1, chapter 1). Nevertheless, the average share of machinery in fixed investment in IIB was 10 per cent points higher than in IIA. Most of this increase came from private investment as the growth of public investment in machinery decelerated dramatically. The share of private investment in

---

40. The reforms have been documented and analysed by Chopra, Collyns, Hemming, *et al.*, (1995), Joshi and Little (1994), Ahluwalia and Little (1998), Srinivasan (2000), Acharya (2001), Virmani (2001b), and Williamson and Zagha (2002) among others.

41. The rupee values of exports and imports have been deflated using the GDP deflator.

fixed investment consequently increased from 52.6 per cent in IIA to 67.6 per cent in IIB. As shown in Virmani (2001b) growth in import of capital goods also decelerated. The growth of fixed investment in manufacturing, that had accelerated sharply during sub-phase IIA decelerated somewhat to 9.7 per cent per annum during IIB, despite an acceleration in the rate of growth of registered manufacturing to 12.8 per cent per annum. GFCF growth in mining and quarrying also collapsed during IIB. Gross fixed capital formation in agriculture, which had collapsed from its green revolution boom of 5 per cent per annum during IB to 1.3 per cent during IIA, withered to 0.6 per cent per annum during IIB. The deceleration in tradable sector investment growth may have (temporarily) affected productivity growth.

Import controls, quantitative restrictions and protective custom tariffs declined during sub-phase IIB. Peak tariff rates, which had risen to 150 per cent by 1990-91, had been reduced to 30 per cent in 2002-03 and to 25 per cent in 2003-04.[42] The net effect on protection was a combination of this reduction and offsetting changes in the nominal exchange rate. The reduction in protection of manufactured goods and minerals would have led to a depreciation of the real exchange rate i.e. a fall in the price of tradable goods relative to that of non-tradable goods. We would, therefore, expect to find during an initial adjustment period, a reduction in the rate of growth of tradable goods relative to the rate of growth of non-tradable services. This is what happened. The growth of the tradable goods sector decelerated to 4.5 per cent during IIB, while that of the non-tradable services sector accelerated to 7.5 per cent, the highest level of any sub-phase. The growth of the services sector excluding government administration accelerated to 7.5 per cent per annum, from 6.4 per cent in sub-phase IIA (Table 2.1). Consequently, the share of tradable goods in GDP declined by 8.4 per cent points over sub-phase IIB compared to a decline of 4.9 per cent points over sub-phase IIA.

## 2. Growth Impulse

The statistical significance of the (temporary) growth boom has already been tested (chapter 1).

---

42. There were a few items up to 300 per cent during 1990-91. In 2003-04 the tariff rate on the automobile sector, a dozen agricultural goods and alcoholic beverages exceeded 25 per cent.

The results suggest that the economic reforms of the early nineties imparted an additional growth impulse to the manufacturing sector. This led the growth boom of Indian economy during 1994-95 to 1996-97. The boom however, petered out in 1997-98. The reasons for this are explored further below.

### 3. Relative Sector Performance

Within the service sector the depth of de-licensing and decontrol affected the speed and degree with which private investment and production expanded. The communication sector with a phenomenal growth rate of over 18 per cent per annum can be called the leading sector in this sub-phase of growth (Table 2.1). Given its small size, it contributed only about 5 per cent to overall growth; this is, however, five times its contribution in the sub-phase IIA (Table 2.2). Clearly the breaking of the government monopoly over telecom, the entry of private competitors, and the early set-up of a regulatory system, however imperfect, have played a vital role in the high growth. Despite initial hiccups and false steps, telecom demonstrates the potential contribution to growth of opening, previously government-owned or monopolised sectors, given a moderately good regulatory system to deal with natural monopoly elements and promote competition.

The financial sector dropped to third place with a lower growth rate of 9.4 per cent per annum (Table 2.1). This brought its contribution to overall growth to 9 per cent from 7 per cent in sub-phase IIA (Table 2.2). The introduction of modern regulatory norms and procedures led to the exposure of hidden NPAs in the banking system (particularly public sector banks) and slowed the growth of the banking system, a cost that had to be paid for past sins. This was partly offset by the growth impulse imparted by gradual de-control of the banking system and the stimulus arising from private entry and competition. The public share in the GCF in banking and insurance fell sharply during sub-phase IIB to half its level in sub-phase IIA, but has risen sharply since 1997-98 (47 per cent in 1991-92, 41.7 per cent in 1997-98). Its share in GDP from this sector declined to 58.4 per cent in 2000-01 from over 78 per cent in 1990-91 (Table 2.3).

The electricity sector was, however, dethroned from its place among the top three performers as its growth rate slowed to 5.7 per cent per annum (Table 2.1). The gradual conversion of the electricity sector from a public utility to a mafia-type operation run for the benefit of employees and political bosses, played a role in this slowdown as organised theft increased to half of the total production in some states.[43] The lack of will to challenge power theft and the absence of a clear policy and regulatory framework for promoting private entry and competition were major factors in the growth slowdown.

Agriculture growth slowed to 3.3 per cent per annum, almost the same rate as seen in sub-phase IA (Table 2.1), reducing its contribution to 13 per cent of the total growth (Table 2.2), given that the share of agriculture had declined to about a fourth of the GDP. The manufacturing sector contributed 17 per cent to overall growth, only marginally less than its contribution in sub-phase IA (Table 2.2). Manufacturing growth accelerated to 6.8 per cent per annum, with both modern (registered) and traditional (unregistered) segments growing faster (Table 2.1). The net effect of increased competition on manufacturing growth was, therefore, positive as improved access to imported technology and inputs and cheaper imports more than offset the reduction in relative prices arising from lower tariffs on output. Intra industry trade (import and export) has also increased across a range of two-digit industries during the nineties, indicating efficiency improvements through increased specialisation (Virmani, 2003). This was also reflected in the remarkable stability of the ICOR, which remained unchanged from the previous two sub-phases.

The measured ICOR for modern manufacturing, however, increased to 8.3 after declining to 6.9 in sub-phase IIA from 9.6 in sub-phase IB (Table 2.4). Entry of new firms and upgradation of technology (by the more competitive firms) through new investment with limited exit of existing firms would raise the ICOR and reduce TFPG (as measured).[44] As labour laws effectively apply only to the registered manufacturing sector, and the exit problem is most acute for large units within this sub-sector, a lowering of manufacturing tariffs could be followed by a period during which measured average TFPG declines. An ICRIER working paper by D.K. Das (2003) shows that TFPG has declined in a majority of (registered) three digit industries during the nineties. In our view this (probably) reflects a

---

43. I use the word 'Mafia' consciously as state electricity board employees reserved the right to cut of electricity to any establishment that did not provide them free services or cash (as appropriate).

44. With no adjustment for capacity utilisation.

decline in capacity utilisation of the so-called 'sick' and other inefficient firms that are not allowed to exit because of controls and policy restrictions. Goldar and Kumari (2003) have shown that capacity utilisation in registered manufacturing increased during the eighties.

Mining sector growth collapsed to 3.8 per cent per annum, only a little higher than its low point of 3.7 per cent in sub-phase IB (Table 2.1). The slowdown was accompanied by a worsening of capital utilisation as the overall ICOR rose to 8.2, from 6.1 in sub-phase IIA, and that for public sector mining increased to 14.6 (Table 2.4). Public sector mining's share in the gross value added declined to 86.7 per cent in 2000-01 from 97.2 per cent in 1979-80, while its share in the GCF went up from 70 per cent to 86.1 per cent (Table 2.3). The liberalisation of the mining sector during sub-phase IIB has been woefully inadequate, with the vital Coal Nationalisation (Amendment) Bill languishing in Parliament for several years, and a clear policy framework and modern regulatory structure still absent for most minerals.

Many other services, besides those considered above, contributed to the acceleration of non-tradable service growth. Among these were hotels and restaurants, which had the second highest growth rate of 10.3 per cent, trade (8 per cent), community, social and private services (7.7 per cent), other transport (7 per cent), and real estate, personal dwellings, and business services (6.3 per cent). Several services grew faster than registered manufacturing (7.1 per cent) during this phase. Contrary to some perceptions, government administration grew by only 6.3 per cent per annum (Table 2.1) and actually pulled down the average for the service sector, even though real government consumption expenditure grew at a faster clip at 6.6 per cent per annum (Table 1.1, chapter 1). Construction, railway, and storage were the other sectors that grew at a lower rate than all manufacturing (6.8 per cent) (Table 2.1). Thus, the gap between the growth rate of tradable goods and services widened to its highest level of any sub-phase.

**4. Reform Puzzle: Constraints to Growth**

In sub-phase IIB, the puzzle is the reverse of that in sub-phase IIA. With much wider, deeper, and more comprehensive reform during this sub-phase (particularly in 1991-92 and 1992-93), why has the growth rate increased only marginally above that seen in sub-phase IIA? There are a number of possible explanations, which are discussed below.

a) Structural Reform: Impact Lags

It can be argued that fundamental changes in the economic policy framework take time to work their way through the economic system as agents take time to learn and respond to new conditions. Many industry-linked economists have asserted that the nineties reforms are leading to profound changes in the way that the industry conducts it self.[45] Though, these changes are visible in only a handful of pioneering companies, they will gradually spread throughout the industry and the macro effects will become apparent over the decade. We have already seen, however, that the reforms initiated in 1991-92 resulted in an industrial boom during 1993-94 to 1996-97 led by the consumer durable sector, including automobiles. Further, the underlying growth rate as measured by the HP filtered series has been declining continuously since the peak of 6.1 per cent in 1994-95 and 1995-96 to reach 4.8 per cent in 2002-03 (Table 1.1). *Prima facie* this does not provide support to this contention in terms of economic lags. One way to validate this assertion at this stage would be to find other countries that went through a similar reform experience followed by a lagged spurt in growth. The statistical analysis of the growth impulse (given above) however does not support this hypothesis.

b) Real Interest Rates

One hypothesis is that growth is slower than warranted by the reforms because interest rates are too high.[46] Using the State Bank of India (SBI) lending rate and the wholesale price index (WPI), we find that the real lending rate during Phase I was negative, averaging -1.9 per cent if we use the WPI and -2.3 per cent if we use the WPI for manufacturing (Table 2.6). The real interest rate increased from -2.8 per cent (-3.7 per cent) in sub phase IA to -0.6 per cent (-0.9 per cent) during sub-phase IB. This increase could have contributed to the decline in the growth rate between these two sub-phases. The low

45. One example of such an economist is Dr. Omkar Goswami of the Confederation of Indian Industry.

46. This stance is favoured, for instance, by Dr. Surjit S. Bhalla of Oxus Research.

interest rate during phase I was not due to the investment demand as it grew at 6.1 per cent per annum, almost the same as the 6.3 per cent per annum, during phase II. Similarly, the rise in real interest rates during sub-phase IB cannot be attributed to increased investment demand as the growth rate of investment declined to 4.5 per cent per annum from 7.9 per cent per annum during sub-phase IA (Table 1.1). At the same time the private saving rate and overall national saving rate continued to grow.

The real interest rate increased dramatically in phase II, averaging 7.8 per cent to 7.9 per cent (Table 2.6). Investment demand grew at a marginally higher rate of 5 per cent per annum during sub-phase IIA than it did earlier (Table 1.1), while the supply of government saving declined progressively over the eighties. The decline in the

**Table 2.6**

*Real Interest Rates (SBI) and Real Effective Exchange Rates (REER)*

*(Per Cent)*

| | *Phase I (1950-51 to 1979-80)* | | | *Phase II (1980-81 to 2001-02)* | | |
|---|---|---|---|---|---|---|
| | | *Sub-phase* | | | *Sub-phase* | |
| *Sector* | *Phase I (1950-1 to 1979-80)* | *I A (1951-64)* | *I B (1965-79)* | *Phase II (1980-81 to 2002-03)* | *II A (1980-91)* | *II B (1992-2000)* |
| SBI Lending Rate (Real) (Deflated by) | | | | | | |
| *WPI (Total)* | -1.7 | -2.9 | -0.6 | 7.8 | 7.9 | 7.8 |
| *WPI (Manufacturing)* | -2.3 | -3.7 | -0.9 | 8.6 | 8.3 | 8.9 |
| Inflation Rate | | | | | | |
| *WPI (Total)* | 9.0 | 7.3 | 10.7 | 7.6 | 8.6 | 6.5 |
| *WPI (Manufacturing)* | 9.6 | 8.3 | 10.9 | 6.9 | 8.2 | 5.4 |
| REER (Calendar Year) (Average Growth Rate) | | | | | | |
| *Export-Weighted Index* | -2.3 | -0.3 | -3.9 | -1.4 | -3.2 | 0.5 |
| *Trade-Weighted Index* | -0.8 | -0.3 | -4.1 | -1.0 | -2.7 | 0.8 |
| Ratio to GDP | | | | | | |
| Fiscal Deficit-Centre | 3.6 | 3.4 | 4.1 | 6.8 | 7.7 | 5.7 |
| Current Account Deficit | 1.4 | 1.3 | 0.7 | 1.3 | 1.8 | 0.9 |

*Source* : RBI (2003); (various years).

*Note* : The REERs are calculated for calendar years because data for financial years are only available from 1975-76 onwards. The REERs from 1950 to 1959 are our estimates.

government saving rate must be one important factor in the rise of real interest rate along with a possible increase in inefficiency of the politically directed banking system ('loan melas' in the 1980s). The higher growth rate during phase II was, therefore, achieved despite the rise in interest rates.

There is little change in the real interest rate between sub-phases IIA and IIB, when measured using the total WPI and a marginal increase of 0.5 percentage points when deflated by the WPI for manufacturing, from 8.3 per cent to 8.8 per cent (Table 2.6). This marginal rise in real interest rates has however, been more than offset by other factors ('animal spirits' activated by the 'new economic policy') with real gross domestic investment accelerating to 7.8 per cent per annum during sub-phase IIB (Table 1.1, chapter 1). Thus, at this broad level of analysis, real interest rates do not explain the growth puzzle.

At the same time, the above analysis does not imply that real interest rates do not have an impact on private investment or economic growth. It is quite possible that the growth rate would have been higher than it was, if real rates were lower. Perhaps manufacturing growth during sub-phase IIB would have been higher if real interest rates were lower. The average real interest rate at 6.9 per cent (7.7 per cent) during 1994-95 to 1996-97, was somewhat lower than the average for sub-phase IIB as a whole, and could have provided some growth stimulus. The small decline in the real rate thereafter, is likely the result of a fall in effective demand from the private sector as growth petered out.

The precise impact of interest rates on these variables will be analysed in the subsequent work. This requires recognition of the fact that Indian credit markets are not as developed, competitive or free as those of the developed countries. The floor on saving deposit rates in banks plays a small role, but other factors are much more important. The legacy of nationalisation of banking (in sub-phase IB) and the introduction of wide and deep structure of controls and directed credit still shapes the monetary system despite the liberalisation of the nineties. The multiple role of the RBI as the government's debt manager (salesman), proxy manager of the nationalised banks, and regulator responsible for the health of the payment system, often results in actions that are not consistent with efficient monetary management. In our view, these contradictions have kept the RBI from lowering the short-term (1 to 7 day) repo rates during periods of low growth and moderate inflation and weak private credit demand since 1997-98. One consequence of these high repo rates has been to put a floor under the overnight inter-bank, call-money rates and thus prop up the entire structure of bank lending rates. Another outcome of this policy has been a rising differential between domestic short-term rates and global short-term rates during 2002. This has attracted short-term capital inflows during 2002-03.

An additional factor in the downward stickiness of bank interest rates is the government monopoly of the banking system with government banks still constituting about 70 per cent of the total bank assets, the highest proportion in the world. With the RBI and the government either exercising regulatory forbearance or conniving in keeping deposit rates high and stable, loan interest rates often do not reflect credit market conditions during periods of low demand/ excess supply.

The inflation rate relevant for determining the real overnight rate is the current rate. Expectations about future inflation are irrelevant in determining such rates. Those who assert that expectations of higher future inflation (because of high fiscal deficit and rising government debt), have kept bank lending rates (for one year or more) high, have been disproved by the flat term structure of interest rates on government paper during 2002-03. The floors on the government provident fund (GPF) and post office saving instruments (so-called small saving instruments), have not kept this from happening.

c) Incomplete Reform: Reform Gaps

Another argument for the under-responsiveness of the tradable goods sector to the trade and other liberalisation of the nineties is the lack of sufficient complementary domestic reforms. These arguments are, however, quite distinct from arguments about the hollowing out of Indian manufacturing or of the manufacturing sector being a drag on overall growth. Manufacturing growth in sub-phase IIB at 6.8 per cent per annum has not only been distinctly higher than the 6.1 per cent per annum in sub-phase IIA but also higher than the 6.6 per cent per annum average during sub-phase IA (Table 2.1).

Though reduction of protection has created the conditions for labour-intensive agriculture and manufacturing to grow and export,

India's tariff rates remain among the highest in the world (Virmani, 2002a). Domestic policy constraints have kept even the limited potential created so far from being fully exploited. Thus, labour-intensive manufacturing continues to be hampered by the anachronistic SSI reservation policy and labour laws, rules, and procedures that have converted labour from a variable to a fixed factor in firms with over 100 employees, with attendant consequences on employment. Minimum wage laws applied to modern (power-using) firms with more than 10 employees and excise tax exemptions for firms with sales up to Rs.1 crore ($200,000), continue to distort the entire system of production and efficient division of labour, such as in the textile sector. This explanation is consistent with the statistical analysis of the growth impulse and its petering out.

As many of these policies were introduced during sub-phase IB, the increase in the share of manufacturing in GDP was only 2.4 percentage points during this period, compared to an average increase of 3.1 percentage points for the countries of S. Asia (Table 2.7). It is not surprising that with the persistence of policy distortions (in some cases even a worsening), the share of manufacturing increased by only 2.3 percentage points during phase II. The share of manufacturing at 17.1 per cent of the total GDP is, therefore, currently less than half that in China (34.5 per cent) and a little more than half that in Malaysia (32.8 per cent), Thailand (31.9 per cent), and the average for East Asia and Pacific (31.8 per cent) (Table 2.7).

Similarly, the lack of reform in the agriculture and allied sector has hampered the growth of agriculture (Virmani and Rajeev, 2002). The state monopoly over electricity production and supply coupled with the organised theft of power (Virmani, 1996) is another factor that affects the growth of modern manufacturing and agriculture.

#### d) Governance Deterioration: Public Goods

One argument made earlier is as follows: the pace of reform has picked up during the nineties and has had a positive effect on growth. This has been offset by a slow but steady deterioration in governance over the last several decades that is beginning to have a significant negative effect on growth (Virmani, 2002b). Thus, the net effect of the positive reform factor and the negative governance factor may be a growth 'plateau'. This explanation is also consistent with the statistical analysis of the growth impulse.

## Table 2.7

*Manufacturing Share in the GDP (%) and Change in Ratio*

*(Per Cent)*

| | *Share in Year* | | | | |
|---|---|---|---|---|---|
| *Country* | *Start of Phase I (1950-51)* | *Start of Sub-phase IB (1965-66)* | *Start of Phase II (1980-81)* | *Start of Sub-phase IIB (1992-93)* | *Last Year of Data in Phase II (2002-03)* |
| India | 8.9 | 13.1 | 13.8 | 15.7 | 17.1 |
| China[1] | | 29.2 | 40.5 | 33.1 | 34.5 |
| Indonesia[1] | | 8.4 | 13.0 | 19.1 | 26.0 |
| Malaysia[1] | | 9.5 | 21.6 | 25.8 | 32.8 |
| Thailand[1] | | 14.2 | 21.5 | 27.5 | 31.9 |
| South Asia[1] | | 13.5 | 15.8 | 16.1 | 15.6 |
| East Asia & the Pacific[1] | | 21.0 | 30.6 | 28.7 | 31.8 |

| | *Change during Period (Percentage Points)* | | | | | |
|---|---|---|---|---|---|---|
| | | *Sub-phase* | | | *Sub-phase* | |
| | *Phase I (1951-79)* | *I A (1951-64)* | *I B (1965-79)* | *Phase II (1980-2002)* | *II A (1980-91)* | *II B (1992-2002)* |
| India | 6.0 | 3.6 | 2.4 | 2.3 | 1.0 | 1.3 |
| China[2] | | | 10.8 | -5.5 | -7.3 | 1.8 |
| Indonesia | | | 3.3 | 14.4 | 2.6 | 11.8 |
| Malaysia | | | 11.0 | 12.8 | 5.6 | 7.2 |
| Thailand | | | 7.2 | 10.8 | 7.2 | 3.6 |
| South Asia | | | 3.1 | -0.9 | -0.6 | -0.3 |
| East Asia & the Pacific | | | | 1.7 | -1.9 | 3.6 |

*Sources* : CSO and World Bank (2002).

*Notes* : 1. The data on manufacturing share in the GDP for other regions and countries are reported for calendar years, i.e. for 1965, 1980, 1992, and 2000 and are available only between 1965 and 2000.

2. The change in ratio for China over sub-phase IB is computed with 1965 as the first year because data for 1964 is not available.

Governance deterioration also has another paradoxical result. As noted earlier, deterioration in the quality and efficiency of 'market distorting institutions' (Virmani, 2004b) during sub-phase IIA, meant that the effectiveness of several controls and licenses was undermined (see chapter 1 Vol. II). Thus, when these controls and licenses were formally eliminated in sub-phase IIB, the effect on growth was less than one would expect if governance quality had remained unchanged, as the degree of 'de-facto' decontrol was less than the '*de-jure*' decontrol.

The deterioration in the electricity and railway monopolies run by the government is an example of this general deterioration in governance. Both these are however 'private' goods and have (less efficient) substitutes in the form of private generation and road transport.[47] More important, these artificially created monopolies can be dismantled through private entry, selected privatisation and independent regulatory systems. This is much more difficult in the case of 'public goods', as private substitutes are an option for a very limited number of the richest and most powerful. Thus, the deterioration in the supply of 'public goods' like law and order, safety and security, courts, police, roads, public health, and civic education and 'quasi-public' goods (drinking water, sewage, sanitation, basic education and rural infrastructure) has a powerful negative effect on the economy and on public welfare.

There is an impression that the government's role in production and supply of goods and services has been reduced during the broad reform sub-phase (IIB). The reality is that the GDP from public sector averaged 25.9 per cent of total GDP during sub-phase IIB, 2.6 per cent points higher than in sub-phase IIA (23.3 per cent). The sharp and continuing rise of the share has, however, been arrested, with the share in 2000-01 (25.8 per cent) almost identical to that at the end of phase IIA (Table 2.3). Thus, there is still considerable scope for eliminating government involvement in the production and supply of private goods and enhancing it in public goods.

The proposed solution to the problem of deteriorating governance is, (a) to get the government completely out of the production and supply of private goods, (b) to narrow its focus on public goods and quasi-public goods (strong externalities) and social security aspects that the government is expected to achieve but has neglected (Virmani, 2002b).

e) Credibility of Reforms

Reform can only have an effect on economic actors if the reforms are credible. The more limited reforms undertaken during the eighties

---

47. Though they have substantial externalities in rural areas.

had great credibility, and their effect on the economy was, therefore, magnified. The reforms undertaken in 1991-92 and 1992-93 were much more comprehensive, but took a few years to gain credibility as they were wrongly perceived (initially) as being driven by the IMF/ World Bank. Agents were afraid that the reforms might be reversed once the crises passed. The reforms gained some credibility by 1993-94 and the effect was felt in the 1993-94 recovery and subsequent boom (1994-95 to 1996-97). Subsequent economic policy actions have been characterised by a 'two steps forward and one step backward' approach that (perhaps) gradually eroded this credibility.

The political economy of Indian reforms since 1993-94 seems to be that whenever reforms are beginning to take-off, someone within the ruling party, the ruling coalition or its supporting organisations feels it is in their interests to undermine and slow down or even halt the entire process.[48] In fact the position may have worsened with 'two-and-a-half steps forward' being followed by 'two steps backward'. The result of this vacillation is a lack of credibility and a repeatedly aborted growth take-off, during the nineties. Thus, the enormous growth potential of the Indian economy is not being realised because of the constraints placed on it by the Indian political system. Some economists have asserted that this is because the opposition parties oppose all reforms when they are not in the government even if they initiate or support reform when they are in power. In our view it is the duty of the opposition to criticise and question change, within limits.[49] The public and economic agents accept such questioning as natural in a democratic country such as India. What is not acceptable is internal criticism, sabotage, and worse, from within the ruling set-up—this has a much more devastating effect on the credibility of reforms.

## 3. GLOBAL COMPARISON

Ahluwalia (1988) states that, "In the period up to the mid-seventies India's growth rate of around 3.5 per cent per year was

48. Whether this is the old 'crab theory' of Indians in operation or something else, this is what we have repeatedly seen in every government since around 1994-95.

49. The limit is not exceeded if for instance the opposition party after criticism and testing of the Treasury benches in the Lok Sabha (ruling coalition has a majority) does not kill reform bills in the Rajya Sabha (where it has a majority).

much lower than the average of about 6.0 per cent achieved by developing countries as a whole. In the past ten years, however, India's growth rate has accelerated, while growth rates in most of the developing world have decelerated. India's growth rate in the period 1981-86 was almost 5 per cent, when all developing countries together grew by 2.5 per cent, while non-oil-developing countries grew at 3.5 per cent per year. In fact India's growth performance in the eighties is exceeded only by some of the fastest growing East Asian economies and China." Bhagwati (1993) states that from the mid-fifties to the end of the seventies, "not merely did India's weak performance in increasing income and per capita income fall below her own aspirations, it also put India behind many developing countries in this race, and way behind the super-performers of the Far East." Ahluwalia (1995) states that, "India's growth performance was close to the bottom of the group during 1965-80 and improved to the middle of the range in 1980-90," in comparison with "not only high-flyers such as Korea, but other large economies such as Indonesia, Mexico, Brazil, and China, on the one hand, and India's small neighbours such as Bangladesh, Pakistan, and Sri Lanka, on the other hand." More recently De Long (2003) concluded that the performance of the Indian economy was about the average of the developing countries prior to 1980.

## A. Socialist Rate of Growth

Since different authors use different periods for comparison a multiplicity of conclusions have been drawn. It is, therefore, useful to compare the performance of the Indian economy in terms of the phases or sub-phases that we have found to be relevant when we look at the performance of the Indian economy in isolation. As comparable data on economic growth during the fifties is available for only a very limited set of countries, we start with the sixties. During 1961-64, India's GDP-growth ranking was 39 out of the set of 73 medium and large economies, those with a GDP at factor cost in 2000 greater than $15 million, for which data is available for this period. Thus, it is quite plausible that India's performance during 1950-64 was around the median of all countries. India's performance deteriorated dramatically during 1965-79 (sub-phase IB), falling to 69th among a slightly larger set of 79 countries for which the GDP-growth data is available (Table 2.8). So, during this period only 6 developing countries had an average growth rate lower than the 2.8 per cent per annum average for India. This, in our view, was an abysmal performance for a country with India's potential. As recognised quite early by a few perceptive Indian economists like Bhagwati and Srinivasan (1974, 1984), the inferior performance was the result of the economic policies introduced during the period.

## B. Bharatiya Rate of Growth

The performance of the Indian economy improved dramatically from the 1980s as documented in Virmani (1999b). India's growth ranking improved sharply to 9th position during the 21-year period from 1980 to 2000 out of a larger set of 86 medium-large countries for which comparable data is available for this period (Table 2.8). Thus, what we have termed the 'Bharatiya rate of growth', was not just better performance relative to our own earlier growth, but also far superior to that of most other countries in the world. India's rank has improved over the last few years despite a fall in its growth rate, because other countries' growth rates have fallen even more. Thus, our rank improves by one position to 8th if we take either the 22 years from 1980 to 2001 or the 23 years from 1980 to 2002. Only China, Singapore, Taiwan, S. Korea, Malaysia, Vietnam, and Thailand had a higher average growth rate than India during the last 23 years. This is a creditable performance by global standards.

India's rank was somewhat lower during the two sub-phases. India ranked 12th during sub-phase IIA (1980 to 1991) with Hong Kong, Indonesia, Pakistan and Cyprus also growing faster during this period. Our rank improved to 10th during sub-phase IIB (1992 to 2002) as the growth rate of S. Korea, Taiwan and Thailand fell sharply after 1997 while the growth rate of Ireland, Uganda, Mozambique and Dominican Republic improved. Thus, only China, Singapore, Malaysia and Vietnam had a higher GDP growth rate than India in the full phase as well as in both sub-phases.

It is interesting that the 23-year growth ranking for India is better than its growth ranking in either sub-period (of 13 years and 10 years, respectively). The reason is the remarkable stability in the growth rate of India relative to some of the other high-growth economies. This is reflected in the growth ranking based on the 10-year moving average growth rate. India's growth rank by this measure has fluctuated between 10th and 15th with a mean position of about 13th (Table 2.8). There were five periods in which the rank was better and two periods in which the rank was much worse. The best 10-year performance has occurred at the start and end of the period, with a rank of 10th for the decade of the eighties (198089) and for the period 1993-2002. The former followed an improvement from 15th for the period from 1979 to 1988. Following the BoP crisis of 1990–91 the rank deteriorated to 17th for the period from 1984 to 1993. There was a sharp improvement in rank following the introduction of the new economic policy in the nineties to 13th for the period 1987-96. After remaining around this level, the position collapsed temporarily to 20th for the period 1991-2000, partly because of the export-led recovery of East Asia (Table 2.8).

## C. Comparison of Service Shares

Our analysis has shown that services played a role in the step up in the GDP growth rate from the mid-eighties.[50] The recovery in manufacturing growth from 1981-82 was, however, equally significant. Consequently, there was little discontinuity in the share of GDP from services. The share of services in GDP at 1993-94 prices rose almost linearly from 32 per cent in 1950-51 to about 58 per cent in 2002-03 (i.e. about 0.5 per cent point per year). The service share has, however, been above this linear trend for the last five years or so.

To see whether the share of services in Indian GDP is excessively high we need to compare it with the share in other countries. We do this by constructing the average share during 1992 to 2000 (sub-phase IIB) along with the average per capita GDP at constant ppp (pcgdpk) and regress one against the other to derive a normative value of the service share at each income level.[51] India's average service share is then compared with this norm. For the 160 countries for which data is available in the World Development Indicators, we find that a third order polynomial in pcgdpk fits the data best. Based on this equation, India's average service share of 45 per cent (+2 per cent) is almost identical to the predicted/normative value of 44 per cent based on

---

50. See also Gordon and Gupta (2003).
51. We use the US GDP deflator to convert from current US$ to constant US$ 1995 prices.

## Table 2.8

*India's Comparative Growth Rate and Global Growth Rank*

| Country | Period Growth Rates | | | | | | | | | | | | | |
|---|---|---|---|---|---|---|---|---|---|---|---|---|---|---|
| | Rank | | | | | | | Growth Rate (%) | | | | | | |
| | Sub-phase | | | | | | | Sub-phase | | | | | | |
| | I A (1961-64) | I B (1965-79) | II A (1980-91) | II B (1992-2002) | (1980-2000) | (1980-2001) | (1980-2002) | I A (1961-64) | I B (1965-79) | II A (1980-91) | II B (1992-2002) | (1980-2000) | (1980-2001) | (1980-2002) |
| 1 | 2 | 3 | 4 | 5 | 6 | 7 | 8 | 9 | 10 | 11 | 12 | 13 | 14 | 15 |
| China | 73 | 25 | 1 | 1 | 1 | 1 | 1 | -1.8 | 6.1 | 9.0 | 9.8 | 9.5 | 9.4 | 9.4 |
| Singapore | 29 | 2 | 5 | 7 | 2 | 2 | 2 | 5.8 | 10.5 | 7.5 | 6.4 | 7.7 | 7.2 | 7.0 |
| Korea, Rep. | 27 | 4 | 3 | 13 | 4 | 3 | 3 | 6.1 | 9.0 | 7.8 | 5.6 | 7.0 | 6.8 | 6.8 |
| Taiwan | | 3 | 2 | 17 | 3 | 4 | 4 | | 10.2 | 7.9 | 5.3 | 7.2 | 6.8 | 6.6 |
| Vietnam | | | | 4 | 6 | 6 | 5 | | | | 7.2 | 6.4 | 6.3 | 6.3 |
| Malaysia | 22 | 13 | 9 | 8 | 5 | 5 | 6 | 6.7 | 7.3 | 6.4 | 6.1 | 6.6 | 6.4 | 6.3 |
| Thailand | 19 | 9 | 4 | 33 | 7 | 7 | 7 | 6.9 | 7.8 | 7.7 | 4.0 | 6.2 | 6.0 | 5.9 |
| India | 39 | 69 | 12 | 10 | 9 | 8 | 8 | 5.2 | 2.8 | 5.5 | 5.8 | 5.7 | 5.6 | 5.6 |
| Indonesia | 68 | 16 | 7 | 37 | 10 | 10 | 9 | 2.3 | 6.8 | 6.8 | 3.8 | 5.6 | 5.5 | 5.4 |
| Hong Kong | 2 | 7 | 6 | 39 | 8 | 9 | 10 | 13.2 | 8.6 | 6.8 | 3.8 | 5.8 | 5.5 | 5.4 |
| Ireland | 52 | 43 | 31 | 3 | 13 | 11 | 11 | 4.2 | 4.7 | 3.5 | 7.4 | 5.3 | 5.3 | 5.3 |
| Uganda | | | 28 | 6 | 16 | 14 | 12 | | | | 6.6 | 5.2 | 5.2 | 5.3 |
| Pakistan | 21 | 35 | 8 | 35 | 12 | 13 | 13 | 6.7 | 5.5 | 6.5 | 3.9 | 5.4 | 5.3 | 5.3 |
| Chile | 46 | 65 | 14 | 11 | 11 | 12 | 14 | 4.5 | 3.1 | 4.6 | 5.8 | 5.4 | 5.3 | 5.2 |
| Cyprus | | | 10 | 28 | 14 | 15 | 15 | | | 5.8 | 4.3 | 5.2 | 5.2 | 5.0 |
| Egypt (EAR) | 17 | 33 | 11 | 26 | 15 | 16 | 16 | 7.1 | 5.5 | 5.5 | 4.4 | 5.2 | 5.1 | 5.0 |
| Bangladesh | 35 | 76 | 16 | 19 | 19 | 18 | 17 | 5.5 | 2.3 | 4.4 | 4.9 | 4.6 | 4.7 | 4.6 |
| Luxembourg | 54 | 66 | 18 | 21 | 17 | 17 | 18 | 4.1 | 3.0 | 4.3 | 4.9 | 5.0 | 4.8 | 4.6 |
| Sri Lanka | 59 | 44 | 17 | 24 | 18 | 21 | 20 | 3.6 | 4.7 | 4.4 | 4.5 | 4.8 | 4.5 | 4.5 |

*Contd. ...*

*... Contd. ...*

| *Country* | *Variation in Rank over Last Two Decades (Based on 10-year Moving Averages)* | | | | | | | | |
|---|---|---|---|---|---|---|---|---|---|
| | *1979-88* | *1980-89* | *1981-90* | *1982-91* | *1984-93* | *1987-96* | *1991-2000* | *1992-2001* | *1993-2002* |
| *1* | *16* | *17* | *18* | *19* | *20* | *21* | *22* | *23* | *24* |
| China | 1 | 1 | 1 | 1 | 1 | 1 | 1 | 1 | 1 |
| Singapore | 5 | 4 | 5 | 5 | 7 | 3 | 2 | 5 | 7 |
| Korea, Rep. | 4 | 3 | 2 | 2 | 5 | 6 | 11 | 15 | 13 |
| Taiwan | 3 | 2 | 3 | 4 | 4 | 9 | 10 | 16 | 16 |
| Vietnam | | 84 | 90 | 91 | 92 | 10 | 4 | 4 | 5 |
| Malaysia | 12 | 12 | 10 | 7 | 9 | 5 | 6 | 8 | 11 |
| Thailand | 7 | 6 | 4 | 3 | 3 | 2 | 30 | 38 | 44 |
| India | 15 | 10 | 11 | 11 | 17 | 13 | 20 | 11 | 10 |
| Indonesia | 10 | 8 | 7 | 6 | 8 | 8 | 34 | 39 | 45 |
| Hong Kong | 2 | 5 | 6 | 8 | 10 | 14 | 32 | 34 | 43 |
| Ireland | 44 | 35 | 23 | 27 | 28 | 16 | 5 | 3 | 3 |
| Uganda | | 85 | 93 | 94 | 29 | 11 | 8 | 7 | 6 |
| Pakistan | 6 | 7 | 8 | 10 | 13 | 21 | 40 | 40 | 47 |
| Chile | 20 | 14 | 22 | 18 | 6 | 7 | 7 | 15 | 14 |
| Cyprus | 8 | 9 | 9 | 9 | 12 | 15 | 36 | 29 | 36 |
| Egypt (EAR) | 11 | 11 | 12 | 12 | 23 | 33 | 33 | 26 | 25 |
| Bangladesh | 16 | 17 | 15 | 21 | 22 | 29 | 26 | 21 | 18 |
| Luxembourg | 31 | 15 | 16 | 13 | 11 | 18 | 14 | 18 | 17 |
| Sri Lanka | 18 | 19 | 18 | 20 | 21 | 26 | 21 | 27 | 21 |

*Sources* : 1. World Bank (2002), 4 (5) years data is missing for Uganda (Vietnam) during the eighties.
2. IMF WEO (recent years).

India's average per capita GDP at ppp during the period. Thus, we conclude that the service sector share during phase IIB was normal.

We repeat this exercise for the period 1980 to 1991 (sub-phase IIA) with the smaller set of countries (148) for which data is available in the World Bank's WDI. In this case we find that the average service share for India was (at 40 per cent) 6 per cent lower than the norm of 43 per cent. The faster growth of services during phase II, therefore, seems to have corrected an imbalance that had emerged earlier.

The exercise for 1992-2000 shows that with the exception of the island economies of Singapore (+1 per cent) and Hong Kong (+28 per cent), most other fast growing economies had an average service share less than the norm for their per capita GDP. These countries (with the average service share in brackets) are Vietnam (-3 per cent), Chile (-4 per cent), Thailand (-8 per cent), Ireland (-13 per cent), Indonesia (-14 per cent), S. Korea (-19 per cent), Malaysia (-21 per cent) and China (-31 per cent). The reason for this contrast between the other high growth economies and India, is the failure of the manufacturing sector in India to grow as fast as it did in these high growth economies. As a consequence, the structural transformation of the Indian economy from agriculture to manufacturing has not taken place. If the manufacturing sector can be freed of the remaining shackles and distortions, the rate of growth of GDP and of employment can be accelerated.

## 4. CONCLUSIONS

In this chapter we argue that each of the two phases of economic growth can be divided into two sub-phases based on the nature of the policy regime and the development focus. The growth rate in one sub-phase of a given phase differs from that in the other sub-phase, but this difference is not statistically significant. From the policy perspective, however, these four sub-phases (quest for commanding heights, socialist rate of growth, modest reform and broader reform), can be thought of as distinct. The growth rate declined from 4.1 per cent per annum during the commanding heights sub-phase to 2.6 per cent per annum in the socialist rate of growth phase. It is hypothesised that this was due to a combination of direct control on private activity and the accumulating burden of government imposed costs. These costs arose from oppressive controls as well as from the crowding out of private production by public sector supply of goods and services unconstrained by compulsions of profitability, efficiency, and quality. Supply-side factors such as the rise in global oil prices, which acted as an external tax on citizens and the inefficiency of public utility monopolies contributed to the slowdown. Credible changes in the direction of economic philosophy that resulted in some liberalisation of industrial (production and investment) controls and the trade regime (particularly with respect to exports and capital goods imports), played a role in the recovery of growth during the eighties.

The conclusion of earlier papers that India's performance during the first three decades was around the average of the developing countries, is not supported by the facts presented in this chapter. This was only true during the commanding heights sub-phase (15 years). In the socialist rate of growth sub-phase (next 15 years), India's performance plummeted to the bottom of the global order, with only six developing and four developed countries having a GDP growth rate lower than that of India.

India's global growth rank has improved dramatically to 8th during the BRG phase, with the rank being 12th during the first sub-phase and 10th during the second sub-phase. The rank for the entire phase is better than that in either sub-phase, because the growth rate has been less volatile than in many other countries.

We seem currently to be stuck at the 'Bharatiya' rate of growth of around 5.8 per cent per annum.[52] In fact, the trend rate in 2002-03, appeared to be about 1 per cent point lower than this because of the very sharp cyclical decline in growth that occurred in 2002-03. With the cyclical recovery of the economy to a predicted 8 per cent plus growth in 2003-04 and a forecast of 6 per cent growth rate in 2004-05, the economy is returning to the 'Bharatiya' rate of growth trend of 5.8 per cent per annum.

Subsequent chapters will however explore, whether there are underlying improvements or structural changes in productivity that have not been translated into higher growth so far, but which could, in future, result in a sustained upward shift in the growth trend.

52. Based on CSO data. The WDI data gives a lower average of 5.6 per cent.

# 3

# Sources of India's Economic Growth

*Trends in Total Factor Productivity*

## 1. INTRODUCTION

Chapters 1 and 2 have analysed the growth performance of the Indian economy since 1950-51. Chapter 1 showed that the trend growth rate of the economy declined gradually from 1951-52 to reach a trough around 1972-73. It then rose more rapidly to reach a peak around 1995-96 and has been on a downtrend since then. The present chapter attempts an explanation of these trends in terms of the standard sources of growth methodology.

There is an extensive empirical literature on total factor productivity growth (TFPG) in India's registered manufacturing sector. Fewer authors have estimated aggregate productivity. Brahmananda (1982), King and Levine (1993, 1994) and Guha-Khasnobis and Bari (2003) have estimated aggregate Total Factor Productivity Growth in India based on National Accounts Statistics (NAS) data on GDP and investment. Of these only Brahmananda (1982) estimated TFPG for GDP sectors. The current study differs from earlier ones in the following respects.[1] Firstly, it covers the entire period from 1950-51 to 2003-04. Second, it derives a time series for TFPG to show the changes in trend over the entire period, by using a Hodrick-Prescott filter. It shows that even the period averages can differ significantly from the period averages derived from the unfiltered series when TFPG is close to zero. Third, it is probably the only study that estimates the aggregate production function with rainfall as an exogenous variable. It then uses the estimated elasticity instead of

---

1. I would like to thank Roberto Zagha for encouraging me to explore TFPG and to Bishwanath Goldar for his comments. My thanks to Gurnain K. Pasricha for research assistance and Manmeet Ahuja for secretarial assistance.

factor shares, which are difficult to estimate in an economy with a large informal sector, characterised by mixed (profits and wages) income of self-employed. Fourth, it covers all major national accounts sectors of the economy (but without the innovation applied to the aggregate). Fifth, it does not account for education.

The chapter is structured as follows. Section 2 gives an overview of the historical growth experience of the Indian economy and the relevant growth trends. Section 3 outlines the standard sources of growth methodology, the estimating equations to determine the sources of growth and the decomposition methodology for determining the contribution sector TFPG and capital deepening to aggregate TFPG. Section 4 discusses the data used and presents the estimated equations and TFPG estimates. The results are then analysed in section 5. Section 6 analyses the determinants of TFPG. Sector total factor productivity trends are estimated and discussed in Section 7. Section 8 concludes the chapter. The appendix presents average TFPG estimates by different periods.

## 2. GROWTH TRENDS

Figure 3.1 shows the annual growth rate of Net Domestic Product at factor cost (NDPfc), the growth rate of the Hodrick-Prescott filtered NDPfc series (NDPhp) and the 3rd and 4th order polynomials fitted to the annual growth rate series. The NDP growth rate trend (as measured by the HP-filtered series) started at 4.8 per cent per annum in 1951-52 and decelerated during the fifties and sixties to reach a low of less than 3.2 per cent per annum during 1971-72 to 1972-73. The trend growth rate accelerated from the mid-seventies to reach a peak of almost 6.2 per cent per annum during 1994-95 and 1995-96. Thereafter, the trend growth rate has decelerated to 4.8 per cent in 2003-04, a rate that is still higher than in 1982-83. The 3rd order polynomial starts in a similar way as the HP filtered series, makes an earlier trough and then keeps rising even after the HP series has peaked. In contrast, the 4th order polynomial starts much lower and remains flat for some time. Its trough in the seventies and peak in the nineties is closer to that of the HP filtered series. Because of these variations with the order of the polynomial we prefer to use the HP filtered series for analysis of growth trends.

## FIGURE 3.1

*NDP Growth Trends: HP Filtered Series and 3rd and 4th Order Polynomial*

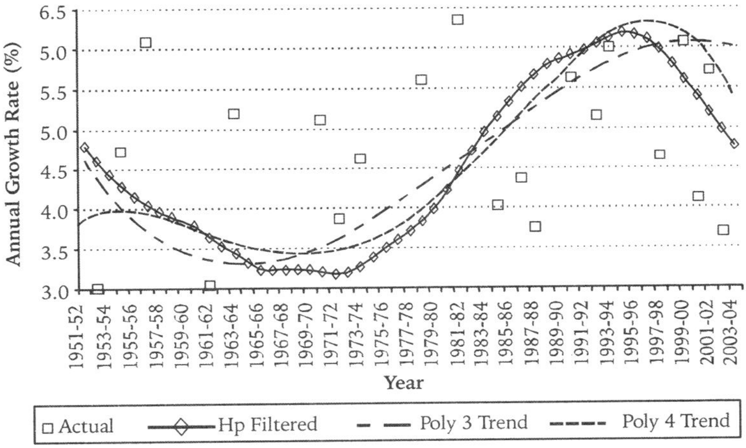


## FIGURE 3.2

*Trends in HP: Filtered Series- NDP, NDPpc and NDPpwrk*

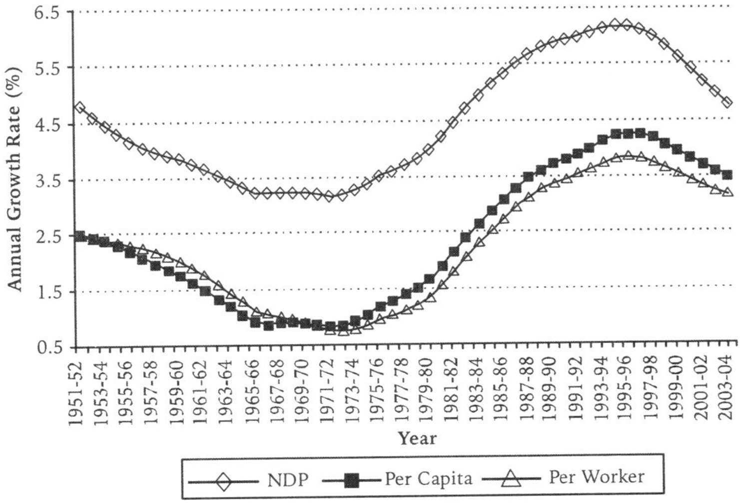

Figure 3.2 shows the growth trends in per capita NDPfc (PCndp) and per worker NDP (PWndp) along with that in NDPfc. Both the per capita and per worker series start at a trend growth of 2.5 per cent per annum in 1951-52. They reach a trough of 0.7 per cent per annum in 1971-72 and 0.8 per cent in 1972-73, respectively. Thereafter, they rise to a peak of 4.25 per cent and 3.84 per cent respectively in 1995-96. Currently (2003-04), the trend rate is 3.5 per cent per annum in per capita NDP and 3.1 per cent per annum in per worker NDP.

## FIGURE 3.3

*Tradable Sector Growth Trends*

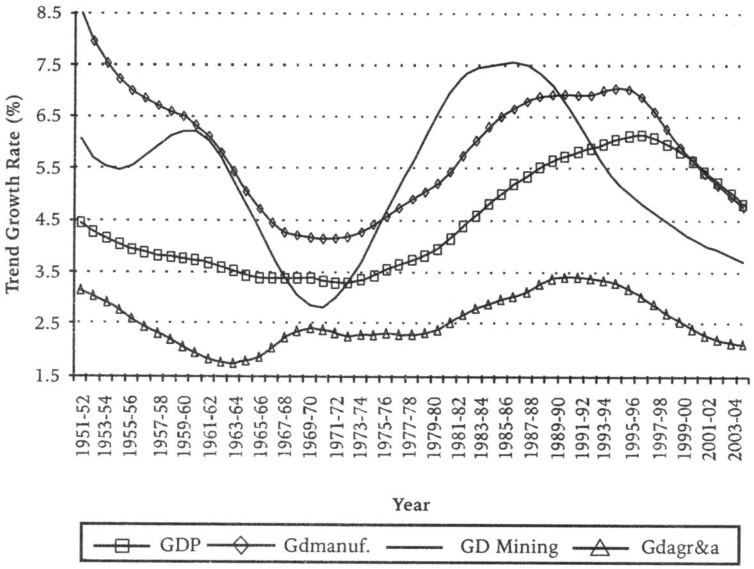


The Figure 3.3 suggests that recent GDP growth trends are driven by the tradable goods sector. The trend growth in manufacturing has been decelerating since 1997-98. The downtrend in agricultural growth started earlier at the beginning of the nineties, while mining growth has been trending down since the mid-eighties with the downtrend continuing in the nineties. Import protection (QRs and tariffs) for the tradable goods sector has been reduced over the nineties. During a transitional phase this would (*ipso facto*) lead to an increase in the rate of growth of the non-tradable sector relative to that of the tradable sector. This has indeed happened. The apparent decline in the trend rate of growth of the tradable goods sectors (manufacturing, mining and agriculture) over the last 5-7 years is however, disturbing and points to the need for domestic reforms related to these sectors (Virmani, 2004a).

# 3. METHODOLOGY

## 3.1 Sources of Growth

We can use the standard growth accounting framework to apportion growth between capital accumulation, labour supply and TFPG. For this purpose we make the conventional assumption of a constant returns to scale production function F. Because of the importance of rainfall to the Indian economy we include rainfall in the production function, assuming that its effect is multiplicative and factor neutral:

$$Y_t = A_t \text{ G(rainfall) F } (K_t, L_t) \text{ and } y_t = A_t \text{ G(rainfall) f}(k_t) \qquad (1)$$

where, $Y_t$ = NDPfc(t), $A_t$ is neutral technical change, $K_t$ = Capital stock, $L_t$ = Labour, $y_t = Y_t/L_t$ (NDPfc per unit of labour), $k_t = K_t/L_t$ (Fixed capital per unit of labour). Rainfall is an area-weighted index of monsoon rainfall all over India. If we assume the fulfilment of the competitive marginal product conditions we would need the share of wages and returns to capital. Because of the large size of the unorganised/self-employed sector as much as 45 per cent of total income is classified as mixed income (labour and capital) in the NAS. A time series for labour/capital income shares is consequently not available. We, therefore, assume a Cobb-Douglas production function and on differentiation of Equation 1, obtain the estimating equation,

$$\text{Gry} = \text{C} + \alpha * \text{Grk} + \text{E} * \text{Drainm} + \text{e} * \text{Drainm}(-1) + \text{U}_t \qquad (2)$$

Where Gry is the rate of growth of y, Grk is the rate of growth of k, Drainm is the per cent variation of rainfall from mean with Drainm(-1) representing the lagged value of the same and $U_t$ is the error term. $A_t$ is commonly set at C when estimating the coefficients of Equation 2. The most direct and immediate effect of rainfall is on crop output and agricultural GDP. The change in the amount of water available in hydel reservoirs also affects electricity generation. The change in availability of surface water also affects the demand for electricity for drawing sub-surface water. The change of income of farmers would, also affect the aggregate pattern of demand and consequently, the sectoral pattern of supply. Earlier studies ignore rainfall and therefore include only the first two terms of Equation 2. This could give biased estimates of elasticity and consequently an under estimate of TFPG.

Once we have obtained the coefficients of this equation, we can calculate the total factor productivity growth as:

$$\text{TFPG} = \text{Gry} - \alpha * \text{Grk} - \text{E} * \text{Drainm} - \text{e} * \text{Drainm}(-1) \qquad (3)$$

The analysis of the previous section suggests that growth rate of $A_t$ could also equal $C_0$ + $C_1$*Dummy.

If we have constant returns to scale production function without rainfall, competitive factor markets and a capital share of $\alpha$, then TFPG would be as follows:

$$\text{tfpg} = \text{Gry} - \alpha * \text{Grk} \qquad (4)$$

Thus, we can obtain an alternative estimate of TFPG using any value of $\alpha$. The estimate obtained by inserting the coefficients estimated in Equation 2 into Equation 3 (TFPG0), however, has one weakness. The entire error term in the GDP growth equation is attributed to/contained within this estimate. We, therefore, need to use some smoothing operation such as the HP filter to purge the series of the error term and derive the underlying trend (TFPG0hp). If TFPG does not have the form $C_0$ + $C_1$*Dummy and has varied over time because of changes in the policy environment, the estimate in equation could also be biased. We, therefore, follow a two-stage procedure. The filtered series (TFPG0hp) is inserted back into Equation 2 to obtain the following equation:

$$\text{Gry} = \text{TFPG0hp} + \alpha'*\text{Grk} + \text{E}'*\text{Drainm} + \text{e}'*\text{Drainm}(-1) + u_t \qquad (5)$$

This equation is estimated to obtain revised values for the co-efficient which are then used in Equation 3 to derive another value for TFPG (TFPG1). The HP filtered version of this (TFPG1hp) then shows the time trend in TFPG. Period averages are, however, obtained by averaging the unfiltered series (TFPG0 or TFPG1).

## 3.2 Determinants of TFPG

The link between investment, capital and growth is the foundation of the standard sources of growth methodology. If technology is capital augmenting, Equation 1 is modified as follows:

$$y_t = A_t\, G(\text{rainfall})\, f(b_t k_t) = (A_t b_t)^{\alpha} k_t^{\alpha}\, G(\text{rainfall})$$

assuming a Cobb-Douglas form. In this case the estimating equations for TFPG remain unchanged. If technology is embodied in capital stock each vintage of capital has different productivity and the measurement of aggregate capital stock requires either the relative price of each vintage or the relative quality. Such information is not available in India.

De Long and Summers (1991, 1992) have emphasised the link between equipment investment and growth. They also showed that equipment prices and equipment investment are inversely related. If technology is embodied in equipment (and not in structures $Ks_t$), augmentation would occur primarily in the machinery and equipment part of the capital stock ($Km_t$). It would, therefore, be necessary to separate out the two forms of capital in the production function:

$$y_t = A_t\, G(\text{rainfall})\, f(b_t km_t, ks_t) = (A_t b_t^{\alpha 1}) km_t^{\alpha 1} ks_t^{\alpha 2}\, G(\text{rainfall})$$

De Long and Summers also found that equipment imports are the best predictor of equipment investment. In a 1993 paper they showed that the effect of equipment investment is primarily through TFPG. Hulten (1992) showed that for capital goods with embodied technology, improvements in quality could explain 20 per cent of the residual (TFPG). Lee (1995) modelled the effect of capital imports and showed that if trade reduces the price of investment and increases real investment there will be faster investment and technological progress. Thus, TFPG may be a function of total or imported equipment investment or their ratio to total capital stock in Equation 1.

$$y_t = A(Iimp_t/I,\ Ime_t/I,\ t)\, G(\text{rainfall})\ f(k_t)$$

$$y_t = A_t\, (Kme_t / K_t)^{\alpha 1} k_t^{\alpha}\, G(\text{rainfall}) \text{ or } y_t = A_t\, (Kimp_t / K_t)^{\alpha 1} k_t^{\alpha}\, G(\text{rainfall})$$

In the developing country context where technical change is largely a consequence of diffusion of technology from the developed countries, most embodied technology would enter through imported capital goods. Technological change could also be affected by the variety of manufactured intermediates available to the producers. Restrictions on the import of capital good and intermediate inputs and the tariffs imposed on them would, therefore, influence import of these goods and the rate of technological change. Such import policy restrictions would also lead to an appreciation of the real exchange rate (XRreal= Pt/Pnt, P=price, t=tradables and nt=non-tradables). Changes in the real exchange rate would capture both the price wedges introduced by QRs and tariffs and the quality differential between domestic and imported capital goods and intermediates. Thus, technical change could be inversely related to the real exchange rate (i.e. an appreciation of the exchange rate is correlated with lower TFPG).

Because of the difficulty of estimating augmented capital stock we assume for our estimation that technological change is either neutral or labour augmenting. TFPG (as in Equation 1) is a function H of investment in machinery and equipment and of changes in import restrictions captured by the growth of the real exchange rate (GrXRreal), i.e.

$$\text{TFPG} = H(\text{Imet}/I, \text{GrXRreal}, t) \quad (6)$$

## 3.3 TFPG by Sector

Equation 4 is also the method used for calculating the TFPG for each sector of the economy based on an estimate of the capital share (a) for that sector. The contribution of TFPG in each sector to aggregate/overall TFPG is estimated as follows (the time sub-script t is dropped):

$$Y = AF(K, L) \text{ or } A = Y/F(K, L),$$

$$Y = \sum_{i=1}^{n} Y_i = \sum_{i=1}^{n} A_i F_i(K_i, L_i)$$

Substituting the second equation in the first we have,

$$A = \sum_{i=1}^{n} S_i A_i, \text{ and } S_i = F_i(K_i, L_i)/F(K, L) = K_i^{\alpha i} L_i^{1-\alpha i} / K^{\alpha} L^{1-\alpha}$$

is the ratio of total factor input in sector i to total factor input (TFI) into aggregate GDP. Differentiating this equation with respect to time we have,

$$dA = \sum_{i=1}^{n} (S_i dA_i + A_i dS_i) \tag{7}$$

The term on the left represents the change in TFP of aggregate GDP. The first term on the right represents the contribution of sectors' TFPG and the second term the contribution of the change in allocation of total factor input among different sectors. The TFPG of sector i contributes a proportion $S_i\ dA_i\ /dA$ to total TFPG while the factor shift to sector i contributes $A_i\ dS_i\ /dA$. If dA is close to zero or negative this fraction can be misleading and it is better to use the absolute numbers $S_i\ dA_i$ and $A_i\ dS_i$ to compare the relative contribution of different sectors.

## 4. EMPIRICAL ESTIMATION

### 4.1 Data

The capital stock series is constructed using fixed investment at constant 1993-94 prices from the NAS, using the perpetual inventory method. The depreciation rate is assumed to be 5 per cent. Starting stock (end 1950-51) is also obtained from the NAS. The same depreciation values are also used to construct NDP from GDP at factor cost. As an annual labour or worker series is unavailable, we use the population aged 15 to 64 to measure potential workers for L. This data is obtained from the World Development Indicators (from 1960 onwards) and from the UN for 1950. The data for the rest of the fifties is constructed by interpolation of the ratio of population 15 to 64 over the total population.

The data problems are more severe when we move from the aggregate to the sector level. Time series on number of workers or worker hour are not available even at the aggregate level. We, however, have data from national census and national sample surveys on the number of workers for about nine distinct years for most sectors. The important exception is insurance, banking, housing, real estate and business services, which is put in the residual category along with government and social and personal services. Approximately, consistent series can be constructed for eight of these years based on the work of earlier authors. Capital share values (a) for all sectors can be derived from Brahamananda (1982). Based on GDP data and the fixed capital series constructed by us, we can calculate TFPG growth rates by sector for these seven periods using Equation 4 (These are given in the Appendix Table A3.2).

These years do not however coincide with the turning points identified in the aggregate data. Nor do they coincide with the phases and sub-phases of growth identified in chapters 1 and 2. To get an idea of the cyclical trends (peaks, troughs and periods of rising or declining productivity) we interpolate the share of workers by sector for the missing years and use the population of 15 to 64 year olds to interpolate the total workers for the missing years. This is then used along with the GDP data and the capital series to derive annual TFPG estimates for each sector (from 1952-53 to 2000-01) using capital share values ($\alpha$) in Equation 4. This allows us to estimate the average productivity growth during the phases and sub-phases of growth identified earlier. We then filter the TFPG series using an HP filter to find the trend in TFPG and then compare these trends as represented by the fitted line.

## 4.2 Production Function and TFPG

OLS estimates of Equation 2 yields the following result:

$$\text{Gry} = \underset{(2.35)^{**}}{0.0148} + \underset{(1.6)^{*}}{0.430}*\text{Grk} + \underset{(5.7)^{***}}{0.202}*\text{Drainm} - \underset{(-3.4)^{***}}{0.118} * \text{Drainm}(-1) \quad (8)$$

$R^2$ = 0.51, $R^2$ (adj) = 0.48, DW = 2.29. When the Equation 8 is re-estimated with AR(1), the coefficient on the AR term is not significant. The negative parameter on previous years' (lagged) rainfall deviation indicates that the short run (one year) effect of rainfall deviation on growth (2/10th of rainfall deviation) is higher than the long-term (two-year) effect (less than 1/10th of rainfall deviation). This is probably due to substitution on both supply side (e.g. agricultural imports, thermal electricity generation) and demand side (e.g. income transfers from government or food for work programmes) that take time to adopt.

These parameters are substituted into Equation 3 and TFPG0hp estimated. TFPG0hp is then used to estimate Equation 5. The results are as follows:

$$Gry = \underset{(4.6)^{***}}{1.11\ TFPG0hp} + \underset{(1.9)^{*}}{0.34*Grk} + \underset{(6.9)^{***}}{0.22*Drainm} - \underset{(-4.0)^{***}}{0.12 * Drainm(-1)} - \underset{(-2.5)^{***}}{0.35*AR(1)}$$

$R^2 = 0.62$, $R^2$ (adj) $= 0.59$, DW $= 2.1$. (9)

The most important change is the reduction in the capital coefficient (implicit profit/capital share). This estimate is almost identical to the capital share (0.35) used by Collins and Bosworth (1996) and by Guha-Khasnobis and Bari (2003). It however differs from that of Brahmananda (1982), who estimated the share of wages in total income for the economy as 75 per cent from 1950 to 1970 and 71 per cent for 1980. This suggests a capital share of 25 per cent in the fifties and sixties, rising to 29 per cent between 1970 and 1980 and perhaps even higher in the nineties. Our estimate of 0.34, therefore, appears quite reasonable. These new coefficients are reinserted into Equation 3 to get a second estimate of total factor productivity (TFPG1). This is again smoothed using the HP filter to obtain the trend value (TFPG1hp).

If we estimate the same regressions using GDP growth as the dependent variable instead of NDP growth the estimated total factor productivity and its trend (as per the HP filtered series is virtually the same. However, the filtered total factor productivity series using GDP is everywhere below the filtered TFPG series derived using NDP.

If Equation 4 is used (instead of Equation 3) to estimate TFPG (tfpg0a) and the HP filtered series (tfpg0ahp) used in the estimation of Equation 5, we obtain

$$Gry = \underset{(4.3)^{***}}{1.04\ TFPG0ahp} + \underset{(2.4)^{**}}{0.41*Grk} + \underset{(6.4)^{***}}{0.21*Drainm} - \underset{(-4.2)^{***}}{0.13 * Drainm(-1)} - \underset{(-2.3)^{***}}{0.32*AR(1)}$$

$R^2 = 0.61$, $R^2$ (adj) $= 0.58$, DW $= 2.1$. (10)

There are two noticeable differences from the estimates obtained using tfpg0hp. One, the co-efficient on the capital per worker appears to be different from that obtained in Equation 9 (0.411 instead of 0.337) and is significant at a higher level of confidence (2 per cent instead of 6 per cent). Two, there is virtually no difference in the co-efficient on the capital per worker from that obtained in Equation 8 (0.43). The estimates that use the TFPG calculated without subtracting the effect of rain fall on ndp growth (0.41) are close to that of Senhadji (1999) who obtains an estimate of 0.42 for the capital share in case of South Asia (when estimated in difference form). These estimates contrast both with our previous estimate of 0.33 and with the non-labour share (0.25 to 0.29) estimated by Brahmananda (1982).

# 5. ANALYSIS AND IMPLICATIONS

## 5.1 Productivity Trends

The values of total factor productivity obtained above (TFPG0, TFPG1) are plotted in Figure 3.4 in filtered form (TFPG0hp, TFPG1hp). The two HP filtered series for TFPG follow a broadly similar pattern, though TFPG1hp is found to be higher than TFPG0hp for all years except the first half of the fifties. Total factor productivity growth started at 2.4 per cent after independence, but was on a declining trend thereafter. TFPG fell below single digit at the beginning of the sixties and bottomed out at 0.39 per cent per annum in 1972-73 (TFPG1hp). TFPG has accelerated steadily during the seventies and the eighties and peaked at 2.62 per cent in 1988-89. This was followed by a temporary setback due to the BoP crises after which TFPG has essentially plateaued out at around 2.7 per cent per annum since 1996-97 (Figure 3.4).

The significant decline in TFPG during mid-sixties to the end-seventies can also be confirmed directly by the introduction of a dummy variable for the period 1965-66 to 1980-81 (D6580) into Equation 8:

$$\begin{aligned} Gry = \; & \underset{(3.9)^{***}}{0.021} - \underset{(3.5)^{***}}{0.020} * D6580 + \underset{(2.0)^{*}}{0.41} * Grk + \underset{(6.0)^{***}}{0.21} * Drainm - \\ & \underset{(-4.4)^{***}}{0.15} * Drainm(-1) - \underset{(2.2)^{**}}{0.3}\; AR(1) \end{aligned}$$

$$R^2 = 0.61,\; R^2\,(adj) = 0.57,\; DW = 2.1. \qquad (11)$$

Equation 11 suggests that TFP growth which averaged about 2.1 per cent per annum during the over fifty year period, fell by 2.0 per cent points to almost zero during 1965-66 to 1980-81. Chapter 2 showed that other exogenous factors such as oil prices do not have a significant effect on GDP growth and therefore the effect of the dummy variables could be interpreted as the effect of the set of policies undertaken during the sub-period. These policies included a comprehensive control regime for the private sector that can be named legislative-bureaucratic-socialism (popularly known as Licence-Permit-Quota Raj and Inspector Raj), which affected not just manufacturing but all areas of business. Even agriculture was not left untouched as the Essential Commodity Act and other restrictions on trade, transport, sale and processing affected agricultural growth. These, along with the after effects of the public monopoly created till the mid-sixties, seem to have played a role in the decline in productivity during 1965-66 to 1979-80.

**FIGURE 3.4**

*Total Factor Productivity Growth (TFPG)*

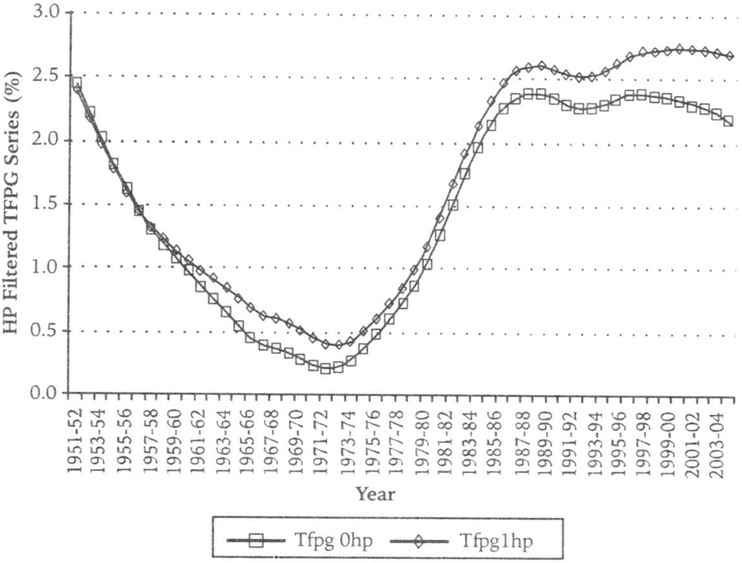

## 5.2 Relative Contribution to Growth

As the annual growth of income and fixed capital are quite volatile, we use the HP filtered series to see the trend in growth of GDP per worker and in the growth of fixed capital per worker. The same series are used to show the trend in the contribution of TFPG and growth of capital per worker to growth of GDP per worker. The growth trend of NDPfc per worker (npwrkhp) has gone through a long cycle stretching over 50 years or so (Figure 3.5). The trend rate of growth of NDP per worker was decelerating during the fifties and sixties, reached a trough in the early-seventies, followed by sustained acceleration till the mid-nineties when it peaked. It has decelerated since then. The trend growth rates of NDP per worker and TFPG were broadly in consonance from the beginning of the period till the mid-nineties, so that the latter appears to be the main driving force for the latter. Thereafter, capital deepening appears to be the main driver of per worker NDP even though the capital per worker cycle seems to lag behind that of NDP per worker (Figure 3.5).

**FIGURE 3.5**

*Sources of Growth (HP Filtered Series): Per Worker NDP/Capital and TFPG*

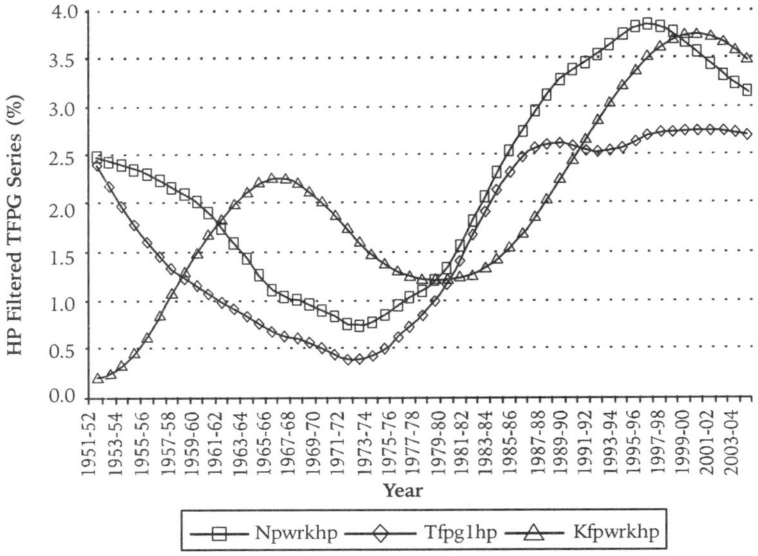

Over the same period, the trend rate of growth of fixed capital per worker (kfpwrkhp) seems to have gone through one and a half cycles (almost two) with one and a half troughs and two peaks (Figure 3.5). The cycle starts mid-way through the first trough at the time of independence and peaks in the mid-sixties. The second trough was at the end of the seventies and the second peak in the mid-nineties, both at a much higher level than the first.

To evaluate the change in the contribution of productivity and capital productivity over time we need to adjust for the volatility in the series. This is done in two ways. First, we multiply the capital per worker series and the rainfall deviation series by the estimated impact coefficients (from Equation 9 for evaluating the contribution of tfpgl). The resultant growth rates for tfpgl and kfpwrkl and rainl are plotted and a 3rd order polynomial fitted to each to show the trend (Figure 3.6). The second method is to subtract the impact of rainfall variations from the growth of NDP per worker and then use this as divisor for TFPG and capital per worker growth, to obtain their relative contribution (share). A third order polynomial is then fitted to find out the trend in relative contribution (Figure 3.7).

## FIGURE 3.6

*Sources of Growth in Per Worker NDP*

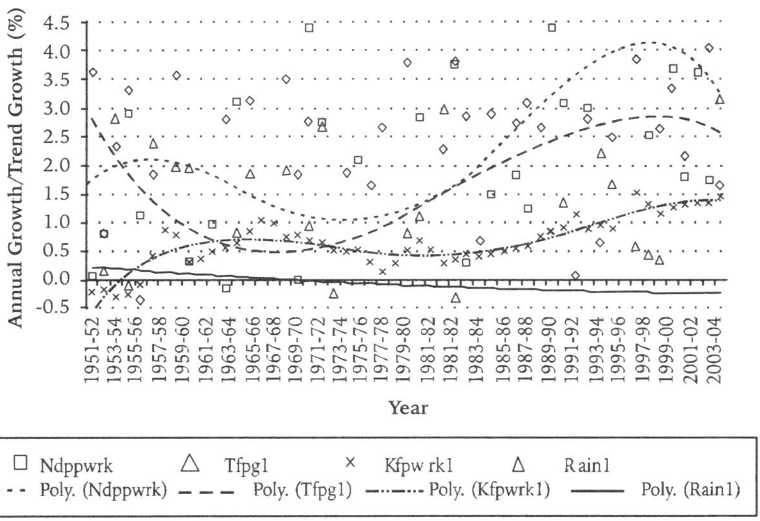

## FIGURE 3.7

*Contribution to Growth of Per Worker NDP:*
*(Adjusted for Rainfall Deviation)*

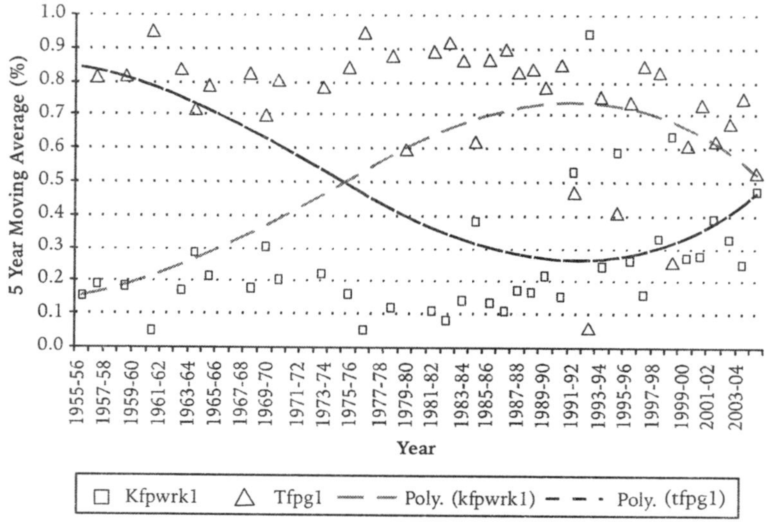


The dotted line at the top of Figure 3.6 shows the trend in the growth of NDP per worker, while the dashed line just below it is TFPG. The third dashed line shows the impact of growth of capital per worker. The contribution of TFPG to growth was initially high and even offset the negative consequence of capital shallowing. As the contribution of rainfall to growth was positive (though falling) the growth of NDP per worker accelerated for about five years till the mid-fifties. The contribution of TFPG declined over time while that of capital deepening increased. As the deceleration of TFPG was sharper than the acceleration in capital deepening, the growth of NDP per worker decelerated after the mid-fifties. The acceleration in growth of capital per worker was driven by a sharp rise in public investment, which more than tripled the public share of fixed capital from about (1/10th) in 1950-51 to more than 1/3rd of the total by 1964-65. Public investment was clearly not driven by the profit motive, but the increase in poverty during this period suggests that the social benefit-cost ratio for this investment (whether borrowed or raised through distorting taxes) was also low. The low productivity of this public capital formation appears to have pulled down total factor productivity growth.

The position was therefore reversed between 1960-61 and 1970-71 when TFPG was at a trough. During this period capital deepening contributed marginally more than TFPG to the growth of NDP per worker. The economic situation worsened from the mid-sixties with the growth of capital stock declining, slowly at first and then in an accelerating downtrend till the late-seventies where it reached a trough. Since 1971-72, the contribution of TFPG has progressively increased relative to that of capital deepening till the mid-nineties after which it has declined marginally/stabilised. The contribution of rain also became negative from 1971-72. Growth of NDP per worker therefore decelerated till the mid-seventies, picking up only after the decline rate of growth of capital per worker slowed and the TFPG accelerated.

The relative contribution of TFPG and capital deepening to the growth of NDP per worker adjusted for rainfall deviations, is depicted in Figure 3.7. The contribution of TFPG fell from about 85 per cent at the beginning of the period to 50 per cent in the mid-seventies while that of capital deepening rose from 15 per cent to 50 per cent. The relative contribution of capital deepening continued to rise till the end of the eighties when it peaked at around 75 per cent and that of TFPG reached a trough of 25 per cent. Since then the contribution of capital deepening has declined to a little over 52 per cent while that of TFPG has declined to a little less than 48 per cent. From the trends, it seems likely that the contribution of TFPG will move above 50 per cent over the next few years, while that of capital deepening will fall.

## 5.3 TFPG during Growth Phases

Chapter 1 showed that there were two statistically distinguishable phases of growth: I) Indian version of socialism (1950-51 to 1979-80) and II) Market Reforms (1980-81 to present). It also highlighted four sub-phases: IA quest for commanding heights, IB legislative-bureaucratic socialism or socialist rate of growth, IIA modest reforms and IIB broader reforms. Table 3.1 shows the average growth rates and TFPG estimates in terms of these phases and sub-phases. The average rates of growth of GDP and NDP were quite similar over the periods and sub-periods, so that the conclusions regarding the sources of growth of NDP per worker and NDP per capita would also apply to GDP per worker.

## Table 3.1

*Sources of Growth in Net Domestic Product*

| | *Phase I: 1950-51 to 1979-80* | | | *Phase II: 1980-81 to 2003-04* | | |
|---|---|---|---|---|---|---|
| *Variable* | *Total* | *IA:(1950-51 to 1964-65)* | *IB:(1965-67 to1979-80)* | *Total* | *IIA:(1980-81 to 1991-92)* | *IIB:(1992-93 to 2003-04)* |
| | | | *(Per cent)* | | | |
| Gross Domestic Product | 3.5 | 4.1 | 2.9 | 5.8 | 5.5 | 6.1 |
| Net Domestic Product | 3.5 | 4.5 | 2.7 | 5.9 | 5.6 | 6.1 |
| Per Capita NDP | 1.3 | 2.5 | 0.4 | 3.9 | 3.4 | 4.3 |
| Per Worker NDP | 1.3 | 2.7 | 0.3 | 3.5 | 3.1 | 3.9 |
| Capital Stock | 3.6 | 2.8 | 4.3 | 5.1 | 4.3 | 5.9 |
| Capital Per Worker | 1.4 | 0.9 | 1.8 | 2.7 | 1.8 | 3.6 |
| Population | 2.1 | 1.9 | 2.3 | 1.9 | 2.1 | 1.7 |
| Pop. 15 to 64 | 2.2 | 1.9 | 2.4 | 2.3 | 2.5 | 2.1 |
| Rainfall Deviation from Mean | 0.5 | 4.0 | -2.7 | -1.8 | -1.7 | -1.9 |
| *Total Factor Productivity Growth* | | | | | | |
| TFPG0 | 0.7 | 1.6 | -0.1 | 2.4 | 2.4 | 2.4 |
| TFPG1 | 0.9 | 1.6 | 0.2 | 2.7 | 2.6 | 2.8 |
| TFPG1hp (HP Filtered tfpg) | 1.0 | 1.4 | 0.6 | 2.5 | 2.3 | 2.7 |
| TFPGs (Share=0.26) | 0.9 | 2.1 | -0.2 | 2.8 | 2.6 | 3.0 |
| *Contribution to Gr. of NDPpwrk* | | | | | | |
| TFPG0 | 0.58 | 0.68 | -0.21 | 0.68 | 0.77 | 0.61 |
| Capital Per Worker | 0.45 | 0.16 | 2.72 | 0.34 | 0.25 | 0.00 |
| Rainfall Deviation from Mean | -0.03 | 0.16 | -1.51 | -0.02 | -0.02 | -0.02 |
| TFPG1 | 0.67 | 0.68 | 0.57 | 0.76 | 0.83 | 0.71 |
| Capital Per Worker | 0.36 | 0.13 | 2.14 | 0.26 | 0.20 | 0.32 |
| Rainfall Deviation from Mean | -0.03 | 0.19 | -1.70 | -0.02 | -0.03 | -0.02 |
| Impact of CG Import on | 1.3% | 1.3% | 1.3% | 2.2% | 2.0% | 2.5% |
| TFPG1 | 1.4 | 0.62 | -7.2 | 0.80 | 0.76 | 0.83 |

*Source* : NAS and authors estimates.

One striking contrast that emerges is as follows: While the rate of growth of NDP per capita and per worker tripled between the socialist and market phases (from 1.3 per cent to 3.9 per cent and 1.3 per cent to 3.5 per cent respectively), the average rate of growth of capital stock per worker only doubled (from 1.4 per cent to 2.7 per cent). The growth of NDP per worker accelerated despite a fall in the average deviation of rainfall from a positive 0.5 per cent in phase I to a negative 1.8 per cent in phase II. Clearly, changes in total factor productivity growth are an important reason for these paradoxes. Equally striking is the fact that the growth of NDP per worker fell from 2.7 per cent in sub-phase IA to 0.3 per cent in sub-phase IB despite a doubling of the rate of growth of capital per worker from 0.9 per cent per annum to 1.8 per cent annum. Here, rainfall variation provided part of the explanation, with a positive deviations of 4.0 per cent from mean during sub-phase IA turning into a negative deviation 2.7 per cent during sub-phase IB.

Turning to the estimates of TFPG, we find that the average TFPG over the periods and sub-periods as estimated in stage one (TFPG0) and stage two (TFPG1) are very similar. The largest difference of 0.3 per cent between the two measures occurs in sub-phase IB. The results are also very similar if we ignore the rainfall effects completely and assume that capital share is equal to 0.26 and use this to calculate TFPG using Equation 4 (TFPGs). The largest difference in this case is 0.5 per cent in sub-phase IA. However, if we take the averages of the HP filtered series for TFPG1 (TFPG1hp), the result is different for sub-phase IB (0.5 per cent) and sub-phase IIA (-0.3 per cent). We will, therefore, use our preferred measure TFPG1 in the discussion, supplemented by TFPG1hp.

A tripling of the growth of total factor productivity from 0.9 per cent per annum in the socialist phase I to 2.7 per cent per annum during the market phase II, was clearly the driver in tripling the rate of growth of NDP per capita over these two phases. Of the 2.2 per cent (3.5 per cent-1.3 per cent) points increase in growth rate of NDP per worker, 1.8 per cent points were due to the increase in TFPG1 and 0.4 per cent points due to capital deepening. Consequently, the contribution of TFPG to per worker growth increased from 67 per cent during phase I to 76 per cent during phase II. As the contribution of rainfall remained virtually unchanged, the contribution of capital deepening correspondingly declined from 36 per cent to 26 per cent (Table 3.1).

The reason for the sharp decline in the growth of per worker NDP during the socialist rate of growth (IB) also becomes clear. More than half the decline of 2.4 per cent points between sub-phase IA and IB is the result of a 1.4 per cent point per annum decline in TFPG1. The rest was contributed by the change from above average to below average rainfall. Thus, almost 6/10th (0.57) of the pathetic growth rate of 0.3 per cent during this sub-phase was due to TFPG1 with the rest coming from capital deepening, which also compensated for the negative effect of weather (0.44= 2.14 - 1.7).

The rate of growth of per worker NDP has increased from 3.1 per cent per annum during sub-phase IIA (moderate reforms) to 3.9 per cent per annum in sub-phase IIB (broader reforms). TFPG has remained almost unchanged over these two sub-phases, increasing marginally from 2.6 per cent per annum to 2.8 per cent per annum (i.e. by 0.2 per cent point). The growth of capital per worker has, however, doubled from 1.8 per cent per annum to 3.6 per cent per annum, contributing 0.6 per cent points to the increase in the growth rate of per worker NDP. As a consequence the contribution of TFPG to the overall growth declined from 83 per cent during sub-phase IIA to 71 per cent during sub-phase IIB, while that of capital deepening increased from 20 per cent to 32 per cent. Thus, the broadening and deepening of reforms during the latter phase seems to have lifted 'animal spirits' leading to greater investment and growth. The effect on productivity has been modest if we go by TFPG1, but reasonable if we use TFPG1hp. In the latter case, 0.4 per cent of the 0.9 per cent point increase in NDP per worker between sub-phase IIA and IIB (44 per cent) is accounted for by TFPG.

We can compare our estimates of total TFPG with those given in Guha-Khasnobis and Bari (2003). For this purpose we have to create decade averages. Our estimates of TFPG1 are 1.3 per cent per annum during the 1960s, -0.1 per cent per annum during the seventies and 3.0 per cent per annum (Appendix Table A3.1). The estimates based on TFPG0 are marginally lower. Our estimates are therefore close to one of their three estimates in which the growth rates are 1.2 per cent, -0.4 per cent and 2.5 per cent for the same three decades. The estimates of King and Levine (1993, 1994) are 0.66, -1.77 and 3.0 and differ most sharply for the seventies. Our analysis suggests that the TFPG for the seventies is underestimated because of the missing variable rainfall (which was unfavourable). To some extent, the same caveat applies to the under estimation of TFPG in the sixties, where the other two estimates of Guha-Khasnobis and Bari (2003) are even lower (0.72 and 0.15).

## 6. DETERMINANTS OF TFPG

A simple regression of the ratio of fixed investment in machinery and equipment to total fixed investment (Ifme/IF) on TFPG yields a highly significant co-efficient:

$$\text{TFPG1} = \underset{(7.8)^{***}}{0.044\ \text{Ifme/IF}} \ \underset{(-2.77)^{***}}{-0.17^{*}\text{GrXRreal}} \ \underset{(-2.3)^{**}}{-0.271\ \text{AR}(1)}$$

$$R^2 = 0.27,\ R^2\ (\text{adj}) = 0.24,\ DW = 2.1 \qquad (12)$$

GrXRreal is the rate of change of the real exchange rate (measured by ratio of implicit GDP deflator for tradable goods/non-tradable services). Thus, investment in machinery and equipment seems to have a productivity enhancing effect in India. Drainm and drainm(-1) are not significant when introduced into this equation for TFPG as expected, as we have taken account of these in calculating TFPG1 (and tfpg0). Similar results are obtained if the dependent variable is Kfme/kf or if the independent variable is TFPGO.

Using the co-efficient of 0.044 we can estimate the impact of machinery and equipment investment on TFPG1. Machinery and investment was responsible for an average 0.18 per cent point, 0.15 per cent point 0.32 per cent point and 0.35 per cent point of TFPG in the sub-phases IA, IIA and IIB respectively. Thus, the contribution of machinery and equipment investment to TFPG growth increased from phase I to phase II. The contribution of the real exchange rate was a fraction of this except in sub-phase IB when an appreciation reduced TFPG by 0.13 per cent point thus nullifying the contribution of machinery investment. Appreciation reduced the TFPG by 0.05 per cent point and 0.06 per cent point in IIA and IIB respectively.

From Equation 11 we know that the dummy for 1965-66 to 1980-81 has a significant effect on TFPG. Introducing this into the above equation we have:

$$TFPG1 = \underset{(-2.5)^{**}}{-0.01\ D6580} + \underset{(8.9)^{***}}{0.05\ Ifme/IF} \underset{(-2.7)^{***}}{-0.17*GrXRreal} - \underset{(-2.8)^{***}}{0.35\ AR(1)}$$

$R^2$ = 0.35, $R^2$ (adj) = 0.31, DW = 2.1. (13)

The co-efficient on Ifme/Ifixed is marginally higher than in Equation 12 but similar. Thus, in addition to import controls and import substitution policies that affected machinery investment and the real exchange rate, TFPG was reduced by 1 per cent point during 1965-66 to 1980-81 due to other polices. In other words approximately 1.1 per cent point of the 1.45 per cent (0.77 per cent) point decline in TFPG1 (TFPG1hp) during sub-phase IB is explained by Equation 13 (last 2 lines of Table 3.1).

One possibility is that the other policies captured by the dummy worked to reduce capacity utilisation. This is suggested by the rise in the co-efficient on machinery investment on introduction of the dummy and the doubling of the rate of growth of capital per worker during sub-phase IB. The policies introduced during this phase could for instance have reduced the rate of capacity utilisation through the following channels: (a) Rise in import duties leading to higher prices paid by consumers for domestic consumer goods and consequent reduction in consumer demand. (b) Higher (income/excise) taxation and consequent reduction in personal disposable income. (c) Over-investment by government in the production of goods and services for which there was no demand from the private sector. This is the sub-period of 'legislative-bureaucratic socialism' that Virmani (2004c) called the "socialist rate of growth (SRG)" period in which GDP growth plummeted.

## 7. SECTOR PRODUCTIVITY TRENDS

### 7.1 Phase I

The TFPG estimates for the sectors are summarised in period averages (Tables 3.2 and 3.3) and also presented in the Figures 3.8, 3.9 and 3.10 in the form of filtered (using HP filter) series. The pattern of TFPG decline in the aggregate series is most clearly mirrored in the TFPG for other services ('finance, real estate, housing and business services' and 'community services and government administration') sector and trade and hotels (Figure 3.8). Except for an initial rise and peak in the TFPG in trade *et al.*, the three series decline till the early seventies, with trade reaching a trough in 1971-72, aggregate in 1972-73 and other-services in 1975-76. The TFPG for trade and hotels, however, falls much more sharply and becomes negative and then recovers equally sharply. This suggests problems relating to capacity utilisation perhaps arising from the negative effect of government appropriating resources from the private individuals and thus having a negative effect on demand for services. The pattern of growth in private consumption is found to mirror that in the aggregate TFPG series with the former reaches a trough in 1970-71 (Figure 3.8), providing support to this hypothesis.

**FIGURE 3.8**

*TFPG by Sector-HP Filtered Series 1*

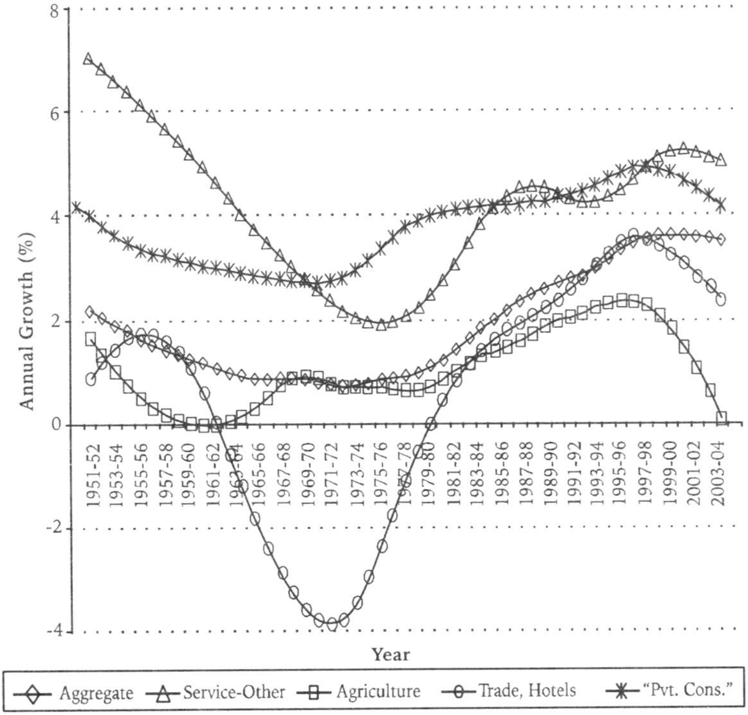

TFPG in agriculture follows a somewhat similar pattern to aggregate TFPG except that the trough occurs early around 1961-62 and there is an additional peak in 1969-70. TFPG in all other sectors is initially negative and becomes positive in the sixties or seventies (Figure 3.9 and Figure 3.10). The negative TFPG in the early-fifties could be due to a sudden discontinuous spurt in government investment, which because of a combination of gestation lags and excessive capacity build-up (not being motivated by profitability/ efficiency considerations) initially resulted in very low capacity utilisation. Longer lifetime assets (with lower depreciation rate), would also tend to show lower measured productivity in initial years and higher measured productivity in later years.

**FIGURE 3.9**

*TFPG by Sector-HP Filtered Series 2*

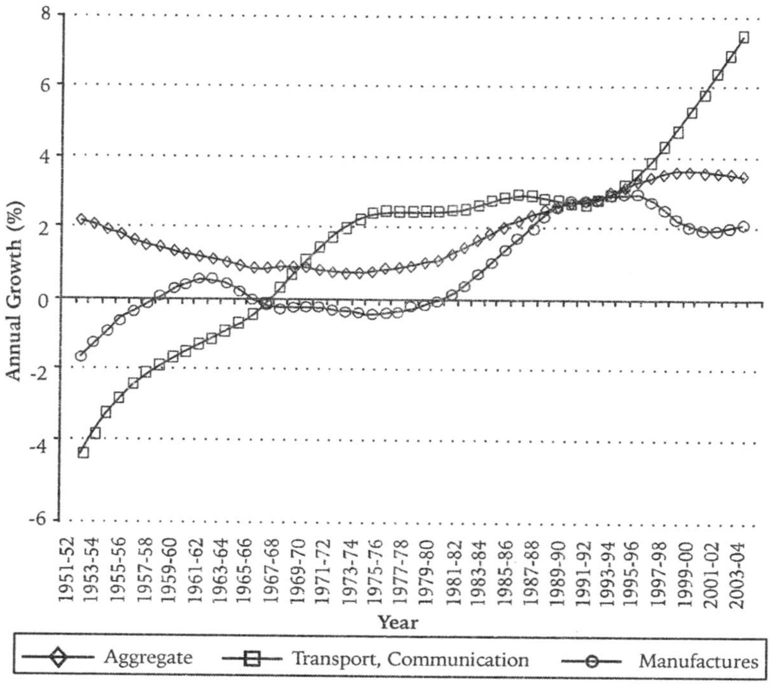

## FIGURE 3.10

*TFPG by Sector-HP Filtered Series 3*

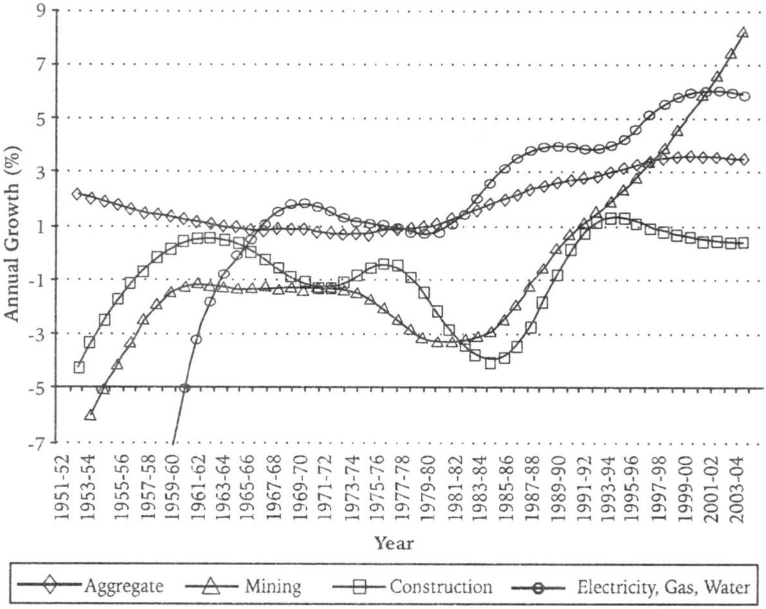


These factors seem to be responsible for the negative TFPG in electricity, mining and transport (road, rail) and communications and construction during the first decade of independence as there was a rapid increase in investment during this period. But this also means that actual TFPG was even lower during sub-phase IB (1965-66 to 1979-80) than our estimates because of the effect of gestation lags and longer lifetime arising from investment in sub-phase IA. Put another way, given the sharp slowing of investment in sub-phase IB, neglect of these two factors would mean that TFPG is overestimated.

As long as sector TFPG is negative, it clearly pulls down aggregate TFPG. TFPG in transport-communications and electricity, generally follows a rising trend with intervening plateau. The trend TFPG in manufacturing, mining and construction made a trough at a negative value in 1974-75, 1979-80 and 1983-84 respectively, after which TFPG rose. The electricity sector has also been on a rising trend since 1978-79.

The TFPG trend (HP filtered series) for manufacturing was positive for only 8 out of the 30 years from 1950-51 to 1979-80 (phase I), mostly during sub-phase IA. According to the unfiltered series TFPG averaged 0.4 per cent in sub-phase IA and -0.3 per cent in phase I as a whole. It was, therefore, effectively zero during this period of 'socialism with an Indian face', characterised by the Mahalanobis model of state led heavy industry (machines for making machines) complemented by small-scale industry reservation.

Given this pattern of TFPG trends in phase I (1950-51 to 1979-80), TFPG was negative in all sectors except agriculture and the residual sector 'other services' (Table 3.2). While agriculture TFPG was positive in sub-phase IA alone, TFPG in 'other services' grew strongly in both phases. As a result TFPG was the sole cause of growth of other-service during sub-phase IB, overcoming even some capital shallowing. In sub-phase IB TFPG was responsible for 85 per cent of the growth with the result that during phase I as a whole TFPG contribution was more than 100 per cent. Given the size of these two sectors, this was sufficient to ensure that aggregate TFPG was positive, with a little help from a positive TFPG in 'manufacturing' and 'trade, hotels and restaurants' in sub-phase IA and a positive TFPG in 'electricity, gas and water' and 'transport and communications' in sub-phase IB.

There was massive decline in factor productivity in the electricity sector in sub-phase IA and a substantial decline in productivity in the mining sector in both sub-phases. Both these sectors were reserved for the government and the share of public sector in total GDP from these sectors went up to 100 per cent in electricity and about 97 per cent in mining by the end of phase I. Gestation lags in investment may have been partly responsible for the mismatch between investment and output, especially in electricity. The government may also have built capacity too far ahead of potential demand on the assumption that supply would create demand through general development (Mahalanobis model). The net result, as in the former USSR, was that nationalisation of these sectors had a negative effect on TFPG even though GDP from these sectors continued to grow due to capital deepening and expansion of manpower.

The negative TFPG growth in manufacturing and in trade, hotels and restaurants in sub-phase IB could have been due to the following:

## Table 3.2

*Total Factor Productivity by Sector*

| Sector | Sub-phase K Share | Phase I: 1950-51 to 1979-80 Total | IA:(1950-51 to 1964-65) | IB:(1965-66 to 1979-80) | Phase II: 1980-81 to 2003-04 Total | IIA:(1980-81 to 1991-92) | IIB:(1992-93 to 2003-04) |
|---|---|---|---|---|---|---|---|
| *Total Factor Productivity Growth (Per Cent)* | | | | | | | |
| GDPfc: Total | 0.26 | 0.9 | 1.9 | 0.1 | 3.0 | 2.5 | 3.6 |
| Agriculture | 0.23 | 0.2 | 1.0 | -0.5 | 2.1 | 2.2 | 2.1 |
| Mining | 0.36 | -3.1 | -4.3 | -2.1 | 2.0 | -0.2 | 4.3 |
| Manufacture | 0.32 | -0.3 | 0.4 | -0.8 | 2.0 | 1.3 | 2.8 |
| Electricity | 0.58 | -7.6 | -17.0 | 0.6 | 4.4 | 4.1 | 4.7 |
| Construction | 0.16 | -0.9 | -0.7 | -1.1 | -0.7 | -1.7 | 0.3 |
| Trade, Hotels | 0.38 | -1.0 | 1.3 | -3.0 | 2.6 | 1.6 | 3.6 |
| Transport, Comm. | 0.33 | -0.2 | -2.1 | 1.5 | 3.8 | 2.8 | 4.9 |
| Service Other | 0.23 | 4.0 | 5.8 | 2.4 | 4.4 | 4.1 | 4.7 |
| *Growth Rate of NDP Per Worker (Per Cent)* | | | | | | | |
| GDPfc: Total | | 1.1 | 1.9 | 0.5 | 4.1 | 3.3 | 5.0 |
| Agriculture | | 0.0 | 0.4 | -0.4 | 2.5 | 2.5 | 2.6 |
| Mining | | 0.9 | 1.2 | 1.0 | 3.8 | 2.0 | 5.7 |
| Manufacture | | 1.6 | 3.6 | 0.2 | 3.9 | 3.1 | 4.8 |
| Electricity | | 5.2 | 7.0 | 4.3 | 7.6 | 6.4 | 8.9 |
| Construction | | 0.4 | 2.7 | -0.7 | -0.7 | -1.8 | 0.6 |
| Trade, Hotels | | 1.6 | 4.6 | -0.8 | 2.5 | 1.8 | 3.3 |
| Transport, Comm. | | 1.2 | 1.1 | 1.6 | 3.7 | 2.6 | 4.8 |
| Service Other | | 3.5 | 5.1 | 2.0 | 4.7 | 4.1 | 5.4 |
| *Contribution of Sector TFPG to Sector Growth* | | | | | | | |
| GDPfc: Total | | 0.26 | 0.41 | 0.04 | 0.52 | 0.46 | 0.59 |
| Agriculture | | 0.05 | 0.21 | -0.18 | 0.36 | 0.39 | 0.34 |
| Mining | | -0.88 | -0.93 | -0.75 | 0.34 | -0.03 | 0.69 |
| Manufacture | | -0.07 | 0.09 | -0.30 | 0.35 | 0.24 | 0.46 |
| Electricity | | -2.13 | -3.69 | 0.22 | 0.76 | 0.76 | 0.76 |
| Construction | | -0.25 | -0.15 | -0.38 | -0.12 | -0.30 | 0.05 |
| Trade, Hotels | | -0.29 | 0.28 | -1.08 | 0.44 | 0.29 | 0.58 |
| Transport, Comm.7 | | -0.05 | -0.45 | 0.52 | 0.65 | 0.50 | 0.80 |
| Service Other | | 1.11 | 1.25 | 0.85 | 0.76 | 0.75 | 0.77 |

*Note*: TFPG for GDPfc differs from that in Table 3.1 because of difference in methodology.
Capital income shares are average values of shares given in Brahmananda (1982).

(a) Declining capacity utilisation. (b) Use of inferior domestic (import-substituting) capital goods consequent to imposition of QRs. (c) Use of inferior imported capital goods from the rupee payment areas (Soviet Union, E-Europe) which were exempt from QRs/bans applicable to import of capital goods from convertible currency areas. The negative TFPG growth in 'transport and communications' in sub-phase IA was due partly to the government monopoly of the railways and communications and partly to the above reasons.

In phase I as a whole TFPG growth in sectors (Table 3.3 based on Equation 7) was responsible for about 17 per cent of overall TFPG.

### Table 3.3

*Contribution of Sector TFPG and TFI to Overall TFPG*

*(Per Cent)*

| *Sector* | *I: Total* | *IA:(1950-51 to 1964-65)* | *IB:(1965-66 to 1979-80)* | *II: Total* | *IIA:(1980-81 to 1991-92)* | *IIB:(1992-93 to 2003-04)* |
|---|---|---|---|---|---|---|
| | *Contribution of Sector (tfpg+tfi) to Total TFPG* | | | | | |
| Agriculture | -36 | 15 | -11 | 6 | 13 | 2 |
| Mining | 2 | 2 | 0 | 2 | 4 | 1 |
| Manufacture | 30 | 22 | 2 | 16 | 15 | 17 |
| Electricity, Gas, Water | 2 | 0 | 0 | 2 | 3 | 1 |
| Construction | 11 | 11 | 0 | 5 | 4 | 5 |
| Trade, Hotels, Restaurant | 25 | 18 | 2 | 20 | 14 | 23 |
| Transport, Comm. | 11 | 3 | 2 | 13 | 8 | 15 |
| Rest: Other Services | 48 | 25 | 5 | 37 | 39 | 36 |
| Total | 94 | 96 | 0 | 100 | 99 | 100 |
| | *Contribution of Sector TFPG to Total TFPG* | | | | | |
| Agriculture | 0 | 27 | -5 | 21 | 31 | 16 |
| Mining | -7 | -4 | -1 | 2 | 0 | 3 |
| Manufacture | -4 | 4 | -2 | 10 | 8 | 11 |
| Electricity, Gas, Water | -3 | -3 | 0 | 2 | 2 | 2 |
| Construction | -8 | -2 | -1 | -1 | -5 | 0 |
| Trade, Hotels, Restaurant | -18 | 7 | -5 | 13 | 9 | 15 |
| Transport, Comm. | 1 | -3 | 1 | 9 | 6 | 10 |
| Rest: Other Services | 56 | 33 | 5 | 33 | 33 | 32 |
| Total | 17 | 59 | -9 | 87 | 84 | 88 |
| | *Contribution of Inter-sector TFI Allocation* | | | | | |
| Agriculture | -36 | -11 | -5 | -16 | -18 | -14 |
| Mining | 9 | 6 | 1 | 1 | 4 | -1 |
| Manufacture | 34 | 18 | 3 | 6 | 7 | 6 |
| Electricity, Gas, Water | 4 | 3 | 0 | 0 | 1 | 0 |
| Construction | 20 | 12 | 2 | 6 | 9 | 4 |
| Trade, Hotels, Restaurant | 43 | 11 | 7 | 7 | 5 | 8 |
| Transport, Comm. | 11 | 6 | 1 | 4 | 2 | 5 |
| Rest: Other Services | -8 | -8 | 0 | 4 | 6 | 4 |
| Total | 77 | 37 | 8 | 13 | 15 | 12 |

*Note* : * TFPG for sub-phase IB is close to zero, so numbers have not been divided by it.

growth with other services being the main contributor (56 per cent). The remaining TFPG growth was the result of a shift of factors from agriculture (33 per cent) and other-services to all other sectors [trade and hotels (43 per cent), manufactures (34 per cent) and construction (20 per cent)]. In sub-phase IA TFPG growth in sectors was responsible for almost 60 per cent of total TFPG with agriculture (27 per cent) and other services contributing almost equally (33 per cent). The remaining contribution came from a shift of factors out of agriculture and other services to the remaining sectors.

If we look at the full (TFPG + TFI share) contribution of each sector to total TFPG, other services is the largest contributor (I: 48 per cent, IA: 25 per cent) but is followed by manufacturing (30 per cent, 20 per cent) and trade, hotels and restaurants (25 per cent, 18 per cent). In phase IB the total TFPG is so small that it is difficult to be sure about the relative contributions (Table 3.3, column 3).

## 7.2 Phase II

Since 1980-81 TFPG was negative only in mining and construction till 1987-88 and 1988-89 respectively (Figure 3.8, Figure 3.9 and Figure 3.10). TFPG trend in every sector except construction (which bottomed out in 1984-85) was rising, with the trend in most sectors peaking between 1992-93 and 1999-2000. The aggregate TFPG also peaked then. The first sector TFPG to peak was construction at 1.3 per cent in 1992-93, followed by manufacturing TFPG at 3 per cent in 1993-94, agriculture TFPG at 2.35 per cent in 1994-95, trade-hotels at 3.6 per cent in 1995-96, and electricity (6 per cent) and other-services (5.2 per cent) in 1999-2000. TFPG in mining (8.2 per cent) and transport-communication (7.5 per cent) is, however, still on an accelerating trend as of 2002-03 with the latter driven primarily by the communication sub-sector. In the case of mining, the share of the public sector in GDP and in GCF has been on a downtrend since the late-1980, so that entry of the private sector could have contributed to rising TFPG. In the case of the communication sector, policy and regulatory reform starting with the opening of the sector to private entry and competition, arising from the introduction divisible mobile technologies has clearly fuelled TFPG and value added growth.

Construction is the only sector in which average TFPG was negative during phase II (1980-81 to 2002-03). Its performance has been abysmal. Much of construction is either carried out by government or procured by government. The procurement standards and procedures adopted by the government, therefore, play a vital role in the evolution of the construction industry. These standard and procedures have not been changed since Independence so that the industry has been stuck in a time warp. As noted in Virmani (2004a), there is an urgent need to modernise procurement and other policies related to the construction sector.

Between phase IB (1965-66 to 1979-80) and IIA (1980-81 to 1991-92) TFPG accelerated most sharply in trade and hotels and electricity sectors and least in construction. Transport and communications and other services, however continued to have above average growth of TFPG during phase IIA and IIB with the former accelerating sharply in IIB and the latter also improving from its high levels.

During phase II, the contribution of sector TFPG to the same sector's GDP per worker ranged from a low of around 35 per cent in mining, manufacturing and agriculture to 76 per cent in 'electricity, gas and water' and 'other services'. The rest was contributed by capital deepening. For both electricity and other services, the contribution of sector TFPG to sector's GDP per worker remained at around 75 per cent in both sub-phases (IIA and IIB). While in agriculture it varied around 36 per cent, it increased from phase IIA to IIB), in manufacturing (24 per cent, 46 per cent), trade, hotels and restaurants (29 per cent, 58 per cent) and transport, storage and communications (50 per cent, 80 per cent).

The contribution of sector TFPG to aggregate TFPG increased sharply during phase II to 87 per cent from the 17 per cent average during phase I and 59 per cent during sub-phase IA. The greatest increase in contribution was in trade-hotels, followed by agriculture and manufacturing. The average contribution of TFPG in other-services declined sharply, but it remained the largest contributor to aggregate TFPG. The contribution of all other sectors increased by small amounts. Inter-sectoral shifts in factors contributed only 13 per cent to aggregate TFPG during phase II (Table 3.3).

The contribution of sector TFPG was marginally lower in sub-phase IIA (84 per cent) and marginally higher in sub-phase IIB (89 per cent). Compared to sub-phase IIA, IIB also saw a smaller contribution from TFPG in agriculture, and a larger contribution from TFPG in trade-hotels, construction, transport-communications, manufacturing and mining. In other words, the sector TFPG contributions were more evenly distributed in sub-phase IIB, even though other-services continued to contribute a little less than 33 per cent (Table 3.3).

TFPG in agriculture has declined sharply during the second half of the nineties (Figure 3.8). Among the potential reasons for this sharp decline are: (a) The deterioration in the fertiliser (NPK) mix because of price distortions arising from subsidies for urea. (b) Lowering of water table due to inadequate public attention to developing and maintaining water systems for regenerating underground water as well as the lack of optimal utilisation of surface water. (c) Over-exploitation of under-ground water because of the provision of free electricity by the State. (d) Deteriorating R & D and extension systems. This highlights the urgency of reforming policies relating to the entire food chain starting from production to retailing (Virmani and Rajeev, 2002; Virmani, 2004a).

The trend growth of TFPG has, after rising to 2.5 per cent per annum in the mid-nineties, regressed to 2 per cent per annum. This is less than the aggregate TFPG estimated in the first part of the chapter and is significantly lower than TFPG estimated by applying exogenous capital shares and ignoring rainfall effects. Thus, manufacturing, instead of acting as a driver of overall TFPG, currently appears to be acting as a drag. Economic reforms related to labour intensive manufacturing should be accelerated to raise TFPG and global competitiveness of this tradable sector.

## 8. CONCLUSIONS

Since Independence, trend growth of GDP and NDP has gone through one complete cycle (growth cycle) with a trough in 1971-72 and a peak in 1994-95. The trend started at around 4.8 per cent per annum in 1951-52 and is currently around the same level. The trends in growth of NDP per capita and NDP per worker were almost identical. This chapter uses the source of growth methodology to explain this growth cycle. It shows that TFPG followed a V shaped pattern between 1951-52 and 1985-86 with the tip of the V in the year 1971-72. Since the mid-nineties TFPG has flattened out with a gently rising trend. Growth of NDP per worker also follows a V shaped pattern but peaks much later in the mid-nineties and turns down thereafter instead of plateauing out. The pattern of capital deepening (growth of capital per worker), in contrast, is quite different, with two almost complete cycles. The first peak occurs in 1965-66 and the second one in 1998-99 to 1999-2000, three years after the peak in growth of per worker NDP.

The contribution of total factor productivity growth to growth of NDP per worker (net of effects of variations in rainfall), consequently fell progressively from 85 per cent in 1951-52 to a little over 25 per cent in 1991-92. The contribution has risen sharply since then to almost 50 per cent (a level it last had around 1975-76). The contribution of capital deepening (growth of capital per worker) has followed the inverse pattern.

The chapter then goes on to link the TFPG estimates to the analysis of growth and policy structures given in chapters 1 and 2. It shows that the collapse of GDP/NDP growth during the sub-period 1965-66 to 1979-80 (sub-phases IB) was due substantially to a sharp fall in total factor productivity growth. Half the decline in growth between sub-phase IA and sub-phase IB was because of the decline in TFPG and the rest because of poor rainfall. The chapter also shows that the recovery of growth during 1980-81 to 1991-92 (sub-phase IIA) was due to an increase in TFPG to 1.6 times the level prevailing in 1951-52 to 1964-65 (sub-phase IA), coupled with a doubling of per worker NDP growth relative to IA. A change of policy direction from an immersion in the Indian version of socialism towards market economics, has been responsible for the acceleration in both these sources of growth.

Formal econometric analysis shows that investment in machinery (relative to investment in structures), and changes in protection (through QRs and tariffs) played an important role in the rate of growth of total factor productivity. It is shown that the ratio of machinery to total investment and the rate of change in the real exchange rate (ratio of tradable/goods prices to non-tradable/service prices) have significant effect on TFPG and explain about 25 per cent of the variation in it. Other policies prevailing during 1965-66 to

1979-80, captured by a dummy variable, explain another 5-10 per cent of the variation in TFPG during the entire period from 1951-52 to 2003-04.

The chapter goes on to estimate total factor productivity for all major sectors of the economy for which data on workers is available. This allows us to examine the relative contribution of TFPG and capital deepening to per worker growth in each sector. The TFPG estimates are also used to estimate the contribution of each sector's total factor productivity growth and capital deepening to the growth of aggregate TFPG. It is shown that the contribution of sector TFPG to aggregate TFPG increased from 17 per cent during 1951-52 to 1979-80 (phase I) to 87 per cent in 1980-81 to 2003-04 (phase II). The greatest increase in contribution was in 'trade, hotels and restaurants' followed by agriculture and manufacturing. TFPG in 'other services, (financial, real estate, housing, business, personal and government services) remained the largest contributor to aggregate TFPG (though the change in it was small). Further, more detailed, work needs to be done to identify the productivity drivers in the service sectors.

## Appendix A3.1

### *Estimates of TFPG by Decades*

As most previous studies and global comparisons are in terms of decades, we summarise below our estimates of TFPG by decade. The most different result is the positive TFPG for the 1970s using the HP filtered series. This is perhaps because the filtering procedure eliminates temporary fluctuations in capacity utilisation that are not accounted for in the estimation procedures used so far.

The share of workers in different sectors and the number of workers (usual status) in each sector are available only for specific years (of which we have chosen eight). We then used our NDP and fixed capital estimates for all sectors to calculate the TFPG. The growth rates used in the estimation of TFPG are compound annual rates for each period. These are shown in the first panel of Table A3.2.

We have constructed the time series for the sector distribution of workers by linear interpolation of the sector shares between these eight years (and also extrapolated it into the future). The time series for the aggregate work force is constructed as follows: For the chosen eight years the ratio of workers to working age population (age 15 to 64) is constructed. The ratio is constructed for all relevant years through linear interpolation and extrapolation. The constructed ratio is then used along with the time series for working age population (World Development Indicators) to obtain total number of workers (us) in every year. These are then used along with interpolated sector distribution of workers to calculate the number of workers (us) in each sector in every time period. This, along with the series for NDP and fixed capital for each sector, allows us to estimate TFPG for each sector for each year.

## Table A3.1

*Sources of Growth in Net Domestic Product*

| *Variable* Decade* => | *1950s* | *1960s* | *1970s* | *1980s* | *1990s* | *2000s* |
|---|---|---|---|---|---|---|
| Net Domestic Product | 3.9% | 4.0% | 2.8% | 5.9% | 5.8% | 5.7% |
| Per Worker NDP | 2.0% | 1.7% | 0.2% | 3.5% | 3.5% | 3.4% |
| Capital Per Worker | 0.4% | 2.2% | 1.4% | 1.6% | 3.3% | 4.1% |
| Workers (Pop. 15 to 64) | 1.8% | 2.1% | 2.5% | 2.5% | 2.2% | 2.0% |
| Rainfall Deviation from Mean | 3.4% | -1.4% | -0.1% | -2.1% | 1.2% | -8.6% |
| Total Factor Productivity Growth | | | | | | |
| *TFPG0* | 1.4% | 1.1% | -0.2% | 2.8% | 2.0% | 2.2% |
| *TFPG1* | 1.4% | 1.3% | -0.1% | 3.0% | 2.3% | 2.7% |
| *TFPG1hp* | 1.7% | 0.8% | 0.7% | 2.2% | 2.6% | 2.7% |
| Contribution to Gr. of NDPpwrk | | | | | | |
| *TFPG1* | 0.70 | 0.76 | -0.33 | 0.84 | 0.66 | 0.79 |
| *Capital Per Worker* | 0.07 | 0.42 | 2.21 | 0.15 | 0.32 | 0.41 |
| *Rainfall Deviation from Mean* | 0.23 | -0.18 | -0.88 | 0.01 | 0.02 | -0.21 |

*Source* : NAS and authors estimates.

*Notes* : * Data for 2000s is only for four years.

Workers = Pop. 15 to 64.

## Table A3.2

*Total Factor Productivity Growth*

| *Sector* | *K Share* | *(1951 to 1961)* | *(1961 to 1972-73)* | *(1972-73 to 1977-78)* | *(1977-78 to 1983)* | *(1983 to 1987-88)* | *(1987-88 to 1993-94)* | *(1993-94 to 1999-00)* |
|---|---|---|---|---|---|---|---|---|
| | *Compound Average Annual (Original Worker Data) (Per Cent)* | | | | | | | |
| All: GDPfc | 0.26 | 1.6 | 0.6 | 1.8 | 0.9 | 1.4 | 2.7 | 4.3 |
| Agriculture & Allied | 0.23 | 0.6 | -0.2 | 2.4 | 0.3 | -1.0 | 2.5 | 2.6 |
| Mining and Quarrying | 0.36 | -4.2 | -1.7 | -1.1 | -4.2 | -4.0 | 2.1 | 5.1 |
| Manufacturing | 0.32 | -0.5 | 0.2 | -1.0 | 0.3 | 0.6 | 2.6 | 2.2 |
| Electricity, Gas, Water | 0.58 | -18.1 | -0.2 | 0.1 | -1.1 | 6.8 | 1.0 | 8.6 |
| Construction | 0.16 | -1.4 | -1.2 | 3.6 | -5.1 | -9.0 | 4.9 | -0.3 |
| Trade, Hotels, etc. | 0.38 | 1.8 | -3.3 | -1.7 | 1.2 | 1.0 | 2.1 | 4.3 |
| Transport, Strg., Comn. | 0.33 | -2.5 | 0.3 | 2.0 | 1.8 | 5.2 | 1.8 | 4.7 |
| Services-other | 0.23 | 6.0 | 3.6 | 1.5 | 2.4 | 6.0 | 3.4 | 6.1 |
| | *Average of Calculated Annual Rates (Per Cent)* | | | | | | | |
| All: GDPfc | 0.26 | 1.6 | 0.7 | 1.9 | 1.0 | 1.4 | 2.8 | 4.3 |
| Agriculture & Allied | 0.23 | 0.7 | 0.0 | 2.7 | 0.7 | -1.0 | 2.7 | 2.7 |
| Mining & Quarrying | 0.36 | -4.4 | -1.7 | -1.0 | -4.1 | -3.8 | 2.2 | 5.1 |
| Manufacturing | 0.32 | -0.5 | 0.3 | -1.0 | 0.5 | 0.6 | 2.7 | 2.4 |
| Electricity, Gas, Water | 0.58 | -20.7 | -0.1 | 0.6 | -0.9 | 6.9 | 1.3 | 8.6 |
| Construction | 0.16 | -1.2 | -1.1 | 3.9 | -4.9 | -9.0 | 4.9 | -0.3 |
| Trade, Hotels, etc. | 0.38 | 1.8 | -3.3 | -1.7 | 1.2 | 1.0 | 2.1 | 4.4 |
| Transport, Strg., Comn. | 0.33 | -2.5 | 0.4 | 2.1 | 1.8 | 5.2 | 1.8 | 4.8 |
| | 0.23 | 6.0 | 3.6 | 1.5 | 2.4 | 6.0 | 3.5 | 6.2 |

*Source* : NAS, Krishnamurthy (1970), Sundaram (2001), Visaria (2002) and authors estimate.

*Note* : Based on estimates of Worker (UPSS).

As a crosscheck we average these for the time period for which TFPG has been estimated using compound annual growth rates between the eight data points. These values are shown in the second panel of Table A3.2. For instance the TFPG for aggregate GDP during the period 1951 to 1961 was 1.6 per cent per annum both by the compound annual average method and by averaging the annual TFPG obtained through interpolation of worker series. In contrast, the TFPG for the electricity sector between 1972-73 and 1977-78 is 0.1 per cent per annum by the compound method and 0.6 per cent per annum (or almost six times) by interpolation method. Overall, except for a few sectors and periods the two sets of TFPG estimates are quite close.

The decade averages for the annual estimates by sector are summarised in the Appendix Table A3.3.

**Table A3.3**

*Total Factor Productivity Growth*

*(Per Cent)*

| *Variable* Period => | *1950s* | *1960s* | *1970s* | *1980s* | *1990s* | *2000s* |
|---|---|---|---|---|---|---|
| All: GDPfc | 1.5 | 1.4 | 0.0 | 3.0 | 3.1 | 3.1 |
| Agriculture & Allied | 0.6 | 0.8 | -0.8 | 2.8 | 2.0 | 0.2 |
| Mining & Quarrying | -5.7 | -0.9 | -3.3 | -0.6 | 3.0 | 6.9 |
| Manufacturing | -1.1 | 0.7 | -0.6 | 2.2 | 1.4 | 3.6 |
| Electricity, Gas and Water | -27 | 0.7 | -0.1 | 4.1 | 4.6 | 4.6 |
| Construction | -2.0 | 0.5 | -1.4 | -3.2 | 1.5 | 0.4 |
| Trade, Hotels, etc | 1.3 | -0.8 | -3.1 | 2.1 | 3.1 | 2.1 |
| Transport, Strg., Comn. | -2.8 | -0.4 | 2.1 | 3.0 | 3.5 | 7.2 |
| Services-Other | 6.2 | 4.0 | 2.1 | 4.5 | 4.6 | 3.3 |

*Note*: Based on estimates of Workers (UPSS).

According to this break-up, aggregate and sector TFPG growth was the worst during the seventies, consistent with the available studies. The negative TFPG results for so many sectors in the 1950s, however, contradicts the results of Brahmananda. The results for the 1990s and 2000s are also new, though the latter are very tentative.

# 4

# China's Socialist Market Economy

*Lessons of Success*

## 1. INTRODUCTION

In the late 1930s Oskar Lange put forward the idea of "Market Socialism," an economy in which assets (means of production) were owned socially (by the communist party or State), but which mimicked the supply-demand price adjustment of the competitive market economy. Aba Lerner, Lange and others then debated this issue during the 1930s. The key element that is common to 'market socialism' *a la* Lange and Lerner and 'Socialism' (*a la* Lenin and Stalin) is socialist (i.e. party) ownership and (managerial) control of assets. The key difference is market based allocations *versus* centrally planned allocations.

In China, the 'market' element has expanded gradually since the start of the agricultural reforms in 1979[1] and the introduction of urban reforms in 1984. In 1992, China publicly stated that its goal is a "socialist market economy with Chinese characteristics." Though China has successfully expanded the scope of the market, 'socialist' (communist) control of factors remains very important. An understanding of these elements is essential to an understanding of the economic performance of China.[2] The chapter starts by giving a stylised version of China's economy in terms of the mix of socialist and market elements. This leads to an explanation of the growth performance of the Chinese economy and appropriate lessons for other countries, particularly non-socialist ones.

---

1. After the third plenum in December 1978.

2. The reforms that China is currently undertaking or plans in future, have no relevance to past performance. The focus of the chapter is on industry so early agriculture reforms are not discussed.

The primary 'market' economy is in products (goods and non-infrastructure services) where even CPC controlled enterprises compete to maximise growth, as in a private corporate economy. The other market elements are external capital (into foreign invested enterprises) and external trade. Exports and foreign direct investments (FDI) have played such an important role in China's economy that its growth has been characterised as 'export-led growth', and could since 1990 be characterised as 'FDI-export led growth'. The extent to which import trade is now free is not entirely clear, though on balance this could be put into the market category. There is also a competitive fringe of individual capitalists/private capital that operates in export production.

The socialist planning system still operates, however, in factor markets (land, labour, capital) and infrastructure and the pricing of these inputs is used to provide (indirect) subsidies to foreign investors and domestic exporters. Cities/provinces can sell land to any buyer at any price. The labour responsibility system determines where a person can work legally and where it cannot. The banking system has evolved little from a government department where loans are decided on the basis of provincial/national objectives and ability to repay is irrelevant (variable cost of capital).[3] Infrastructure pricing and supply (particularly to foreign invested enterprises) is similarly decided on the basis of national/provincial/city objectives and can vary with enterprise. This is also true to some extent for the output of the state owned enterprises (SOEs) which remain subject to central department (their bosses) orders and directions.

In moving from the 'Socialist' to the 'Socialist Market Economy', China has borrowed aspects from the 'Nationalist Market Economies' of developing Japan, S. Korea and Singapore. The primary objective of the latter's government's was to catch-up with the advanced countries through fast growth of average income. They, therefore, developed a national consensus to maximise GDP growth. The whole nation was mobilised to achieve this goal. The simplicity of this objective (growth, investment, production) made it much easier to decentralise it and ensure accountability at every level including that of the private

3. For SOEs it varies downward from the formal rate to zero. The implicit interest rate could be negative if partial repayment is expected. For non-SOEs it varies upward from the formal rate for SOEs plus 20 per cent.

corporate sector (e.g. Zaibatsu, Chaebol). Democratic accountability was however stronger in these countries, so that much greater attention had to be paid to democratisation of the gains from growth, and the welfare of all citizens.[4]

Both types of economies contrast with 'democratic market' economies like India that are driven primarily by democratic concerns in which the multidimensional nature of welfare maps into multiple, often contradictory, objectives. The means adopted to achieve one objective often contradict those required to achieve another, resulting in cross-cutting actions. Multiple objectives lead to diffusion of accountability and provide liberal scope for pursuing one's personal goals (agency problems), as failure to achieve any one objective can always be blamed on the need to ensure another.

## 2. SOCIALIST ELEMENTS

### 2.1 Leninist Party

The standard Marxist-Leninist description of the Communist ruled State is the "dictatorship of the proletariat". In China this means the dictatorship of the Chinese Communist Party (CCP).[5] To quote Perkins (1994), "All political power in China is monopolised by the Chinese Communist Party, a party that is organised along Leninist lines. Power is centralised at the top and not easily challenged from below." The party is a hierarchy stretching from the party general secretary at the top to the party honcho in the smallest settlement/ village. The objectives and broad approach to their implementation is decided at the top as are the parameters within which lower levels can take initiatives. Within this framework, there is a multi-level decision making process from the national to provincial, metro cities and town and village level. This decentralisation is not a post-1978 development

4. Even though in theory we can always devise a set of assumptions that shows welfare maximisation and growth maximisation as equivalent, we are talking about the effect of adopting and trying to implement the two approaches in the real world (outcome).

5. The only reasonable benchmark is the former USSR/Soviet Union. North Korea is a personal dictatorship, not a party (proletariat) dictatorship. Similarly, Cuba is better described as a kind of feudal or virtual dictatorship. Even though Castro is the unchallenged dictator of Cuba, his stature in the party, rather than use of terror, ensures that nobody challenges him (i.e. he is a virtual dictator). Therefore, to say that China is far removed from North Korea and cannot, therefore, be called a 'dictatorship', is a red herring.

but has evolved since the 1960s, with the decentralisation of planning authority first to the provinces and then to the county.[6] The degree of operational freedom and flexibility within the designed and designated sphere of operation of the lower levels has however, increased since 1980. China's governance system is, therefore, a mix of centralised and decentralised elements, with the latter much wider than it was in the Leninist USSR.

The party has undoubtedly changed and evolved over the last 25 years and is different from what it was under Chairman Mao's Cultural Revolution. But it is also very different from any ruling party in a genuine democracy or 'quasi-democratic' State. For instance, one of the most important departments of the party is the personnel department. This department (at different levels), vets and selects all official appointees to positions with decision-making authority[7] and every CEO of every government owned/controlled company/firm/organisation. These appointees are, therefore, not just state officials or company/co-operative CEOs, but part of the network of the CCP. Even if the CEO is not a party member, there will be a party member (or group of members) ostensibly junior(s) in the organisation who can over-rule him on 'ideological' grounds.

Within the overall structure of decentralisation, the degree of autonomy and nature of accountability for managers of organisations and enterprises can vary from province to province, from township (village) to township (village) within the same province. Thus, appointment of the CEO by the party/government can go along with a relatively high degree of operational autonomy for the CEO in a production firm.[8] For instance, the town or village CCP boss who appoints the Town and Village Enterprise (T&Vs) CEO could leaves him free to maximise the growth of the firm subject to specified obligations to the village/town administration (e.g. local purchase or hiring) and/or the local party boss.[9] Similarly the CEO of a joint venture may be free to pursue a growth/sales maximisation strategy

6. To quote Perkins (1988), "By the 1970s a large proportion of Chinese enterprises were under the authority of the provinces rather than Beijing. In most cases, particularly with large enterprises and strategic sectors, Beijing retained effective control even if planning formally was at the provincial level."
7. Equivalent to our Joint Secretary and above.
8. But not in the financial sector where the party/government still controls capital flows.
9. Indian public sector managers have always enjoyed this type of freedom. This does not mean that we can arbitrarily classify the Indian public sector or the T&VEs as private.

subject to either promoting exports (with any losses covered by State loans i.e. disguised as NPAs) or below cost supply of intermediates to an FDI investor to attract it to that area. On the other hand, the professional CEO of an investment company or bank, may have limited market autonomy, with most of his decisions vetted or reviewed by a committee of party members (formally junior to him in his and other organisations).

Other vital departments of the CCP are the ideology and propaganda departments. The management of information is one of the important responsibilities of the party and its senior leadership. Democratic country citizens' too readily forget that the communist state has to ensure that its citizens believe, decade after decade, that every thing the party does is for their good. Good chits from foreign business partners are also helpful in this endeavour, so it is important to ensure that foreigners believe the party line. In any case, positive expectations among foreigners is essential for maximising FDI, exports and investment all of which are critical to the attainment of CCP objectives.

China is not immune to the deterioration in governance that is seen in many non-OECD countries, particularly those that try to control economic activity. The systems of government and party are, therefore, fraying as in these countries, leading to increased corruption. The lack of control arising from the general deterioration in governance can easily be confused with a deliberate decision to reduce, dismantle or eliminate the control network, given the level of transparency regarding internal working of CCP.

## 2.2 Factor Markets

The socialist control over factor markets is pervasive, compared to any 'democratic market economy', though it may appear liberal relative to the former USSR or Mao's China. This includes the land, labour and capital Markets.

### *2.2.1 Land*

All land is owned and controlled by the State. Many urban municipalities in market economies own urban land that is normally acquired rural land on the outskirts of a city for conversion into urban land. They have, however, to operate within a system of zoning laws, rules and procedures. In a socialist economy, land use can be changed overnight at the stroke of a pen. To whom, at what price and for what purpose the land is given, can vary with the category of the person/ firm. For instance, the acquisition of new land for involved complex negotiations with suburban communities or townships in which it gives up part of its land in exchange for guaranteed jobs for some of its members (Perkins, 1988). Buying and selling of long term leases was allowed in urban areas in the 1990s, but the process of acquisition of rural land for factory purposes remained unchanged. Citizens can be evicted from the land if the CCP/government decides to rebuild an urban area or build a new township on rural land.[10] Alternatively, the land price can be reduced to a fraction or nil for a 100 per cent foreign invested firm that brings in skills, technology or products that are thought desirable or one that commits to export a part or whole of its output.

*2.2.2 Labour*

In every communist country, the party controlled the labour unions and therefore the terms and conditions of work. This is also true in China and therefore the overall policy approach to terms and conditions of employment, work hours and wages is decided by the CCP (at an appropriate geographical level or level of government). If the CCP decides to apply different work and pay rules in a particular province, sector, industry or type of enterprise (e.g. foreign invested) from those applied to general domestic enterprises, neither the (so-called) labour unions nor the employees can do anything about it. They can either like it or lump it.

In addition, in China the labour market is also controlled through the *Hukou* system that determines where a person is entitled to live and work and receive State provided social benefits. If people move without formal CCP permission they are, in effect, illegal migrants with no rights. Surplus labour in rural areas (due to underemployment) was estimated to be about 100 million, of which the 'floating population' of illegal migrants from rural to urban areas constituted 'tens of millions' (Perkins, 1994). When the Special Economic Zones (SEZs) were first opened, all labour contracts were with a Chinese labour

10. 30 million people have had their land taken over by property developers since 1994. According to Gao Zhi Sheng, a public interest lawyer, a majority of Chinese judges are members of the CCP and therefore ensure that its objectives are fulfilled.

bureau (CCP controlled) that effectively controlled terms and conditions of employment. Later when the demand for unskilled labour exceeded the local labour pool, people were brought in from neighbouring areas and by this act given (temporary) legal right to live and work in that SEZ. If every unskilled labourer was expected to work 100 hours a week, 52 weeks a year in the SEZ, the new migrants would 'voluntarily' even 'happily' do so. There was no other option to earn that kind of annual wage in their own place of legal residence and the legal right to work/live in the SEZ could and was easily revoked if (s)he was not willing to accept the rules decreed by the CCP. If FDI investors were willing to produce and export labour intensive goods if a docile pool of unskilled labour willing to work day and night, was available, this was ensured by the local party bosses. The extreme restrictions on labour have undoubtedly eased over time, but likely remain stricter than in any market economy (or one that claims to be a 'market' economy).

Formally, labour is allowed to work for 76 hours a week of which 40 is normal and 36 overtime. Reports suggest that 100 hours a week (at normal wages or piece rates) is not uncommon in labour intensive units producing for export.[11] This ironically results in a reduction in per hour productivity below what it would be if working hours were the same as in SOZs.

### 2.2.3 *Capital*

#### 2.2.3.1 Ownership and Management

In 1980, hundred per cent of capital assets were owned and controlled by the State/CCP. The management of these assets was (is) distributed to different levels of government, which in turn was (is) controlled by different levels of the party. Some were (are) controlled at the national level through the departments of the central government and their CCP bosses. Others are managed/controlled at the provincial, city and village level (village co-operatives, T&V enterprises). All industrial enterprises (now SOEs) were what in Indian parlance would be called Departmental Public Enterprise. Some

---

11. As an increasing number of western companies have made commitments to stake holders to enforce labour standards in their overseas production units and suppliers, records are falsified and labour coached to provide the 'right' answers to visiting social auditors.

of these industrial enterprises have been converted into (what in India we call) public sector units (PSUs), i.e. companies that may or may not be listed on the stock exchange. In China, the listing could also be (solely) on the Hong Kong Stock Exchange or even a foreign exchange. This does not convert them into private enterprises as management control remains with the same CCP boss or his nominee/appointee.[12]

Similarly, T&VEs, though (in theory) collectively owned by the workers, are subject to local govt. direction (Perkins, 1988; 1994).[13] This would in practice mean that the CEO is appointed by the local party boss/government and works under his supervision/direction within the operational autonomy given by the latter. It would be an extremely foolhardy T&V manager who could ignore the objectives and guidelines set down by the local party boss/govt. However, party appointed managers have a sphere of autonomy assigned by the CCP/ government within which they run the firm and compete in a market environment. Thus, managers of county firms may maximise value added, so that they can increase the benefits (wages, perks, employment of children) to enterprise employees. This would result in competitive behaviour in input/output markets.[14] As long term value added maximisation is the same as growth maximisation, the conflict between local and national goals is minimised. Fierce competition in product markets (both inputs and output side) is also consistent with party appointed management, given the growth objective.

China's SOEs can be formally owned/managed by the national, provincial or municipal governments. Listed companies are largely national or provincial SOEs as even collective enterprises were not allowed to raise capital on these exchanges till 1997.[15] TVEs are classified as non-state sector, but often this is mistaken as private

---

12. In India, the Tatas exercised absolute control over TELCO and TISCO with 6-8 per cent of the share holding till the mid-nineties.
13. The township was basically the old commune which carried out both production and government functions. Even in (so-called) 'individual private' enterprises started by workers or managers, the local govt. would invariably play a role and have a share in their earnings.
14. Competition can however be thwarted by local/provincial protective barriers to trade.
15. Regional stock exchange on which the latter raised capital were abolished in 1995. Listing quotas were abolished in 2000.

sector.[16] TVEs are SOEs controlled by the lowest level of government with a greater degree of autonomy in terms of market operation.[17] However, township governments own and operate township enterprises and village enterprises have substantial and numerous ties to village government. Village committees perform government functions but village officials are not civil servants.

Urban collective enterprises can be wholly owned subsidiaries of SOEs or township promoted or hived off units.[18] Thus, they have organic links to the government. By way of comparison, co-operatives in India, operate under explicit rules and regulations and can be termed as private, even in those cases in which their dependence on government funds, makes them vulnerable to government interference.[19]

### 2.2.3.2 Banks

The policy banks and commercial banks are 100 per cent owned by the national government while the regional banks are owned by local governments, state owned enterprises or business federations (govt. controlled).[20] Till 1998 there was a formal lending quota system operated by the central bank for SOEs. The only financial intermediary that could be called private, the Urban Credit Cooperatives (UCC) was compelled to hand over a majority of shares to the municipal governments in 1995 (Huang, 2003). Up to 1998, only the urban and rural credit cooperatives, whose deposit base was limited to the non-state firms were allowed to lend to private firms.

In the Communist State, capital has no price or cost. Even in China, banks are not intermediaries but instruments of the State (departments) for channelling capital into desirable activities.

---

16. The correct picture as painted, for instance, by Gelb and Byrd (1990) and Perkins (1988, 1994) seems to have been lost along the way.
17. According to Huang, (2003), the revenue objectives of the local officials are much more closely aligned with the profit maximisation objectives of the enterprise as both depend on income maximisation, in contrast to higher levels where many macro objectives come into play and dilute autonomy and accountability (pp. 140, 127, 106).
18. With the township contributing old machinery from existing township production unit but legally owning the entire enterprise even it is subsequently nurtured/built-up by the managers with their own funds.
19. They have a choice not to get funds from the govt. If they choose to become dependent on govt. funds, then they have to abide by the conditions imposed on provision of these funds.
20. Minsheng bank is owned by the All-China Federation of Industry and Commerce, a government organisation overseeing private firms.

According to Perkins (1994), "Though formally commercial banks were separated from the Central bank early in the reform period, in reality they follow the direction of the central bank and of the government policy makers in general." Below market interest rates are standard (Perkins, 1988 and 1994). More important, capital costs can vary by borrower (in the same category) among borrowers of different categories in the same industry, place and time. Interest rates on loans to non-state firms (i.e. non-SOEs), have to be equal to or greater than the rate of interest to SOEs plus 20 per cent.

According to official figures, NPAs for the four commercial banks were 25 per cent in 1998 of which 20 per cent were loss assets. NPA's constituted 30 per cent of GDP.[21] NPA has no meaning for loans to SOEs, because credit is given if it is needed to maintain an activity or organisation that has an assigned role in the economy. In other words, if partial or no repayment is expected when the loan is made, it is a misnomer to call it an NPA later when the expected happens (in this situation full repayment is a low probability event and therefore, unexpected). The repeated capitalisation of China's 'banks' shows that this description is not far from the truth, for a large share of loans.[22] Such bailouts since the Asian crisis aggregate to between 50 per cent and 100 per cent of GDP.

This stylised picture for the entire period till 2004 should not be taken to mean that there is no liberalisation/market reform over time or that in 2004 truly market oriented lending based on technical criterion is nil. The extent of such lending is, however, very hard to know accurately and is likely to be a much smaller fraction of the total than is assumed by conventional wisdom. Further, sale of some shares to foreign banks or the public will not dilute CCP (management) control of these commercial banks in any way.[23] It will merely result in transfer of technology and skills to the bank for them to use within the circumscribed autonomy authorised by the CCP, perhaps with a gradually expanded scope for market lending over the next few decades.

---

21. See Lardy (1998) for a detailed discussion of NPAs.
22. A Mckinzie journal volume on China (2004) gives just a hint of this.
23. A recent (2005) report in the *Financial Times* quoted the Chairman of one of the Commercial Banks complaining about how all his decisions were subject to review (and were reviewed monthly) by a committee consisting of party cadres holding mid-level positions in the financial system.

### *2.2.4 Technology and IPR*

Realising the extent of its industrial backwardness in 1979, China did not hesitate to send thousands of students to the US and the West to close the gap in education and skills. Most of these early students were the children and kin of party officials who could be trusted to collect as much information and knowledge and bring it back for socialist dissemination. Even later, a large fraction of students was connected to CCP.

Technology as a factor is largely a part of the socialist system (collective ownership). There is no genuine market for technology in socialist China in the sense that individual buyers and sellers of technology can transact among themselves. In the socialist system, if any government firm acquires technology from abroad, either through purchase or through a joint venture with a foreign firm, that technology could be disseminated to every government firm that needs it.[24] Reverse engineering, where feasible, would also be viewed as part of the natural right. Even in the case of ostensibly private firms, such acquired technology may be transferred to others.

China has partly avoided the pitfalls of stagnating commercial technology that was one of the factors in the falling behind/collapse of the USSR, by allowing relatively free import of capital goods (embodied technology) and welcoming FDI. FDI helps avoid stagnant or negative technical change in the civil economy (i.e. all non-strategic areas) that characterised the last decade of the USSR. China has also tried to undertake research in new scientific areas with some success. The output of Chinese scientists as measured by the citation index increased rapidly to respectable levels.

## 2.3 Infrastructure

As in many developing countries a large part of China's basic physical infrastructure is owned by the State. Other countries also control prices and implicitly cross-subsidise certain categories of users such as low and lower middle-income consumers. Some do the opposite by setting lower rates for industry. China, however, has the ability to tailor supply, including the supply price, to the individual

24. A research oriented company in each industry may be selected to import, adapt, modify and develop technology for that industry and then disseminate it to all SOEs in that industry. This perhaps includes reverse engineering of imported capital goods.

user to meet other objectives such as exports or FDI. Thus, for instance a distribution line could be laid or a road constructed to a new FDI investor's location, if this is necessary to attract it. Utility prices could be similarly changed to suit any requirement if that helps meet an objective. There is no incentive for the receiver of this munificence to disclose or publicise such hidden subsidies, because they could just as easily be withdrawn.

# 3. MARKET ELEMENTS

## 3.1 Product Market

The most important market innovation that China introduced into its socialist economy was the product market. In 1979, it started with agriculture output markets. Initially, agriculture markets were partially liberalised in a manner similar to that used in India for sugar and other markets in the sixties. This was a 'dual pricing and distribution' system in which part of the produce continued to be handed over to the government at a controlled price, while the rest could be sold freely at the market price.

Many of the rules circumscribing small-scale service activities were also abolished or ignored, resulting in a boom in collectively and individually owned restaurants and shops. Labour contracting services also developed in the interior provinces to supply construction workers to urban areas.

Dual pricing in industrial goods was introduced by China in 1985-86, with prices on the market channel allowed to fluctuate according to market conditions.[25] At this point, more than half of all industrial goods were still distributed at administered prices. Product liberalisation was gradually extended to the entire manufacturing sector. It has also been selectively extended to the real estate sector and retail trade.

Domestic markets are however far from perfect, particularly for goods and services that were produced and traded at the county level and at the province level (to a smaller extent). As the county/province owns the local/provincial firms there is a tendency to modify

25. "Low level government officials did extract informal payments of various kinds," Perkins (1994).

regulations to favour local production and create protective barriers against import of competitive goods from other counties/provinces. This tendency will be least in cities and provinces whose CCP bosses are part of the central party leadership and therefore more interested in national growth. Further, the collective enterprises that constitute the most competitive firms are limited in their physical reach by capital, transport and other constraints. Inter-provincial market integration has increased from very low to moderate levels.

## 3.2 International Markets

### *3.2.1 Foreign Trade*

In the early years external trade was carried out largely by state trading companies and provincial trading companies and by 1993 there were 4000 such government controlled foreign trade companies. External trade can now be taken as largely market based even though the system retains a strong bias against imports. Though policy biases against imports by domestic firms have been gradually removed, government and managers have an asymmetric attitude to exports and imports. In 1979, reforms were introduced to facilitate exports of manufactures and (for the first time) to allow for foreign investment (Lardy, 1992). SEZs (export processing zones) were set up to free foreign investors and other exporters from red tape. Input tax offsets and export subsidies were introduced. The currency was devalued from 1.7 yuan per US dollar in 1981 to 2.9 yuan per USD in 1985. Though exports grew rapidly from 1977 onwards, imports remained tightly controlled till the mid-1980s (Perkins, 1988).

### *3.2.2 Exchange Rate*

In early 1980s foreign exchange was tightly controlled by the Bank of China even for foreign investors who needed to repatriate profit or import inputs for export. To attract export oriented FDI from Hong Kong and other overseas Chinese, government created 'foreign exchange adjustment centres' or swap markets on which those with surplus foreign exchange (e.g. joint venture hotels) could sell their surplus FE to foreign firms at market determined rates. The establishment of these centres effectively freed imports for FDI producers. The currency was devalued further to 4.8 Yuan per USD in

1990, the dual exchange rate integrated in 1994 and current account convertibility formally introduced in 1995. External trade was, therefore, effectively freed for foreign producers between mid-1980s and mid-1990s.

### *3.2.3 FDI*

The third important market element is foreign capital in the form of FDI. Compared to the control exercised over domestic capital, FDI is attracted through the application of market principles. Namely, FDI will only come if the expectation of profit is high. Conditions have therefore been created using every socialist control (indirect subsidy) at its command to attract FDI to China and to ensure that it finds it profitable to keep expanding exports. Policy has been liberalised whenever it was necessary to keep inflows of FDI and outflows of exports from faltering. This has included fairly early opening of both the real estate sector and of retail trade.

The first FDI investors to take advantage of the freeing of trade were producers from Hong Kong and Macao who shifted their export production to Guangdong SEZs in China starting in the mid-1980s.[26] In 1990, 55 per cent of all (realised) foreign investment came from Hong Kong and Macao and by 1992 Hong Kong's share in the total Chinese exports had risen to 44 per cent. Producer-exporters from Taiwan (to Fujian) and other overseas Chinese followed with the shift from their home countries to China accelerating in the early 1990s.

## 3.3 Private Fringe

There is also a small proportion of the domestic (i.e. non-FDI) manufacturing sector that could be classified as a genuinely private sector. This consists mostly of individual (atomistic) producers who supply labour intensive goods to exporters and FDI producers. Though there is no direct management control by the CCP, the latter always has the residual power to destroy anyone who steps too much outside the limits acceptable to higher party authorities.

---

26. In 1979, 22.6 per cent of China's total exports were to Hong Kong, of which only 21 per cent were exported. By 1987 the shares had increased to 31.1 per cent and 62 per cent. Hong Kong's share in China's manufactured exports was even higher ranging from 46 per cent in textiles to 62 per cent in clothing to 87 per cent in machinery (Sung, 1991).

Genuinely private enterprises consist of two types: Individual (e.g. push carts) and those with one or more employees. In 1998, the former constituted 99.8 per cent of the 6 million such enterprises. Further, out of the total 56 per cent were in the service sector (mainly food and retail). Thus, there were probably as little as 6000 (1/2 of 0.2 per cent of 6 million) private manufacturing enterprises in 1998. Some progressive provinces/cities such as Guangdong (Shunde) and Wenzhou (Zhejang) did try to promote private entrepreneurship and privatisation (Huang, 2003: 110, 129). Given existing laws, this required innovative steps like joint govt.-private structure and labelling of firms as collective enterprises.

## 4. GROWTH MODEL

China is a nationalist State with a clear vision of national power through economic growth and technological catch-up. The CCP translates this vision into explicit objectives suitable for different levels (nation, province, city, firm) that are broadly coherent but far from perfect (not devoid of contradictions). Among the sub-goals that this translates into are increased sales/production, value added investment and technology transfer from the advanced countries. The growth strategy for achieving these objectives has evolved over time. Starting from the mid-1970s, it first became an export-led growth strategy and then from the mid-1980s an FDI-export led growth strategy. Underlying these has been the development of domestic product markets and the evolution of the management structures of government enterprises to meet the challenges of competition in domestic and global markets.

### 4.1 Objectives

In general terms, the objective of the CCP is to increase China's global power subject to retaining power indefinitely. In the process of achieving the primary objective, the people should be reasonably content and no significant sub-group should become so unhappy as to revolt against CCP rule. More formally, the objective is the maximisation of economic growth subject to the maintenance of existing welfare of all groups. The objective is similar to that adopted by 'nationalist market economies', or 'corporate states', such as Japan and S. Korea prior to their becoming high-income countries, with the difference that growth maximisation was subject to rising welfare of all groups of citizens. The approach contrasts with the social welfare maximisation objective of the governments of most 'democratic market economies'.

The growth maximisation objective percolates down the CCP network and becomes the major, if not primary objective of every level of government (province, city, town, village) as well as of the managers of firms appointed by them. There is enough flexibility in the system to adapt the objectives to the particular circumstances and constraints of each level and the area in which it operates. At the level of the firm, the growth maximisation objective could be translated either into a market share objective similar to corporate capitalism or a value added maximisation objective that combines the interests of labour/managers and capital. Thus, even CCP appointed managers compete in product markets. Unlike managers in corporate capitalism, however, they are subject to the guidelines and constraints arising from national/provincial/city objectives set (and conveyed) by the CCP (boss). They, therefore, often have to balance (trade-off) firm against national or provincial objectives (e.g. employment).

## 4.2 Means

The primary means of achieving high growth is high investment rate. This has two prongs. One is government/public investment and the second is FDI. This is combined with an unprecedented degree of export orientation. Thus, public investment, FDI and exports are the three pillars of China's successful growth maximisation strategy. The policy framework and the CCP network has been moulded to maximise these three critical elements of the growth strategy. Everything else has a secondary or marginal role in explaining non-agricultural growth to date, though it may become more relevant in future. FDI-export led growth has earlier been an important part of the growth strategy of Singapore, Thailand, Malaysia and Indonesia, but China has taken this to a new level and scale. China has (so far) successfully combined this with levels of public investment not seen since the collapse of the USSR.

## 4.3 Foundation: Public Investment

The public ownership of assets has been an important contributor to the fast growth of China's economy as it allows a motivated government to use these profits either for public investment or to provide subsidies to FDI or exporters and thus indirectly boost investment. Unlike a democratic market economy like India, China does not need to generate funds for public investment (or subsidies) through taxes that distort markets and reduce efficiency and productivity. Government appointed/controlled managers cannot, however, match the innovativeness of private entrepreneurs or the efficiency of growth maximising private firms (e.g. Zaibatsu, Chaebols). Though public ownership of assets has driven growth so far, it can become the greatest source of weakness as public profits decline and disappear reducing public investment and stalling the entire economy. Past strength and future weakness are two sides of the same coin.

A very large fraction of assets are still owned and controlled by the State/CPC network, which appoints the top management in listed companies, co-operatives, T&V enterprises and state owned enterprises. The State, therefore, has a high share of national profits and consequently the ability to have both low tax rates and very high investment rates (including in infrastructure). For instance, when the State owned 100 per cent of the capital assets, a capital-output ratio of 4 along with an 8 per cent rate of return on assets would have resulted in non-tax revenues of 32 per cent of GDP.[27] Thus, reinvestment of public returns to capital along with FDI inflows of 8 per cent of GDP (7.4 per cent in 1993), would result in a 40 per cent investment rate without recourse to any taxes. Gross fixed investment was less than 31 per cent of GDP till 1992 and reached 40 per cent in 2002, when gross FDI was about 5 per cent of GDP. High rates of investment in infrastructure since the mid-1990s reflected a change in the allocation of public expenditure. This was initially driven by the unemployment created by SOE closure and weaker export demand during the Asian crises.[28]

---

27. According to Prof. Xianon Xue of the China Europe International Business School, Shanghai, the earning before interest and tax (EBIT) has fallen from 12 per cent of assets in 1992 to 4 per cent in 2003. He also indicated that FDI was 7 per cent of total investment and that the bulk of investment was still made by government firms.
28. Around 1994-95, many SOEs were shut resulting in large pockets of unemployment. The Asian crisis added to this by the weakening of global demand for China's exports, thus increasing the losses from exports by government owned firms. Infrastructure spending was therefore increased in the second half of the nineties so as to increase job creation (Keynesian aspect). The positive effect on China's image were soon recognised and publicised effectively to attract more FDI, including export oriented FDI.

The USSR's early growth was also founded on high levels of government investment. Growth, however, stalled after the economy reached middle-income, because the USSR was largely cut-off from the global economy and the global technology pool. This lack of concern for social benefit-cost means that the marginal product of public capital may fall to zero or even become negative because of excess capacity. We know from the USSR experience that this can lead to un-saleable inventory stock, falling capacity utilisation and collapse. Though inventory investment reached a peak of 10.4 per cent of GDP in 1989, it had declined to 0.2 per cent of GDP by 2002.[29] China, therefore, appears to have successfully dealt with this problem so far by liberalising output/product markets and orienting its system to push exports. The former helps avoid obvious mismatches between consumer/user demand and public sector output. Despite this, exports are an important channel for utilising excess capacity in tradable goods, a version of the old 'vent for surplus', with marginal cost pricing and indirect subsidies aiding this effort. Such exports can help in exploiting scale economies by building plants with a capacity larger than domestic demand. The unabashed promotion of export-oriented FDI has proved to be a vital means for achieving efficient and sustainable export growth. Because global export shares have to be raised at such a frenetic pace, a fall in unit values is inevitable in some goods and markets.[30]

Rising implicit subsidies and declining returns to public capital will eventually make it difficult to maintain such high rates of public investment. Listing of government owned companies and banks on foreign and domestic stock exchanges is a clever way to get foreign equity capital to finance public investment. This suggests that the return on capital may already be so low as to create a shortage of funds for investment and implicit subsidy. Lardy (1999) estimates that the rate of return on capital in state owned enterprises has fallen from 25 per cent at the start of reform to 6 per cent in 1997.[31] Lardy also estimates that the consequent decline in public saving from 30 per cent of GDP to 20 per cent, has been more than offset by a rise in

---

29. The previous peak was 8.4 per cent of GDP in 1978.
30. This is happening for instance in textile exports to the USA.
31. If ROC has fallen over a decade by 8 per cent points in (show piece) publicly listed companies (Prof Xue, foot note 27), then the ROC in other govt. firms is likely to average between 0-4 per cent.

household saving from 0 per cent to 20 per cent of GDP (overwhelmingly, in banks or currency). It would not surprise if international capital markets readily provide these funds on the illusion that this means privatisation of government companies or banks.[32] If these funds are not forthcoming or when they run out China will have to alter its development strategy more fundamentally.

## 4.4 Engine: FDI and Exports

FDI is the second pillar of China's growth. China has learnt from and built upon the experience of Singapore, Thailand and Malaysia, the pioneers of FDI-export led growth. It has aggressively pursued FDI by identifying potential FDI investors across the globe, including in other successful low and middle-income countries. It has then laid out a red carpet for every FD investor that can help raise China's technological levels, skills and expertise or can directly or indirectly raise the level of exports on a sustainable basis. The welcome mat included all inducements needed to ensure that they set up base in China (including capital subsidies).

FDI and exports have been the engine of efficient economic growth since 1985. Adoption of an FDI-export led growth strategy converted China from an autarchy into an essential link in the global production chain developed between 1965 and 1985 by the newly industrialising economies and the ASEAN 4. China created conditions (suspension of labour rights, capital subsidies to counter every negative) for a wholesale shift of labour intensive (LI) production by Chinese entrepreneurs from Hong Kong, Taiwan and other countries in S. E. Asia to the SEZs and regions. 59.3 per cent of FDI between 1978 and 1999 came from Hong Kong, Taiwan and Macao.[33] The share was much higher in the initial years and has declined over time. It was 68.2 per cent in 1994 and 40.2 per cent in 2003.(Prasad and Wei, 2005). Detailed data for 1995 shows that the share of foreign invested enterprises (foreign equity share $\geq$ 25 per cent) in manufactured exports was 51.2 per cent. FIE's share in exports of electronics and telecommunications was 94.5 per cent, in instruments 71.8 per cent,

32. As Abraham Lincoln said, "You can fool all the people some of the time," perhaps in China a lot more time than he imagined.
33. Almost 50 per cent was from Hong Kong during 1979 to 1999 (Huang, 2003: 36, 48).

in plastic products 77.2 per cent, in printing and record pressing 79.4 per cent, in furniture 79.4 per cent, in leather products 73.2 per cent, in metal products 61.1 per cent and in garments and footwear 60.5 per cent (Huang, 2003: Table 1.4). Another 17 per cent of manufactured exports take place through export processing where the buyer supplies the inputs, detailed designs and specifications and quality inspection and control personel and gets back the output for export.[34] Thus, these labour intensive (LI) export goods are now highly competitive. Along with the support system provided by the socialist-corporate state, this gives China a comparative advantage in organised labour intensive mass manufacturing.

The conventional wisdom is that China's phenomenal success in LI exports is due to the superior productivity of Chinese workers. In reality, the per-hour worker productivity is not much different from that in any other country at a similar level of income (perhaps lower). The output per man-month is however much higher because hours worked per week/month are up to 100 per cent higher than in equivalent democratic market economies, being unconstrained by (implementation of) bourgeois labour laws. Now that China has developed a comparative advantage in mass manufacturing and construction, it is likely to persist even if hours worked gradually decline from 'socialist' to 'democratic' levels.

Non-labour intensive exports (even those produced by FDI) are not necessarily competitive. The banking system provides loans to state enterprises (e.g. SOEs) and provincial/city governments producing intermediate goods and infrastructure services respectively at zero or negative effective capital cost. These implicit subsidies are then transformed through below cost prices, into explicit subsidies to the FDI-export complex and to hi-tech industry.[35] This is a significant factor in attracting hi-tech/skill intensive FDI and capital-intensive exports. Through this process, some competitive items are undoubtedly discovered or created and these, along with less than competitive items, are part of the set of capital intensive (KI) and skill-intensive (SI) exports.

---

34. Huang (2003) p. 15. The share of HK and Taiwan in FDI was 61.8 per cent in 1995, and another 4.9 per cent was from Singapore.
35. The prices of intermediate goods in China are reportedly less than their price on the high seas outside India–i.e. before taxes, delays or red tape.

The banking losses arising from these implicit subsidies have been repeatedly capitalised by the government budget during the last five years. If this is a real rather than a paper transaction, the enterprise profits available for re-investment will be reduced. In this case, either taxes on the FDI-export sector have to increase or the supply of free public services has to be reduced.[36] The former either undermines the usefulness and sustainability of the high public investment that is the foundation of China's growth maximisation strategy or offsets the subsidies given to the FDI export sector (increasing inefficiency).

In the last five years, the first class infrastructure in and around the FDI-export hubs is advertised as an important factor in the high share/growth of KI and SI exports from China. The building of showpiece infrastructure well ahead of demand certainly helps in attracting attention and approbation from investors and adds to the attractiveness of China as an FDI location. Further, even if infrastructure is highly under utilised, it is a permanent asset that will become useful at some time. However, if its marginal social return is zero or negative, the sustainability of the public reinvestment strategy becomes doubtful as returns dwindle, making it necessary to raise distorting taxes. It should also not be forgotten that poor infrastructure in Jakarta, Indonesia and Bangkok, Thailand did not prevent these two countries from growing fast for decades.

Tseng and Zebregs (2002) estimate that FDI contributed 2.5 per cent per annum to TFP growth and about 3 per cent per annum to overall GDP growth. This suggests that the difference between China's and India's growth rate since 1980 can largely be explained by the difference in FDI inflows (including export-oriented FDI).

## 5. RESULTS

### 5.1 Income Growth

If we go by the official statistics, China's economy grew at an average rate of 9.5 per cent per annum during 1980 to 2003, the fastest in the world. During this period the world share of China in merchandise trade saw the largest expansion and China became the largest recipient of FDI. Collins and Bosworth (1996), corroborated

---

36. The latter is related to the income distribution point discussed below.

later by the World Bank and IMF, have shown that China's growth from 1980 to end-nineties was overestimated by 1 per cent to 2 per cent. Young (2000) shows that non-agricultural growth is over-estimated by 2.5 per cent. If we make an adjustment of 2 per cent, China has demonstrated its ability to sustain growth at about 7.5 per cent per annum over 25 years. This is still the fastest in the world, but only 30 per cent higher than India's the 9th fastest growing economy.[37] The IMF (2004) has, however, shown that China's growth so far (as measured by official statistics) is on a trajectory similar to that of Japan and the NIEs in a similar period of their development, though it is faster than that of the ASEAN-4.

In the last few decades, China's growth has benefited from the demographic dividend. As the demographic transition is coming to an end, this dividend will soon be reduced to zero.[38] The 1990s were a period of above average international trade growth and the current decade could see a slower growth in goods trade. As China's share of the world's goods exports rises to US levels, its export growth will slow. China has also benefited from the large gap between its per capita income and its manufacturing wage relative to India and other labour intensive exporters. The gap is likely to be eliminated as its per capita income rises to upper-middle income levels and then to high-income levels. The closing and inversion of the wage gap will contribute to the slowdown in export growth and FDI inflows. Most observers have been forecasting a slow down in China's growth rate and a few have even predicted a dramatic slowdown.[39] On balance, China's growth rate is likely to decline gradually to more normal levels from the stratospheric rate of 9.5 per cent!

## 5.2 Income Distribution

The distribution of income has worsened dramatically since 1979. Part of this deterioration is the reversal of unsustainable levels of equality reached during the Maoist years. The rest of the deterioration was a conscious decision to accelerate growth by focussing subsidies

---

37. About 60 per cent higher in terms of per capita growth.
38. After a decade or two it will become negative because of the rapid aging of its population.
39. See IMF, World Bank and ADB reports on China and Chang (2001). See also Virmani (1999b and 1999c).

and infrastructure development into the FDI-export areas in the coastal regions during 1985 to 2000. Given the restrictions on internal movement of workers (the labour responsibility system) this translated into growing income inequality. Out of a total of 127 countries, China ranks 91st in terms of the Gini co-efficient of inequality, and 94th in terms of the consumption share of the poorest 20 per cent of the population. Further, the retreat of the State from provision of social goods has also translated into greater inequality in the receipt of public and quasi-public goods. Rising inequality and declining public social services have a potential for socio-political upheaval and counter repression that could disrupt growth.

## 5.3 Risks

The FDI-export drive is critically dependent on building and sustaining optimistic expectations about the economy and the Asian crises demonstrated the vulnerability of this model. The obverse of high social ownership of domestic assets and consequent high investment rates is a low share of private consumption in GDP. The rate of capacity build up is much faster than the growth of private consumption, leaving exports as the only means for balancing supply and demand. China's membership of WTO and rising job fears in OECD countries will result in increased scrutiny of and resistance to subsidised exports. Its socially regressive labour rules for export oriented manufacturing, may also be questioned more seriously, if not by governments then by Western Labour unions and NGOs.

Given the continuing generation of NPAs, China is somewhat more vulnerable on these issues than the Asian crisis countries.[40] Its income distribution is also worse than in other successful Asian economies. On the other hand, China's large economy has domestic strengths and bargaining power that were absent in the smaller Asian countries. These will result (in our judgement) in a slowing of growth and not a sudden collapse if the CPC/Government continues to adapt its policy to the changing circumstances and imperatives as it has repeatedly done since 1980.

---

40. Which have resulted in a national debt of 50 per cent to 100 per cent of GDP. See Jia Kang and Zhao (2001).

### 5.4 Politics

There are political arguments for a sharp slowdown in economic growth arising from rising inequalities and social tensions. Some have gone further to argue that there is an inherent contradiction between the market economy whose success requires competition and plurality and the centralised political system that suppresses independent democratic thinking and impulses.[41] If the contradiction cannot be managed, it has within it the seeds of a socio-political explosion that will bring growth to a halt for a substantial period of time (after which it could resume at a much slower rate). This contradiction is much more than it was in S. Korea (say) and the latter eventually succumbed to the democratic impulse. The counter argument is that dictators can and have maintained highly repressive regime for decades after upheaval. Whether growth rate can be maintained along with repression, depends on the response of the rest of the world.

## 6. COMPARATIVE PERFORMANCE: INDIA

### 6.1 Reform Impact: J Curve

According to India's National Accounts data, GDP and per capita GDP have grown at an average of 5.8 per cent per annum and 3.8 per cent per annum, respectively, during the last 25 years (1980-81 to 2004-05).[42] The comprehensive reforms instituted in the 1990s have increased competitive pressures on the Indian economy while at the same time enhancing its ability to compete globally. The growth rate has however increased by only about 0.6 per cent point.[43] The opening of the economy to international trade seems to produce a J-curve effect: The direct negative effects of competition appear immediately as capacity utilisation falls in un-competitive product lines. With capital immobile, reduction in capital stock is limited by the rate of depreciation. The positive effects of competition on productivity appear gradually. New technology is first adopted by the pioneers and

---

41. K. Subrahmanyam *et al.* (1995).
42. The WDI data underestimate the GDP growth rate substantially though the per capita GDP growth rate is almost the same.
43. From 5.5 per cent per annum during 1980-81 to 1991-92 to 6.1 per cent during 1992-93 to 2003-04. Per capita GDP growth accelerated by 1 per cent point from 3.3 per cent to 4.3 per cent per annum.

effected through new investment. It diffuses gradually to other firms in the industry.[44] Improvements in productivity will, therefore, appear at the aggregate level only after a lag. We, therefore, expect the underlying trend rate of growth in India to move up to around 6.5 per cent over the next few years.

The growth rate is projected to rise further to 7 per cent thereafter on the assumption that reforms will continue at the average pace seen since 1991. These include removal of controls on a host of sectors and sub-sectors that are the basis of the jungle of red tape and lead to bureaucratic delays, labour reform, and lifting of entry restrictions in education (Virmani, 2004a).[45] Three specific (modern services, FDI, demographic transition) and three general factors make this increased growth feasible and sustainable.

## 6.2 Services: Exports to GDP

First, the one area in which the improved competitiveness of the Indian economy is clearly visible is in the double-digit (20 per cent to 30 per cent per year) growth of Information technology (IT) and IT enabled services (ITES) export. Though such non-traditional (i.e. excluding transport and tourism) service exports are already a significant share of India's total exports, they constituted a very small part of the economy. Therefore, the impact on GDP growth was limited. With the continuing high growth of non-traditional service export, they are now becoming large enough to have a measurable impact on GDP and their contribution to GDP growth could rise from 0.5 per cent to 1.5 per cent points over a decade.[46] India is likely to become one of the largest suppliers of non–traditional services to the world over the next few decades (including R & D, financial, medical, educational and social services). OECD ageing citizens will benefit greatly from the universalisation of medical services that their lower cost will make possible.

---

44. There are numerous cases of firms that have transformed their systems and shown large increases in productivity. The effects of these are not however available in the sector data.
45. This book summarises the reforms proposed in a series of internal papers done in the Ministry of Finance (Department of Economic Affairs), Government of India, from 1995 onwards. The underlying theme of these suggestions is to increase competition in every market and sector by removing the distortions introduced by the Indian version of socialism and to focus government effort on the supply of public and quasi-public goods and services. See Virmani, 2004a for details.
46. Starting at the lower end and going up to the higher end of the range.

## 6.3 FDI: Unexploited Potential

The second factor is the un-exploited potential of FDI. The proportion of FDI in total investment and GDP is very low in India compared to other high growth Asian countries such as Singapore, Malaysia, Thailand, China, Indonesia and Vietnam. In contrast to China's FDI-export led growth model, India's growth has been led by domestic investment and entrepreneurship.[47] The positive role of FDI in growth (marketing, technology, management systems) is, therefore, largely un-exploited. A doubling of FDI flows from the recent levels of $ 3.5 to $4 billion to $8 billion to $10 billion per annum will give a substantial boost to productivity and growth.[48] India is already an attractive location for skill-intensive manufacturing because of the high quality and availability of middle management/technical skills and knowledge workers. Several areas of competitiveness related to such skills are already visible, namely biotechnology, auto engineering (parts) and specialised chemicals.[49]

With China's per capita income more than twice that of India's, its hourly wage will eventually attain the same ratio. Membership of the WTO and scrutiny by global NGOs will make it increasingly difficult for foreign invested firms in China to make people work 100 hours a week. India will therefore become a more attractive location for small and medium scale labour-intensive manufactured exports *vis-à-vis* China. The new SEZ law can reduce red tape/bureaucracy, introduce the much needed flexibility in labour laws, rules and procedures and accelerate development of high quality infrastructure, thus expediting this process. FDI can play a critical role in integrating India into the global supply chain for a host of products. If domestic hurdles to global operation are removed, FDI could add at least a point to growth.

## 6.4 Demographic Dividend

The third important factor is the demographic transition that is taking place across the world. The high growth of E. and S.E. Asian countries was to a substantial degree due to the demographic transition (Bloom *et al.*, 2001). This is the Ç (inverted U) shape followed by the

47. See Khanna and Huang (2003) for a comparison with China.
48. Several ICRIER working papers by Rashmi Banga have shown the positive effects of FDI in India.
49. With the introduction of a product patent regime from this year, the protection of the legal system will now be available to drug developers.

ratio of labour force to population.[50] With the supply of labour rising faster than population, per capita GDP growth accelerates. Further, the changes in the age profile also result in a rise in the aggregate saving rate ensuring sufficient funds for investment. China is nearing the end of its demographic transition while India has entered its most positive phase. We estimate that this could add between 0.5 per cent to 0.8 per cent points to the growth of the Indian economy.

In addition, the population of Europe and Japan is aging rapidly and there will be a great demand from these economies for 'youth-intensive' goods and services.[51] Over the next half century, India will have the youngest labour force in the world. India is, therefore, likely to become the largest exporter of such items.[52]

## 6.5 Intangibles

There are also several general factors that will sustain growth. One is the existence of a large under-utilised pool (20 million to 100 million) of free thinking, autonomous working, high IQ people. The normal distribution of IQ in a population, means that 2 per cent of population has very high IQ and 10 per cent has high IQ. Applying this to India we get 20 million and 100 million people respectively. Bad economic policies till 1980 contributed to gross under-utilisation of this resource.

The second is the high quality and diversity of India's institutions and the social capital built over centuries.[53] The democratic system, including the relatively new non-governmental institutions and free and vibrant media, is a great source of long-term strength. Rodrik and Subramanian (2004) estimate that India's (China's) income level is 15 per cent lower (higher) than that predicted by the quality of its institutions. India's income will, therefore, rise to the predicted level with the correction of wrong policies, while China will not be able to sustain the same growth at higher income levels where these institutions are critical.

50. The dependency ratio follows a U shape first falling then rising.
51. For instance a study has shown that Nobel prize winners in Physics did their most productive work below or around the age of 25.
52. As China's population will age much earlier than that of India, it is not in a position to exploit this opportunity.
53. China had similarly high levels of social capital but much of this was destroyed during the Communist Revolution and the Cultural Revolution.

The third is the experience of working with citizens of very diverse backgrounds (religious, ethnic, language, sub-culture) and the facility with English. This pluralism and language facility is a unique advantage in the globalised 21st century. India is also ideally placed to partner OECD countries in the emerging global knowledge economy of the 21st century. These specific and general factors are sufficient to overcome any negative growth factors, to raise growth to a sustainable 7 per cent or so.[54]

## 6.6 Poverty

There are some questions raised by India-sceptics about poverty and inequality in India, which have to be viewed in the light of the following facts. India is a low-income country, so the proportion of poor is still high (about 23 per cent).[55] The absolute number of poor is, thus, larger than the total population of all but two countries (USA and China). It is democratic, so the poor are free to live and work anywhere and are therefore visible everywhere. India's income distribution is, however, among the top quarter of the 127 countries for which the Gini co-efficient is available.[56] It does very well for the poorest 10 per cent whose consumption share is the 6th highest among these 127 countries.[57] India is one of a handful of high growth countries whose income distribution has not worsened significantly during the high growth period.[58] By 2010, when India becomes a lower-middle income country, the poverty rate will be reduced to about 15 per cent.[59] Poverty is likely to be completely eliminated by the time it becomes an upper-middle income country around 2025.[60]

---

54. A more optimistic scenario is also possible in which growth reaches the 7.5 per cent-8 per cent range and remains there for a decade or so. The probability of this is 10-15 per cent in our view. Surjit Bhalla has been asserting for the last 3 years that India's growth rate will soon exceed 8 per cent.
55. The poverty rate or head count ratio is 29th out of 87 countries for which data is reported.
56. 32nd to be precise.
57. 14th for consumption share of bottom 20 per cent and 25th for bottom 40 per cent of the population.
58. Cornea and Court (2001).
59. Based on official rate in 1999-2000 (26 per cent) adjusted for survey changes (i.e.28 per cent-29 per cent). We assume a decline of 1 per cent point per year based on the average decline since 1980.
60. Before that, the national poverty line will probably be raised.

## 6.7 Governance Issues

The greatest long-term weakness is on the political side. Infirmities in its political system have led over the last four decades, to a deterioration in the quality and quantity of public goods (roads, policing, legal system) and quasi-public goods supplied. The high fiscal deficit is merely a symptom of this deterioration in governance. The governments' lack of success in suppressing Maoist and other insurgencies in the interiors of the country is a reflection of this failure. Political/governmental reforms are necessary over the next decade to ensure that the system remains on even keel.[61] This down trend in governance must and will be reversed. Though Indian democracy responds slowly to such intangible threats, it has always been able to deal with them in a democratic and non-disruptive manner. However, because we anticipate a slow correction of these weaknesses, the Indian economy is unlikely to grow above seven per cent despite other strengths.

# 7. LESSONS

In this section, we summarise some of the lessons arising from the above analysis of the Chinese economy, viewed from the perspective of the Indian economy and India's growth experience. These lessons, therefore, implicitly incorporate an India-China comparative perspective.

## 7.1 Welfare or Growth Maximisation

In theory, we can always construct a set of assumptions in which growth maximisation is identical to social welfare maximisation. The issue here is about the outcome of one or the other strategy in practice.

A growth maximisation strategy is clear, focussed, easy to understand and implement. Growth maximisation is related to maximisation of value added, sales/production, and long term employment at the firm and local government level. It can therefore be relatively easily decentralised down to the lowest levels of government and implemented more efficiently even with low quality

61. See Virmani (2004a) or Virmani(2002b) for the new development paradigm needed for high growth in India.

of governance. The public sector can also be integrated into this objective without creating dissonance.

A welfare maximisation strategy leads to multiple, often contradictory, objectives. Though rational trade-offs are possible in theory they are not made in practice and confusion and cross cutting actions are common. This in turn leads to, (a) detailed rules regulations and procedures for making choices—red tape and bureaucratic functioning, (b) lack of accountability—it is easy to use one or more objectives (those that are hardest to measure) as an excuse for non-achievement of all others. It also becomes easier to substitute ones personal objectives for the official ones by disguising the former as the latter, and (c) given serious agency problems in governance, particularly in democratic systems, this provides an incentive for inefficiency and corruption.

A growth maximisation strategy subject to reasonable social welfare constraints is superior to a welfare maximisation strategy implemented through subsidiary growth objectives. The former is much more likely to take the largest number of citizens from low income to high-income category in the shortest possible time. The latter provides greater opportunity to those charged with implementation to increase their own welfare in the name of the poor, consequently resulting in faster deterioration of governance *ipso facto* (other things equal).

## 7.2 Institutions: Micro-Structures

The importance of Institutions, defined as laws, rules and social conventions in long run growth is now widely accepted. There are also studies showing the importance of social capital. Institutional micro-foundations or micro-structures, the organisations that implement these laws, rules and conventions have a critical role in economic growth (Virmani, 2004b). One of the lessons that we draw from our study of China and India's growth is, 'Do not destroy institutions, modify and adapt them to your development objectives'. It is very easy to destroy institutions, very difficult and time consuming to build them.

The Communist Party Government that came to power in China in the middle of the last century systematically destroyed what it considered 'capitalist' institutions and organisations. But they also built Communist Party run organisations during the next 50 years. The post-Mao reformers have adapted the latter to fill the gap left by the former. China has shown that, (a) even a communist/socialist institution like the CCP can be used to nurture and support capitalist growth, and (b) that communist controlled and managed co-operatives, which in the Maoist period undertook a combination of governing and production functions at the local level, can be converted into competitive production organisations (town and village enterprises).[62]

The destruction of centuries old social and market institutions (e.g. private entrepreneurs) under Chairman Mao will, however, prove costly in the long run. Such institutions are particularly important at high income levels, when investors from countries at the same (high income) level are unlikely to find it as advantageous as it is today to set up either export oriented or high tech operations in a 'socialist market economy' like China relative to a 'democratic market economy' like India.

## 7.3 FDI and Trade Liberalisation

FDI bundles capital, 'technology' and entrepreneurship, where 'technology' is defined broadly to include information, knowledge, and skills relating to management, marketing and production. The technology part of the bundle is much more important than capital for countries like India and China. For China, the entrepreneurial role of FDI has also been very important.

FDI can be an extremely effective instrument for growth if it helps a country enter the global supply chain. A successful diaspora in a more advanced country is even more effective if it still has a connection to and an interest in the development of the country of origin. The effectiveness of trade liberalisation in promoting growth is enhanced if it can be coupled with the attraction of export oriented FDI. FDI-export led growth has clearly worked in Asia, even if there are both positive and negative examples from other parts of the world. Democratic market economies are unlikely, however, to be able to replicate the breakneck expansion of exports and FDI seen in China's socialist market economy (and perhaps even in some 'nationalist market economies').

62. Even ostensibly negative social institutions such as Caste organisations could have been used by India for productive purpose e.g. for promoting literacy or group credit.

Technological change (embodied in capital goods or intermediates or disembodied), is greatly facilitated by free imports and therefore import restrictions on these have added costs. When bureaucrats decide (QRs) what and from where capital goods and intermediate goods should be imported by entrepreneurs, innovation inevitably suffers.

## 7.4 Labour Laws and Rules

The special labour laws and rules for foreign invested enterprises and export producers in China has undoubtedly played a role in attracting export oriented FDI and increasing labour intensive exports. India is at the other extreme with very socially advanced labour laws and rules since 1950s (similar at that time to those in the richest countries). These were implemented in a manner that introduced extreme rigidity and restriction in the organised labour market. Rigid rules and bureaucratic procedures, have limited the inflow of export oriented FDI, discouraged the mass production of labour intensive exports (e.g. garments, toys and consumer electronics) and resulted in slower employment growth in the modern manufacturing sector. India's workers could obtain the full benefits of an open economy if these laws and rules provided for greater flexibility. There is no need for India (or any other country) to go to the other extreme typified by China.

## 7.5 Competition and Public Monopoly

Artificial monopolies, created by reserving industries for the government/public sector i.e. exclusion of private investment, have the most negative effect on efficiency and growth (as they have no redeeming merit). Setting up of government production companies *per se* is not obviously bad, creation of government monopolies and oligopolies clearly is. A competitive market structure is much more important than private ownership for efficient economic growth. Growth maximising and profit maximising monopolies, whether private or public can, theoretically, be equally (in) efficient initially, but eventually succumb to X-inefficiency. Highly motivated political and administrative leadership (as in post-independence India or post-Mao CCP rule) can even be more effective initially, but this level of motivation and honesty is seldom sustained over long periods.

The public sector is, however, more likely to be characterised by multiple and incompatible objectives and agency problems. This is primarily responsible for the negative effect of public ownership. Soft budget constraints, poor selection of managers and lack of incentives arise in a context in which everyone and no one owns the firm. Public monopoly multiplies these problems. A monopoly/oligopoly structure coupled with social objectives (even secondary ones) and agency problems, distorts incentives for managers and can be disastrous for efficient growth. This applies in banking as much as in manufacturing.

The threat of imports (even where imports are low) is the greatest competitive force. In general, free access to imports (i.e. no bans or QRs) is the simplest way to ensure competition, a method that is available to economies of all sizes. Only large economies have the luxury of limiting themselves to domestic competition, but even in their case there will always be some products for which market size and minimum economic scale do not permit much competition.

## 7.6 High-Risk, High Return Policies

India invested well ahead of demand in higher education in the 1960s just as China is doing in infrastructure since mid-1990. In India's case there was a clear imbalance between investment in basic education relative to higher education. In China's case, there is an imbalance between private and public consumption relative to public investment. In hindsight, India's higher education strategy appears to have been highly successful (vide IT and other service exports).

The supply of infrastructure in ASEAN high growth economies generally lagged behind demand for it, in complete contrast to China, which is building well ahead of demand (8 lane highways where 4 lanes would be sufficient). China's infrastructure investment strategy appears, so far, to be equally successful. India's investment could have been totally wasted if globalisation did not provide a channel of migration and utilisation of skills for which there was no demand in India. China's investment in rich country style infrastructure could still be wasted if growth slows dramatically. Both are, therefore, high-risk high-return policies. Large countries like India and China can have diversified portfolio of policies, including a few high risk, high return ones. Small, poor countries should be extremely cautious in adopting any such strategy.

### 7.7 Democracy *versus* Dictatorship

Oligarchies such as Communist Party ruled China or dictatorial democracies such as Singapore, post-war Japan and S. Korea, appear to have been more successful in organising a country to develop from low-income to high-income category. They also have an advantage in mass production and large-scale organised activity including construction The disadvantages of dictatorship include the stamping out of diversity (language, culture, religion) and dissent.

'Democratic market economies' like India, appear to be more successful at generating entrepreneurship, independent thinking and individual responsibility, which is an advantage in the service sector. Even the humblest service provider has greater scope for individual initiative than an assembly line worker and these characteristics are more important in services than in modern manufacturing. These skills are also advantageous in moving from the bottom to the top of the high-income category. India, with its great diversity, coupled with English language facility has an additional advantage in the globalised 21st century. Most managers and professionals have worked with others of different ethnicity, religion, native language, etc. and can, therefore, work easily with people of any nationality or background.

There is, however, a simultaneity problem in comparing dictatorship with democracy. The former group seem to have adopted a growth maximising strategy and the latter group a welfare maximising one. Would a swapping of objectives make the latter more successful even in the low and middle income range?

## 8. CONCLUSION: FDI-EXPORT LED GROWTH

Many eminent scholars have studied China's phenomenal growth rate and come to the conclusion that it has basically adopted the 'East Asian model of growth'. An essential element of this model is 'export led growth'. Though the approach to growth among these countries has common elements, there is also a great deal of variation. Singapore, for instance, lacked domestic capitalists and initially depended heavily on FDI as a source of capital, technology and entrepreneurship. Though the role of the State in investment gradually expanded, the importance of FDI is still very high, perhaps the highest among Asian countries. Singapore, therefore, followed an

FDI-export led growth model rather than an export-led one. China, for its own political reasons and socio-economic dynamics, shares with Singapore this significantly greater emphasis and dependence on FDI as a source of entrepreneurship, technology and competitive growth. During the eighties and early-nineties, it moved gradually from an export-led growth strategy to an FDI-export led growth one. This strategy and the associated policies (whatever their short term costs and long term risks), have been a very important engine of growth in China during the last 25 years.

The greatest difference between China and the other countries of E. Asia that followed the East Asian Model was that at the start of reforms China was a Marxist 'Socialist' State ruled by a Leninist Communist Party. Most of the E.A. States in their early years of reform/growth could perhaps be classified as authoritarian (one man or one party) democracies. There is a fundamental difference between the two. The socialist state (communist party) owns all the means of production, controls all factors and manages all production and sale of goods and services. China's reforms have moved the economy from socialist economy to a 'socialist market' economy with a mix of old 'socialist' and new 'market' elements. The 'socialist' party/government still controls around 95 per cent of domestic assets (i.e. excluding FDI).

As is well known, the market has two key elements: Individuals and organisations that supply and demand a good and a mechanism for determining prices by matching the total supply and demand for that good. The efficiency and productivity depends on the behaviour of the supplier (objectives, incentives and skills) and the structure of the market (competition). The external elements of the market are well understood technically and relatively easy to institute. For instance, 'dual' pricing and distribution systems were used as an intermediate step in moving agricultural goods from a rationed/ controlled system to a market based one in India during the mid-sixties. In the 1970s such transitional arrangements were applied in India to controlled manufactured goods well before the reforms in China. It is much more difficult to design, introduce and operationalise systems of management in which the government owns and controls virtually all the capital/assets.

At the start of reforms in late 1970s China had an administrative system that combined a high level of centralisation of policy making with a relatively decentralised system of governance and production. The lowest level of government, the townships and villages had a level of autonomy that was greater than in democratic India with a free and competitive agriculture sector. Similarly, the level of production decentralisation was much greater than in the USSR or Eastern Europe, partly due the disastorous Maoist experiments in decentralising manufacturing of steel and other capital intensive goods to the local level. These experiments facilitated the creation of (party controlled) organisations and managers with experience of producing goods and services at the local level. With the creation of output markets these organisation, formed the nucleus of the T&VEs, which played a vital role in the success of market reforms during the 1980s. Governance decentralisation also facilitated the closer matching of the objectives and incentives of local governments and T&VEs than was possible at the provincial and national levels.

China's economic growth has been driven by a highly motivated CCP leadership that had fast growth and income catch-up with richer/ advanced countries as its primary objective. This objective was successfully diffused and decentralised to the lowest level of the government, the towns and villages, to a degree that was perhaps unmatched even by Japan and S. Korea that had similar objectives in the corresponding point in their development.[63] This objective did not necessarily exist from the beginning of the reforms in 1977 or 1978, when the focus was on correcting the abysmal policies of the past decade that had put the economy well below its 'normal' trajectory. In 1975, China's GDP at PPP was about 81 per cent of India's and its per capita GDP at PPP was about 54 per cent of India's. Market reforms in agriculture led to a growth spurt in this sector. Renewed interest in exports to generate FE for imports helped support this growth and helped spread growth to the other sectors. The growth spurt between the mid-1970s and early-1980s represented normalisation of agriculture and foreign trade (export thrust) policy from a self-

63. Singapore also had similar objectives, but decentralisation is not an issue in a city state.

destructive Maoist extreme. As a consequence, the GDP gap with India had been closed by 1982-83.[64]

Product market and managerial reforms then shifted to manufacturing sector and the policy focus shifted to an export led growth strategy. This evolved into an FDI-export led strategy. The policy could be described as a combination of attracting FDI at any cost and promoting exports at any cost. The public ownership of capital assets and land has provided the profits that were used to push up public investment and provide the subsidies needed to maintain incredibly high rates of export and FDI growth. The output of this investment was absorbed by further investment, consumer demand expressed through output markets and exports.

Though economic policy has constantly evolved to expand the scope of the market and to develop market institutions, a large area of socialist inefficiency remains. The strengths and weakness of socialist ownership are two sides of the same coin. Government ownership of most domestic assets eliminates the need for high taxes that create distortions and disincentives for private entrepreneurs. In combination with absolute control of individual saving it allows high rates of public investment and high levels of subsidies to attract FDI and push capital intensive exports. The other side of the coin is that rates of return to public capital have progressively declined and will continue to decline as long as centralised social ownership and control (of national and large provincial SOEs) is maintained. At some point, therefore, both the amount of subsidy and the rate of public investment must fall, leading to a lower growth rate. Though, in principle, policy reform that expands the scope of the (genuine and more efficient) private sector can help maintain growth, this appears unlikely to happen at a speed that will keep the rate of growth from declining albeit gradually.

64. It took another decade to close the income gap.

## Appendix A4.1

*OLS Growth Regressions for China*

The following OLS growth regressions for China for the period 1982 to 2002 based on data available in World Development Indicators 2002, are suggestive:

$$
\begin{aligned}
\text{GrPcGdp} = \; & \underset{(1.0)}{0.54} + \underset{(3.6)^{***}}{0.24^{*}\text{GrGfcf}} + \underset{(3.9)^{***}}{0.12^{*}\text{GrGfcf(-1)}} + \underset{(4.6)^{***}}{1.03\ \text{GrGwrld}} \\
& + \underset{(2.5)^{***}}{0.017^{*}\text{GrFDIg\$}}
\end{aligned}
$$

$R^2$ = 0.96, $R^2$ (adjusted) = 0.95, DW = 2.1. Numbers in bracket are t values. *** is significant at 1 per cent level.

All variables are in growth rates (represented by the preface Gr). The independent variable is Growth rate of per capita GDP. Dependent variables are the rates of growth (Gr) of gross fixed capital formation (GFCF), world GDP (Gwrld) and FDI gross in US $ (FDIg$). Similar results are obtained using TSLS.[65] If we replace gross FDI by net FDI the equation becomes:

$$
\begin{aligned}
\text{GrPcGdp} = \; & \underset{(1.8)^{*}}{132}\underset{(-1.8)^{*}}{-0.07^{*}\text{Year}} + \underset{(7.6)^{***}}{0.26^{*}\text{GrGfcf}} + \underset{(4.0)^{***}}{0.1^{*}\text{GrGfcf(-1)}} + \underset{(3.6)^{***}}{0.78^{*}\text{GrGwrld}} - \\
& \underset{(-2.1)^{*}}{0.54^{*}\text{GrFDIn\$}}
\end{aligned}
$$

$R^2$ = 0.94, $R^2$ (adjusted) = 0.92, DW = 2.1. Numbers in bracket are t values. * is significant at 10 per cent level, *** is significant at 1 per cent level.

FDIn$ is the net FDI inflow in US $. If the same equation is run with TSLS, year and FDIn$ become non-significant. If year is dropped from the equation, FDIn$ is significant at the 10 per cent level.

These regressions show the strong investment led nature of China's growth and the role of world demand GDP on China's growth. The latter represents the opportunity for exports at unsubsidised rates or without lowering unit values. FDI plays an

65. Instruments include growth rates of world imports, China's population and labour force and exports (lagged).

important role in China's growth. These results are consistent with an FDI-export led growth.

The importance of FDI is also brought out by the following sources of growth equation (estimated for 1966 onwards) in which the prefix Gr represents the growth rate, Gdp_L represents GDP per unit of labour and Kf_L is fixed capital per unit of labour:[66]

GrGdp_L = 1.47+0.832*GrKf_L+0.283*AR(1)
(1.9) (2.9)*** (1.9)*

$R^2$ = 0.29, $R^2$ (adjusted) = 0.24, DW = 1.79.[67]

Using the parameters of this equation we can calculate TFPG as,

TFPGa = GrGdp_L – 0.832*GrKf_L or TFPG= TFPGa-1.47. Then by OLS,

TFPG = 478 – 0.24*year + 0.04*FDIg$z
(4.4)*** (-4.4)***(5.9)***

$R^2$ = 0.83, $R^2$ (adjusted) = 0.81, DW = 1.88.

This equation shows that, (a) FDI is a driver of productivity growth. (b) There is a secular down trend in productivity growth. We hypothesise that this is the result of excessive investment by the CCP/government either directly or because of provision of capital subsidies, resulting in declining marginal productivity of capital.

66. The capital stock series is built using perpetual inventory method using GFCF and assuming a five per cent depreciation rate.

67. Capital's share is much lower (0.54) and DW very low if we estimate from 1977 onwards.

# Section II

## Global Growth, Power and International Relations

# 5

# Tripolar World: India, China and USA

## 1. INTRODUCTION

This chapter is about the economic basis of global power and the 'power potential' of nation states (details in chapter 8). Power potential is measured by an index, first presented in Virmani (2004e), which we christen VIPP or $VIP^2$. This forms the foundation of relative power of countries and its evolution over the first half of the 21st century.

The correlation between 'potential' and 'actual' power is not, however, perfect. The economic basis of power really takes us only as far as the 'power potential' is concerned. Actual power depends on many other factors besides the economic. We will not go into details about these non-economic factors. There are very complex models built by people like Ashley Telles etc. to measure actual power.

Our basic approach is that the power potential of a country depends on its economic strength. The two papers use the same basic economic analysis and power potential indices to explore different aspects of international relations. Virmani (2004e) discussed the implications of this approach for global governance and UN reforms, in terms of the natural balance of power (chapter 7). Virmani (2005a) focused on the balance of power between countries, the evolution of these balances till 2050 and the impact on international relations and international security. This chapter puts these issues in the context of the demographic and economic developments of the last few decades and their evolution over the next few decades.

In our formulation of economic strength the size of an economy, correctly measured and its growth play a critical role. The economic drivers of the changing balance of power are two developments: globalisation during the second half of the 20th century and in early

21st century and the phenomenon of 'catch-up growth' in Asia. This is the underlying driver of the forecasts for the set of 20 large countries that can be considered as potential global players.

To preview the results, we can think of three quarter centuries, ending in 2000, 2025 and 2050. The mean scenario that we present brings out clearly that the world is unipolar at the end of the first quarter, but will become bipolar at the end of the second and tripolar at the end of the third. This is the fundamentally different conclusion of this chapter (and of chapter 8) from that of scholars and statesman who have discussed and debated multi-polarity or uni-polarity till now.

The world currently gives the illusion of emerging multi-polarity because there are a number of powers today of comparable size or power (China, Japan, Germany, France, UK, Russia and India). Their power is, however, still a fraction of that of the USA. Thus, the world is clearly unipolar. The common/implicit assumption of the multi-polar school has been that all/most of these countries will grow relative to the USA and in co-operation convert the world into a multi-polar one. This presentation shows why this is improbable.

The key outcome will, therefore, be the emergence of two new powers China and India to make it a tripolar world by the middle of the 21st century. Recalling Keynes' words that in the long run we are all dead, most practical men may prefer to focus on the medium term, (till 2025). That is the bipolar challenge of China to USA power, first in Asia and then perhaps on a wider canvas. Even in the medium term, we show that India's role in the world economy and its global power will become the third highest. India's relations with the USA and China will, therefore, play a critical role in Asian security and global peace.

For a lot of people, talk about bipolarity and 'balance of power' raises the specter of 'cold war' 'containment' and 'military alliances'. In our view, the 21st century is going to be different from the 19th and 20th centuries because of (a) the much higher degree (width and depth) of economic globalisation and economic interdependence, and (b) the possession of nuclear weapons by the great powers. The ways in which power is expressed will gradually change and evolve. This will not, however, make national power and military strength irrelevant (*a la* 'End of History'). Relative power and power relations will, we believe, still determine the risk of conflict and the emergence of a stable balance of power in Asia will be vital for peace.

India-US partnership needs to be strengthened and India-China bilateral relations normalised. This will be in the interests of other Asian countries as it will enhance their security and freedom of action. We need to develop inclusive structures, perhaps an Asian Economic Community patterned on the EEC, that enhance mutually beneficial co-operation.

## 1.1 Economics of Power: Current Size

Let us start with the size of the economies, which is the basis of national power. The size of the economy has two components: population and per-capita Income (GDP = population x per capita GDP). The size of the economy is critical to determining its relative power.

Figure 5.1 shows the share of world's GDP of the 18 largest countries. The countries have been ordered by size i.e. the share of GDP at purchasing power parity (PPP). The largest economy in the world, the USA is on the extreme left, followed by China, Japan and India. What this measure (PPP) does, is to value every good and service (shirts, cars, milk, telephone calls, restaurant meals, soldiers etc.) at the same (relative) prices for every country.

India is now the fourth largest economy with six per cent of the world's GDP. There are two other things to note here. Firstly, China is still half the size of the US economy while India is half the size of the Chinese economy. So, when we mention tripolarity, we are not talking about the current situation, which is very clearly unipolar. We are talking about the future—what is going to happen in the next five, ten or more years.

What about multipolarity? The other large rich countries, Japan is still the third largest and Germany the fifth largest, are past their peak in the sense that their size relative to the USA is likely to decline. And then there are a number of middle income countries such as Brazil and Russia, with less than three per cent of the world's GDP. As Brazil is a large important country, it must be kept in perspective. Its size is half that of India's economy, with the Russian economy being even smaller.

## FIGURE 5.1

*Relative Size of Countries: Share of World GDPppp (Per Cent)*

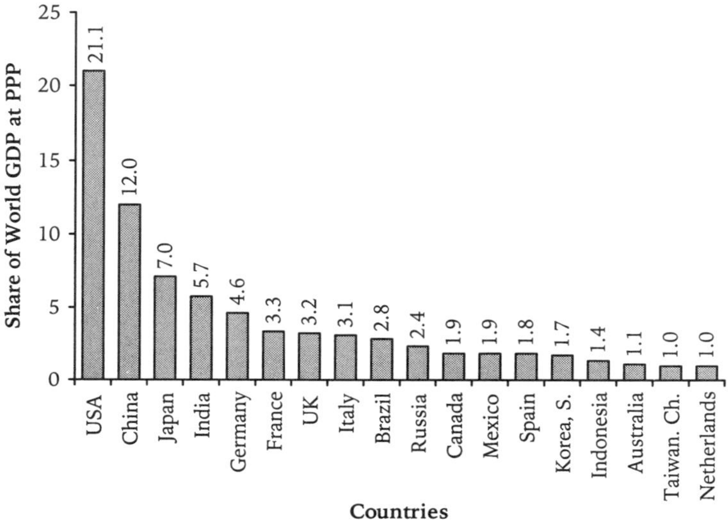


*Source*: World Development Indicators, CD.

### 1.2 Size: Population and Per Capita Income

Population is an important but relatively exogenous component of economic size, in that changes in it occur relatively slowly. Figure 5.2 shows the share of each country in global population, with the most populated on the left. China, as is well known, has the largest population in the world, about 20 per cent of the world total, followed by India with 17 per cent of the world total. The USA, the third most populated country, has only 5 per cent of the world's population, which is 1/3rd that of India and 1/4th that of China. And this again will have implications for the future.

Ranked next to the USA in population are Indonesia, Brazil and Russia. The last two have received a lot of positive attention in the recent past, but not the first. To the extent that population share is relevant to future potential, Indonesia's potential is greater than that of Brazil and Russia.

FIGURE 5.2

*Country Shares of World Population*
*(Per Cent)*

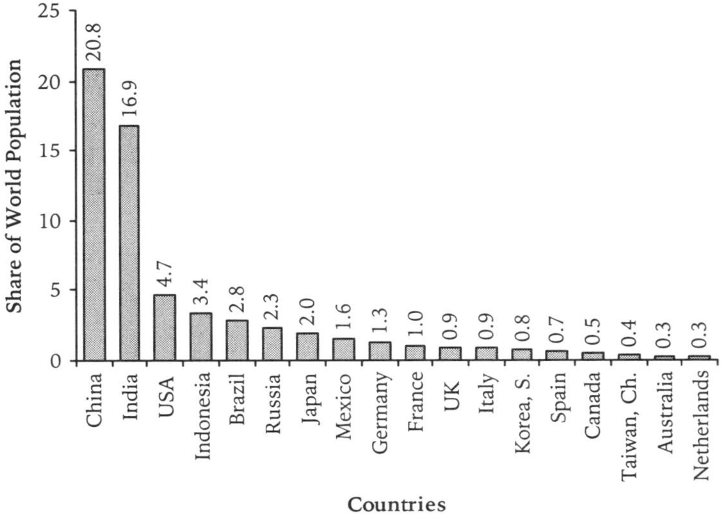


*Source*: World Development Indicators, CD.

The second component of size is per-capita income and in some ways that determines the potential for catch up. In Figure 5.3, the per capita GDP of each country is depicted relative to the USA which, therefore, is at 100 per cent. The USA is followed by Canada the second richest among the large countries, Netherlands the third richest and so on. India is still a very poor country. Among the large countries, India is at the bottom (extreme right) with per capita GDP about 8 per cent that of the US. Indonesia is next with 13 per cent of the per capita income of the USA. Indonesia has the greatest potential for catch-up after India and can play an important role in the catch-up story once its political transformation stabilises. Though, China is now a lower-middle income country, it is still relatively poor, coming just above Indonesia. It has the 3rd highest catch-up potential among the set of large countries.

Brazil and Russia, being 4th and 5th from the bottom among the large countries, also have catch-up potential. Just having the potential is however, not enough. Pritchett (1997) has shown that for the

200-300 countries constituting the world, income divergence (falling behind) is the norm not income convergence (catch-up). We will, therefore, have to show how and why the catch-up story applies to the countries that are the focus of our attention and conversely, to which of these 18 large countries it does not apply.

**FIGURE 5.3**

*Relative Per Capita GDP (Per Cent)*

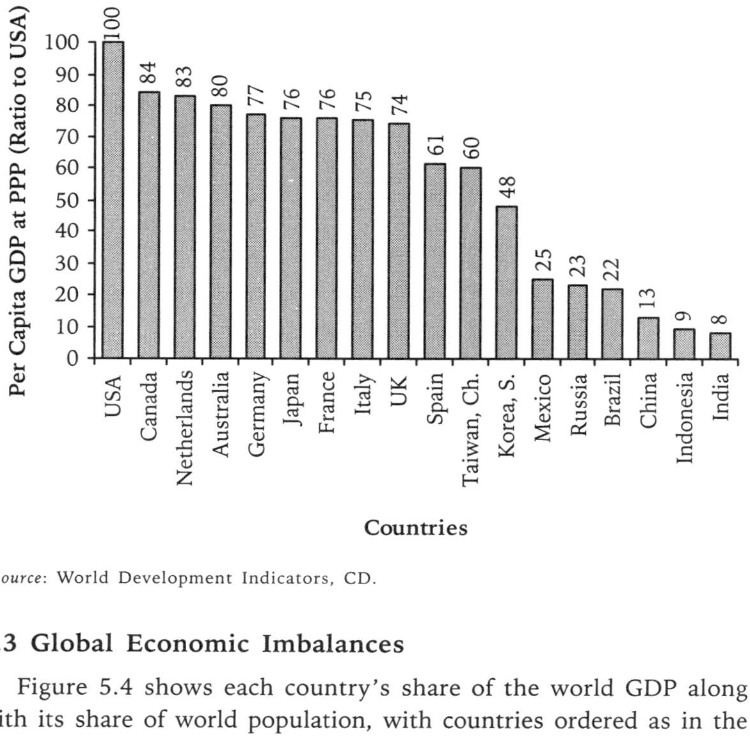


*Source*: World Development Indicators, CD.

## 1.3 Global Economic Imbalances

Figure 5.4 shows each country's share of the world GDP along with its share of world population, with countries ordered as in the Figure 5.1. As one can see, the US has a very high share of GDP while its population share is much lower. Three other countries, China, Japan, and India stand out clearly as having large differences.

More important at this stage, is the identification of the countries for which the gap is small i.e. the dog that did not bark! Brazil and Russia stand out as the only two among this group of countries whose share in the world GDP is almost the same as their share in the world population. In other words their current weight in the world economy is also their natural and due—there are no imbalances one way or the other, that may be corrected in future. They are, therefore, not relevant in the context of the closing of such gaps.

**FIGURE 5.4**

*Gaps between GDP and Population Shares*

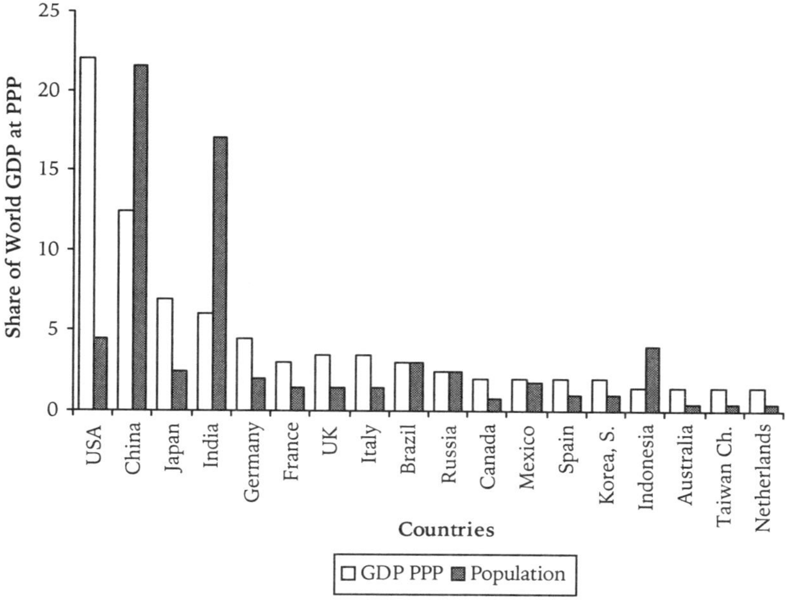


If they grow at a rate faster than the world economy, they would develop a positive imbalance. However, even if Brazil grows at a rate that is 50 per cent faster than our assumptions, this will not happen. Russia is projected by us to grow faster than the world economy, but its population will simultaneously decline. The scope for Russia to grow faster than our projections is limited. The global picture is, therefore, unlikely to be significantly affected by this over the next 25 years or so.

We can summarise these gaps in a new figure that clearly brings out the current global imbalances and their location. Figure 5.5 shows these global imbalances by subtracting each country's share of the world GDP from its share of the world population. Thus, for instance, the US's share of the world GDP minus the US's share of the world population equals about 15 per cent and it has positive imbalance of this amount. These imbalances and the extent to which they will be corrected will be critical to the future of global power relations.

Figure 5.5 shows that there is positive divergence for the USA, Japan, Germany, France, UK and Italy. And there is negative divergence for Indonesia, China and India. The key element underlying our conclusions is the closing of these gaps over the 21st century.

The sceptics, quite rightly note that several of these gaps and imbalances have existed for two to three centuries, some since the start of the Industrial Revolution in 1600s. They can justifiably ask why we think these gaps are going to close in the 21st century? The answer to the sceptics is given by the performance of these countries in the past 25 years, to which we turn.

### FIGURE 5.5

*Global Imbalance: GDP Share-Population Share*

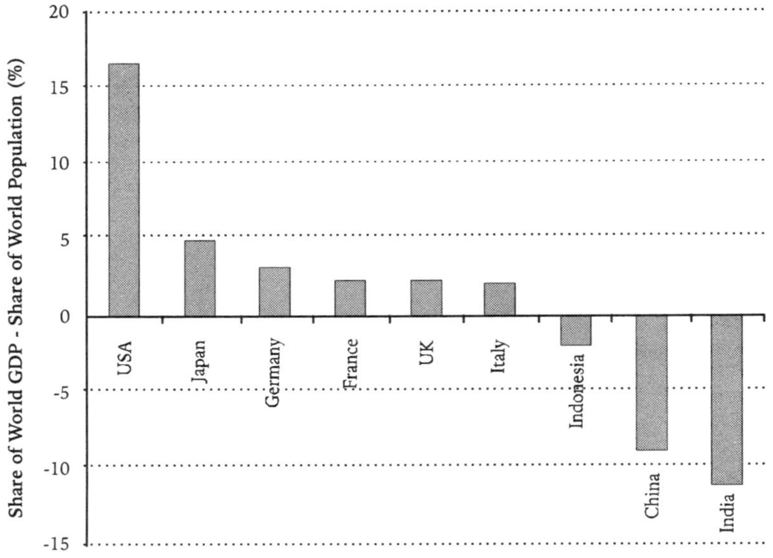

## 1.4 Economic Performance

The following Table 5.1 answers two related questions. Why we think catch-up growth is relevant and why the GDP-population share gaps identified above will close. Table 5.1 shows the growth rates of per capita GDP of the fastest growing medium-large economies in the world ranked by the rate of growth.

**Table 5.1**

*Per Capita GDP Growth: 1980 to 2003*

| *Economy* | *Rank* | *Average* |
|---|---|---|
| China, PR | 1 | 8.2 |
| Korea, Rep. | 2 | 5.6 |
| Taiwan, China | 3 | 5.3 |
| Thailand | 4 | 4.7 |
| Vietnam | 5 | 4.6 |
| Ireland | 6 | 4.5 |
| Singapore | 7 | 4.2 |
| Hong Kong | 8 | 3.9 |
| India | 9 | 3.7 |
| Luxembourg | 10 | 3.7 |
| Indonesia | 11 | 3.6 |
| Malaysia | 12 | 3.6 |

*Source*: World Development Indicators, CD.

The most noteworthy fact is that ten of the twelve fastest growing economies in the world over the last quarter century were in Asia. The rate of growth was faster than the rate of growth of the global economy. In other words, Asian countries have been converging. The second noteworthy fact is that five of these fast growing economies are also in the list of the 20 largest economies in the world. Three of these, India, China and Indonesia had the largest imbalance.

China as everyone knows, has been growing very fast—although its 8.2 per cent per annum growth per capita has been rightly questioned by several eminent scholars. These scholars calculate that the growth rate may have been overestimated by 1 to 2.5 per cent. Even if we reduce the official growth rate by 2 per cent to 6.2 per cent, China still remains the fastest growing economy in the world during the past 25 years.

What some may not know is that India has been the ninth fastest growing economy at 3.7 per cent per annum over these 24 years. Table 5.1 shows that Indonesia, a country we highlighted earlier as having the third highest negative imbalance, comes out only a little behind India during this 24 year period. It may also be noted that S. Korea and Taiwan (China) are the only other large economies that figure in our list of the 10 fastest growing economies during this period.

Thus, for the three economies with the largest imbalances, India, China and Indonesia, the gap has been closing for the last 25 years. This has happened because economic policy reform has allowed them to exploit the opportunities opened up by globalisation (which have themselves been expanding during this period), and to accelerate the pace of catch-up growth. We expect these three economies to continue this process of catch-up growth (at least) till they reach the high-income level, based on the assumption that they will continue the process of economic and institutional reform.

More specifically, China and India will remain among the 3 to 5 fastest growing economies in the world during the next 20 years or so. So, we expect the gaps to close and the imbalances to be reduced over the next 50 years.

To summarise the main points, there is scope for catch up given the gap between India, China and the USA. India is still a low-income country, meaning a poor country. The income status is going to change to lower-middle income in the next five years or so, but poverty will not be eliminated for another 15 years. China is a lower middle income country. There is a huge catch up potential for both the countries.

In this context, a number of people working on economic growth issues talk about the innovative capacity of a country, the number of inventions etc. But in our view these matter only after a country reaches the high-income category and it really doesn't matter so much in the catch-up stage, when the country is going from low-income to high-income.

## 1.5 Population Projections: Tripolar Bias

To make projections for these economies we need population projections and per capita growth forecasts. The population projections are taken unmodified from the UN (2004). These are depicted in Figure 5.6 for 2025 and 2050, with the 2002 population shares also given for comparison.

The first point is, that the US's share of the world population remains almost unchanged over these 50 years. There are two sets of changes over this period. One is in the relative population of China and India. China's population, which is currently larger than India's, is projected to become smaller by 2050, with the cross over occurring around 2035. The second is that Japan and Russia's population share, (and to a lesser extent Germany's), will decline significantly, while the share of other countries declines marginally or remains unchanged, relative to the US.

## FIGURE 5.6

*UN Population Projections*

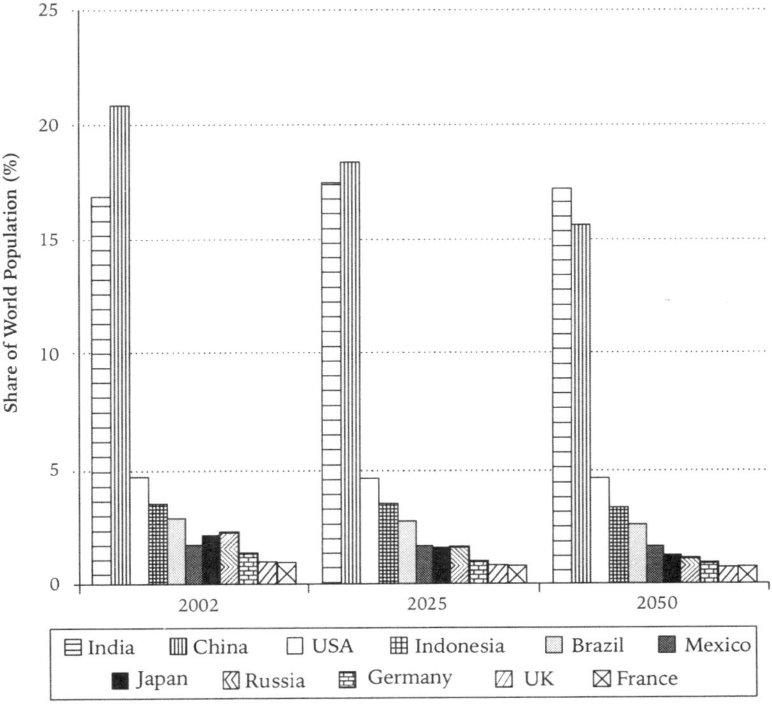


*Source:* UN, 2004.

The key insight that comes from the population comparison (current and projected) is that only two nations, China and India, are potential contenders for multi-polarity over the next fifty years. As the population of all others is a fraction of that of the USA and this fraction will either decline or remain unchanged, their per capita income would have to be significantly greater than that of the USA to reach comparable levels of GDP. There is little prospect of this happening in the next 25-50 years (based on our analysis).

The European Union (EU) is often posited as a contender for multi-polarity in the medium-long run. There are two points to note in this case. The population of the EU as well as that of non-EU, European countries is on a declining trend. Second, the EU could be a pole in a multi-polar world if it becomes a virtual state like the former Warsaw Pact. This requires a surrender of national power to a EU government. The consequent emasculation of national power is unlikely to be acceptable to the voters of the large member countries (France, UK, Germany, Italy, Netherlands) in the next 25 years.

## 1.6 Growth Projections

We turn next to the second component of the size forecast, the trends in growth of per capita GDP. On these, the critical question is how quickly will China slow down and can India maintain or raise its growth rate? But before discussing the growth prospects of China and India in detail, we look at the overall projections. Table 5.2, presents the projected average growth of per capita GDP for each country by period. The countries are ordered by the growth rate in the first forecast period.

For China, based on the official figure of 8.2 per cent for the past, we expect growth will slow down in the next 15 years to an average of around 6.6 per cent. For India the growth rate is projected to rise over the next 15 years. The annual trend, is assumed in the projections underlying these averages, to reach 6 per cent per annum by the beginning of the next decade, stay around that level for around 5 years and then start declining again. The peak rate will translate into a GDP growth rate of about 7 per cent per annum given a population growth rate of about 1 per cent per annum at that time.

**Table 5.2**

*Per Capita GDP Growth Projections*

| | *Growth Rate–Per Capita GDP at PPP (Per Cent)* | | | | |
|---|---|---|---|---|---|
| | *(1980-2002)* | *(2003-2015)* | *(2016-2025)* | *(2026-2035)* | *(2036-2050)* |
| China | 8.2 | 6.6 | 5.6 | 4.9 | 4.0 |
| India | 3.6 | 5.2 | 6.0 | 5.7 | 4.8 |
| Russia | | 4.9 | 4.5 | 4.1 | 3.6 |
| Korea, S. | 5.7 | 4.3 | 4.0 | 3.7 | 2.6 |
| Indonesia | 3.7 | 3.3 | 3.7 | 3.6 | 3.5 |
| Taiwan, Ch. | 5.4 | 3.3 | 3.1 | 3.0 | 2.3 |
| Spain | 2.3 | 3.0 | 2.8 | 2.6 | 2.2 |
| Canada | 1.6 | 2.5 | 2.3 | 2.2 | 2.2 |
| Australia | 2.0 | 2.5 | 2.4 | 2.1 | 2.2 |
| UK | 2.0 | 2.2 | 2.2 | 2.2 | 2.4 |
| USA | 1.8 | 2.0 | 2.0 | 2.0 | 2.0 |
| Japan | 2.0 | 1.8 | 2.0 | 2.1 | 2.0 |
| France | 1.6 | 1.8 | 2.0 | 2.1 | 2.3 |
| Netherlands | 1.8 | 1.8 | 2.0 | 2.0 | 2.0 |
| Mexico | 0.8 | 1.8 | 2.1 | 2.3 | 2.3 |
| Italy | 1.8 | 1.6 | 1.9 | 2.0 | 2.0 |
| Germany | 1.6 | 1.4 | 2.0 | 2.1 | 2.2 |
| Brazil | 0.7 | 0.7 | 1.5 | 1.5 | 2.2 |

*Source:* UN, 2004.

Going down the Table, Russia, Korea and Indonesia's growth also comes in high according to our estimates. This has implications for Korea, as pointed out to me by a renowned professor from Korea recently. In the case of Russia, the growth rate assumption is perhaps a little higher than the average forecast. Our forecast for Japan is similarly optimistic, relative to many who have doubts about its growth prospects. This is done deliberately to ensure neutrality *vis-à-vis* India.

The forecast for Brazil, based on its performance over the last 25-30 years is perhaps more pessimistic than the one made by those who base their expectations on its stellar performance till the mid-1970s. The structural change that would be essential for moving the economy from the former to the latter forecast is, however, not visible to many Brazilian observers. Even if Brazil grows at a rate 1.5 times the assumed rate the broad global scenario is unaffected.

## 1.7 China Forecast

To make the China forecast we had to look deeply at its economy in the previous chapter.

The perspective of this chapter was that China is a 'socialist market economy'—as per Chinese Communist Party (CCP) terminology. Focusing only on the 'market' part and ignoring the 'socialist' element can be very misleading. Oscar Lange's (1971) book on 'Market Socialism' provides a useful starting point for understanding such an economy. We build a stylised model of the economy, to capture the main features of the 25 years, fast growth, period that will explain the growth performance and help us draw lessons for other countries. The key elements of this stylised model are as follows:

Market elements of China's Socialist Market economy include product markets for goods, non-infrastructure services etc., basically the bright thing they did in 1970s and 1980s was to start freeing up the goods market. And of course FDI—the big emphasis on FDI and equally important is the freeing of foreign trade particularly exports. Till the 1980s, imports and most exports were channeled through party/government controlled trading organisations and enterprises.

All other elements of the economy are under various degrees of socialist planning and control. All factors (land, labour, capital) are under social control to an extent that is difficult to imagine in a market economy. Going to the other extreme of communist economy like Stalinist USSR or N. Korea can be a convenient red herring! To talk about the banks in China, which are basically like government departments, as if we are considering a market economy, can be highly misleading. We have here a former Deputy Governor of the RBI who oversaw the nationalised banks in India. Even in the most interventionist phase, Indian banks enjoyed a lot of managerial freedom compared to China's banks. Having worked and lived in India we understand this. But most market people in the West have no experience or stylised model to comprehend how these things work in Communist Party ruled China.

Infrastructure, in most developing countries is under state ownership or control. But in China, the supply and price of infrastructure can be determined on an individual basis so as to channel subsidies (capital or revenue). Thus, it is used to promote exports, attract FDI inflows and ensure technology transfer. The flip side is that detailed controls always breed corruption and we also have this in China.

The CCP controls virtually everything in the country. Product markets exist and Foreign Direct Investors (FDI) have a relatively free market environment as a result of a deliberate decision of CCP (there is however, no legal/institutional constraint on their ability to interfere at will in these markets). Second, those using the USSR economic model to analyse China are led astray because the USSR was very centralised, whereas China is highly decentralised, in terms of governance and the government owned production structure. So, China's socialist economy is a mix of centralisation and decentralisation and this must always be kept in mind.

Their goals and objectives are very clear. The objective is national power. With economic strength clearly recognised as the basis of power, this translates into an objective of growth maximisation subject to the CCP retaining power. So the CCP leadership is very focused and this is ensured at all levels—nation, province, city and firm. At a disaggregated level, it is analogous to 'corporate capitalism' or corporate growth maximisation in a market economy.

The growth maximisation strategy leads directly to maximisation of investment. This has two components—what may be called the 'foundation of growth' and the 'engine of growth'. The foundation of growth is public investment. In 1978, 100 per cent of the assets were owned by the government and the return on them was fairly high (24 per cent for SOEs). As there is no pressure on the party/government to distribute these profits to citizens/consumers/workers, it can invest 100 per cent of these profits. This makes possible a very high rate of public investment without introducing distorting taxes. Though the governments share of assets has declined (perhaps by 5-10 per cent) as has the rate of return (6 per cent in SOEs), this socialist element (heritage), when coupled with product market competition, has proved advantageous. Thus, despite public sector inefficiency, public investment has been one of the drivers of growth.

The engine of growth is FDI, and coupled with exports is the big driver of economic growth. There is a consensus among China scholars that export-led growth *a la* ASEAN has been an important driver of growth. Two additional points emerge from our analysis. One, that it is much more of an FDI-export led growth (even more so than in Singapore which come closest) than in ASEAN countries. Two, all exports are not necessarily as competitive as labour-intensive exports associated with non-resident Chinese entrepreneurs. Many capital/skill intensive exports may be fueled by direct or indirect subsidies. These subsidies may be hidden in the supply of intermediate goods from SOEs, in infrastructure supply and its pricing and in the so-called non-performing assets of Banks.

There is a flip-side to China's success. On each area of successful policy, there is a weakness. For instance, China's clear growth objective is a great strength but it also means they did bother too much about the income distribution, which has worsened tremendously. Similarly, the FDI-export model has risks which have been shown in the Asian crisis and are more serious for China, because the build-up of 'public capacity' can only be sustained through exports (vent for surplus or export at any cost).

Our conclusion is that the growth rate will decline gradually and not collapse. This differs from two important schools of thought. One, which argues that the contradiction between 'Market economy' and 'Stalinist politics' will result in a Chinese collapse. In our view, the possibility of this happening, while it is a middle income country, is remote. The other school argues that China can grow even faster if the socialist part of the economy is transformed into a market one. We disagree. In our view the strengths and weaknesses of China's current system are two sides of the same coin. Surgically excising the weakness will also remove the strength. Gradual reform of the sources of weakness while building alternatives to past strength can however sustain growth till the country reaches high income levels. The rate of growth, will however, decelerate. More fundamental changes may become necessary at high income levels and the probability of sharper slow down will rise if these are not made.

## 1.8 India Forecast

In the case of India, you may recall, we made an assumption that its growth rate will rise in the future. One reason for this assumption is what we call the 'J curve of liberalisation', by anology with the 'J-curve' in the foreign trade literature. Our hypothesis is as follows. When a country undergoes dramatic reforms (the kind initiated by Dr. Manmohan Singh and implemented by Mr. Montek S. Ahluwalia), any negative effects are immediate, but the positive effects take time to appear. That is because of immobility of capital and the S-curve of technology diffusion: Uncompetitive lines of production are immediately affected, with profitability and measured productivity falling dramatically, as capital cannot be shifted to other uses. Though, new competitive lines of production emerge, it takes time to develop them by acquiring technology and making investment. The diffusion of technology takes time. So, you get the negative effect immediately while the positive effects build up gradually.

So, what we've seen so far in India is a rise in growth rate by about 0.6 per cent. It is about 6.1 per cent for the 12 years since the 1990 reforms started. Figure 5.7 shows that the underlying growth trend is rising. We believe that it will go up to about 6.5 per cent as a result of the reforms which have already happened.

**FIGURE 5.7**

*J-Curve of Liberalisation: India's Rising Growth Trend*

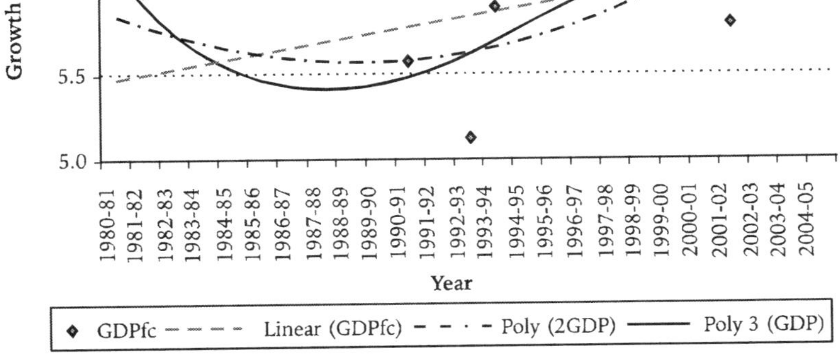

Further reforms (see e.g. Virmani, 2004a and Mid-term appraisal of the 10th Plan) can raise this growth rate further. We forecast that these reforms will continue at the average pace seen so far and, as a consequence, the growth rate will gradually rise to 7 per cent and stay there for about ten years (i.e. growth forecast is conditional on forecast of continuing reforms). In principle, the growth rate could be accelerated above 7 per cent (slow below 6.5 per cent) if the pace of reform accelerates above (slows down below) the average pace seen so far.

For the India sceptics, who generally forecast a GDP growth rate of 5 per cent to 5.5 per cent, there are six other factors, which will support a rise in India's growth rate above its current level. One, is the increasing share of business service in GDP. Till the 1990s this share was very small, so the double digit growth of IT & ITES exports had a very small effect on GDP growth. The size of the sector is now large enough for the continuing double digit growth of service exports to have a visible impact on GDP growth. During this and the next decade, the effect of fast growth of business service exports will be to raise overall growth by 0.5 per cent to 1.5 per cent point per annum.

The second positive factor is the demographic transition and demographic bonus. We have seen in many countries including East Asia and China, that this raises the growth rate. Based on these studies we estimate that the demographic bonus could raise India's growth rate by 0.5 per cent to 0.8 per cent point per annum. Further, India will have the youngest labour force in the world, when most advanced countries are aging rapidly. This will increase the demand for 'youth intensive' exports from India.

The third factor is strong 'indigenous entrepreneurship'. A Harvard Business School study has shown that India's growth has been fuelled by domestic entrepreneurship in contrast to China which is basically driven by FDI. Another study puts the impact of FDI on China's growth at 3 per cent points per annum. We estimate that if India can double its FDI from $ 4 billion to $ 8 billion, there could be a growth bonus of around 1 per cent.

The fourth factor, is India's large institutional and social capital based on its culture and civilisation. There are studies by Rodrik and others, which say that India's growth is about 15 per cent lower than is predicted by the quality of its institutions. Though old (mainly govt.) institutions have deteriorated, this has been offset by the development of new ones like non-profit organisations (NGOs) and an independent media. Though, China also had civilisational strengths, institutions related to the market were deliberately destroyed (entrepreneurs killed) by the Communist revolution.

The fifth is the 'Global Indian manager'. Most of our managers are used to dealing with very diverse religious, ethnic, sub-cultural bunch of workers, colleagues and consumers. We are, therefore, advantageously placed in the emerging globalised economy.

Sixth is what we call 'underutilised brains'. When media reports how intelligent/brainy/skilled we are and how we are taking the world by a brain storm, my reaction is a bit unconventional. The IQ (Intelligent Quotient) distribution is universal and applicable to all sub-populations of the world. The top 2 per cent and 10 per cent of any country/world's population can be classified as brilliant and very bright respectively. For India, this means 20 mi brilliant and 100 mi very bright people. Earlier, most of them were either hidden in remote rural areas or were condemned to the job of clerks in Delhi or taxi drivers in Mumbai. The big change is that globalisation and economic reforms is making it possible to utilise more and more of these underutilised brains in Silicon Valley and Bangalore.

Many visitors to India ask me whether India will be able to maintain its growth rate given the poverty and income distribution. Underlying the questions are the horrifying experiences of seeing real poor people, perhaps for the first time in their life (on their way from the airport). The following is addressed to them.

Why are there lots of poor people in India? Because India is a low income i.e. poor country and our population is large. India's average per capita income is less than Indonesia's and much less than (lower-middle income) China's. A poverty rate of 23 per cent (judgement based on a review done at ICRIER) translates into 230 million poor people. That is larger than the population of every country in the world except USA and China. India is a free country, the poor can live and work anywhere. They gravitate naturally to where the jobs are, normally in the high growth cities and towns. Misguided urban policies (e.g. Urban land ceilings, Rent control) make returns negative on private provision of one room apartments for the poor, and concentrate them in illegal slums. This means high visibility in Mumbai, Delhi etc. The fact that a lot of poor people are visible on the drive from the airport to the city does not mean that poverty is increasing or income distribution is bad!

For this we have to look at the comparative statistics across countries (e.g. WDR 2005) In terms of the Gini Co-efficient, a widely accepted measure of distribution, India comes in the top quarter of countries (31 out of 127 countries). In contrast, China is in the bottom third (91 out of 127 countries). Another fact, which is not well known is that the consumption share of the poorest (bottom) 10 per cent of India's people, is the 6th highest in the world out of 127 countries. If there is no contest between India and China on economic growth, this is equally true in reverse with respect to income distribution.

There is one great weakness in India, the deterioration in governance. This is our biggest challenge. The excellent governing institutions of the 1950s have been deteriorating over the last 30 years. This has affected the provision of public goods and services (police, legal system, administration, agriculture R&D and extension, recharge of aquifers, roads). Over time it is going to effect growth. So political reforms are needed but happen slowly. Governance reforms will take place, because we have a free and responsible media, judiciary and NGOs. Dr. Manmohan Singh has the knowledge and statesmanship to undertake long term reforms that do not have immediate pay-offs.

## 1.9 Global Scenario

Now we come to the mean scenario. Figure 5.8 shows the projections for each country's GDP at purchasing power parity (ppp) relative to the USA. The line in the middle which is at 100 per cent therefore represents the USA, which is also growing, but its ratio to itself is by definition constant (flat line). One of the two striking results of this projection is the exponential rise of China's economy.

Though, the basic facts about China's rise are known, perhaps the exponential nature of this rise in the 21st century was not fully comprehended. In fact a knowledgeable American told me about a year ago, that the US CIA's (US Central Intelligence Agency) projections for China were of moderate (not serious) concern to analysts and decision makers. The CIA projections of a year ago merely talked about India being a swing economy/power. Late in 2004-05 a CIA assessment was put in the public domain that for the first time expressed some concern about China and also acknowledged the positive global role that India could play. This assessment must have been done around the same time as Virmani (2004e), which first gave projections till 2035. Both this paper and Virmani (2005a) have been sent to scholars, journals and decision makers in the US.

## FIGURE 5.8

*GDP at PPP: Relative to the USA*

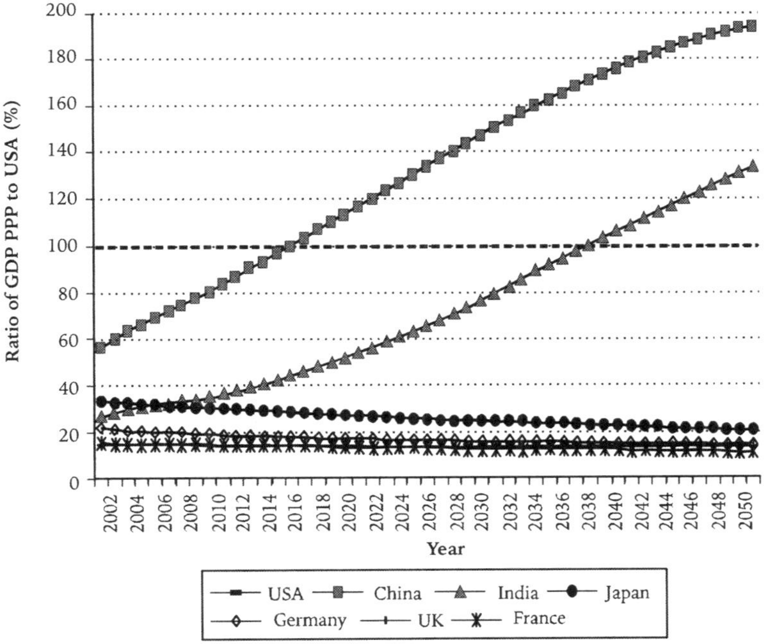


One is not aware of any study that brings out as clearly as Figure 5.8 the dramatic rise of China and its competitive challenge to the USA. It shows that China's economy will equal that of the US within 10 years and could by 2050 be double that of US. This has huge implications for the US, which they still do not put a very high probability on. This is our mean scenario with a probability of 75 per cent.

The second striking result of this exercise is the equally dramatic rise of India a couple of decades behind China. This is something, which was clearly not recognised by anybody. Right now India is the fourth largest economy, but its size is close to many other countries. The projection shows that within five years India's economy will be larger than Japan's.

Within 20 years, India will become the third most important economy in the world. Though not self-evident today, this will become quite clear, even to sceptics, in 10-15 years. This forecast is quite conservative, as the GDP growth rate is assumed to be less than 6.5 per cent during the rest of this decade and rising gradually to a maximum of 7 per cent during the next decade. This contrasts with the forecasts by many financial analysts and business organisations of 7 per cent to 8 per cent growth, which is also the revised target for India's 10th Five Year Plan.

Figure 5.8 shows that by 2040 India's economy would become as large as the US economy (conditioned on maintaining the pace of our policy reforms). This is the second major implication of the projections, a point not made previously by any scholar (to our knowledge). The projected development will transform the global economy and international relations.

Recall that the measurement of economic size/GDP is at Purchasing Power Parity (ppp), because there is no other way to compare the size of different economies. The potential impact on the world economy—the economic impact on other countries in terms of trade, capital flows etc, is however, not very well measured by GDP ppp. So we can do some alternative projections that measure the incremental impact of GDP on the world economy.

Figure 5.9 shows the annual change in GDP measured in terms of 2002 exchange rates and prices for each country (the usual widely available measure of GDP) relative to the annual change for the USA. Though the Chinese economy is now the second most important in terms of annual impact, it will take around a quarter century for it to equal that of the USA. Many have recognised China's influence on the world economy. Despite our 1999 forecast (paper on ICRIER website), few have realised that within ten years, India's impact on the world economy will equal that of Japan and in 15 years will exceed it.

This has implications for India's fundamental approach to the outside world. We must abandon our post-colonial, pre-independence fears and self perception of a small helpless non-aligned (African/ Caribbean/Pacific) country buffeted by the rich and powerful ones. Acting confidently does not, however, mean amnesia about our high poverty or illiteracy rate (30 per cent), nor should it lead to a slackening of efforts to reform economic policy and institutions.

**FIGURE 5.9**

*Change in GDP: At 2002 Exchange Rate*

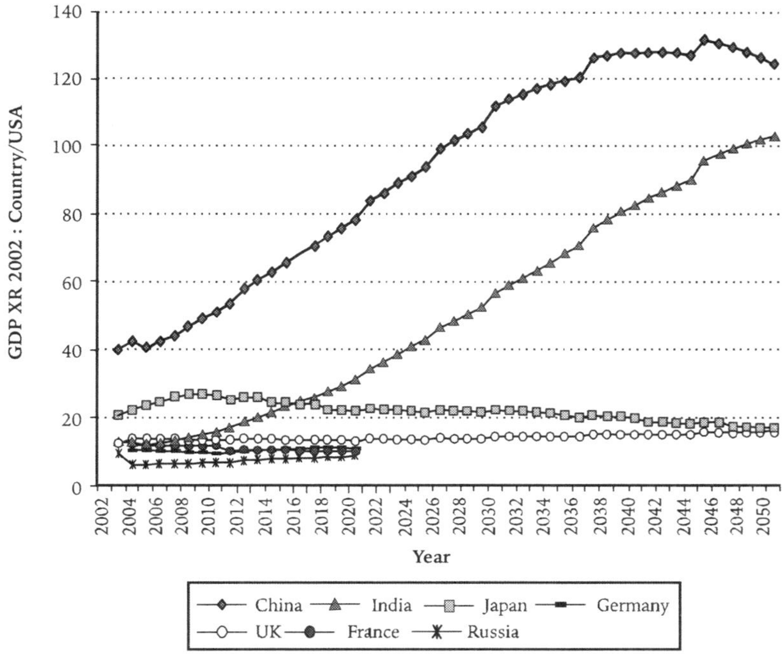


To summarise, China is already the second largest growth driver after the USA, while India will overtake UK in about three years to rank 4th in terms of incremental impact. India will overtake Japan in about ten years in terms of incremental importance. If we look 20 years and beyond, China will likely overtake the US in first place within 25 years and India's incremental impact could become the second largest by mid-century.

## 1.10 Virmani Index of Power Potential: VIPP or VIP$^2$

Given these economic facts we move on to the power potential index that we have constructed, the details of which are in the following chapters. Compared to the complex models built by others, it is a very simple concept. Basically we identify a proxy for technology and put a weight on it that is additional to its natural weight in the aggregate production function of an economy. The production function expressed in per capita terms, adequately captures the technological capabilities, skills and capital needed to produce output at that level. In a globalised economy, if all technical flows are free and subject only to commercial considerations, the size of the economy adequately measures its power potential, as the inherent capability can be used to produce/procure any set of goods or services.

However, it does not adequately measure a country's power potential when there are controls on strategic and dual use technology. As strategic technology is restricted and not subject to the normal commercial considerations, a country needs to develop its own strategic technology. Relative per capita GDP is an adequate measure of a country's relative capability to develop and use new technology. Therefore, to measure the power potential we put a weighting factor on per capita GDP *vis-a-vis* population. For various reasons, it is reasonable to assume a weight of 0.5.

As mentioned earlier, one should not take 'potential power' as 'actual power' VIP$^2$ is an index of power potential and not actual power. Actual power depends on many other things such as the will or desire of a country to be globally powerful. For example, after the World War, Japan consciously abandoned 'will to power' by aligning with the USA and following its foreign policy. So if a country doesn't have the will to become powerful, it will not become so. Another factor is the allocation of funds among different public goods such as strategic R & D and defence. This choice can change the actual power. The third element is alliances. There are many countries (such as Israel), which because of their alliances with other countries, have benefited greatly through transfer of technology and equipment. The resources so saved can be used for other public goods thus multiplying the benefit in terms of power.

## 1.11 Tripolar World

Figure 5.10 shows the evolution of the power potential, based on VIP$^2$ with a parameter value of 0.5. In contrast to the earlier graph of economic size, this has greater implications for foreign relations etc. The evolution of power potential is more reassuring for the US. It will be at least 20 years, before China's power potential will get within hailing distance of the USA. Similarly, it will take another 50 years before India's power potential gets close to the US.

At the same time we must remember that power does not have to be exactly equal among three countries for the world to become tripolar. Though it is hard to be precise, when the power potential of the challenger reaches 40 per cent or 50 per cent of the incumbent the former is likely to become another pole.

### FIGURE 5.10

*Index of Power Potential, VIP$^2$ (with a=0.5)*

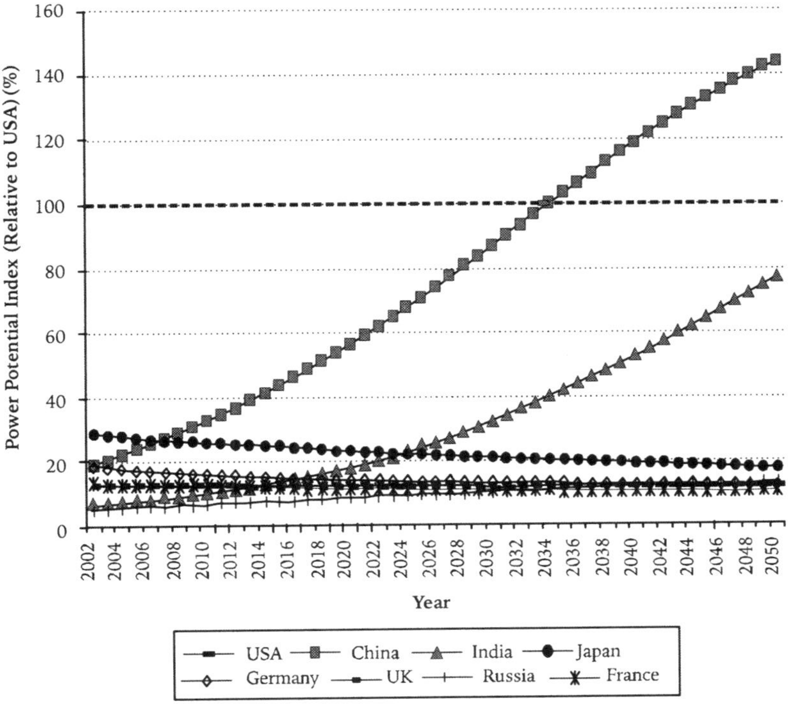

The reason why Japan, UK, Germany and others cannot challenge the US today is because they have less than 20 per cent of its power potential. And as the figure shows, Japan's power potential will remain highly significant during the next 50 years despite its declining trend arising from a shrinking population. Russia, which is projected to increase its power potential gradually doesn't increase it significantly. Even if Russia catches up in terms of income (as projected), a population decline of 25 per cent will offset part of its impact on size and power potential. The position is similar for many other countries.

$VIP^2$ suggests that China's power may equal that of the USA in 30 years. What is the reason for this? China's population will be about 3.8 times that of the US in 2035 and its per capita income about 43 per cent of that of the US. At this point its GDP ppp will be 1.6 times that of the USA. The technological disadvantage of lower per capita income is, thus, implicitly offset by the advantage of a larger scale to produce an economy with equivalent power potential. A further increase in China's per capita income relative to the US after 2035 could make it more powerful than the USA. There is, however, a probability of its growth rate slowing more sharply than we have assumed, after it reaches high income levels between 2025 and 2030.

## 1.12 China–India Gaps

Figure 5.11 shows the evolution of India's size and power relative to China's. The upper line is the relative GDP (ppp) and the lower one is relative power. Twenty five years ago, India's GDP was larger than that of China (not shown). Over the last 20 years it has fallen behind and is now less than 50 per cent of China's. Its relative power has declined even more rapidly. In terms of the mean scenario this gap is going to increase till about the middle of the next decade and thereafter it will start closing. The gap will not close completely till the last quarter of the century because China is projected to continue to grow faster than the global economy till then.

We believe, that it is in the interest of the advanced democratic countries, including the USA, to help India close this gap as rapidly as possible. There are several reasons. One is philosophical. Both as peoples and nations we share fundamental human and democratic values and aspirations, whose propagation and strengthening will make the world a better place for all.

## FIGURE 5.11

*India-China: GDP at PPP and VIP*[2]

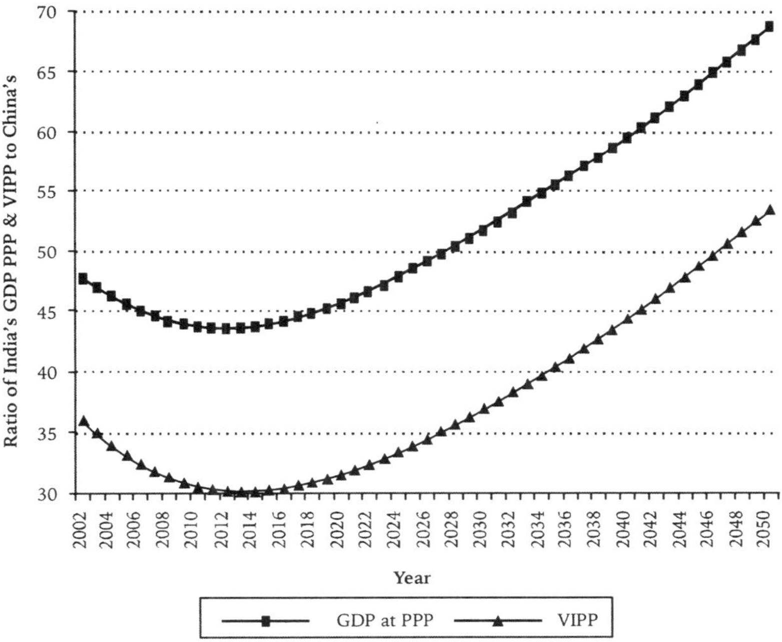


Two, is pragmatic self interest. A more symmetric balance of power in Asia will reduce the risk of conflict in Asia and increase the freedom of action of the smaller Asian countries. This, in turn, will have two economic benefits for advanced countries. (i) It will expand the scope for profitable economic interactions (trade, capital flows etc.) with all countries of Asia. (ii) It will ensure that the economic policies of smaller countries are not biased towards one Asian neighbour at the expense of all democratic countries.

Three, is correction of past mistakes. The ban on transfer of dual use and strategic technology to India after its 1974 nuclear test constrained India's growth and development. China was positively favoured (space, missile and defence technology) and Pakistani transgressions (illegal purchases from Netherlands, Germany and the USA, transfers by NPT signatory China, ISI-Khan black market network) were ignored. In contrast, India was even denied fuel for its civilian nuclear power plant (Tarapur). These policies are partly responsible for the opening of the gap and should be reversed to close it.

India must aim to get complete exemption from the post-1974 controls on technology transfer, whether incorporated in old or new denial regimes. India's democratic polity (including the 220 million poor) will not accept the expenditure of limited tax resources on responsibilities undertaken for countries that deny it technology needed for development.

## 2. CONCLUSIONS

To summarise, we believe there is a very high probability that in terms of global power, the world will become bipolar by 2025 and tripolar by 2050. India will be the weakest pole in this tripolar world of the 21st century, according to the mean scenario underlying these conclusions. China's economy is likely to equal the USA economy in size by 2020 and to become about twice its size by 2050. By then, India will be the second largest economy (ppp), having overtaken the USA around 2040. The gap in 'power potential' between China and the USA will be eliminated by 2040. China's economy/power in 2050 will likely be about 20 per cent smaller/less than that of the US and India combined. The balance of power among the three countries USA, China and India and the relationship between them will be critical to the peace and stability in Asia and the World.

China's economy and power in 2050 will equal that of the six larger democracies of Asia—India, Japan, Indonesia, Russia, South Korea and Australia. This makes it imperative for them to increase economic and technological cooperation among themselves so as to preserve their freedom of action.

The predicted emergence of a tripolar world has important implications for relations between the USA, India and China. From India's perspective there are two implications. First, an India-US partnership for peace in Asia is in the interests of both countries. Second, China and India must normalise and strengthen bilateral relations, to the point that they are no weaker than China-USA and China-Japan relations were at their high point.

Strengthening of USA-India relations has to be viewed from a 21st century perspective in which every economy will continue to engage all the others in this globalised world economy. The 19th and 20th century concepts of military alliances and containment are not appropriate. A partnership between India and the USA means a quantum jump in the width and depth of mutually beneficial economic relations and technology transfers. As it is in the mutual interest of the USA and India, both (particularly their democratic representatives and bureaucrats) need to think in new ways.

Among the steps that could be taken are:

(1) A comprehensive economic cooperation agreement (Indo-USA CECA) covering trade, FDI and movement of professionals.

(2) Strategic partnership whose elements are (a) Decontrol of dual-use technology transfer to India. (b) Free trade with India in nuclear plants, equipment and materials. (c) Defence technology transfer to India. (d) Cooperation in space (production, launch, etc.). (e) Joint R & D in strategic and defence systems.

(3) Co-production of defence systems (including naval vessels).

(4) Due role in global governance (permanent seat with veto in UNSC).

It is equally important to normalise the relationship between India and China as this is going to be critical for peace and security in Asia. Fortunately, the first steps in this direction have already been taken. An ICRIER study by Amita Batra has shown that there is a large unutilised or un-actualised bilateral trade potential. This should be fully exploited for mutual benefit by removing trade barriers and constraints and by facilitating better communications and transport.

In addition, there are three keys to developing trust and enhanced cooperation between China and India (and China being the stronger country will have to take some positive steps). First, a fair and equitable border settlement, at least no worse than what was offered by the Chinese Premier, Chou En Lai, in the 1960s. Second, stop nuclear proliferation to countries that are hostile to us. Only the proverbial ostrich can miss the implications of the Chinese atomic bomb designs found in Libya, courtesy Dr. A.Q. Khan and Pakistani military rulers. And third, realise India's due role in Asia and the world.

On the first and third steps, China has already begun to move. This is indicated by the first concrete steps to a border settlement and a public statement that China would not oppose India's permanent membership in the UNSC and possibly even veto power. The lifting off of that opposition is a positive step. The second issue is still left (with routine denials about passing on bomb/missile technology to various countries).

Besides improving bilateral relations, we need to build inclusive economic structures. Though the 21st century is going to be different from the 20th, there is nothing automatic about it. Imbalances in power can still result in conflict. We need to build structures of interaction that will reduce the threat of conflict and enhance the gains from peace. European history provides some lessons. The European Commission started with the iron and steel community and the coal community. Perhaps we can learn from that history. India's oil minister has initiated oil and energy cooperation and we could think of building an Asian oil and energy community. Indian Prime Minister has talked about building an Asian Economic Community. India is taking an active positive role in East Asia and has recently been invited to the plenary session of the East Asian Economic Community. That could be a step towards the Asian Economic Community.

And finally, a USA-India partnership does not mean abandonment of multiple interests and multi-polar diplomacy by either country. The USA will continue to pursue its interests in Asia (Pakistan, Iraq, N. Korea, Iran) regardless. India must obtain the frontier strategic technologies wherever they are available (e.g. Russia, France) and develop those that are unavailable but necessary for its independence and security (ICBMs, nuclear ballistic-missile submarines).

# 6

# VIP$^2$: A Simple Measure of a Nation's (Natural) Global Power

## 1. INTRODUCTION

The USA is often referred to as the most powerful nation on earth, particularly since the collapse of the USSR in 1990. It is well known that the US economy is the largest in the world. But does the size of an economy measure a nation's power in a global context? During the Cold War between the US and NATO, and the USSR and Soviet Bloc, the world was treated as being bipolar, i.e. the two countries USA and USSR were recognised to be the two most powerful in the world of the time. The most visible part of their competition was in space, nuclear, defence and other technology. The possession of advanced military equipments such as ICBMs, submarines, aircraft carriers, bombers and fighters was also an element of the relative power of these two nations. Since then, complex models have been built to define and measure a nation's global power. Economic and technological factors play a major role in these models (Tellis *et al.*, 2000). Other factors are natural resources, education and skills and investment in R & D and technology development.

State power is the "extent that [one] effects others more than they affect [one]" (Waltz, 1979). It is, therefore, a "combination of its capacity to resist the unwelcome influence of others and, conversely, to influence others to behave as it wants them to." International relations experts have been divided on the relative importance of economic strength and military might in the global power of a nation. We resolve this conflict by decomposing national power into two elements: (a) the 'power potential' of a country, which depends on economic strength and general technological capability, and (b) military capability. This includes defence and strategic equipment and specific technologies needed for attaining military superiority.

Together these define the actual power of a country. International ambition and determination, the 'will to power' play a role in transforming the 'power potential' into 'actual power'.

Virmani (2004e, 2005a) proposed a simple index of 'power potential'. In this chapter we present the index (christened $VIP^2$), discuss its rationale and calculate the value of this index for all the medium and large countries in the world. We also define an index of actual power (VIP) based on $VIP^2$, which requires a separate measure of military capability.

The next section discusses the economic basis of national power. Section 3 defines the $VIP^2$ (Virmani index of power potential). This index is then calculated for about 113 countries (Appendix Table A6.1). Section 4 and Section 5 present and discuss the results for the global and regional Powers. Section 6 gives a sensitivity analysis on the key parameter used on the index. Section 7 discusses the likely evolution of the $VIP^2$ clubs. Section 8 analyses the implications for permanent, veto bearing membership of the UN Security Council. Section 9 concludes the chapter.

## 2. ECONOMIC STRENGTH AND NATIONAL POWER

An appreciation of the role of economic size and technological potential on the global balance of power has grown since the Second World War. Prof. Paul Kennedy, in his *Foreign Affairs* article and subsequent book, *The Rise and Fall of Great Powers* gave economics considerable weight in the evolution of the global balance of power. He made the following points:

- Traditional field of International Relations has not fully appreciated the role of economic strength, with the role of economic factors relatively neglected!
- Military power rests on and is sustained by economic power.
- The rise and fall of great powers can be traced to the change in their economic strength.
- Relative rather than absolute economic strength is the relevant variable.
- There may be leads and lags between the change in economic power, military power and national power.

Economic power is the foundation of national power. Economic strength is the only sustained and sustainable basis for national power and relative economic power is the basis for national power. Even though military power disproportionate to economic power can be used to enhance national power for a certain period of time, this is not sustainable over long periods. This was illustrated by the break-up of the USSR, where the military and strategic competition could not be sustained by a declining economy. The role of economic factors in international affairs is, likely to be much greater in the 21st century than it has been in previous centuries. With the growth of communication and the increased mobility of goods and services, labour, capital and technology, much technical knowledge is becoming the common heritage of mankind in reality. General technological capability is increasingly part and parcel of economic evolution, and 'economic factors', therefore, encompasses this technology. The process of modernisation and global economic integration has expanded the gains from economic co-operation between states, reduced the gains to the winner from war, and increased the potential losses to third parties from active war between states. The lags between the rise or decline of economic power and the rise or decline of great powers are also likely to shorten during the 21st century.

Tellis *et al.*, (2000) have developed a comprehensive and complex model for measuring power in terms of the ability of a state to achieve and sustain global hegemony. In their model military capability, is the outcome of an interaction between national resources and national performance. National resources consist of five building blocks of power, technology, enterprise, human resources, financial/capital resources and physical resources. National performance contains three factors, infrastructural capacity, ideational resources and ideational resources that augment or detract from the utilisation of these natural resources.

The factors mentioned in the Tellis model are all inputs into the productive capacity of an economy, though their economics nomenclature and definition may be different. Thus, a country's natural resource (e.g. oil), physical capital stock (including the stock of infrastructure), human capital (education and skills) and technology (including management, marketing and entrepeneurship) are all inputs into the production of national output and are formally included in the aggregate production function of the economy.[1] The gross domestic product (GDP) of a country, which is the output produced by all these inputs, given the external (e.g. technology denial) and internal (e.g. quality of governance, social divisions/ conflicts) constraints facing economic agents, is therefore a summary index of its 'national resources' and 'national capacity'. Even more broadly the growth of a country's GDP and the level it has reached reflects both the strengths and weakness of its society (social capital, religion, culture, family) and institutions (political, market regulating, non-profit organisations, civil) in addition to its national policies.[2]

## 2.1 Commercial and Strategic Technology

There is need to distinguish between two categories of technology: commercial and strategic.[3] Commercial technology is part and parcel of normal trade, financial flows and movement of managers and skilled personnel between open economies. FDI normally bundles two or more of these together. Any specific commercial technology (not available at a given time in the country) can, therefore, either be purchased from global markets or be attracted to the country through FDI (joint ventures etc.).

Strategic technologies are the technologies of power. They include military related technologies as well as nascent technologies that may play a critical role in future defence systems. Because of the uncertainty inherent in forecasting the future, less developed technologies may at one stage be classed as 'commercial' and at another stage as 'strategic'. By definition, strategic technologies are critical to national power and are not traded on commercial considerations. General technological capability forms the foundation of strategic technology, but its development requires specific and focused attention. It has either to be developed through national effort or acquired through strategic/military alliances.

General technological capability, therefore, has a dual role: It is the foundation of the productive capability of the economy and also the

1. $Y = F((K, H, R, T)$, where Y is GDP, K is the stock of physical capital, H is the stock of human capital (education and skills), R represents natural resources (e.g. oil, minerals), and T is the level of technology (broadly defined).
2. The quality of institutions is an important determinant of growth. Social capital and related variables are also found to be significant.
3. Dual use technologies represent the overlap between the two types.

foundation for the development of specific strategic technologies. Thus, in the real world in which nations guard their strategic technological knowledge, those with higher technological capabilities have a greater ability to develop strategic technology and therefore have greater power potential.

## 3. INDEX OF POWER

### 3.1 Productive Capability

The economic capacity of a country at any point in time is measured by its GDP. This represents its output of goods and services during the year. The same economy can produce different goods and service in different amounts, with the actual pattern of output depending on the pattern of demand. In general two economies can differ not only in their productive capacity but also in the pattern of demand. So how do we know that one economy is larger than another i.e. has greater productive capacity? The only way to compare the size of different economies is by valuing all goods and services produced in each, by using a common set of relative prices. Such a measure of a country's economy is referred to as Gross Domestic Product at Purchasing Power Parity (Y).[4]

The technological capability of an economy depends on many factors. Virmani (2004e) has used the principle of OCCAM's razor to define technological capability in the simplest possible way. This is done by using the familiar concept of an aggregate production function.[5] When viewed from the perspective of productive capacity, an economy consists of different productive resources such as unskilled labour, stocks of physical capital, human capital in the form of education and skills, natural resources such as oil and minerals, disembodied technology (organisations) and technological capabilities embodied in capital goods and human beings. The aggregate production function shows how these resources can be combined to

4. If the economy is open and competitive it also follows that it is producing things in which it has a comparative advantage and importing those which others produce relatively efficiently. If the policy distortion prevent this from happening, the economy's productive capacity will be reduced and this will be reflected in GDP at PPP.
5. Familiar to economists and particularly macro-economists.

produce output i.e. it summarises the productive capacity of the economy. The aggregate production function and the related concept of aggregate factor productivity can be used to define the general technological capability of an economy.

The concept of total factor productivity growth (TFPG) is commonly used in economics to measure technological change in an economy. Conceptually the level or value of total factor productivity (TFP) could represent the technological capability of a country. Its operationalisation, however, requires the assumption that technology is disembodied and neutral.[6] As we have indicated, technology is often embodied in capital and labour i.e. it is inseparable from the physical capital or the labourer/employee.[7] In addition, historically we observe that capital intensity (capital per unit of labour input K), the education/skill level of the labour force (human capital per person H) and technology (T) move broadly in tandem as an economy develops. In other words, for new/better technology to be translated into higher output per person, an appropriate complement of better skills and more capital per person is also needed i.e. they form a package that together produces a higher level of productivity. Labour productivity or output per unit of labour is a summary measure of the level and quality of this package of technology, capital intensity and skill intensity. As is also much easier to define and measure than TFP, it is operationally a more useful measure of an economy's technological capability than TFP.[8] Per capita GDP at purchasing power parity or GDP per person ($y = Y/L$, with $L$ = population) can therefore be used as a summary measure of the 'general technological capability' of an economy.

## 3.2 Power Potential: VIP$^2$

A nation's power potential (NPP) can therefore be defined as the multiple of the size of its economy measured by the GDP at

---

6. That is the aggregate production has a form $Y = T(t)\ F\ (K, H, R, L)$ in which the technology factor $T(t)$ is separable from the factor inputs, capital (K), human capital (H), natural resources (R) and unskilled labour (L). In this case $T(t)$ = TFPG.
7. It has the form $Y = F(\ A(t)K, B(t)L, H, R)$ or $Y = F(\ A(t)K, B(h, t)L, R)$. The definition and measurement of TFPG is very complex and difficult in this case.
8. Labour Productivity $y = f(A(t)k, h, r, T(t))$, where $k = K/L$, $h = H/L$, $r = R/L$. In this case it does not matter if $T(t)$ is non-separable as shown or separable as follows: $y = T(t)\ f(A(t)k, h, r)$.

purchasing power parity (Y) and its technological capability measured by its per capita GDP (y):

$$NPP = Y * y^{\alpha}, y = Y / L,$$

L is the population and $\alpha$ is a parameter that can have a value between 0 and 1.

If we substitute Y = y * L in the above equation and put $\beta = 1 + \alpha$, we obtain;

$NPP = L * y^{\beta}$ where $\beta$ is a parameter that can have a value between 1 and 2.

The Virmani Index of Power Potential (VIPP) or $VIP^2$, in short, is the power potential of a country (as defined above) relative to the USA.

(1) $VIP^2 = (Y / Y_{usa}) * (y / y_{usa})^{\alpha}$, where $0 \leq \alpha \leq 1$

Or equivalently as

(2) $VIP^2 = (L / L_{usa}) * (y / y_{usa})^{\beta}$, where $1 \leq \beta \leq 2$

A number of conclusions follow from these equations:

If $\alpha = 0$ ($\beta = 1$) then,

(a) The power potential of a country is measured by its GDP (at purchasing power parity) relative to that of the USA. A country with a higher GDP is potentially more powerful than one with lower GDP. Implicitly, population and per capita income (GDP) have equal weight.

If $\alpha$ is non-zero, then

(b) If two countries have the same GDP but one is richer than the other (higher per capita income/GDP)[9], the richer country will be potentially more powerful. As per capita income is an indicator of general technological capability, this multiplies the power potential of a given GDP. Overall, it also means that technology (per capita income) has a greater weight in determining power potential than population (number of people). In applying this index to measure the relative power of countries, we assume that $\alpha = 0.5$ ($\beta =$

9. The other country therefore has a large population.

1.5).[10] The power potential of all countries with a GDP at purchasing power parity of more than $ 15 billion in 2002 (WDI 2004) is estimated using this index.

## 3.3 Actual Power: VIP

'Actual power' will however depend (among other things), on the proportion of national resources spent on developing these strategic technologies and in translating them into weapons systems. As both these items are classified as public goods, the difference between actual and potential power will depend on the allocation of expenditure on public goods as a whole as well as on the allocation to different types of public goods. Strategic alliances with a more powerful country can achieve the same objective at lower resource cost if the more powerful country transfers strategic technology to the less powerful one. Clearly, the more powerful country will only do this if the less powerful one is able to enhance its power or welfare in some other way (e.g. provision of bases, supply of soldiers/guerilla fighters, oil contracts, help in anti-terrorist operations).

In the national accounts, expenditure on public goods like defence and strategic technology, is treated as current expenditure valued at current cost. From the perspective of national power it is more like an investment in capital equipment. Further, as it is not a commercial tradable good or technology its value is not equal to the cost or notional price at which it is acquired. The shadow price of a strategic good for a country that does not have the capability to produce it is much higher than the cost expended by the country which has already produced it. If we are to compare the diverse range of investments by different countries, we must use the same shadow price for all countries.[11] If the value of this investment over time can be correctly cumulated into a stock of strategic technology and equipment this would explain a substantial part of the difference between 'potential' and 'actual' power.

---

10. For this set of medium-large countries, we estimated for 2002 the relationship between per capita GDP measured at current exchange rate x and per capita GDP at purchasing power parity y. On running a cross section regression for 2002 data, we find the following relationship: $x = A\, y^{0.5}$. This was one of the reasons for selecting $\alpha = 0.5$ after simulating the index for a range of $\alpha$ values from 0.25 to 0.75.

11. This will be higher than the highest cost incurred by any country.

Formally this can be written as,

$$K^s_t = p_t E_t - \delta K^s_{t-1},$$

where at time t, $K^s_t$ is the stock of strategic technology t, $E_t$ is the expenditure on this technology valued at the shadow price $p_t$ and $\delta$ is the rate of depreciation of the stock. The Virmani index of actual power (VIP) could then be defined as,

$$VIP = VIP^2 * K^s / K^s_{us}$$

The former USSR spent a lot of resources on strategic technologies and goods (E) and, thus, attained a level of VIP that was much greater than its $VIP^2$.[12] This level of expenditure on one public good perhaps led to the neglect of others. The USSR was ultimately unable to sustain such high levels of public expenditures on strategic technology and collapsed under the burden. The accumulated strategic knowledge ($K^s$), though it has deteriorated over time, has not been lost. Though the economy of Russia is much smaller than the USSR and the Warsaw Pact, the reduction in the 'power potential' was greater than the reduction in the strategic capability ($K^s$). Therefore, the gap between its 'power potential' and its 'actual power' remains much larger than is usually observed among normal nation states.

Conversely, Japan after its defeat in World War II became a pacifist nation, which deliberately reduced expenditure on strategic technology, defence systems and forces. It also gave up any ambitions of being an independent power in Asia. Its 'actual power' is therefore lower than its 'power potential'. Post war Germany also has some of these characteristics. In addition some very small economies with low power potential (e.g. Israel, Pakistan) have skillfully used formal or informal alliances to attain a level of actual power, far in excess of their power potential. In general, however, country expenditure on such technology/systems is highly correlated with GDP, and consequently, so is actual power and power potential.

## 4. GLOBAL VIP²s

After calculating the index of power potential for each country in the world for which GDP and population data is available in the World

12. Further, its power potential was related not just to the economic size of the USSR but to the economic size of the Warsaw Pact which was more like a Soviet empire. The Warsaw Pact was, in the context of power, more integrated than the current EU.

Bank WDI for 2003, we rank them from the most powerful to the weakest. We also use the IMF GDP data for 2004 and its projections till 2006, to calculate the index for all medium-large countries for 2005 (Appendix A6.1). For selected countries we extend the forecast up to 2008 and beyond. We define the global VIP$^2$s by using a cut-off value of the index of 5 per cent.[13] This gives us 13 global VIP$^2$s and one borderline case (Table 6.1).

According to our index, China is now the third strongest power in the world and will displace Japan in second place in the next few years. The larger rich countries of Europe—Germany, France, UK and Italy—are long time members of the global VIP$^2$ club and will remain more powerful than India for some time even though the latter's economy is the fourth largest in the world.[14] India has just moved into 8th rank in the global VIP$^2$ club displacing G7 member Canada. Its GDP will become larger than Japan's in the next three years, and its power will exceed that of Italy a year or so later. Its power potential is greater than that of Russia, which is in 10th place behind Canada. As noted earlier, Russia's actual power is greater than its 'power potential' because of the historical legacy of the Soviet empire. The other members of the global power club are Spain, Brazil and South Korea. S. Korea's power potential is rising relative to that of Spain and Brazil, and is likely to exceed it in the next five years.

The set of global VIP$^2$s is not necessarily identical to the set of global powers. The latter would constitute a sub-set of the former. Countries with a VIP$^2$ of less than 10 per cent cannot lay claim to being global powers and a cut-off value double this appears reasonable. The benchmark could therefore be 20 per cent. By this criterion, only China and Japan qualify today (in addition to the USA). Germany, which was a potential global power till a decade ago, is no longer one.

## 5. REGIONAL POWERS AND VIP$^2$s

The academic debate and general discussion of international relations often refers to regional powers. Is there any way of

13. The alternative would be to take the top 10 or 15.
14. In GDP at PPP is the only way to compare the size of the economy. Their GDP converted at the current exchange rate is much larger than India's.

## Table 6.1

*Global VIP²'s in 2005*

| Economy | VIP² Rank | | | | | | | GDP Rank | | | Index of Power: VIP² (Per Cent) | | | | | | |
|---|---|---|---|---|---|---|---|---|---|---|---|---|---|---|---|---|---|
| | 2003 | 2005 | 2007 | 2010 | 2012 | 2016 | 2023 | 2003 | 2005 | 2007 | 2003 | 2005 | 2007 | 2010 | 2012 | 2016 | 2023 |
| **Global Powers** | | | | | | | | | | | | | | | | | |
| United States | 1 | 1 | 1 | 1 | 1 | 1 | 1 | 1 | 1 | 1 | 100 | 100 | 100 | 100 | 100 | 100 | 100 |
| Japan | 2 | 2 | 3 | 3 | 3 | 3 | 4 | 3 | 3 | 4 | 28 | 27 | 26 | 25 | 24.8 | 23.7 | 21.8 |
| China | 3 | 3 | 2 | 2 | 2 | 2 | 2 | 2 | 2 | 2 | 22 | 25 | 29 | 34 | 39 | 48 | 67 |
| **Regional Powers** | | | | | | | | | | | | | | | | | |
| Germany | 4 | 4 | 4 | 4 | 4 | 5 | 5 | 5 | 5 | 5 | 18 | 17 | 16 | 15 | 14.8 | 14.1 | 13.2 |
| France | 5 | 5 | 5 | 5 | 7 | 7 | 7 | 6 | 6 | 6 | 13 | 12 | 12 | 12 | 11.7 | 11.3 | 10.8 |
| United Kingdom | 6 | 6 | 6 | 6 | 6 | 6 | 6 | 7 | 7 | 7 | 13 | 12 | 12 | 12 | 11.7 | 11.6 | 11.3 |
| Italy | 7 | 7 | 7 | 8 | 8 | 8 | 11 | 8 | 8 | 9 | 12 | 11 | 11 | 10.2 | 9.8 | 9.2 | 8.2 |
| India | 9 | 8 | 8 | 7 | 5 | 4 | 3 | 4 | 4 | 3 | 7.8 | 8.5 | 9.3 | 10.8 | 11.9 | 14.9 | 22.3 |
| Canada | 8 | 9 | 9 | 9 | 9 | 10 | 10 | 11 | 11 | 11 | 8.0 | 7.8 | 7.9 | 8.0 | 8.1 | 8.2 | 8.2 |
| Russia | 11 | 10 | 10 | 10 | 10 | 9 | 8 | 10 | 9 | 8 | 6.0 | 6.5 | 6.9 | 7.4 | 7.7 | 8.5 | 9.7 |
| Spain | 10 | 11 | 11 | 11 | 12 | 12 | 12 | 13 | 13 | 13 | 6.5 | 6.4 | 6.4 | 6.5 | 6.5 | 6.6 | 6.6 |
| Brazil | 12 | 12 | 13 | 13 | 13 | 13 | 13 | 9 | 10 | 10 | 5.7 | 5.8 | 5.7 | 5.7 | 5.7 | 4.5 | 5.1 |
| Korea, Rep. | 13 | 13 | 12 | 12 | 11 | 11 | 9 | 14 | 14 | 14 | 5.5 | 5.5 | 5.9 | 6.4 | 6.7 | 7.4 | 8.5 |
| Australia | 14 | 14 | | | | | | 16 | 17 | | 4.8 | 4.7 | 4.8 | 4.8 | 4.9 | 5.0 | 5.0 |

objectively defining these regional powers. We can use our index with a cut-off percentage of 1.5 per cent to first define the set of regional $VIP^2$s i.e. the members of the regional VIP club. These are given in Tables 6.2 and 6.3. Among the different regional groupings, unsurprisingly, Europe has the largest number of regional $VIP^2$s (14), followed by Asia with 9 (including global powers). Latin America and Carribean (LAC) and N. Africa and Middle East have only 3 regional $VIP^2$s each, while Sub-saharan Africa has only one.

**Table 6.2**

*Global Ranking of Europe Region $VIP^2$s*

| *Country* | *$VIP^2$ Rank* 2003 | *$VIP^2$ Rank* 2005 | *GDP Rank* 2003 | *GDP Rank* 2005 | *$VIP^2$ (Per Cent)* 2003 | *$VIP^2$ (Per Cent)* 2005 |
|---|---|---|---|---|---|---|
| **Regional Powers** | | | | | | |
| Germany | 4 | 4 | 5 | 5 | 18 | 17 |
| France | 5 | 5 | 6 | 6 | 13 | 12 |
| United Kingdom | 6 | 6 | 7 | 7 | 13 | 12 |
| Italy | 7 | 7 | 8 | 8 | 12 | 11 |
| Russia | 11 | 10 | 10 | 9 | 6.0 | 6.5 |
| Spain | 10 | 11 | 13 | 13 | 6.5 | 6.4 |
| **Other Regional $VIP^2$** | | | | | | |
| Netherlands | 17 | 17 | 19 | 24 | 3.9 | 3.7 |
| Poland | 21 | 19 | 24 | 23 | 2.2 | 2.3 |
| Belgium | 18 | 20 | 29 | 30 | 2.3 | 2.4 |
| Austria | 22 | 26 | 33 | 34 | 2.0 | 2.0 |
| Sweden | 27 | 27 | 34 | 35 | 1.9 | 1.9 |
| Switzerland | 26 | 28 | 36 | 37 | 1.9 | 1.9 |
| Norway | 30 | 31 | 42 | 42 | 1.6 | 1.6 |
| Greece | 31 | 32 | 37 | 36 | 1.5 | 1.5 |

The 'regional powers' constitute a sub-set of the regional $VIP^2$s. One sub-set that comes naturally to mind are those members of the global $VIP^2$ club whose index is below the benchmark for a 'Global power' (Table 6.1). By this criterion there are six regional powers in Europe, two in Asia and one each in North America and Latin America.[15]

15. Leaving aside the three global powers, USA, China and Japan.

**Table 6.3**

*Global Rank of Other Regional $VIP^2$s*

| Region/Country | $VIP^2$ Rank | | GDP Rank | | $VIP^2$ (Per Cent) | |
|---|---|---|---|---|---|---|
| | 2003 | 2005 | 2003 | 2005 | 2003 | 2005 |
| **Asia** | | | | | | |
| *Global Powers* | | | | | | |
| Japan | 2 | 2 | 3 | 3 | 28 | 27 |
| China | 3 | 3 | 2 | 2 | 22 | 25 |
| *Regional Powers* | | | | | | |
| India | 9 | 8 | 4 | 4 | 7.8 | 8.5 |
| Korea, Rep. | 13 | 13 | 14 | 14 | 5.5 | 5.5 |
| Australia | 14 | 14 | 16 | 17 | 4.8 | 4.7 |
| *Other $VIP^2$s* | | | | | | |
| Taiwan, China | 16 | 15 | 17 | 16 | 4.0 | 4.5 |
| Thailand | 24 | 22 | 21 | 19 | 1.9 | 2.2 |
| Indonesia | 23 | 25 | 15 | 15 | 2.0 | 2.1 |
| Hong Kong, China | 32 | 30 | 41 | 40 | 1.4 | 1.6 |
| **Latin America & Carribean** | | | | | | |
| Brazil (Regnl. Power) | 12 | 12 | 9 | 10 | 5.7 | 5.8 |
| Mexico | 15 | 16 | 12 | 12 | 4.2 | 4.2 |
| Argentina | 19 | 18 | 23 | 22 | 2.3 | 2.5 |
| **Sub-Saharan Africa** | | | | | | |
| South Africa | 20 | 21 | 20 | 21 | 2.3 | 2.4 |
| **N. Africa & Middle East** | | | | | | |
| Turkey | 25 | 23 | 18 | 18 | 1.9 | 2.1 |
| Iran (IIR) | 28 | 24 | 22 | 20 | 1.8 | 2.1 |
| Saudi Arabia | 29 | 29 | 28 | 28 | 1.6 | 1.7 |

## 5.1 Europe

Twelve of Europe's 14 regional $VIP^2$s are the known rich countries of Western Europe. Poland and Russia are the only two regional $VIP^2$s from Eastern Europe. Russia has been placed in Europe because much of its GDP arises in that continent, even though much of its physical area lies in Asia. Germany, France, UK, Italy and Spain along with Russia can be classed as regional powers in Europe. The last could perhaps also be categorised as a regional power in Asia also.

If all the members of the EU, including the regional powers listed above had surrendered their entire power to the EU (voluntary emasculation), they would no longer be regional VIP$^2$s. The EU would thereby, become a 'virtual state' with a VIP$^2$ of about 80 per cent i.e. a global power second only to the USA. The world would then be bipolar (neither unipolar nor multi-polar).[16]

If EU member states surrendered half their power to an elected EU government with complete and unfettered right to exercise these powers, EU would be a global power with the second highest VIP$^2$ (about 40 per cent). But the individual power of Germany, France, UK and Italy would become less than that of Canada and India, though it would still be more than that of Brazil and S. Korea (except for Italy's).

## 5.2 Asia

Though Asia has nine members in the regional VIP$^2$ club, one of these is politically a part of China and another is claimed by it. This leaves only seven countries in the club, almost half the number in Europe. Among the seven, four countries are also members of the global VIP$^2$ club.

Of these, China and Japan are potential global powers. India is clearly a regional power, while S. Korea is also a potential regional power. The other three members of the Asian regional VIP$^2$ club are Australia, Thailand and Indonesia. Of these three, Australia could also be considered a regional power as its index was only marginally less than the cut-off level for the global VIP$^2$ club and is likely to exceed the cut-off in a few years.[17]

As ASEAN's economic integration is minimal compared to the EU, it would be highly premature to discuss its possible emergence as a

16. A common stand on WTO negotiations or a common tariff should not be confused with being a'virtual state'. Any group of independent nations can have a common stand on one or more issues (G8, G4, G20, G5). Even though the EU's stand may have a greater degree of permanence because they are institutionalised, there is no EU government deciding on or acting on these issues without the approval of member states.

17. Pakistan's power potential is less than Egypt's and neither country meets the benchmark for being classed as regional VIP$^2$. The low rank of Pakistan (48), below Egypt (46) and Algeria (47) and just above Vietnam (51) and Bangladesh (52) suggests that it has enhanced its actual power above its 'potential', through the use of alliances. Similarly, Egypt's importance to the USA/West increased with its peace treaty with Israel.

regional power, even though its $VIP^2$ would be above the benchmark we have set (i.e. about 6.5 per cent).

### 5.3 Other Regions

The LAC region has a total of three nations who qualify as members of the regional $VIP^2$ club, of which one, Brazil is a member of the global club. The other two are Mexico and Argentina, with the former a competitor of Brazil. Brazil's power potential is, however, currently half that of Italy's and 68 per cent of India's. It is projected to be half that of India in about six years (and more than half of Italy's). The only reason for considering Brazil for permanent membership would be if it represents the whole of LAC instead of itself.

South Africa is the sole member of the Sub-saharan Africa regional $VIP^2$ club with an index less than that of Argentina. The index for the three members of the middle-east regional club, Turkey, Iran and Saudi Arabia have an even smaller power potential index than South Africa. One noteworthy fact is that two countries, often mentioned as regional powers, Egypt and Nigeria do not meet even the less stringent criterion of membership in the regional $VIP^2$ club. Nor does Nigeria, whose power potential index is a small fraction of that of S. Africa. Talk of Nigeria being a permanent member of the UNSC, therefore, appears to be divorced from reality.

Brazil is the only regional power in LAC, while Africa and the Middle East have no countries that meet the regional power threshold of a $VIP^2$ of 5 per cent. South Africa's power potential is 2/5th that of Brazil's. There is thus even less justification for S. Africa to have a permanent seat on the UNSC than there is for Brazil. If it was representing the whole of Africa or at least Sub-saharan Africa, a case could be made.

## 6. SENSITIVITY OF $VIP^2$ TO PARAMETER

The choice of the value of 0.5 for the technology weighting parameter is based on judgment. It is, therefore useful to test the sensitivity of our results on the $VIP^2$. We do this by measuring the impact of a change in $\alpha$ from 0.5 to 0.55 (i.e. by 10 per cent) on the $VIP^2$ for the set of global $VIP^2$s. The results are summarised in Table 6.4. The elasticity of $VIP^2$ with respect to the parameter $\alpha$ is given in column 2 and the per capita GDP at PPP in column 3. It is seen that the elasticity is inversely related to the per capita GDP. The elasticity is negative up to a threshold level of income (around 2/3$^{rd}$ of US income) and positive above it. Thus, $VIP^2$ decreases/increases with $\alpha$ below/above the threshold. Thus, below the threshold, if $\alpha$ is raised above 0.5 (as assumed), the $VIP^2$ of the poorer countries will fall proportionately more than for richer countries. Among the set of global $VIP^2$s, India's relative position worsens (improves) most as $\alpha$ increases (decreases), followed by the relative position of China and Brazil.

**Table 6.4**

*Elasticity of $VIP^2$ w.r.t. $\alpha$*

| Country | Elasticity $VIP^2$ w.r.t. $\alpha$ 2005 | Per Capita GDP (Relative to USA) (Per Cent) | Population (Relative to USA) | Per Capita GDP at PPP | Pop. 2005 |
|---|---|---|---|---|---|
| Canada | -0.11 | 80 | 0.1 | 31865 | 32.2 |
| Australia | -0.12 | 78 | 0.1 | 31006 | 20.3 |
| Netherlands | -0.14 | 73 | 0.1 | 28906 | 16.4 |
| Japan | -0.16 | 75 | 0.4 | 29807 | 127.9 |
| Germany | -0.17 | 71 | 0.2 | 28392 | 60.2 |
| France | -0.17 | 72 | 0.3 | 28433 | 82.6 |
| UK | -0.17 | 71 | 0.2 | 28365 | 59.7 |
| Italy | -0.18 | 69 | 0.1 | 27390 | 22.7 |
| Taiwan | -0.18 | 70 | 0.2 | 27792 | 57.8 |
| Spain | -0.26 | 59 | 0.1 | 23392 | 41.9 |
| Korea, S. | -0.35 | 49 | 0.2 | 19316 | 48.4 |
| Russia | -0.64 | 27 | 0.5 | 10535 | 142.1 |
| Mexico | -0.69 | 24 | 0.4 | 9610 | 104.9 |
| Brazil | -0.76 | 21 | 0.6 | 8216 | 181.4 |
| China | -0.91 | 14.8 | 4.4 | 5897 | 1304.6 |
| India | -1.18 | 8.1 | 3.7 | 3216 | 1096.9 |

Another way of looking at the same results is as follows. The elasticity for high income countries is fairly small with most falling in the range of 0 to - 0.18. The elasticity is significantly lower for middle income countries, ranging from -0.2 to -1. The elasticity in the case of low income countries is below -1. This suggests that the band of uncertainty in measuring power potential using our index $VIP^2$ is considerably higher in the case of low income countries and this uncertainty declines as a country's per capita income rises.

Given the higher uncertainty in the measure of power potential of poorer countries, we hypothesise that alliances, formal or informal, can make much more difference to their actual power than they do for high income countries.

## 7. POTENTIAL GLOBAL POWERS

A comparison of Table 6.1 and 6.4 also brings out clearly that India and China are still relatively poor countries and their high rank in the global power club is due to their large population (relative to the USA and other countries) and despite their relatively low per capita income. The other side of this coin is that they have the greatest potential for increasing power, by raising their per capita income. For instance, if Russia's and Brazils per capita income was raised to the level of the USA, their 'power potential' would still be 50 per cent and 60 per cent that of the USA respectively. In contrast, China and India's power potential would equal that of the USA if their per capita income was about 50 per cent of that of the USA today.

The potential for closing the power gap is illustrated in Figure 6.1, which shows all countries with the greatest gap between their share of world GDP at PPP and their share of the world population. India, China and Indonesia have the largest negative gap, while USA, Japan and Germany have the largest positive gap followed by France, UK and Italy. The other countries in the global power club such as Russia and Brazil have negligible gaps and are consequently not shown here. Indonesia is still not a member of the global power club, and will only become a serious contender once it reaches there in the next two decades or so. Among the members of the global power club, India and China have the greatest gap (Table 6.4 and Figure 6.1) and therefore, the greatest opportunity for closing it.

Population changes slowly over time and UN population projections till 2050 do not show major changes in relative population, with the exception of Russia and Japan whose population will decline by 25 per cent and India whose population will increase to equal that of China. Thus, the major increases in power potential will come only through increases in per capita income relative to USA's. China and India have been among the 10 fastest growing countries in the world for the past 25 years. Virmani (1999b and c) had forecast that they are likely to be among the 3-5 fastest growing economies in the next two decades. Thus, the current unipolar world can only become bipolar or tripolar over the next 25 to 50 years if either or both of these countries continue to grow at a much faster rate than the USA. Otherwise, it will remain unipolar, as there are few signs of the EU turning into a virtual State that could act as another pole. The reason is that the larger countries of the EU would have to emasculate themselves in the process of transferring power to the EU virtual State and the people of these countries are not likely to agree to do so in the next few decades.

**FIGURE 6.1**

*Global Imbalance: GDP Share–Population Share*

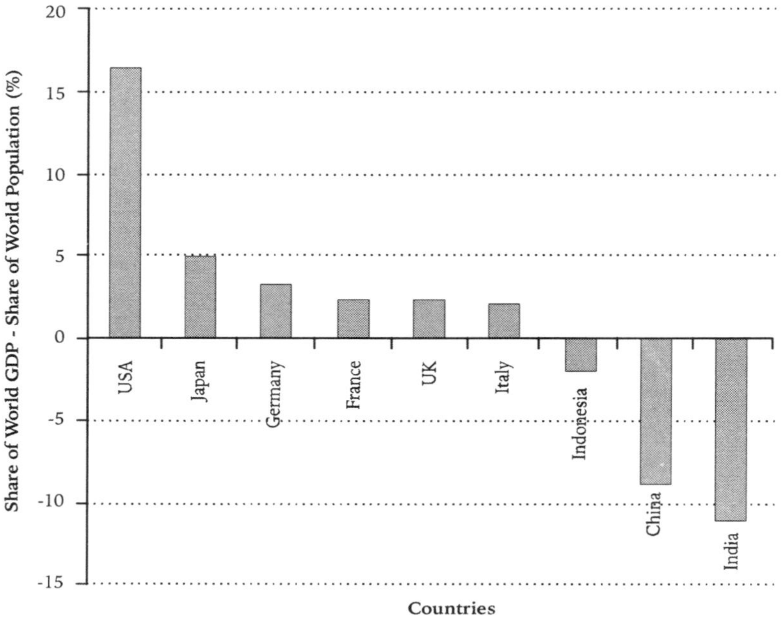

Table 6.1 (also) gives the projected evolution of the power potential of members of the global $VIP^2$ club. The growth rate assumptions are primarily those used in Virmani (2005a) (Appendix A8.2 to chapter 8). A few minor corrections are made for the period 2006 to 2008 because new data is available from WDI and IMF WEO. As noted, China will become the second strongest global power and continue to catch up with the USA, reaching about 50 per cent of the USA's power potential by 2025.

The other noteworthy change is the projected rise in India's power ranking over the next 25 years. India will become more powerful than Italy in about five years, and France and UK in about seven years. In about 10 years (2016) it is projected to become more powerful than Germany. By 2022, India's power potential will exceed 20 per cent, making it a (potential) global power along with China and Japan (in addition to the USA). As shown in chapter 5 (Virmani, 2005b) and reflected in our projections, no other country has the potential to join the ranks of global powers over the next 25 years. Within 20 years India's power potential will exceed that of Japan (Figure 6.2).

## FIGURE 6.2

*India: An Emerging Global Power*

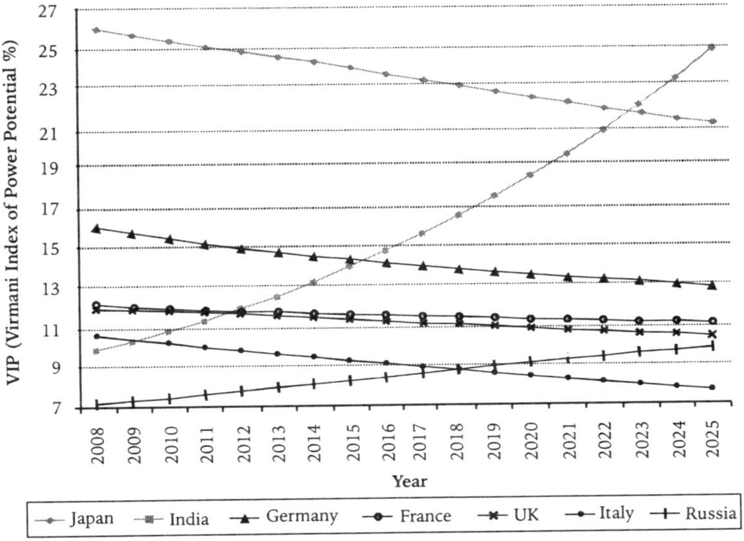

## 8. GLOBAL POWER AND UNSC

Virmani (2004e) has argued that the 'natural balance of power' as measured by the relative size of GDP (at PPP) or 'power potential' is a possible basis for reform of the UNSC. In principle, either the $VIP^2$ or GDP (at PPP) could be used as benchmark or criterion for membership of the UNSC. As permanent veto-yielding membership of the Security Council at the time the UN was formed was based on victory in WW II, $VIP^2$ would appear to be the favoured criterion. The inclusion of China in the original UNSC and recent calls for regional representation in an expanded UNSC on the other hand, imply that population should get greater weight. This suggests the use of the GDP criterion, which gives greater weight to population.

To be considered for UNSC permanent membership with veto power, either a country's GDP (at PPP) or its $VIP^2$ or both, must be greater than the GDP/$VIP^2$ of the lowest ranked member of the current UNSC, namely Russia. Using the data for 2005, only four countries, Japan, Germany, Italy and India, satisfy both criteria. Canada's $VIP^2$ is higher than Russia's but its GDP is lower.

If the current (2005) power potential and GDP is the basis for veto-bearing permanent membership of the UNSC, Japan has the strongest case, given that it has the highest power potential and largest GDP. Germany has a stronger case than India or Italy because its power potential is much higher, even though its GDP is lower than India's. Among the last two India has a better case than Italy, given its significantly higher GDP and only one rank lower power potential. UNSC reform does not, however, occur very frequently. The issue of UNSC reform has come up after 50 years and choices made today could remain in place for another 25 years or more. Therefore, any additions to the UNSC must take account of the likely evolution of power potential over this period. As shown by the projections in Figure 6.2 (and Table 6.1), India's claim to permanent membership of the UNSC is stronger than that of Germany's as its GDP is already larger than Germany's and its power potential will exceed Germany's in about 11 years and Japan's in about 18 years. India's GDP will become larger than Japan's in the next few years and is projected to be 1.5 times Japan's in 10 years. Given a time horizon of 20 years,

India has a stronger case than Japan. India's case becomes even stronger if giving representation to the poor of this world is an additional criterion, as India with about half the world's poor is in the best position to represent them. This is partly offset for Japan if reward for UN contributions is given weight.[18]

## 9. CONCLUSIONS

In this chapter we presented a simple index of power potential, the $VIP^2$ that can be easily applied to any one of the 200 or so countries for which GDP and population data is available. The index measures potential power relative to the USA, which is therefore has an index value of 100 per cent. We specify benchmark values of the index for a country to be considered a global power (20 per cent) or a regional power (5 per cent). We find that there are currently two potential global powers, China and Japan in addition to the undisputed and unique USA. Germany, which was a potential global power till a decade ago, is no longer one.

As expected, the largest number of regional powers are found among the rich countries of Europe, namely Germany, France, UK, Italy and Spain (somewhat more surprisingly). Canada, another rich country meets the grade, while Australia just misses it today but is likely to meet it in a few years. Asia is clearly a rival to Europe in that it now has two global powers and three regional powers, India, S. Korea and Australia. Brazil is the sole regional power in Latin America, while no country in Africa or the Middle–East meets the criterion.

Projecting into the future, the number of global powers will increase from three to four in less than 20 years, with the addition of India. At that point, China's power potential would be about 65 per cent of the USA's while the sum of Japan and India's power potential would be 3/4th of China's. Virmani (2005a) forecasts, that the world

---

18. China is highly likely to veto Japan's permanent membership (with veto power) and be neutral/abstain in the case of India. The other veto bearing members would probably not veto either country (if only the two were being considered for veto power).

would become bipolar by 2025 and tripolar by 2050.[19] This is elaborated in this chapter. Recent developments in US-India relations suggest that the US will support faster economic and technological development of India, so that India's rise to global power is accelerated. This will delay the onset of a bipolar world and accelerate the arrival of a tripolar one. In other words the period of bi-polarity will be shortened, an outcome that is in the mutual interest of both the USA and India.

Thus, the bold decision of President Bush to remove all restrictions on the flow of commercial nuclear technology to India and to facilitate the flow of dual use and strategic technology could transform power relations in Asia and the world just as President Nixon's opening to China did.[20] It must be remembered, however, that after the first opening, it took China 10 years to emerge from its isolation, 20 years to make its mark in the global economy and 30 years to become a global power. During this period, it did not let future power go to its head and worked modestly and diligently to acquire the economic and technological wherewithal from every country including the USA.[21]

Finally, the emergence of China and India on the global scene may force the residents of the large countries of the EU to reconsider their stand on EU integration. Twenty years from now, they may decide to set up an elected EU government based on direct elections by all citizens of the EU with complete powers to act on all matters connected with international relations (defence, foreign affairs, international economic relations). Such an EU would be a global power and the world would be tripolar in 2025 and quadri-polar in 2050.

---

19. A game theoretic approach suggests other possibilities. For instance, one speculative scenario could be for India and Japan to unite in an alliance to make the world Tripolar in 2025. If we add Russia and S. Korea to this alliance, the aggregate power potential almost equals that of China. Such an alliance is even more fanciful. There is little likelihood of this scenario fructifying, as long as Japan remains closely tied to the USA, in the US-Japan defence pact. Another even more speculative scenario could be for China, Japan and India to combine to challenge US power in Asia. This scenario is even less likely as long as China remains a one party communist party ruled state that nurses strong historical grievances against Japan.

20. This will, in my view, be one of the decisions that mark President Bush's (and his Indian counterpart Dr. Manmohan Singh's) place in history.

21. There is a lesson in this for India. Size gives it an advantage that smaller less populated countries do not possess, but the large number of poor people reduce the influence and respect that it enjoys. Though projections indicate that size will increase and poverty, as currently defined, will be eliminated in 15 to 20 years, analysts should be realistic, remembering both the strengths and weaknesses.

## Appendix A6.1

*Global Ranking by the Virmani Index of Power Potential ($VIP^2$): 113 Countries*

| | $VIP^2$ Rank | | GDP Rank | | $VIP^2$ (Per Cent) | | GDP, PPP (Mi.) | |
|---|---|---|---|---|---|---|---|---|
| | 2003 | 2005 | 2003 | 2005 | 2003 | 2005 | 2003 | 2005 |
| **N. America** | | | | | | | | |
| USA | 1 | 1 | 1 | 1 | 100 | 100 | 10923376 | 11780533 |
| Canada | 8 | 9 | 11 | 11 | 8.0 | 7.8 | 970326 | 1027421 |
| **Europe** | | | | | | | | |
| Germany | 4 | 4 | 5 | 5 | 18 | 17 | 2291007 | 2346285 |
| France | 5 | 5 | 6 | 6 | 13 | 12 | 1654018 | 1712405 |
| United Kingdom | 6 | 6 | 7 | 7 | 13 | 12 | 1610579 | 1693698 |
| Italy | 7 | 7 | 8 | 8 | 12 | 11 | 1563332 | 1582092 |
| Russia | 11 | 10 | 10 | 9 | 6.0 | 6.5 | 1323839 | 1497208 |
| Spain | 10 | 11 | 13 | 13 | 6.5 | 6.4 | 920292 | 979184 |
| Netherlands | 17 | 17 | 19 | 24 | 3.9 | 3.6 | 476454 | 487945 |
| Poland | 21 | 19 | 24 | 23 | 2.2 | 2.5 | 434626 | 507713 |
| Belgium | 18 | 20 | 29 | 30 | 2.3 | 2.4 | 294001 | 323570 |
| Austria | 22 | 26 | 33 | 34 | 2.0 | 2.0 | 243458 | 266116 |
| Sweden | 27 | 27 | 34 | 35 | 1.9 | 1.9 | 239576 | 265706 |
| Switzerland | 26 | 28 | 36 | 37 | 1.9 | 1.9 | 224557 | 245233 |
| Norway | 30 | 31 | 42 | 42 | 1.6 | 1.6 | 171850 | 190290 |
| Greece | 31 | 32 | 37 | 36 | 1.5 | 1.6 | 220148 | 247535 |
| Ireland | 34 | 33 | 47 | 47 | 1.4 | 1.5 | 150725 | 174166 |
| Denmark | 33 | 34 | 43 | 45 | 1.4 | 1.5 | 169508 | 186303 |
| Portugal | 35 | 37 | 40 | 41 | 1.2 | 1.2 | 189303 | 206075 |
| Finland | 37 | 39 | 49 | 51 | 1.1 | 1.2 | 143951 | 159573 |
| Ukraine | 41 | 40 | 31 | 29 | 0.9 | 1.2 | 265534 | 332741 |
| Czech Rep. | 40 | 41 | 44 | 43 | 1.0 | 1.1 | 166877 | 187241 |
| Hungry | 43 | 43 | 48 | 48 | 0.8 | 0.9 | 147705 | 166531 |
| Romania | 50 | 49 | 46 | 46 | 0.6 | 0.7 | 158234 | 183257 |
| Slovak Rep. | 55 | 56 | 58 | 59 | 0.4 | 0.4 | 72730 | 83443 |
| Luxembourg | 58 | 58 | 87 | 87 | 0.3 | 0.3 | 27910 | 31167 |
| Kuwait | 60 | 60 | 72 | 73 | 0.3 | 0.3 | 43248 | 47783 |
| Slovenia | 62 | 62 | 75 | 76 | 0.2 | 0.3 | 38204 | 43407 |
| Croatia | 63 | 63 | 67 | 68 | 0.2 | 0.3 | 49249 | 55883 |
| Belarus | 65 | 64 | 64 | 62 | 0.2 | 0.3 | 59803 | 70518 |

*Contd. ...*

*Contd. ....*

| | $VIP^2$ Rank | | GDP Rank | | $VIP^2$ (Per Cent) | | GDP, PPP (Mi.) | |
|---|---|---|---|---|---|---|---|---|
| | 2003 | 2005 | 2003 | 2005 | 2003 | 2005 | 2003 | 2005 |
| Lithuania | 68 | 65 | 73 | 72 | 0.2 | 0.2 | 40420 | 48616 |
| Latvia | 76 | 77 | 93 | 91 | 0.1 | 0.1 | 23836 | 28266 |
| Estonia | 80 | 79 | 101 | 101 | 0.1 | 0.1 | 18318 | 21457 |
| Cyprus | 81 | 83 | 106 | 109 | 0.1 | 0.1 | 14874 | 16656 |
| Bosnia, Herzegovin | 83 | 85 | 92 | 90 | 0.1 | 0.1 | 24703 | 28327 |
| Iceland | 90 | 90 | 113 | 113 | 0.1 | 0.1 | 9029 | 10428 |
| Macedonia, FYR | 102 | 101 | 109 | 110 | 0.1 | 0.1 | 13922 | 15899 |
| Albania | 105 | 103 | 107 | 106 | 0.0 | 0.1 | 14526 | 17179 |
| **Asia** | | | | | | | | |
| Japan | 2 | 2 | 3 | 3 | 28 | 27 | 3567804 | 3697387 |
| China | 3 | 3 | 2 | 2 | 22 | 25 | 6446033 | 7693663 |
| India | 9 | 8 | 4 | 4 | 7.8 | 8.5 | 3078024 | 3527323 |
| Korea, Rep. | 13 | 13 | 14 | 14 | 5.5 | 5.5 | 861042 | 934875 |
| Australia | 14 | 14 | 16 | 17 | 4.8 | 4.7 | 589116 | 629856 |
| Taiwan | 16 | 15 | 17 | 16 | 4.0 | 4.5 | 545437 | 629858 |
| Thailand | 24 | 22 | 21 | 19 | 1.9 | 2.2 | 470992 | 558941 |
| Indonesia | 23 | 25 | 15 | 15 | 2.0 | 2.1 | 721533 | 802314 |
| Hong Kong | 32 | 30 | 41 | 40 | 1.4 | 1.6 | 185250 | 217541 |
| Malaysia | 39 | 35 | 35 | 33 | 1.1 | 1.2 | 235662 | 280258 |
| Philippines | 38 | 38 | 25 | 25 | 1.1 | 1.2 | 352191 | 405532 |
| Singapore | 46 | 44 | 55 | 55 | 0.8 | 0.9 | 104046 | 124111 |
| Pakistan | 48 | 48 | 26 | 26 | 0.7 | 0.8 | 311258 | 368273 |
| New Zealand | 49 | 50 | 57 | 57 | 0.6 | 0.7 | 90538 | 101085 |
| Vietnam | 53 | 51 | 38 | 38 | 0.5 | 0.6 | 202502 | 243545 |
| Bangladesh | 52 | 52 | 32 | 32 | 0.5 | 0.5 | 244402 | 286447 |
| Kazakhstan | 56 | 55 | 56 | 56 | 0.4 | 0.5 | 99254 | 123307 |
| Sri Lanka | 67 | 67 | 59 | 58 | 0.2 | 0.2 | 72654 | 84144 |
| Turkmenistan | 77 | 78 | 85 | 84 | 0.1 | 0.1 | 28881 | 34896 |
| Azerbaijan | 86 | 81 | 84 | 82 | 0.1 | 0.1 | 29782 | 38024 |
| Bahrain | 87 | 86 | 111 | 112 | 0.1 | 0.1 | 12888 | 15044 |
| Uzbekistan | 84 | 87 | 71 | 71 | 0.1 | 0.1 | 44638 | 49265 |
| Nepal | 98 | 99 | 78 | 79 | 0.1 | 0.1 | 35015 | 39820 |
| Cambodia | 100 | 100 | 88 | 88 | 0.1 | 0.1 | 27856 | 31091 |
| **Latin America & Carribean** | | | | | | | | |
| Brazil | 12 | 12 | 9 | 10 | 5.7 | 5.7 | 1375756 | 1555413 |

*Contd. ...*

*Contd. ...*

| | $VIP^2$ Rank | | GDP Rank | | $VIP^2$ (Per Cent) | | GDP, PPP (Mi.) | |
|---|---|---|---|---|---|---|---|---|
| | 2003 | 2005 | 2003 | 2005 | 2003 | 2005 | 2003 | 2005 |
| Mexico | 15 | 15 | 12 | 12 | 4.2 | 4.2 | 937836 | 1058063 |
| Argentina | 19 | 18 | 23 | 22 | 2.3 | 2.4 | 445148 | 520588 |
| Colombia | 36 | 36 | 27 | 27 | 1.2 | 1.1 | 298799 | 339492 |
| Chile | 45 | 45 | 45 | 44 | 0.8 | 0.8 | 162067 | 186926 |
| Peru | 51 | 53 | 51 | 50 | 0.5 | 0.5 | 142791 | 163760 |
| Venezuela | 54 | 54 | 53 | 52 | 0.4 | 0.5 | 126279 | 153908 |
| Dominican Rep. | 64 | 68 | 65 | 65 | 0.2 | 0.2 | 59622 | 64007 |
| Costa Rica | 70 | 71 | 74 | 75 | 0.2 | 0.2 | 38469 | 43414 |
| Guatemala | 72 | 73 | 66 | 67 | 0.2 | 0.1 | 51056 | 56732 |
| Uruguay | 75 | 76 | 86 | 86 | 0.1 | 0.1 | 27987 | 33471 |
| El Salvador | 79 | 82 | 83 | 85 | 0.1 | 0.1 | 31237 | 34307 |
| Panama | 87 | 87 | 98 | 98 | 0.1 | 0.1 | 20452 | 23460 |
| Paraguay | 84 | 88 | 89 | 89 | 0.1 | 0.1 | 26430 | 29064 |
| Trinidad, Tobago | 93 | 92 | 107 | 107 | 0.1 | 0.1 | 14132 | 16759 |
| Bolivia | 100 | 101 | 95 | 95 | 0.1 | 0.1 | 22800 | 25977 |
| Honduras | 106 | 106 | 99 | 101 | 0.0 | 0.0 | 18572 | 21060 |
| | | | **Sub-saharan Africa** | | | | | |
| South Africa | 20 | 21 | 20 | 21 | 2.3 | 2.4 | 474137 | 528279 |
| Nigeria | 66 | 66 | 50 | 49 | 0.2 | 0.2 | 143238 | 165749 |
| Equatorial Guinea | 82 | 70 | 112 | 100 | 0.1 | 0.2 | 12599 | 22267 |
| Sudan | 74 | 74 | 61 | 61 | 0.1 | 0.2 | 64088 | 77205 |
| Ecuador | 73 | 75 | 69 | 69 | 0.1 | 0.1 | 47362 | 54536 |
| Ghana | 78 | 80 | 70 | 70 | 0.1 | 0.1 | 46253 | 53670 |
| Angola | 92 | 84 | 82 | 78 | 0.1 | 0.1 | 31701 | 42776 |
| Cameroon | 91 | 92 | 80 | 80 | 0.1 | 0.1 | 34077 | 39428 |
| Mauritius | 95 | 95 | 110 | 111 | 0.1 | 0.1 | 13795 | 15847 |
| Ethiopia | 99 | 96 | 68 | 66 | 0.1 | 0.1 | 48780 | 60423 |
| Uganda | 96 | 97 | 77 | 77 | 0.1 | 0.1 | 36827 | 43350 |
| Botswana | 97 | 98 | 105 | 107 | 0.1 | 0.1 | 15010 | 17096 |
| Congo Dem. Rep. | 106 | 104 | 76 | 74 | 0.0 | 0.1 | 37026 | 44240 |
| Kenya | 104 | 105 | 81 | 83 | 0.1 | 0.1 | 33099 | 36849 |
| Zimbabwe | 103 | 106 | 90 | 97 | 0.1 | 0.0 | 25335 | 25700 |
| Cote d'lvoire | 108 | 108 | 91 | 92 | 0.0 | 0.0 | 24857 | 27696 |
| Mozambique | 110 | 109 | 98 | 98 | 0.0 | 0.0 | 20984 | 25520 |
| Guinea | 109 | 110 | 104 | 105 | 0.0 | 0.0 | 16582 | 18538 |

*Contd. ...*

*Contd. ...*

| | *VIP² Rank* | | *GDP Rank* | | *VIP² (Per Cent)* | | *GDP, PPP (Mi.)* | |
|---|---|---|---|---|---|---|---|---|
| | *2003* | *2005* | *2003* | *2005* | *2003* | *2005* | *2003* | *2005* |
| Senegal | 111 | 111 | 103 | 103 | 0.0 | 0.0 | 16875 | 19869 |
| Tanzania | 112 | 112 | 97 | 94 | 0.0 | 0.0 | 22300 | 26523 |
| **N. Africa & Middle East** | | | | | | | | |
| Turkey | 25 | 23 | 18 | 18 | 1.9 | 2.1 | 478891 | 565189 |
| Iran (IIR) | 28 | 24 | 22 | 20 | 1.8 | 2.1 | 464394 | 547111 |
| Saudi Arabia | 29 | 29 | 28 | 28 | 1.6 | 1.7 | 297967 | 336845 |
| Israel | 42 | 42 | 52 | 53 | 0.9 | 0.9 | 133981 | 150959 |
| Egypt (EAR) | 44 | 46 | 30 | 31 | 0.8 | 0.9 | 266853 | 303825 |
| Algeria | 47 | 47 | 39 | 39 | 0.7 | 0.8 | 194389 | 222727 |
| Morocco | 57 | 57 | 54 | 54 | 0.4 | 0.4 | 120578 | 135682 |
| Tunisia | 59 | 59 | 60 | 60 | 0.3 | 0.3 | 70863 | 82522 |
| Bulgaria | 61 | 61 | 63 | 64 | 0.3 | 0.3 | 60483 | 70313 |
| Oman | 69 | 69 | 79 | 81 | 0.2 | 0.2 | 34960 | 38960 |
| Syrian Arab Rep | 71 | 72 | 62 | 63 | 0.2 | 0.2 | 62165 | 70384 |
| Lebanon | 89 | 91 | 95 | 95 | 0.1 | 0.1 | 22820 | 26177 |
| Jordan | 93 | 94 | 94 | 93 | 0.1 | 0.1 | 22929 | 26809 |
| Yemen, Rep. | 113 | 113 | 102 | 104 | 0.0 | 0.0 | 17044 | 18897 |

*Sources*: For GDP at purchasing power parity and population or per capita GDP: World Bank, World Development Indicators, 2005 (2003 data) and IMF WEO, April 2005 (for 2005 projection). Rest of the data is from Virmani (2005) and author's calculations.

# 7

# Economic Performance, Power Potential and Global Governance

*Towards a New International Order*

## 1. INTRODUCTION

The end of the colonial era, coinciding with the end of the Second World-War, has led, in the second half of the 20th century, to a post colonial world in which conquest of other nations and people is no longer seen as a legitimate means of expressing national power. As Francis Fukuyama noted (1989, 1992), the strengthening of the democratic impulse and recognition of individual (as against states') rights has played an important role in this process. Over the same period, the forces of globalisation have increased the mobility of capital, goods and services and technology across countries. Temporary movement of people across countries in the form of tourism has increased dramatically. As a result, both, competition and co-operation among countries and their people has increasingly focussed on the economic domain. Social cultural interaction has increased and 'soft power' has become more important.[1]

This does not, however, mean that the role of military power in relations between states has been eliminated. The threat of use of force can itself increase risk and thus harm economic interests and

---

Some of these ideas were first outlined in remarks made while chairing a session of the Indo-German Dialogue on Security Issues: "Dynamics of the Future International Order," organised by the Institute of Defence Studies and Analysis and Konrad Adenauer Foundation, at IIC annex on November 29-30, 1999. The relationship to Global Governance Issues was outlined at an EU-India-USA Trilogue organised by the Hans Siedel and Konrad Adenauer Foundations in Brussels on 30th September, 2004. My thanks to K. Subrahmaniam,Vice Admiral Prem Vir Das (retd.), B.K. Zutshi and Nitin Desai for their detailed comments and to Air Commodore (retd.) Jasjit Singh Henry A. Kissinger, Shashank, Lalit Mansingh, Alexander Nicoll, Admiral Gulab Hirnandani (retd.), Bharat Karnad and Brahma Chellaney for comments on earlier versions of the chapter. Any shortcomings remain the author's responsibility.

1. The first use of this word is attributed to Joseph Nye. See also Held *et al.*, (1999).

well being. The nature of this role, therefore, needs to be redefined in the 21st century. As Paul Kennedy (1988) emphasised, "Economic power is the foundation of national power." Even though military power disproportionate to economic power can be used to enhance national power for a certain period of time, this is not sustainable over long periods. This is particularly so in the post-colonial world, as the option of colonial conquest to expand economic power and thus eliminate the discrepancy has virtually disappeared.

Diplomacy, partnerships, strategic relationships and alliances also retain their relevance. Gerald Segal (1999) pointed to the skill with which China has mastered what he called the 'Diplomacy of Power'. The skill lay in making the established world powers believe that China is the second most powerful nation in the world (which it is in GDPppp), rather than the seventh (as per GDPus$). India, in contrast, has been singularly ineffective in making the world recognise it as one of the five largest powers.[2] Its democratic, open and free civic and political system would entitle it to be part of a new democratic concert, perhaps an expansion or modification of the G7 (G8).

This chapter argues that the new order must be based on natural power potential defined primarily in economic terms. The nineteenth century concept of 'balance of power' must gradually give way to the 'natural balance of power' that has economic size at its base. This balance of power can also be a 'Stable Balance' if the international order recognises, promotes and preserves the natural balance. There will, however, be heightened risks during the transition because of the tectonic shifts taking place in national power potential. To minimise the risks, we need to build a new system of global governance that reflects the natural power potential. The old systems of global governance like the United Nations and its institutions, are widely recognised to reflect the power relations that existed at the end of the Second World War. The world has changed dramatically since then. The most important of these is the rise in the share of Asia in the global economy and the gradual decline of the shares of the USA and Europe. This trend will continue in the 21st century and become more prominent. The new global system of governance must reflect these shifts in the global economy if a stable and peaceful world order is to

2. It has been included in the Group of 20 (G20) formed in 1999.

be established in the 21st century. Global institutions must either be reformed to reflect the new realities or new institutions built.

The rest of the chapter is in four sections. The next section defines and presents trends in the relative size of large countries. It then goes on to define a simple measure of national power potential (NPP) based on economic concepts. Section 3 explores the concept of natural balance of power. Section 4 spells out the implications of these for reforming the structures of global governance in the light of certain principles of fairness and realism. Section 5 presents economic projections for the largest economies and their likely NPP. Based on these, it suggests the likely shift in the global balance of power and explores some of the implications for the USA, EU, Japan and India. Section 6 concludes the chapter.

## 2. ECONOMIC SIZE AND POWER

As already discussed in chapter 6, Tellis *et al.*, (2000) have developed a comprehensive and complex model for measuring power in terms of the ability of a state to achieve and sustain global hegemony. In their model military capability is the outcome of an interaction between national resources and national performance. National resources consist of five building blocks: technology enterprise, human resources, financial/capital resources and physical resources. National performance contains three factors: infrastructural capacity, ideational resources and ideational resources that augment or detract from the utilisation of these natural resources.

This chapter takes an economic perspective and applies the principle of Occam's razor, i.e. it presents the simplest possible indicators of power grounded in economic reasoning.

The Gross Domestic Product (GDP) of a country contains different types of goods and services among which 'public goods' like defence/ military (police, roads). The potential for producing military related goods and services is therefore also captured by the total GDP. Military capability is, however, the outcome of an interaction between this potential, the special external constraints that apply to military technology and a nation's 'choice' on how much of the output should be in the form of military goods and services. The GDP of a country is, therefore, a good measure of economic strength and a basic measure of military potential. The relative GDP of two counties is therefore the simplest measure of relative NPP. A more general measure of overall NPP is presented subsequently that has this as a special case.

## 2.1 Relative Size: GDP at PPP

The GDP of an economy combines population (N) and per capita income (y), in the most natural way. Namely,

$$\text{GDP (Y)} = \text{Population} * \text{Per Capita GDP} = N * y \quad (1)$$

Population N represents the manpower potential which can be used for both economic (workers) and military (soldiers) purposes. Per capita GDP y represents the average productivity of the population and summarises its diverse capabilities. These two variables have often been used historically as indicators of national power, along with GDP.[3]

The GDP of each country is normally measured in local currency units (LCU) and must be converted to a common unit of account before it can be compared with another. The best way to compare two country's economic size and per capita income is to measure GDP (Y) and per capita GDP (y) at purchasing power parity (PPP). Technically this method solves the index number problem of comparing two different baskets of goods and services. Normally, this is done by using a common set of prices to aggregate all goods and services in each basket. This is the approach taken by Heston-Summers in deriving PPP estimates for countries. These estimates are available for most countries from 1975 onwards. The ratio of GDP measured at PPP is, therefore, the best available measure of relative economic size and the simplest measure of relative NNP.

A common method of converting GDP measured in LCU to a common currency (US$ say) is by using the current US$/LCU exchange rate. The argument of those using this measure of GDP (X) is based on a theoretical construct that is applicable in the (very) long run. That is, if there are no controls or taxes on imports and exports, relative prices of all goods in all countries will converge and the exchange rate will reach a PPP equilibrium. Clearly, if and when all

3. Singer, Bremer and Stuckey (1972).

prices converge across countries, this measure is equally good or even better and can be used to compare GDP of different countries. It can, therefore, be used to convert and compare the different baskets of goods and services (X). Econometric tests have however shown that the exchange rate reaches a PPP equilibrium (even for the set of OECD economies) only over long periods (20-30 years). For countries at very different levels of development, relative prices of non-tradable services will not converge as long as per-capita incomes have not converged. Nevertheless, the GDP at current exchange rate (X) is relevant for comparing international trade (exports and imports) and financial flows between countries as these take place at the current exchange rate.

## 2.2 Evolution of Global Economy

### *2.2.1 Trend in Shares of World GDP*

During the last 30 years or so, the weight of the world economy has shifted from the USA and developed Europe (OECD) to Asia (South, Southeast and East). Within Asia the weight has similarly shifted from Japan towards China and India (Figure 7.1 and Figure 7.2). OECD Europe has seen the greatest decline in global GDP share by 4.9 per cent points, followed by USA and Japan with a decline of about 1 per cent points each. The share of Latin America and Africa in world GDP has also declined by about 1 per cent point each. With the gradual inclusion of much of E. Europe (former USSR) in the European Union and the faster growth of these economies, the sharp downtrend in European Union (and Europe's) share is likely to be halted and perhaps reversed. Any reversal is however, likely to be short-lived because of declining populations in many European countries.

Within Asia, the declining global share of Japan since 1990 has been more than made up by the rising share of China and India (Figure 7.2). During the seventies and eighties ASEAN, and during the eighties S. Korea along with China and India also contributed to the rising share of Asia in world GDP. Between 1975 and 2002, Japan's share of world GDP fell by 1 per cent point while that of S. Korea, ASEAN, India and China rose by 1 per cent, 1.2 per cent, 2.2 per cent and 9.2 per cent respectively. Thus, India's gains since 1980

## FIGURE 7.1

*Shifts in the World Economy: GDP Shares at PPP (Current Int. $)*

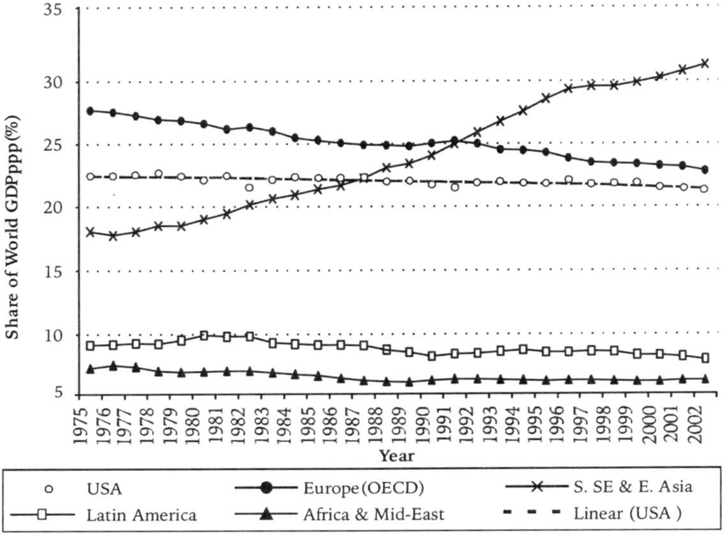


## FIGURE 7.2

*Share of Asian Countries in World GDP at PPP (Current Int. $)*

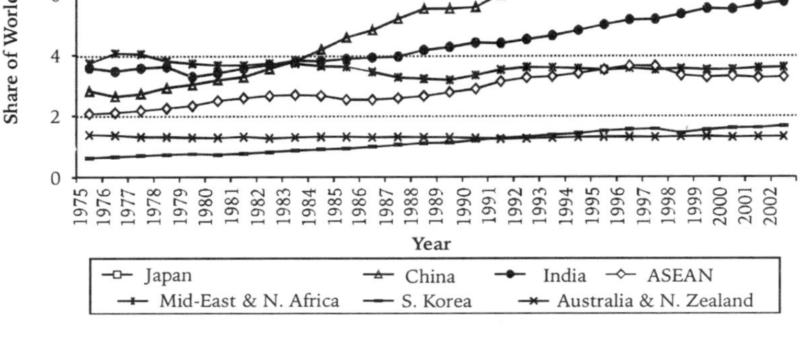

have been much larger than ASEAN and S. Korea but much less than those of China.

### 2.2.2 *High Growth Economies*

Underpinning these trends in the rising share of Asia in the global economy are the fastest growing economies in the world. The 10 fastest growing economies in the world during the period 1980 to 2003 were in Asia (including the mid-east). Though several scholars have pointed out, and the IMF and World Bank have acknowledged, the growth rate of the Chinese economy may be over-estimated by about 2 per cent points during the 1980s and 1990s, no adjustment has been made for this factor in Table 7.1. Even with such an adjustment, China with an average growth rate of 7.5 per cent per annum is the fastest growing economy during this period. The growth performance of what were called the NICs, Singapore, S. Korea, Taiwan, China and Hong Kong has long been recognised, even though the last is no longer in the top ten (12th rank). The growth performance of the ASEAN countries, Malaysia, Thailand, and Indonesia was recognised and appreciated, along with that of the NICs in the World Bank's Asia Miracle Study.

**Table 7.1**

*Average GDP Growth: 1980 to 2003*

| *Table A: GDP Growth (1980 to 2003)* | | | *Table B: Per Capita GDP Growth (1980 to 2003)* | | |
|---|---|---|---|---|---|
| *Economy* | *Rank* | *Avg.* | *Economy* | *Rank* | *Avg.* |
| China, PR | 1 | 9.5 | China, PR | 1 | 8.2 |
| Singapore | 2 | 6.7 | Korea, Rep. | 2 | 5.6 |
| Korea, Rep. | 3 | 6.7 | Taiwan, China | 3 | 5.3 |
| Vietnam | 4 | 6.5 | Thailand | 4 | 4.7 |
| Taiwan, China | 5 | 6.5 | Vietnam | 5 | 4.6 |
| Oman | 6 | 6.5 | Ireland | 6 | 4.5 |
| Malaysia | 7 | 6.2 | Singapore | 7 | 4.2 |
| Thailand | 8 | 6.0 | Hong Kong | 8 | 3.9 |
| India | 9 | 5.7 | India | 9 | 3.7 |
| Indonesia | 10 | 5.3 | Luxembourg | 10 | 3.7 |
| | | | Indonesia | 11 | 3.6 |
| | | | Malaysia | 12 | 3.6 |

*Note:* Authors calculations based on data from WDI, 2003 and WEO April 2004.

Vietnam ranked 4th and India 9th have been referred to along with China as the new Asian miracle economies. Few still know that India has been the 9th fastest growing economy for the 24 years from 1980 and not just since 1992. There is also very little volatility in this growth rate, compared to the other Asian economies that have grown faster than India. As a consequence of the Asian crisis of 1998 and the competitive pressure from China in terms of manufacturing FDI and Exports, most of the ASEAN economies as well as S. Korea have slowed and are unlikely to grow as fast as they have in the past. Thus, India is likely to move up the growth rankings even if its growth rate remains unchanged.

### *2.2.3 Relative Size in 2002*

At the start of the new millennium, the ranking of the 20 largest economies in terms of size is shown in Table 7.2. USA, the largest economy, is almost two times the size of the next largest economy, China, and about three times the third largest economy, Japan. The fourth largest economy, India, is a little over one-quarter the size of the US economy. The next five positions are taken by the big four of Europe: Germany (which was overtaken by India at the end of the decade), UK, France and Italy. Brazil and Russia bring up the rear of the 10 largest economies. It should be noted that Japan, India, Germany and Brazil have staked their (joint) claim to permanent seats on a reformed UN Security Council. This would leave Italy, whose economy is 12.5 per cent larger than that of Brazil, as the only one among the top 10 without a permanent seat on a 'new' Security Council.

Relative size should not, however, be confused with average income. As the size of GDP is the product of population and per capita income, and India and China are the two poorest among the 10 largest economies, their large economic size is based on their large populations. These two, along with Indonesia, are the three poorest among the 20 largest economies (Table 7.2). The fact that two of the five largest economies in the world have much lower per capita income than the other large economies is, historically speaking, a very unusual situation, however. Despite the increase in their size and power they will remain much poorer than the currently rich countries for at least a century. This may affect the interplay between them in a manner different from what has been historically observed.

## Table 7.2

*Relative Size of the 20 Largest Economies in 2002*

| Economy | GDP at PPP | | | | GDP at Exchange Rate | | | | $Z=(Y+X)/2$ | | $NIP^2$ ($\beta=1.4$) | | Pop. |
|---|---|---|---|---|---|---|---|---|---|---|---|---|---|
| | (Int.$Bi.) | Rank | World Share | P. Capita | (US$Bi.) | Rank | World Share | P. Capita | World Share | Rank | World Share | Rank | World Share |
| USA | 10308 | 1 | 21.3% | 35746 | 10383 | 1 | 32.3% | 36006 | 25.7% | 1 | 27.2% | 1 | 4.7% |
| China PR | 5861 | 2 | 12.1% | 4577 | 1266 | 6 | 3.9% | 989 | 8.8% | 3 | 6.8% | 3 | 20.7% |
| Japan | 3425 | 3 | 7.1% | 26937 | 3993 | 2 | 12% | 31407 | 9.2% | 2 | 8.1% | 2 | 2.1% |
| India | 2800 | 4 | 5.8% | 2670 | 510 | 11 | 1.6% | 487 | 4.1% | 5 | 2.6% | 8 | 16.9% |
| Germany | 2236 | 5 | 4.6% | 27102 | 1984 | 3 | 6.2% | 24051 | 5.2% | 4 | 5.3% | 4 | 1.3% |
| France | 1601 | 6 | 3.3% | 26921 | 1431 | 5 | 4.5% | 24061 | 3.8% | 7 | 3.8% | 5 | 1.0% |
| UK | 1549 | 7 | 3.2% | 26155 | 1566 | 4 | 4.9% | 26445 | 3.9% | 6 | 3.6% | 6 | 1.0% |
| Italy | 1525 | 8 | 3.1% | 26429 | 1184 | 7 | 3.7% | 20528 | 3.4% | 8 | 3.6% | 7 | 0.9% |
| Brazil | 1355 | 9 | 2.8% | 7766 | 452 | 13 | 1.4% | 2593 | 2.2% | 9 | 1.9% | 10 | 2.8% |
| Russia | 1186 | 10 | 2.4% | 8229 | 347 | 16 | 1.1% | 2405 | 1.9% | 12 | 1.7% | 12 | 2.3% |
| Canada | 925 | 11 | 1.9% | 29484 | 714 | 8 | 2.2% | 22777 | 2.0% | 10 | 2.3% | 9 | 0.5% |
| Mexico | 905 | 12 | 1.9% | 8972 | 637 | 10 | 2.0% | 6320 | 1.9% | 11 | 1.4% | 14 | 1.6% |
| Spain | 878 | 13 | 1.8% | 21457 | 653 | 9 | 2.0% | 15961 | 1.9% | 13 | 1.9% | 11 | 0.7% |

Contd. ...

*Contd. ...*

| *Economy* | *GDP at PPP* | | | | *GDP at Exchange Rate* | | | | $Z=(Y+X)/2$ | | $NIP^2$ $(\beta=1.4)$ | | *Pop.* |
|---|---|---|---|---|---|---|---|---|---|---|---|---|---|
| | *(Int.$Bi.)* | *Rank* | *World Share* | *P. Capita* | *(US$Bi.)* | *Rank* | *World Share* | *P. Capita* | *World Share* | *Rank* | *World Share* | *Rank* | *World Share* |
| Korea, S. | 807 | 14 | 1.7% | 16946 | 477 | 12 | 1.5% | 10006 | 1.6% | 14 | 1.6% | 13 | 0.8% |
| Indonesia | 683 | **15** | 1.4% | 3225 | 173 | 27 | 0.5% | 817 | 1.1% | 17 | 0.7% | 18 | 3.4% |
| Australia | 556 | 16 | 1.1% | 28262 | 409 | 15 | 1.3% | 20822 | 1.2% | 15 | 1.3% | 15 | 0.3% |
| Taiwan, China | 477 | 17 | 1.0% | 21293 | 282 | 17 | 0.9% | 12586 | 0.9% | 18 | 1.0% | 17 | 0.4% |
| Netherlands | 470 | 18 | 1.0% | 29105 | 418 | 14 | 1.3% | 25886 | 1.1% | 16 | 1.1% | 16 | 0.3% |
| South Africa | 457 | 19 | 0.9% | 10074 | 104 | 35 | 0.3% | 2299 | 0.7% | 21 | | | 0.7% |
| Turkey | 445 | 20 | 0.9% | 6388 | 184 | 25 | 0.6% | 2638 | 0.8% | 19 | | | 1.1% |
| Iran | 438 | 21 | 0.9% | 6687 | 108 | 34 | 0.3% | 1652 | 0.7% | 23 | | | 1.1% |
| Thailand | 432 | 22 | 0.9% | 7009 | 127 | 31 | 0.4% | 2060 | 0.7% | 22 | | | 1.0% |
| Argentina | 413 | 23 | 0.9% | 11312 | 102 | 37 | 0.3% | 2797 | 0.6% | 25 | | | 0.6% |
| Poland | 408 | 24 | 0.8% | 10556 | 189 | 23 | 0.6% | 4894 | 0.7% | 20 | | | 0.6% |
| Philippines | 333 | 25 | 0.7% | 4171 | 78 | 43 | 0.2% | 975 | 0.5% | 30 | | | 1.3% |

*Note*: Authors calculation based on data from World Development Indicators.

## 2.3 Power Potential

Many have argued that technological prowess is a separate input into the relative power of a country. This argument has weakened with globalisation. Technological mobility with regard to civilian technology has increased dramatically during the 20th century. The extent of this mobility is apparent from the fact that the USA (and EU) have, during the 1980s and 1990s, encouraged transfer of sophisticated technology to NPT nuclear member China, the country most likely to challenge their power in the 21st century. To the extent technology is mobile, it is already reflected in GDP (and in growth). There are, however, restrictions on transfer of 'dual use' technologies and on advanced military technology, technologies that can be referred to as the 'technologies of power'. These restrictions are imposed so as to maintain an oligopoly or monopoly over strategic technology that can be translated into military power. Therefore, inherent technological prowess is still a factor in determining national power.

### 2.3.1 *Power Potential Index*

We can define a measure that gives much greater weight to technological achievement. In economic terms, per capita GDP (y), is closely correlated with capital intensity (average capital stock k), level of education/skills (h) and level of technology (T). Formally, the aggregate production function defines the relationship between these as,

$$y = T\,f(k, h, r), \tag{2}$$

Where f is a function of k, the per capita capital stock and h the per capita human capital (combination of education and skills) and r the per capita domestic availability of natural resources. Therefore, technology level T is not directly measurable, but is implicitly defined by inverting the production function, i.e.

$$T = y/f(k, h, r) \tag{3}$$

The level of technology is formally defined by T. Per capita GDP y however captures the level of technology along with the physical and human capital needed to convert this potential into actual goods and services (including military) as well as the efficiency with which it is being done. NPP can therefore be defined as a weighted average of population (N) and per capita GDP at purchasing power parity (y):

$$\text{NPP (Population)} * (\text{Per capita GDP})^{\beta} = N * y^{\beta}, \text{ with } 1 < \beta < \beta_m \tag{4}$$

$\beta_m$ is the maximum value of $\beta$, which in this chapter we will take as 1.4. If $\beta = 1$, NPP is identical to GDP at purchasing power parity (GDPppp or Y). A value of $\beta$ greater than 1 would give greater weight to technology than GDPppp, with the weight given to technology increasing with the value of $\beta$. On rearranging Equation 4 we obtain,

$$NPP = T_f * Y, = T_f = y^{\alpha}, \text{with } 0 < \alpha =< \beta - 1 < \beta_m - 1 \qquad (5)$$

This equation shows that the NPP is the product of a technology factor $T_f$ and the GDP at purchasing power parity Y (same as in Equation 1). We can convert the NPP into an index NIPP (or $NIP^2$) by dividing the NPP of each country j by the implicit NPP for the world i.e. Average per capita GDP at purchasing power parity for the world ($y_w$) and world population ($N_w$):

Equation 6: $NIP^2{}_j = A * (N_j * y_j{}^{\beta}) /* (N_w * y_w{}^{\beta}) = A * (T_{fj} / T_{fw}) * (Y_j / Y_w)$

This index is similar in form to the share of a country's GDP in world GDP (A=0.713 in this chapter).

### 2.3.2 *GDP at Exchange Rate*

The gap between per capita GDP measured at current exchange rates (x) and the per capita GDP measured at purchasing power parity (y), is found to be inversely related to the latter. That is, the gap is the highest at low incomes and declines as income rises. This can be summarised as follows:

$$x = C\, y^a \qquad (7)$$

The log form of this equation log (x) = Log (C) +a * log(y) can be estimated using the cross-country data for medium-large countries in 2002 to yield C = 0.0147, a = 1.38.[4] Thus, Equation 7 becomes:

$$x = 0.0147\, y^{1.4} \qquad (8)$$

On comparing this with Equation 4 for NPP it is seen that if the value of $\beta = 1.4$, PP is identical to per capita GDP at current exchange rate, except for a multiplicative constant (0.0147).[5] In other words,

4. That is, all countries with GDP at PPP of $15 billion or more.

the relative share and relative ranking given by the two (X and NPP with $\beta = 1.4$) will be broadly the same except for short-term deviations arising from large devaluation. For instance, India because of a devaluation of 25 per cent in 1992, which at one stroke reduced the USD value of its GDP (X), ranks much lower in terms of X than in terms of NPP with $\beta = 1.4$ (Table 7.2).

In general, however, the relative share of world GDP at PPP and the relative share of world GDP at current exchange rate represent the range of possibilities for measuring the relative power potential of nation states (if $\beta_m = 1.4$)

## 2.4 Actual Power: Strategic Public Goods

### *2.4.1 Military Power*

NPP is a measure of national power potential not actual power, because the technological capability associated with higher per capita income has to be used to develop military and dual use technology and translated into military strength before it becomes effective. The starting point is the 'will to power' (i.e. national motivation to achieve national power and the organisation of national security systems to achieve it). From this arises a strategic vision and the appropriate allocation of public resources for strategic purpose. As military expenditure and military R & D are technically 'public goods', two countries with the same level of "potential power" may choose to spend different amounts on different types of public goods. One country may spend more on military R & D and armaments and another on highways, urban amenities, forest conservation and the environment. We expect actual power to rise with the ratio of strategic expenditure to public welfare expenditure up to some limit after which it starts declining (inverted U shape). In the rising portion of the curve therefore, of two countries with equal NPP, a country that spends more on strategic public goods would be more powerful than one that spends more on other public goods. If the expenditure ratio

5. In any regression estimate, there is also an error term. In other words, individual countries will not lie exactly on the estimated curve but above and below it. For instance, India, because of a major devaluation in 1992 lies below the long term curve. In other words, its ranking in terms of GDPxr is lower than would arise from the index which represents the long run position.

(strategic to other public goods) moves beyond the peak it would represent 'strategic over-stretch' and would ultimately undermine actual power.

The 'actual' power of Russia and Japan relative to their NPP illustrates these aspects. Russia's effective/actual power appears to be higher than its 16th rank in GDP at current exchange rate, 12th rank in $NIP^2 1.4$ (i.e. with b=1.4) and perhaps even its 10th rank in GDP at PPP ($NIP^2 1$ $\beta = 1$). This is because of its historical legacy of the USSR, whose global ambition converted the world into a bipolar one, and the R & D and military development that it undertook to achieve this goal. Similarly Japan's power is lower than that indicated by its ranking according to either criteria (Y 3rd rank, X 2nd rank) because of its pacifism since World War II and its deliberate policy (till very recently) of underplaying its own strength.

### 2.4.2 *Alliances*

Formal alliances and informal arrangements have been used to overcome inherent technological differentials through transfer of strategic technology and thus change the 'actual' power, and to some extent, the 'power potential'. The transfer of military technology allows the recipient country to spend less on developing these technologies and to divert revenues to other public goods including weapons. For instance, transfer of missile and nuclear technology from the USSR to China during the fifties and sixties was a major factor in the development of China's strategic defence capabilities. China, in turn, is reported to have informally passed on these technologies including an atomic bomb design to Pakistan.[6] Pakistan is a state whose inherent technological potential is not even in the top 25. It in turn, has passed on elements of this technology to Iran, Libya, Saudi Arabia and N. Korea (which also received technology directly from China) that are even further down the technology ladder.[7]

---

6. Pakistan had the additional advantage of complete designs for a uranium enrichment plant from Netherlands (*a la* A Q Khan Xeroxing activity in URENCO) and access to the supply network of URENCO spread over Germany, Netherlands, UK, etc. for critical components.

7. K. Subramanium raised the possibility of such transfer when Saudi Arabia purchased M19 and other missiles from China decades ago. Both Saudi Arabia and Libya were identified by him and others as financiers of the Pakistan nuclear programme and the possibility of a *quid pro quo* was also raised in discussion of Bhutto's 'Islamic Bomb.' Sale of technology to Iran was, however, less anticipated by Indian strategic analysts.

India acquired nuclear weapons capability in 1974 (first nuclear test), six years after China (1968), because its inherent technological potential (as measured by NIP[2]) was higher than that of China's till the mid-1980s.[8] The denial of technology to India by the West since then, contrasts sharply with China's favoured access during the eighties and nineties and has been a factor in the growth of China's power *vis-á-vis* India.[9] Formal and informal alliances can therefore, play an important role in determining 'actual power' *vis-á-vis* 'potential power' and if used productively (i.e. to promote growth instead of consumption), can also affect the NPP of the recipient country.

### *2.4.3 Index*

Though a standardised approach to measurement of power is useful, it can be partially negated by geopolitical arrangements. An alternative would, therefore, be to construct a completely separate index of military technology and capabilities and then combine it with the measure of relative size (Y) to get a measure of power. A new global system based on this would, however, give too much incentive to develop military technologies, convert them into arms and to assert military power. The post-war UN Security Council reflects such a system based largely on military and technological achievements and the views of the World War II victors.

## 3. NATURE OF POWER IN THE 21st CENTURY

The world is gradually moving towards the recognition of democratic rights of all human beings living in this world and globalisation has increased the interdependence between economies. The world will, in our view, gradually move towards a concept of power grounded in relative economic strength and economic inducements rather than on military might and military threats. The concepts of 'realism' and 'balance of power' will however continue to have relevance in the relations between nation states for the foreseeable future. These two concepts can be synthesised to derive the concept of 'NPP'.

---

8. The NPT was signed in 1972, only two years earlier by all major powers except India. One option would therefore be to extend the NPT cut-off date for acceptance of nuclear status to 1974 and, thus, incorporate India as a nuclear power under the NPT.
9. What K. Subramanium dubbed "Nuclear Aparthied" a word later picked up by Jaswant Singh.

### 3.1 Globalisation and Interdependence

The globalisation that has occurred in the 20th century will influence the evolution of the 'new global order' in the 21st century. The essence of globalisation from this perspective is the removal of barriers and the reduction of costs and risks of, the flow of commercial technology, financial capital, goods and services and people between countries. The last mostly covers temporary flow e.g. tourism, while medium-long term migration flows remain much smaller than they were in the 19th century. The global economy, including both the rich and powerful countries and the relatively poor and less developed ones, depend on such global flows. Thus, there is much greater economic inter-dependence on a continuing basis than in earlier centuries. The dark side of globalisation is the increased access to weapons of mass destruction (WMD) and greater ease in undertaking cross-border terrorism. It is now easier for determined individuals with sufficient funds, to procure WMDs and to cross international borders to engage in terrorist acts.[10]

### 3.2 Realism

Prof. Kissinger (1994), the best known recent practitioner of 'realism' and analyst of the 'balance of power' in international relations, has said: "In the emerging international order, nationalism has gained a new lease of life. Nations have pursued self-interest more frequently than high-minded principle and have competed more than they have co-operated. There is little evidence to suggest that this age-old mode of behaviour has changed, or that it is likely to change in the decades ahead."[11] "The balance-of-power system ... when working properly, ... was meant to limit both the ability of states to dominate others and the scope of conflicts. Its goal was not peace so much as stability and moderation."[12] The observations of Profs. Kissinger and Kennedy have to be integrated and modified to account

10. Though the issues of terrorism/fundamentalism and WMD are outside the scope of this book/section, both these factors will tend to reinforce one of the conclusions of this book/section, that the powerful democracies of N. America and Europe need to strengthen India (with which they share many fundamental human values) in their own interest and for mutual benefit. See also Huntington (193, 1996).
11. Page 19 of Kissinger (1995).
12. Page 21 of Kissinger (1995).

for the influence of democratic forces in truly open and democratic societies, countries where people's sovereignty is not just a façade and elections a ritual for propaganda purposes.

An ideal (but unrealistic) world order could legitimately be based on the democratic principle of one-person one vote, no matter what the ethnic or national identity of the person. This would effectively mean that power is proportional to population.[13] This is clearly unacceptable to those populations, which have greater achievements in the field of economics, technology or military. Economic and technological achievements of a nation translate directly into per capita GDP and are closely correlated with per capita income. Economic size (Y = GDPppp), based as it is on a multiplicative combination of population and economic achievement (per capita GDP), is therefore, a more realistic basis for a world order.

## 3.3 Natural Balance of Power

The 19th century power balance was conceived largely in terms of military power (essence of 'realism'). The development of nuclear weapons has made conventional military balance less important. For instance, even though Russia's economic power is a fraction (1/5th) of that of China the latter is unlikely to threaten the former militarily because of its formidable nuclear deterrence. Military power does not however, free it completely from economic and diplomatic pressures.[14] Military strength and conventional balance of power have, therefore not necessarily become irrelevant as some analysts have implied. For instance, a pacifist Japan without nuclear weapons and small defence forces and with an economy about half the size of China's, would likely bend to Chinese pressures if it was not covered by the US nuclear umbrella.[15] India, with an economy less than half of China's,

---

13. At the other extreme, a colonial world was based purely on the military superiority of nations, philosophically justified by ideas similar to those that justified slavery and serfdom.

14. For instance, China's controlled media recently objected to the visit of the Dalai Lama, a Buddhist leader, to Russia (despite his having repeatedly and publicly declared that his objective is to preserve the cultural and religious autonomy of Tibet within China). It is doubtful if Russia would be able to resist such pressures if it did not still have some of its historical military and technological power.

15. Despite this, Japanese Prime Ministers have repeatedly and routinely apologised to China for World War II and given aid under pressure, while China (reportedly) supported the development of WMDs by N. Korea.

will not be able to maintain its decision-making autonomy if the size gap widens, unless it has a credible nuclear deterrent and sufficient military power.

To discriminate between legitimate and illegitimate use of national power in the modern world we can define a concept of, 'natural balance of power' based on the economic definition of national power potential NPP (Equation 5). The natural balance of power can be defined as one in which national power, international standing and global rights and responsibility are proportional to relative NPP (Equation 6).[16] Such a system would be consistent with peaceful economic competition among states and provide an incentive for diverting competition from the military to economic dimension.

The natural balance of power can be a stable balance of power if:

a) Relative military strength is proportionate to relative economic strength. Such a military posture is, in general, rational and legitimate.

b) Initiators of 'disproportionate/aggressive' military build-up (i.e. in excess of economic strength) can in principle be identified and isolated by the international system/global power(s) before a 'defensive/reactive' build-up by potential victims.

c) Changes in relative economic power are accommodated by mutual adjustment of international power relations. The international standing of high growth economies is allowed by the established powers, to rise while (established) low growth economies gracefully accept the fall in their international standing. The system of global governance is periodically (every decade or two) adjusted in accordance with the changes that are taking place.

d) Co-operative and inclusive regional and global structure of economic relations exist, which increase interdependence and raise the costs to any nation that disrupts the global economy through aggressive actions.

Cataclysmic changes in the economic balance can however disturb the natural balance. More than in the domestic context, "Power

16. Adjustments would have to be made for unsettled borders and the number of hostile neighbours.

corrupts and absolute power corrupts absolutely." So too, the sudden acquisition of enormous national power in the hands of a ruling oligarchy can corrupt its intentions and global ambitions for the nation. In such a period of transition, the classical 19th century concepts of 'balance of power' may still be relevant for avoiding hegemony and maintaining peace.[17]

During the 21st century, the world is likely to move towards this concept of 'Natural balance of power' in global relations. The speed with which it does so, depends partly on the adoption and propagation of this concept by the global community and partly on the spread of democratic ideals and practices.

## 4. GLOBAL GOVERNANCE

The current institution of global governance is the UN system (Security Council and General Assembly) along with the associate organisations like the World Bank and the IMF. The UN Security Council reflects the power balance at the mid-point of the 20th century. As the world economy has changed considerably since then, there is a widely felt need to review the entire system. A credible reform has to be based on the principles of democratic legitimacy and natural power potential.

### 4.1 Global Parliament: Double Majority

Global governance in the 21st century must be based on two principles: One is the Democratic Principle, that "All men are created equal." In the domestic context, this means 'one person one-vote' and that all are equal before law (rule of law). In the global context, we can interpret this to mean proportional representation of the world's population in institutions that will take decisions regarding social and human development polices (health, environment, education etc.) that have, direct bearing on people e.g. policy regarding negative global externalities such as global warming and HIV-AIDs.

On the basis of population in 2002, the people resident in China would have the highest vote share of 21 per cent, followed by

17. An imbalance of power allows a hegemonic power to fearlessly proliferate nuclear and missile technology to a potential rival's hostile neighbour and thus undermine the rival's security without directly threatening it militarily. The net result is the same. Such 19th century real politics, requires offsetting arrangements by the adversely affected nations.

residents of India with 17 per cent, USA with 5 per cent and Indonesia and Brazil with about 3 per cent each and Russia and Japan with over 2 per cent.

The proportional representation can be implemented in two ways: Either country governments would have a weighted vote in such organisations that are proportional to their population or that people would democratically elect representatives to such global body/bodies under rules, regulations and procedures that are globally determined and monitored. The former is more realistic to start with, but gives undue power to dictatorial regime *vis-à-vis* their own citizens as well as the citizens of the world. The latter would be closer to genuine democracy and empowerment of global citizenship. It is an extension of what is beginning to happen in the European Parliament *vis-à-vis* the world Parliament.

Unlike in a National Parliament, the Global Parliament is unlikely to have in the near future any independent revenue sources, as richer states are unlikely to cede the right of taxation of their citizens to a global authority. The Global Parliament will, therefore, be dependent on the contributions of member states. Each member state would have to contribute in proportion to its 'natural power' and would be entitled to a weighted vote in proportion to this power.[18] A weighted majority vote would be required for passing the social budget, which would include expenditures on global public goods and global social concerns.

There could, however, be a conflict of interest between the economic majority that contributes the finances and the population majority that decides what social policies are in the best interests of global citizens. A double majority vote could, therefore, be required to pass the social (non-security) expenditure budget.

## 4.2 Global Security Council

### 4.2.1 *Principles: Democracy and Power*

The second issue is that of global security and the reality of power. In the domestic context, the nation state has the monopoly of violence over its citizens. It uses this power (or is supposed to use) for

18. If a country does not want to contribute as much as its vote share, its voting rights must be correspondingly reduced.

protecting its citizens from deviants and external aggressors. No state is going to cede this monopoly of violence over its own citizens to a global government, in the foreseeable future. Thus, the power of global government to ensure global security can only be a co-operative aggregation of the power of nation states for global purpose. Thus, each nation must have a fair share of power in a new global Security Council responsible for global security. We have argued that the natural balance of power based on relative economic strength represents such a fair sharing of power in a peaceful world. A fair and equitable system of global governance, is therefore, one in which each nations' rights and responsibility for global security are commensurate with the natural balance of global power.

The above principle has two major implications, one relating to permanent membership and veto power, and the other relating to regional representation. Permanent (P-V) membership and 'veto' power must go together, with the 'veto' re-formulated as follows. Each P-V member would be assigned a weighted vote in proportion to its natural power potential. A total weighted vote of $\underline{v}$ per cent by the permanent members would constitute a veto, where $\underline{v}$ could be 1/3rd or 1/2. The P-V members have to be selected from a set of countries ranked according to their ability to act globally by applying a cut-off to this ranking. The cut-off point has to be based on a trade-off between compactness of the Council and the comprehensiveness of the power represented. The vote shares would be updated at pre-determined intervals (every decade say) to account for continuing changes.

Regional organisations cannot be P-V members because they neither have the security forces nor have the right to taxation of their citizens. Even the EU, which is just starting on this path, may take decades to reach a point where it has exclusive rights over the security forces and the right to taxation of EU citizens. Regional representation must, therefore, be in the form of non-veto yielding non-permanent membership (NP-NV). The system for selecting regional representatives must be fair to the regional powers. Either the probability of being in the Council or the proportion of years that in they are on the Council, must therefore, be proportional to the nations' relative power. Thus, for instance Nigeria and S. Africa are both important regional powers in Sub-Saharan Africa, but their natural power is relatively weak (Table 7.2). Though, they cannot be

P-V members, they should be represented on the Sub-Saharan NP-NV seat in proportion to their 'natural power potential' in Sub-Saharan Africa.

4.2.2 *Permanent Members: Weighted Veto*

As outlined in section 2.3 the NPP of a country can be characterised by the parameter $\beta$, which ranges from 1 to 1.4. When $\beta = 1$, the relative NPP of a nation can be represented by its share of world GDP measured at purchasing power parity (Y). When $\beta = 1.4$, the NPP of a nation can be approximated by its share of world GDP at current exchange rates (X).[19] We can also define an intermediate case in which the NPP is defined by the average Z=(Y+X)/2 of the two extremes.

The shares calculated for the year 2002 are shown in Table 7.2 with the countries ordered by country size (i.e. Y). Figure 7.3 (A and B) also show the share of GDP (Y, X and Z) on the vertical axis with the countries ordered by size on the horizontal axis. The greatest changes occur in the relative ranking of India, China, Russia and Brazil, if we move from one measure of NPP to another. Thus, to an extent, the choice of a measure cannot be divorced from a decision on what role these countries will play on the global stage.

The cumulative GDP share of countries included grows fairly rapidly with the addition of the first 10 countries but much more slowly after the 15th (Figure 7.3B). Thus, the share of world GDP at purchasing power parity (Y) of the top 5, 10 and 15 countries is about 51 per cent, 66 per cent and 74 per cent respectively. Adding another five members adds only 5 per cent of world GDP (Y). The share of the top 5, 10 and 15 countries in world GDP at current exchange rate (X) is about 56 per cent, 72 per cent and 80 per cent respectively. Adding another five members adds only 4 per cent of World GDP (X). This suggests there should be around 10 permanent members of the global Security Council, along with a similar number of regional non-permanent members representing the rest of the world GDP.[20]

19. Recall that a large devaluation disturbs the concordance by reducing ranking sharply. For instance India in 2002 is correctly ranked 8th according to $NIP^2 1.4$ ($\beta = 1.4$) and wrongly at 11th according to X.

20. Under the conventional approach. An alternative is to have only the 20 largest countries as members, with no regional representation.

## FIGURE 7.3

*Distribution of World GDP: PPP, Exchange Rate and Average*

### A: Share of World GDP

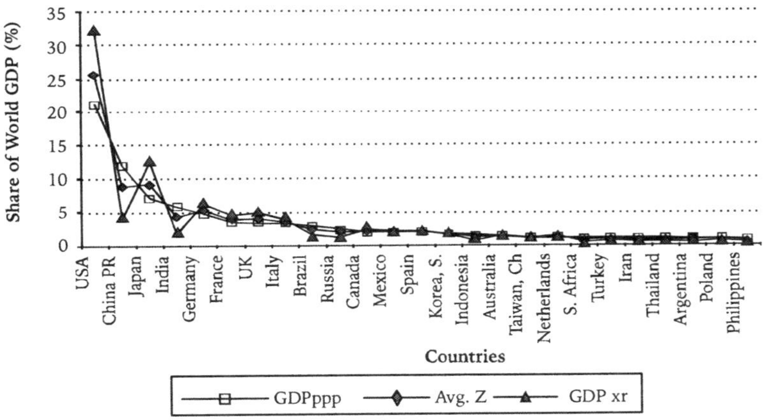


### B: Cumulative Share of GDP

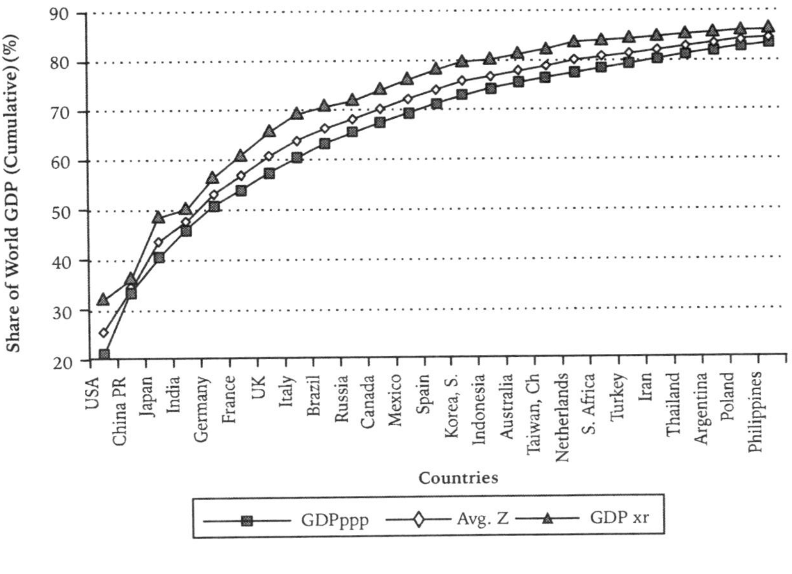

The choice of the measure for applying the cut-off runs into the Russia problem. Russia is the 10th largest country in terms of GDPppp (Y), 16th largest in terms of GDP at current exchange rate (X) and 12th ranked in terms of the average Z. The second criteria (X) applied fairly while including Russia would make the Security Council too unwieldy, unless there is no regional representation. We are, therefore, left with a choice of either Y or Z as the cut-off criteria. The vote shares of the selected countries could, however, lie between that determined using relative size Y or that determined using X. Thus, the US share would be between 21 per cent and 32 per cent, China's share between 4 per cent and 12 per cent, Japan's between 7 per cent and 12 per cent and India's between 1.5 per cent and 5.8 per cent.

Though, many variations are possible, there are two basic options: One is a hybrid that uses the Y ranking to determine those who will become permanent members and uses Z to assign the weighted voter or voter share. The other is to use only Z for both purposes. If we use the first option there could be 10 permanent members with the following shares: USA (25.7 per cent), Japan (9.2 per cent), China (8.8 per cent), Germany (5.2 per cent), India (4.1 per cent), UK (3.9 per cent), France (3.8 per cent), Italy (3.4 per cent), Brazil (2.2 per cent) and Russia (1.9 per cent). In the second option, there would be 12 members. This option has the interesting property that the top 7th, 8th, 9th and 12th ranked countries (as per Z) are identical to the top 7th, 8th, 9th and 12th ranked countries according to Y.

### 4.3 The United Nations

The system of representation used in the United Nations is clearly outdated. Representation in the General Assembly is based on the concept of one nation one vote. This violates both the principles outlined earlier. It is clearly undemocratic in that a nation with 100,000 people has the same vote as a nation of 1 million and a nation of 1 billion people. Such a system provides an incentive for nations to split into smaller and smaller units to get greater representation. It also violates the principle of fair division of power by giving the same vote to a country with a GDP of $1 million as that to one with $1 billion or $100 billion. It gives an incentive for those nations with higher GDP to purchase the votes of those with lower

GDP by bribing them through aid and other inducements.[21] If the UN is to have any legitimacy, it must be reformed to give nations a vote share in the General Assembly, that reflects the distribution of population. An adjustment may have to be made for the fact that authoritarian governments cannot be assumed to reflect the will of their people. Initially, there could also be a minimum (e.g. 1 million) and maximum (1billion) cut-off. Tiny nations would be allowed to band together to attain this minimum size and claim one vote in the General Assembly.

The UN Security Council similarly fails to reflect the power reality of today. The reality is that in 2002 the share of world GDP at Purchasing Power Parity (Y) of the USA and other four permanent members of the Security Council is 21 per cent and 21.3 per cent respectively. In contrast, the GDP of the other five members of the top ten who are not permanent members is 23.4 per cent of world GDP. Further, Japan, India and Germany with 7.1 per cent, 5.8 per cent and 4.6 per cent of world GDP respectively are not permanent members while France and UK with 3.3 per cent and 3.2 per cent of world GDP, respectively, are. A Security Council with 12 of the largest countries as permanent members would encompass 69.4 per cent of world GDP. Similarly, the USA has started ignoring the UN Security Council, because its single positive vote or the (effectively) 100 per cent negative vote of the other permanent members, does not reflect the current balance of power. If we want the USA to be bound by the discipline of the global governance structure, its vote share in the Council must at least reflect its relative economic power (i.e. about 1/4th of the vote).

The nature of the veto would also change. Either a 33.1 per cent or a 50.1 per cent vote against a proposal by the permanent members of the Council could constitute a veto. If the vote share is as proposed in the last paragraph of the previous sub-section, the sole super power would have to garner another 8 per cent or 25 per cent votes from the permanent members, if it wants the Security Council to support its actions. Conversely, for any other nation to veto its proposal would require getting the vote of a number of permanent members. This will make it much more difficult for China, Russia, France and UK to veto

21. The bribe need not distribute income from the richest to the poorest, as nations with low population can be bribed at lower cost even if they are better off.

US action than it is at present. This will be both a recognition of the USA's primacy as well as of the limits on its ability to act unilaterally without loosing its legitimacy and primacy. A majority vote (in terms of assigned vote shares) of the full council would also be required for any action ('double majority'). There could also be certain types of decisions requiring a higher vote share (e.g. pre-emptive attack or rules changes).

The non-permanent seats to represent the remaining 30.6 per cent of the world economy could be assigned on a regional basis. On this basis, and excluding the 10 permanent members, the vote shares would be as follows: Western or OECD Europe would have the highest vote share of 7.7 per cent, followed by East Asia with about 5.1 per cent, Latin America (LAC) with 4.5 per cent, E. Europe and Central Asia with 3.6 per cent. The Middle East and N. Africa would have a vote share of 3 per cent, Sub-Saharan Africa 1.9 per cent, Australia, New Zealand and pacific about 1.4 per cent and S. Asia 1 per cent. Mexico and Canada with a combined share of 3.9 per cent could, in principle, be classed in N. America.

The representative of each region should, logically, be elected by the nations constituting the region, with their vote share proportional to their size. The election should be transparent and supervised by the UN, if necessary. OECD Europe could, in principle, be assigned three seats with an average vote share of 2.56 per cent and E. Asia two seats with an average vote share of about 2.55 per cent. LAC is a borderline region that could also have two non-permanent seats. Thus, there would be about 10 non-permanent seats (i.e. without veto power), representing regional interests. However, some regions could choose to have a different format of representation. For instance, the EU may prefer a single seat to represent its non-permanent members (from W. and E. Europe) with the vote share of the member states assigned to it. In this case, it would be a non-veto yielding renewable semi-permanent membership (in that its constituents would repeatedly elect it).[22]

With rights come responsibilities. Contributions to UN security operations would have to be in proportion to the vote share. Any

22. Though EU may prefer a single permanent seat with the total vote share of all its members, the UK and France and perhaps even Germany are unlikely to agree.

country that desires to contribute less than its vote share would have to have a commensurate reduction in its vote share.

### *4.3.1 Reform Reality*

UN reform cannot happen unless the five permanent members of the Security Council as well as a majority of members of the General Assembly approve of the reform. Any reform means that there will be some losers in the process. The losers will not only oppose the reform but also generate opposition by raking up old rivalries. The permanent members can of course veto any reform that weakens their role in the UN. It is, therefore, useful to ask what would be the best compromise between the principles and analysis given in the previous sub-section and the reality.

Firstly, reform of the General Assembly along the lines proposed appears unlikely and therefore would have to be abandoned so as to get the best possible outcome on reform of the Security Council. Radical reform of the Security Council in the form of weighted voting shares is likely to be vetoed by one or more of the permanent members. Thus, the most realistic option during the next few years is to add some permanent members to the Security Council. In our judgement the following is a possible compromise: (a) Add Japan, Germany and India as permanent members of the Security Council with veto power. (b) Add Brazil as a permanent member without veto. (c) Have a permanent seat without veto to be shared by S. Africa and Nigeria (i.e. a rotating semi-permanent seat).

As none of the existing powers will be very keen to undertake any reform that dilutes their own power, UN reform may in any case take a decade. An alternative would therefore be to support these natural instincts of the current veto powers so that it does not take place during the next ten years. A radical transformation of the UN structure may become feasible in 10-15 years, when the transformation of the world along the lines spelled out below, would be too clear for any country to ignore.

India's diplomatic focus should be on publicising the likely shape of the world in 10-15 years time when India will be a major player. It should highlight how absurd it would be for India to be a second class member of such a UN Security Council in the world of 2015/2020.

## 4.4 World Bank, IMF and WTO

Unlike the global Security Council there is no veto power in the economic institutions. The current system of representation is broadly acceptable, but the voting rights and responsibilities need to be updated to reflect the current situation. Because these organisations deal with the interactions between States (Aid and BoP support respectively) and the high income countries that are the source of funds have a right to a greater say in how these funds are used, GDP at current exchange rates is relevant.[23] On the other hand, the World Bank deals extensively with internal policies that affect the population of these countries, while the IMF has imposed conditions on its lending that relate to domestic policies. Such policies affect people and GDP at PPP, which gives equal weight to population and per capita income, remains relevant. Therefore, for these economic organisations the option of using Z both to determine inclusion and vote shares is probably the most realistic.

The 20 top ranked countries in terms of Z with about 81.4 per cent of the global share in 2002 could be directly represented on the board of directors of these bodies, with a weighted vote share in proportion to their share of Z (Table 7.2). As is the practice today, the remaining countries could select the large member from their sub-region to represent them, with their Z share added to its own share. For instance, if India continues to represent Bangladesh, Sri Lanka and Nepal their share would be added to its own share of 4.1 per cent. The weighted share would be adjusted periodically, perhaps every 10 years to reflect changes in the global economy.

In the WTO, voting rights are based on 'one country one vote' and are therefore, clearly undemocratic. The General Agreement on Trade and Tariffs (GATT) is purely a trade related organisation and a vote share based on the share in world trade could have been a basis of representation. But even in this case, the deviations from zero tariffs, the subject of GATTs attention, are justified by their impact on the economy of the country and on others. Thus, GDP at current exchange rate would have been the natural basis for weighted vote share. The WTO has in contrast, extended itself into many areas besides merchandise trade, such as internal subsidies, TRIMS, TRIPS

23. Recall that this will give greater weight to countries with higher per capita income.

and GATTs (modes 3 and 4). The so-called Singapore issues go even deeper into domestic policy matters and domestic social and development concerns, blurring the distinction between trade and domestic issues. The share of world GDP at PPP would, therefore, be a candidate for determining the vote share weights, given that the population is likely to be affected by such basic changes in the scope of WTO (rules of the game). Given the current situation, the use of a weighted vote share based on Z, as in the case of the World Bank and IMF would be a fair balancing of interests.

### 4.5 Time Lags

The detailed vote shares based on 2002 should be used if reforms are expected to be completed before further data become available. In practice, any reforms e.g. UN reforms, would be preceded by years of discussion and negotiation. The latest available data should be used. There should also be a provision for periodic update of vote shares based on changing shares. An imperfect alternative would be to base the share on the projected data for the mid-point of the expected duration of the new system. For instance, if the new system was assumed to last unchanged for 30 years, then it must be based on the GDP shares (Y or Z) that are expected to prevail 15 years later.

## 5. NEW INTERNATIONAL ORDER

A new global order will emerge during the 21st century, along with new institutions of global governance. Some of these will be adaptations of existing institutions, while others may be completely new ones. This is not likely to happen very quickly, however, because of resistance from declining powers, which currently have disproportionate power in the current system. It is, therefore, important to project the past economic developments into the future to see how the distortions in the current system will grow. At some point these distortions will force a re-alignment.

### 5.1 Economic Forces and Projections

#### *5.1.1 Population*

Population has reached stable or declining levels in the rich, developed and Eastern European countries. European population has peaked in 2000 and is now declining. The population of other continents will continue to grow during the first half of the century but the rate of growth is decelerating. Within Asia, Japan's population will peak in 2010 and that of China will peak in 2030 while that of India will continue to rise till 2050. Sub-Saharan Africa, North Africa and W. Asia will have the most rapid expansion of population during this period. By 2025, both N. America's and Asia's share of the world's population will decline marginally by 0.2 per cent point to 5 per cent and 60.2 per cent respectively. The population share of Europe and China will decline substantially by 3.1 per cent points and 2.6 per cent points (to 18.4 per cent) respectively. USA's share of the world population will remain almost unchanged. The population share of India will increase to 17.4 per cent by 2025 and stabilise at that level, so that China's share (17.3 per cent) will fall below India's by 2035.

In 2025, the USA's population will be about 1/4th that of India or China's. The population of the next three most populated countries (Brazil, Russia and Japan) will be 16 per cent, 9 per cent and 9 per cent of India's respectively. The population of Europe will be about half of India or China's.

The share of population aged 15 to 64, which forms the base (catchment area) of the active labour forces follows broadly the same pattern (UN projections). In 2030, China and India will have 18.3 per cent and 18.1 per cent, respectively, of the world population aged 15 to 64. China's share of potential workers will fall sharply to 17.1 per cent by 2035 when India's share peaks at 18.2 per cent. Thus, India will have the largest share of the world's potential workers around 2030, about five years before its share of total population peaks. As far as this element of relative economic size and power is concerned, India will catch up with China between 2025 and 2035.

### *5.1.2 Globalisation and Catch-up*

The last two decades of the 20th century have been characterised by a rising share of Asia in world GDP. This has been driven by the phenomenon of fast catch-up growth. A set of countries which had relatively low income in the middle of the century, stepped up their growth rate well above that of the high income countries and started closing the gap between the two. These countries were labelled as 'emerging markets' (Garten, 1997). Among the reasons are globalisation and economic policy reforms. The 'Catch-up' phenomenon has occurred in the most sustained and effective way in Asia. Among the reasons is the fact that Asia's civilisations are millennial and most countries of Asia have had governing institutions for centuries. Over the centuries, these institutions have evolved and adapted to the changing environment with varying speed and effectiveness. The presence of these institutions is a source of great strength and continuity. For instance, it has been shown in global cross-country regressions that India's per capita income is about one-fourth of that predicted by the quality of its institutions, implying that further policy reforms will accelerate growth (Rodrik and Subramanium, 2004).

Globalisation has resulted in freer flow of commercial technology, financial capital, goods and services and people (tourism) between countries. Though, the precise national policies needed to convert this potential into a reality in any specific country are still a matter of discussion and debate, it is quite clear that policy reform has played a role in converting the potential of globalisation into 'catch-up' economic growth.

### *5.1.3 Per capita GDP Growth*

During the last two decades of the 20th Century (1980-2003), eight of the ten best performing economies in the world, in terms of growth of per capita GDP, were in Asia. India ranked 9th (Table 7.3). In the first decade of the 21st Century, China and India will be among the five best performing economies. Nine of the ten best performers are also likely to be from Asia. Despite this fast growth there will still be, in 2025, a substantial gap between the per capita GDP of China and India on the one hand, and the USA, Japan Germany and other OECD countries, on the other hand.

Asian economies (Singapore, Hong Kong, Taiwan China, Thailand, Malaysia, China PR, Vietnam and India) have benefited the most from globalisation during the last quarter of the 20th century. India has been the most cautious and slowest growing among them. Given its comparative advantage in services and 'labour-medium skill' intensive manufacturing and young labour force, it is poised for a bolder opening and globalisation to accelerate growth above that of the others.[24]

The rate of growth of GDP and GDP per capita is projected till 2035 based on past performance. These growth assumptions are given in Appendix Tables A7.1 and A7.2 and discussed there. Population growth rates are taken from the UN (mean) projections. These growth rates are used to project GDP at PPP (which forms the basis for Appendix Table A7.3, Table 7.4 and Figure 7.4) and per capita GDP at PPP. The latter is used along with the population projections to derive the NPP and GDP at 2002 exchange rates according to the formulas presented in section 2.3 (which forms the basis of Appendix Table A7.4, Table 7.4 and Figure 7.5).

*5.1.4 Relative Size and Power*

The economic development of the major countries during the next few decades has been projected and is depicted in Table 7.4, Figure 7.4 and Figure 7.5.[25] A historic transformation of the world economy is underway, with a dramatic rise in the relative size of China to be followed some decades later by that of India. This will be offset by a decline in the relative size of Europe and Latin America. The world economy will however, continue to grow at around the same average rate it has in the past 25 years, so that there is no structural break in the growth of demand for natural resources.[26]

China will become the largest economy in the world within 15 years. At that point, it will also be the second strongest power after the USA (in terms of Z, Table 7.4). Its size (Y) will be almost double that of the USA by 2035 (Figure 7.4). This scenario assumes that China will be able to sustain the 'FDI-Export' cum 'Zero capital cost'

24. FDI should be allowed in currently closed service sectors with a phased increase of foreign equity limits in the service sectors in which it is currently less than 100 per cent (manufacturing is already 100 per cent). Peak tariffs should be reduced to 10 per cent by 2006 and to 5 per cent by 2008. Above–peak exceptions should be limited to 60 per cent and brought down proportionately to 30 per cent by 2006 and 15 per cent by 2008.

25. A number of caveats apply. First, the range of uncertainty increases as we project further out into the future. Second, the precise numbers are less important than the relative position of the different countries and the changes in these over time *i.e.* trends in these ratios. There can be other equally valid scenarios of economic evolution.

26. Energy demand could still grow faster than in the past if the energy efficiency of the fastest growing economy China is lower than that of countries that will be growing slower. This aspect needs to be investigated further.

model of fast growth that gives it a knife edge character.[27] Though the decline in USA's share will be more gradual, its power will inevitably be challenged in Asia. This phenomenal change in relative power poses major challenge to the economies of Europe, N. America, and Asia that very few seem to fully understand or appreciate.

## FIGURE 7.4

*Projected Ratio of Country to USA GDP at PPP: 2002 Int. $*

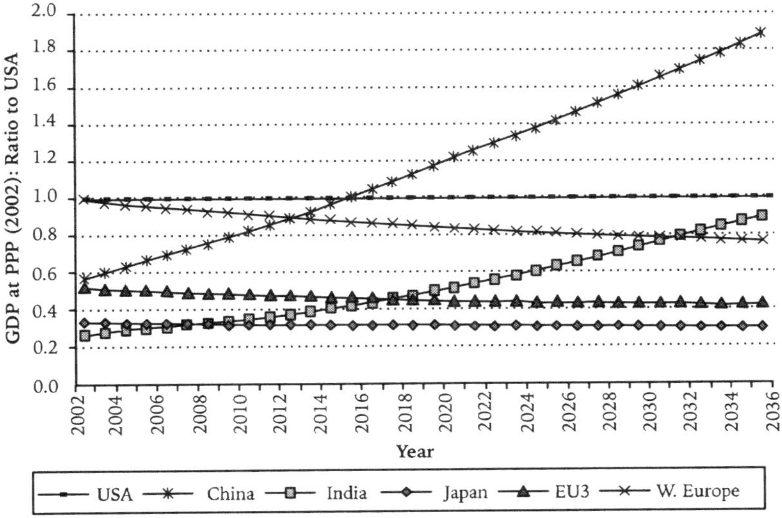


India's economy will become larger than Japan's in about five years taking it to 3rd place behind USA and China. By 2015, it will become the fourth strongest power in terms of power potential measured by Z. Within a few years thereafter, its size (Y) will be larger than the total of the three largest European powers and a little less than half that of the USA (Figure 7.4). By 2035, the Indian economy is likely to be larger than that of W. Europe and by 2050, that of the US.

27. The Asian crisis exposed the weakness of this model. It is heavily dependent on creating and sustaining optimistic expectations and in burying firm level inefficiencies in the government controlled banking system (implicit fiscal subsidies). It is, however, hard to predict what kind of exogenous shock will knock the economy of the high growth knife-edge path to more normal sustainable growth rates.

## Table 7.3

*Per Capita GDP Growth Rate: Average*

| *Economy* | *1980 to 2003* | | *2005 to 2010* | |
|---|---|---|---|---|
| | *Rank* | *Gr. Rt. %* | *Rank* | *Gr. Rt. %* |
| China, PR | **1** | 8.2 | **1** | 6.9 |
| Korea, Rep. | **2** | 5.6 | **4** | 4.6 |
| Taiwan, China | **3** | 5.3 | | |
| Thailand | **4** | 4.7 | **3** | 5.3 |
| Vietnam | 5 | 4.6 | **2** | 6.3 |
| Ireland | 6 | 4.5 | | |
| Singapore | 7 | 4.2 | | |
| Hong Kong | 8 | 3.9 | | |
| India | 9 | 3.7 | **5** | 4.6 |
| Luxembourg | 10 | 3.7 | | |
| Indonesia | 11 | 3.6 | | |
| Malaysia | 12 | 3.6 | | |

*Source* : WDI CD ROM, 2003 and WEO, 2004.

## FIGURE 7.5

*Projected Impact of Country Growth on World Economy: GDP at 2002 Exchange Rate*

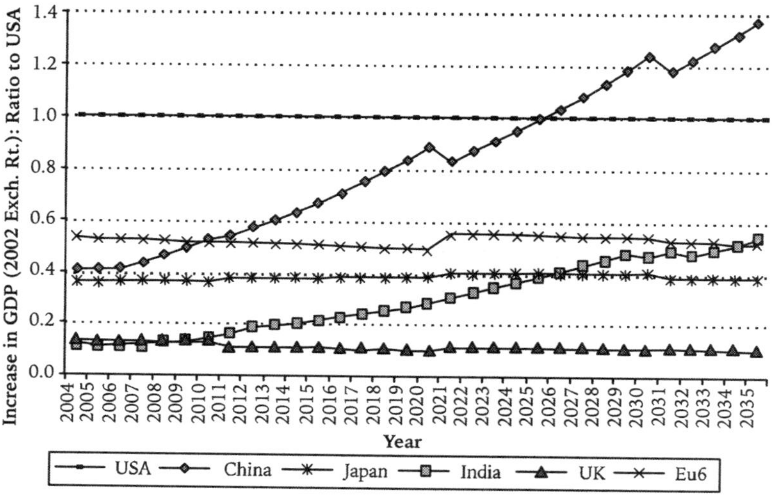

## Table 7.4

*Relative Size and Power Potential in 2015:*
*In 2002 $; 18 Largest Economies in 2002*

| Economy | GDP at PPP (Y) | | | | GDP Exch. Rt. (X) | | | | Z=(X+Y)/2 | | Pop. World |
|---|---|---|---|---|---|---|---|---|---|---|---|
| | Rank | Value | World share | P. capita | Value | Rank | Incremt. | Rank | Value | Rank | Share |
| USA | 1 | 15152 | 19.6% | 45962 | 16752 | 1 | 592 | 1 | 15952 | 1 | 4.6% |
| China | 2 | 15087 | 19.5% | 10759 | 4542 | 3 | 396 | 2 | 9814 | 2 | 19.5% |
| India | 3 | 6389 | 8.2% | 5126 | 1495 | 8 | 223 | 3 | 3942 | 4 | 17.3% |
| Japan | 4 | 4786 | 6.2% | 37622 | 6349 | 2 | 127 | 4 | 5567 | 3 | 1.8% |
| Germany | 5 | 2721 | 3.5% | 32980 | 2602 | 4 | 67 | 5 | 2662 | 5 | 1.1% |
| France | 6 | 2145 | 2.8% | 34139 | 2080 | 6 | 59 | 8 | 2113 | 7 | 0.9% |
| UK | 7 | 2090 | 2.7% | 34110 | 2337 | 5 | 64 | 6 | 2214 | 6 | 0.9% |
| Russia | 8 | 2050 | 2.6% | 15368 | 761 | 13 | 44 | 10 | 1406 | 9 | 1.9% |
| Italy | 9 | 1904 | 2.5% | 34296 | 1631 | 7 | 17 | 18 | 1768 | 8 | 0.8% |
| Brazil | 10 | 1700 | 2.2% | 8416 | 587 | 16 | 42 | 11 | 1144 | 14 | 2.8% |
| Korea, S. | 11 | 1464 | 1.9% | 29467 | 1066 | 11 | 40 | 12 | 1265 | 11 | 0.7% |
| Canada | 12 | 1367 | 1.8% | 40047 | 1186 | 9 | 38 | 13 | 1276 | 10 | 0.5% |
| Mexico | 13 | 1331 | 1.7% | 11125 | 1022 | 12 | 45 | 9 | 1176 | 13 | 1.7% |
| Spain | 14 | 1326 | 1.7% | 32211 | 1121 | 10 | 62 | 7 | 1223 | 12 | 0.6% |
| Indonesia | 15 | 1325 | 1.7% | 5738 | 418 | 18 | 28 | 14 | 872 | 15 | 3.2% |
| Australia | 16 | 837 | 1.1% | 38484 | 692 | 14 | 27 | 15 | 765 | 16 | 0.3% |
| Taiwan, Chi | 17 | 740 | 1.0% | 32697 | 544 | 17 | 26 | 16 | 642 | 17 | 0.3% |
| Netherlands | 18 | 634 | 0.8% | 37772 | 622 | 15 | 21 | 17 | 628 | 18 | 0.2% |

### *5.1.5 Global Growth Engines*

Because the western economies grew relatively slowly in the last few years, while China has continued to boom, the latter was described in the press as a new engine of growth for the world economy. Cyclical factors clearly played a role in this perception. Our long-term projections allow us to explore whether this is a permanent phenomenon and more generally, whether Asia is likely to replace the USA and Europe as the driver of growth for the world economy. In this case, we are interested not in the relative size of the economy but the impact on the rest of the world. We had noted earlier that the GDP converted to US$ at the exchange rate is the best measure of the potential for trade and financial interaction between countries. Changes in this measure of GDP give us an idea of the growth impact (world demand and supply of goods) of an economy on the rest of the world's economy.

The trends in the impact of the global growth poles over the next 30 years are shown in Figure 7.5. Thus, by the end of the decade, China will become a larger driver of global growth than the EU's six largest economies and India will be a larger growth driver than the United Kingdom—the most significant growth pole in the EU. At this time the combined impact of the three Asian giants will exceed that of the USA. By 2025, China's impact on world's growth is likely to be larger than that of the USA and India's larger than that of Japan. By 2035, even India is likely to be a larger growth driver than the EU6, though its impact will be a little over half that of the USA. China's impact will, however, be about 40 per cent more than that of the USA, if China is able to maintain its knife edge growth path. Table 7.4 also shows the global impact of the other large economies in 2015. For instance, Canada and Russia are ranked 11 and 12 in terms of impact, which is less than a third of that of India at that time. The S. Korean economy in contrast, comes in at 7th rank with an impact that is half that of India's. Brazil's impact is projected to be much lower than that of Mexico.

## 5.2 Shift in Balance of Power

Several observers have talked about the emerging shift of global power from the Atlantic to the Pacific dubbing it a "Pacific century" while others have referred to the "Asian century"—a shift in the weight of the world economy towards Asia (Mahbubani, 1995). By the end of the first quarter of the 21st century, China's communist oligarchy will have the economic power to actively challenge the USA's predominance in Asia, even though it will not be in a position to challenge its predominance outside Asia till the middle of the century. By the end of this quarter India will also start playing an important role in Asian affairs and by the middle of the century in global affairs. Though, the EU matches the USA in size, its institutional capacity to translate this into commensurate global power is uncertain given the strength of national sentiment among its constituent nation states.

The NPP of a country lies in a band indexed by a parameter lying between 1 ($NIP^2 1$) and 1.4 ($NIP^2 1.4$). As noted, the relative country share of GDP at Purchasing Power Parity (Y) and GDP at exchange rate (X) approximate the limits of the band.[28] We explore each of these in turn, to trace the possible evolution of global power balances over the first half of the 21st century. The actual power balances are likely to lie within this band.

### *5.2.1 Bipolar or Tripolar World?*

The 'NPP' ($NIP^2 1$) captured by the size distribution of GDP at PPP (Y) puts the power of China and India at the upper limit of the band *vis-à-vis* USA, Japan and W. Europe. The world will become bipolar in terms of size during the next two decades and tripolar over the subsequent two decades. Figure 7.3A shows clearly the unipolar nature of the world in 2002 with the GDP share dropping sharply as we move from the USA to the lower ranked countries. The evolution of this distribution over the first half of the 21st century is projected in Figure 7.6A (base scenario). While the unipolar nature of the size distribution is quite clear in 2005, the distribution becomes bipolar by 2015 with the emergence of China.

As the relative share of the USA falls and that of India rises, the latter emerges as the third pole in terms of relative size of GDP. If

---

28. This was true in 2002 except for an error term. The parameter that was estimated to $\beta$ 1.38 in 2002 may change in future.

power-potential is accurately measured by $NIP^2 1$ (i.e. $\beta = 1$), then the world will become tripolar by 2050 with China, USA and India constituting the three poles. At that point, China's economy is projected to equal that of the USA and India combined.

All the other countries that are either currently members of the Security Council or aspire to become so will therefore, have relatively small shares. Japan the largest among them, will have a share of about 5 per cent while the others (including Russia) will each have 2.5 per cent. They would be considered regional players but be greatly in demand as partners and allies by the weaker pole(s). The forecast based on $NIP^2 1$, therefore, contrasts sharply with an earlier forecast by Prof. Kissenger that there would be five great powers in the 21st century, namely USA, European Union (EU), Russia and China, with a possible fifth India in the latter half of the century. The possibility of the EU acquiring most of the characteristics of a nation-state in the next two decades is low but cannot be ruled out. Another scenario in which the EU emerges as a fourth pole converting the world into a multi-polar one is possible. In this case, India and EU, as the weakest of the four poles ($NIP^2 1$), would have a great incentive to become strategic partners if not allies.

### 5.2.2 *Half Century of Uni-Polarity!*

The upper limit of the NPP band represented by $NIP^2 1.4$ (i.e. with $\beta = 1.4$), puts the power of China and India at its lowest level *vis-à-vis* the USA, Japan and W. Europe. Figure 7.6B shows the projected changes in $NIP^2 1.4$ ordered by the projected ranking in 2025.[29] The unipolar nature of the world in 2005 is again quite clear from this graph, with 2nd ranked Japan having about 40 per cent of the potential of the USA.[30] If power-potential is more accurately reflected by $NIP^2 1.4$, then the unipolar world will last about 30 years longer than if power is better measured by $NIP^2 1.4$ In 2035, China would have 70 per cent of the NPP of the USA, Japan 40 per cent and India 25 per cent.[31] Though, the USA's lead over China is reduced

29. This is calculated from projected per capita GDP at Purchasing Power Parity by using the equation for power potential with $\beta = 1.4$.
30. Which it has never translated into actual power.
31. Japan's potential relative to USA is the same as in $NIP^2 1$.

# FIGURE 7.6

*Changing Size Distribution of GDP and National Power Potential*

**A: Changing Size Distribution and Power**

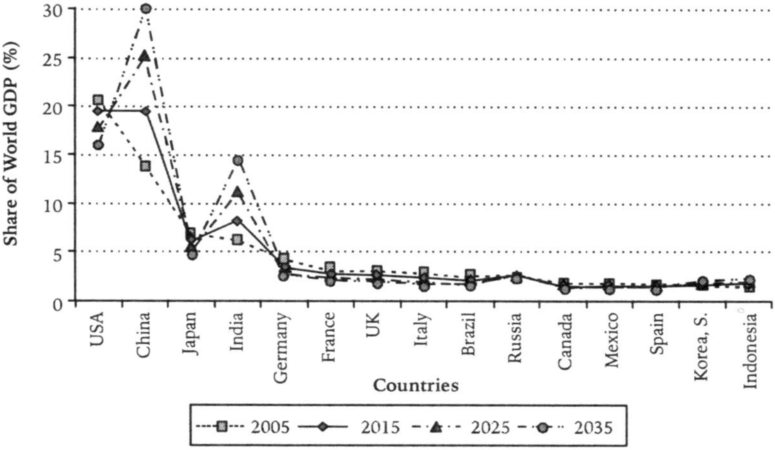


**B: Changing Power Potential (β=1.4)**

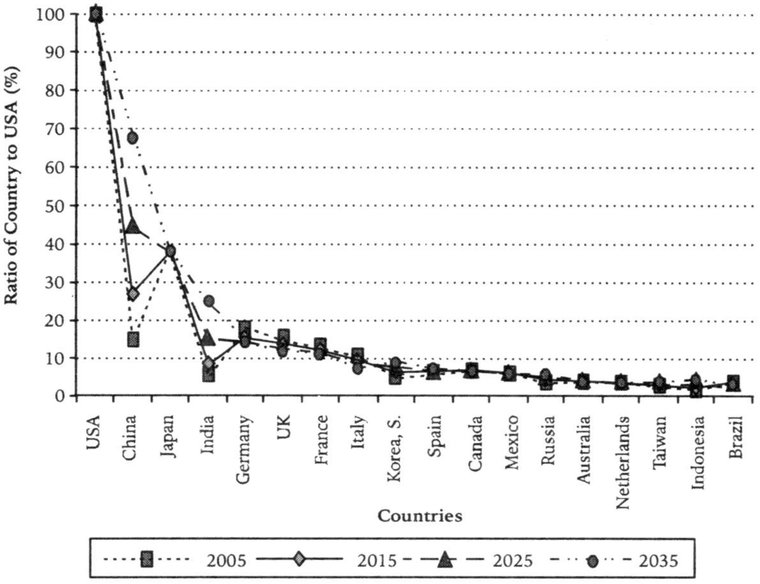

substantially, it can retain its sole super-power status well into the middle of the century by strategic alignment with India. The USA's traditional ally, Japan can contribute if it throws off its earlier diffidence to develop its power in accordance with its potential.[32]

The relative NPP of Germany (14.7 per cent), France (11.6 per cent), UK (12.4 per cent), Italy (7.8 per cent), Russia (6.1 per cent) and Brazil (2.9 per cent) would be lower than under $NIP^2 1$.[33] Thus, even if the NPP is more accurately measured by $NIP^2 1.4$, Brazil would remain a regional player and Russia seems headed in that direction.

The trend in NPP $NIP^2 1.4$ for India represents the lower bound scenario for its rise as a global power. The gap between India's relative size and relative $NIP^2 1.4$ arises from the gap between the inherent technological capability represented by the gap in productivity per person or per capita GDP y. Even by this measure, India's NPP will overtake that of Mexico, Spain and Canada within the next 10 years (Figure 7.7). In the subsequent 10 years, it will go on to overtake Italy, France, UK and Germany. During that period, China would (likely) have overtaken Japan in terms of this measure ($NIP^2 1.4$), so that India would be fourth ranked behind Japan.

### *5.2.3 Asian Balance*

A stable balance of power in Asia will be critical to Asian and consequently, world peace in the second half of the 21st century. The second quarter of the 21st century is likely to be the most sensitive period for Asian stability. During this period, the relative position of India *vis-à-vis* China will be unbalanced while the unipolar system with the USA as the sole super-power will be under a strong challenge from China. According to our base scenario, the gap between (ratio of) China and India's per capita GDP will be the highest around 2020. Given the logic of catch-up, the gap is likely to start closing thereafter, and to be significantly narrowed by 2050. The gap between China's GDP will be highest around 2015, but the gap between China's NPP

32. This is particularly so given the other challenges it faces (terrorism and WMD) that are not considered in this book/section.
33. Numbers in Parentheses are for 2035.

and India's potential power will reach a peak around 2020 (Figure 7.8). The weakness of China's model of development ('FDI-export led' plus 'zero capital cost' intermediate supply) is bound to show itself some time after 2020. That is, the probability of China falling off the knife-edge growth path will increase progressively after 2020 if the growth rate has not moderated to normal levels.

## FIGURE 7.7

*Trends in National Power Potential as Measured by NIP$^2$1.4*

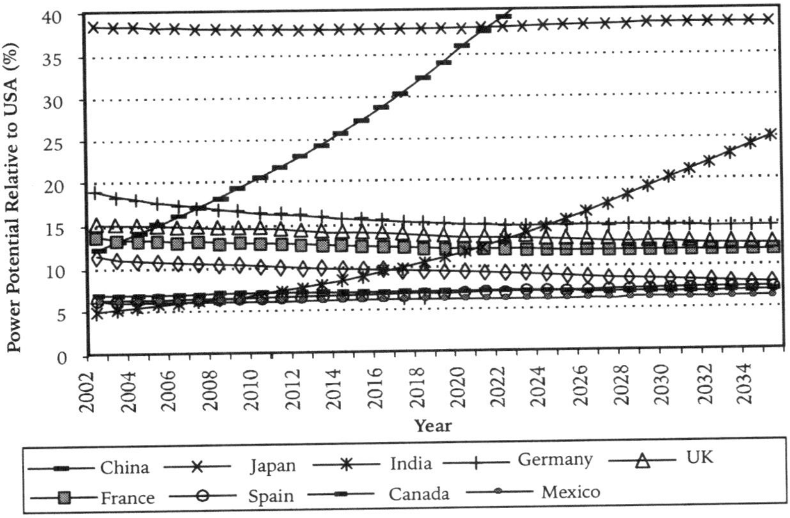


In contrast, some of the weakness of governance in India, which results in poor supply of public goods and services, will reduce as incomes increase and poverty declines. The entrepreneurial, social (capital) and institutional strengths of India will then assert themselves more strongly. By 2035, India's population will have reached that of China and the population balance restored (Figure 7.8). China's dependency ratio as well as the average age of its labour force will also be rising relative to that of India.

## FIGURE 7.8

*Projected Size of China Relative to India*

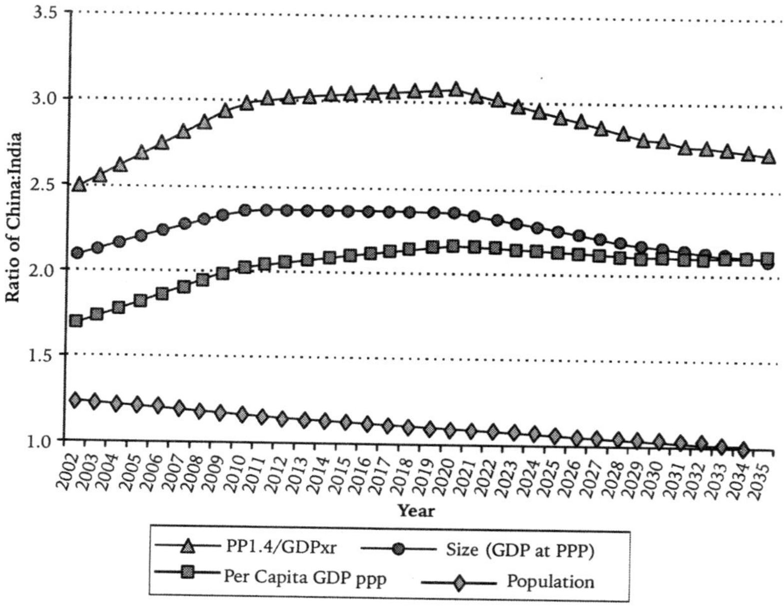


As a stable balance of power in Asia will be critical to peace in Asia in the first half of the 21st century, it is useful to look at the relative balances in Asia. Figure 7.9 shows the size of the major countries of Asia relative to the size of India. There are two interesting facts that emerge from these projections. Firstly, there is great imbalance in the relative size of large Asian countries and this imbalance will be accentuated in future.[34] Thus, China's size is more than twice that of India. Japan's economy in 2005-06 will be approximately the same size as India (while ASEAN countries together are about 70 per cent of India). The next largest economy, Russia, is about 40 per cent, S. Korea and Indonesia about 1/4th and Australia about 1/5th of India's size, respectively. The size of these economies is projected to decline relative to that of India with Japan 3/4th and Russia 1/3rd the size of India by 2015 (Figure 7.9).

34. The imbalance is however nowhere near what it was in the Americas with respect to the USA.

FIGURE 7.9

*Projected Size of Asian Countries Relative to India*

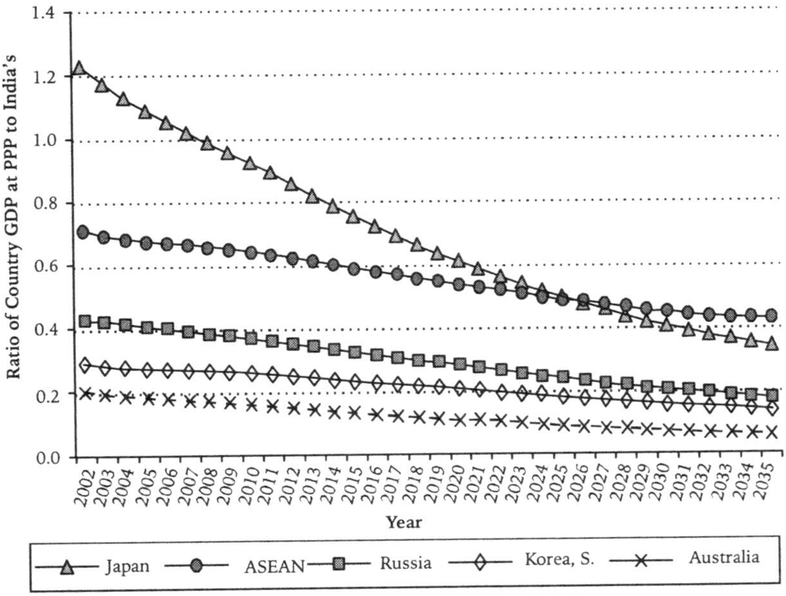


The second noteworthy fact is that China's economy (NIP²1) in 2004 will be marginally larger than that of India and Japan together. By 2017, China's economy/NIP²1 will be larger than the combined economy/NIP²1 of India, Japan, ASEAN, Russia, S. Korea and Australia. If NIP²1.4 is a better measure of NPP, then China's NPP will not exceed that of Japan till after 2020. In this case, Japan still has time to realign its actual power with its NPP to produce a 'natural balance of power', in Asia that is also more stable. In the 19th century world of military oriented 'balance of power', an alliance between the middle powers would have appeared inevitable. The 21st century version of 'realism' requires more imaginative responses.

As India and China will be the two most populous countries in the world by a wide margin, establishment of a 'natural balance of power' between the two will be critical to Asian and global stability. Our projections suggest that the relative size and power (NIP²1) of China *vis-à-vis* India will rise during the current decade, stabilise during the next decade and start declining during the third decade of this century (Figure 7.7). China's relative size and power (NIP²1) is projected to peak at 2.5 to 2.8 times that of India's. The USA and the EU can play a critical role in ensuring that the rising power with its governing nationalist-communist oligarchy is not tempted to assert its power by force of arms. They can do this through whole-hearted and unambiguous support to a democratic and free India with which it shares fundamental human values and belief in the rule of law. The main focus of this support has to be in terms of technology transfer to correct emerging imbalances (such as the need for nuclear power to moderate oil demand) and FDI that helps close the per capita income gap faster than projected. If, as a consequence, India were in a position to balance the economic power of China by 2025, the temptation, for aggressive nationalists within its power structure, to assert their hegemony in Asia in the second quarter of the century, would be moderated. This would allow the peaceful evolution of Asia and the global power structure.

### 5.2.4 *Imbalance and Hegemony?*

As the Appendix indicates, there is a possibility that the rate of growth of India and Japan may be lower than in the base forecast. The maintenance of high growth in China for a longer period than assumed (helped by euphoric expectations among OECD countries), cannot also be ruled out. In this case, the imbalances in Asia would be accentuated and the risks would be much greater, as historically major changes in global power have been marked by violent upheaval.

The global system will be severely challenged to ensure that the rise of China is peaceful.[35] Though, incorporation of Taiwan (China) into the mainland by force poses risks to mainland China's FDI-export driven growth, the Communist Party may be tempted, particularly if its authority is being undermined (e.g. by democratic pressures within the mainland). As China establishes its paramount status in Asia, its approach to various issues will reveal the extent to which its attitude is non-hegemonic. For instance, attempts to exclude specific countries

35. The phrase, "the peaceful rise of China," that was mentioned by the General Secretary and other officials of the Chinese Communist party, and the President and Prime Minister of China have subsequently been replaced by the, "peaceful development of China."

from regional economic co-operation arrangements could indicate a hegemonic intent to deny them a due role in Asia. Among the issues are: (a) The development of an East Asian community that excludes potential rivals so that Japan's financial resources can reinforce its own to establish ASEAN's financial dependence on it. (b) Use of bilateral and regional Free Trade Arrangements to undermine support of other countries' claims on the South China Sea and ensure an effective takeover of its natural resources. (c) Creation of a nuclear capable N. Korea that undermines the security of S. Korea and Japan.[36] (d) Use of Pakistan as a conduit for proliferation of China's nuclear technology and as a 'Trojan horse' to undermine the security of potential rivals. (e) A nuclear Iran that strengthens its position in W. Asia *vis-à-vis* Israel/USA. (f) Choice of approach (reason and mutual respect or economic/military power) to solution of border disputes. If the hegemonic impulse that has characterised such historical shifts in power, cannot be diffused and defanged, 19th century balance of power politics may become inevitable.

In our view, the risk of conflict can be reduced by building co-operative and inclusive structures and systems in Asia that respect the natural balance of power and give a due share of power (and responsibility) to each nation. It is in the interest of Asian countries, including China that believes in 'peaceful rise', to build an inclusive system that ties the major Asian powers and ASEAN into co-operative economic systems. One such structure could be an 'Asian Economic Community' (eventually Asian Common Market). A positive approach by the most powerful nation in Asia, for example, with respect to border settlement, can ensure that neighbours are not pressured to look outside the region for alliances to strengthen their security.

## 6. CONCLUSIONS

Significant changes have taken place in the global economic power since the Second World War. These changes are grounded in the differential economic performance of nations spurred, in part, by economic globalisation and economic reforms. The pace of change has accelerated in the last few decades. Consequently, changes in the

---

36. This assumes a US veto of S. Korean and Japanese nuclearisation.

natural balance of power during the first quarter of the 21st century, are likely to be larger than in the latter half of the 20th century. There is an urgent need to reform the institutions of global governance to reflect the changes in global power balances (past and projected). Co-operative economic structures would have to be built in Asia to minimise the risks of conflict and demonstrate peaceful intent towards each other.

Because of the tectonic nature of the changes underway, global governance reforms may not be enough to avoid conflict. A 21st century version of the 19th century balance of power politics may be temporarily needed to minimise hegemony and avoid violent upheaval during the high-risk period between 2025 and 2050. A particular responsibility devolves on free, democratic nations in N. America and Europe to strengthen those democratic nations in Asia who share their fundamental human values and can help insure its peaceful evolution. This requires recognition of the changes taking place in Asia and perhaps the evolution of a long-term vision to temper the universal temptation of short-term gains from exports of embodied and disembodied technology to the fastest growing economy in the world.

The projections in this chapter indicate that India will have the potential to become a global power in a couple of decades, while other nations (besides USA and China) will be reduced to regional status. To what extent it does so, will depend on its 'will to power'. The extent to which India is able to translate its NPP into actual power will depend on the success of its political system and its elite in developing a strategic culture and an understanding of global power politics.

The USA, EU and India are democratic, free and culturally open societies that share fundamental human values. It will be in the interests of the USA and EU to strengthen India's economic and technological capability over the next two decades for mutual benefit, peace and stability in Asia. The Indian elite and political system must abandon the lingering cold war mentality, suspicions and approach that still survives in some corners. A true partnership requires mutual dependence.[37] India must be willing to share the US (and EU's) global responsibilities in return for USA and EU's willingness to modify the national laws and international arrangements they have put in place (after India's first nuclear test in 1974), to cut India's access to strategic technology. The scenarios presented in this chapter are merely one among many possibilities that so often surprise forecasters. The USA, EU, Japan, India and other democratic countries can, by their enlightened and determined actions, help bring about a world that is much more beneficial to all their citizens than is suggested by these scenarios.

---

37. According to K. Subramaniam, instead of fearing India's dependence on the USA, India must strive to develop a 'reverse dependence'.

# Appendix A7.1

*Forecasts*

## India and China

The rate of growth of GDP and GDP per capita is projected till 2035 based on past performance. These growth assumptions are given in Tables A7.1 and A7.2. The most significant departure from past trends, the assumed spurt in the Indian economy, and the slowdown in the Chinese economy need some elaboration. According to India's National Accounts data, GDP and per capita GDP have grown at an average of 5.8 per cent per annum and 3.7 per cent per annum respectively, during the last 24 years (1980-81 to 2003-04).[38] The comprehensive reforms instituted in the 1990s have increased competitive pressures on the Indian economy while at the same time enhancing its ability to compete globally. In our view, an opening of the economy to international trade produces a J-curve effect: The direct negative effects of competition appear immediately as capacity utilisation falls in un-competitive product lines as capital is immobile (so, reduction is limited by the rate of depreciation). The positive effects of competition on productivity appear only after new technology adopted by the pioneers and fructifies through new investment and gradually diffuses to the rest of the industry.[39] Improvements in productivity will, therefore, appear at the aggregate level only after a lag and we expect the underlying trend rate of growth to gradually move up to around 6.5 per cent.

There are a number of other factors that suggest India's growth rate could accelerate further. One area in which the improved competitiveness of the Indian economy is clearly visible is in the double-digit (20 per cent to 30 per cent per year) growth of non-traditional service exports (commonly referred to as IT & ITES exports).[40] Though, such exports are already a significant share of

---

38. The WDI data underestimate the GDP growth rate substantially thought the per capita GDP growth rate is almost the same.
39. There are numerous cases of firms that have transformed their systems and shown large increases in productivity. The effects of these are not however available in the sector data.
40. We call transport, tourism and communication as traditional service exports and the rest as non-traditional.

India's total exports of goods and services, this sector constituted a very small part of the economy. Therefore, the impact of the GDP growth was limited. The sector is now becoming a significant part of the economy and it contributes between 0.5 to 1.5 per cent points per year to aggregate GDP growth rates.[41]

The second factor is the un-exploited potential of foreign direct investment (FDI). The proportion of FDI in total investment and GDP is very low in India compared to the other high growth Asian countries such as Singapore, Malaysia, Thailand, China, Indonesia and Vietnam. In contrast to China, which has followed an FDI-export led growth model, India's growth has been led by domestic investment and entrepreneurship. The positive role of FDI in growth (marketing, technology, management systems) is, therefore, largely unexploited. A doubling of FDI flows from the current low levels of $4 billion to $8 billion to $10 billion per annum could have a substantial positive effect on the growth rate of the economy. India is already a highly attractive location for skill-intensive manufacturing because of the high quality and availability of middle management/technical skills and knowledge workers. With China's per capita income more than twice that of India's, we would normally expect hourly/daily wages to be twice that in India. China has so far kept monthly wages lower than that in India by allowing workers in FDI invested enterprises to work 60 to 80 hours a week (double that permitted in India). This advantage will disappear very soon. India could, therefore, become a more attractive location than China, for labour-intensive manufactured exports if the new Special Economic Zone law can reduce red tape/ bureaucracy and introduce much needed flexibility in labour laws, rules and procedures.

The third important factor is the demographic transition that is taking place across the world. The high growth of E. and S.E. Asian countries was to a substantial degree due to the demographic transition (the U-shaped curve followed by the dependency ratio/ inverted U of the labour force to population ratio). China is now near the end of its demographic transition while India has entered its most positive phase. This could add between 0.5 per cent to 0.8 per cent points to the growth of the Indian economy. In addition, the population of Europe and Japan is aging rapidly and there will be a

41. Starting at the lower end and going up to the higher end of the range.

great demand from these economies for 'youth-intensive' goods and services.[42] Over the next half century, India will have the youngest labour force in the world. India, is therefore, likely to become the largest exporter of such items. As China's population will age much earlier than that of India, it is not in a position to exploit this opportunity.

The biggest downside risk to Indian growth scenario comes from the infirmities in its political system that have led to a deterioration in the quality and quantity of public goods (roads, policing, legal system) and quasi-public goods over the last four decades. The high fiscal deficit is merely a symptom of this deterioration in governance. It is necessary, however, to distinguish between levels and trends. The quality and diversity of India's institutions and its social capital built over centuries, is very high. The democratic system, including the free media and the non-governmental institutions is a great source of long term strength. Dani Rodrik has estimated that India's growth is 2 per cent to 2.5 per cent lower than predicted be the quality of its institutions (see Rodrik and Subramanian, 2004a). The trends in governance are, however, disturbing and need to be corrected: There is, however, still enough time for the Indian political system and civil society to reform the governance system.

On China, Collins and Bosworth (1996) followed by the World Bank and IMF have shown that its growth from 1980 to end-nineties was overestimated by 1 per cent to 2 per cent. Young (2000) has asserted that China's growth is over-estimated by as much as 3 per cent. If we assume an over estimation of 2 per cent, China seems to have the ability to sustain growth at about 7.5 per cent per annum over decades. Most observers have, however, been forecasting a slow-down in this growth rate (Virmani, 1999 b and c). The 1990s were a period of above average international trade growth and the current decade will see a slower growth. China's export growth will, therefore, slow as its share of world exports rises to the top and per capita income/wages reach upper-middle income levels.

China has used a dual model of high growth that combines FDI-export led growth (like Thailand and Indonesia) with zero-capital cost

---

42. For instance, a study has shown that Nobel prize winners in Physics did their most productive work below the age of 25-30.

for critical intermediates.[43] The latter represents a channelling of subsidies through the banking system (which is effectively like a government department) into state enterprises producing intermediate goods and infrastructure services and from there, through low prices, into the FDI-export complex.[44] Though the labour intensive (LI) export goods produced by Hong Kong, Taiwanese and other non-resident Chinese entrepreneurs are highly competitive, this is not so for other (non-LI) exports. The FDI-export drive is critically dependent on building and sustaining optimistic expectations about the economy and the Asian crises demonstrated the vulnerability of this model. Given the continuing generation of non-performing assets (50 per cent to 100 per cent of GDP), which are in reality an implicit cross-tax subsidy, China is somewhat more vulnerable. On the other hand its large economy has domestic strengths that were absent in the smaller Asian countries. It is, therefore, very difficult to predict if and when a growth crisis could occur in China. We, therefore, assume a gradual slowing down of China's economy.

Our assumptions for Japan are perhaps more optimistic than justified by its growth over the last 25 years. They should, therefore, be viewed as upper bounds. If Japan's growth is slower than assumed (as is quite likely) and India's growth does not match up to the forecast, Asian and global balance of power will be even more unbalanced than in our base scenario.

---

43. S. Korea has used the latter approach to a much more limited extent in that the subsidies were restrained.
44. The prices of intermediate goods in China is, reportedly, less than their price on the high seas outside India—i.e before taxes, delays or red tape.

## Table A7.1

*GDP Growth Rate: PPP, Constant 2002 International $*

| *Country* | *Average Growth Rate (%)* | | | *Projected Growth Rate (%)* | | |
|---|---|---|---|---|---|---|
| | *(1980-2002)* | *(1990-2002)* | *(1998-2002)* | *(2003-2015)* | *(2016-2025)* | *(2026-2035)* |
| China | 9.5 | 9.3 | 7.6 | 7.5 | 6.5 | 5.8 |
| USA | 2.9 | 2.8 | 3.0 | 3.0 | 2.9 | 2.8 |
| India | 5.6 | 5.4 | 5.4 | 6.6 | 7.0 | 6.5 |
| Japan | 2.5 | 1.4 | 0.1 | 2.6 | 2.6 | 2.6 |
| Germany | 1.8 | 1.6 | 1.5 | 1.5 | 2.2 | 2.5 |
| France | 2.1 | 1.9 | 2.6 | 2.2 | 2.4 | 2.5 |
| UK | 2.2 | 2.1 | 2.4 | 2.3 | 2.2 | 2.3 |
| Russia | -0.1 | -2.4 | 3.8 | 4.3 | 3.8 | 3.3 |
| Italy | 1.9 | 1.5 | 1.7 | 1.7 | 1.8 | 1.6 |
| Brazil | 2.4 | 2.0 | 1.6 | 1.8 | 2.2 | 2.0 |
| Korea, S. | 6.8 | 6.2 | 4.6 | 4.7 | 4.3 | 3.8 |
| Canada | 2.7 | 2.6 | 3.8 | 3.1 | 2.7 | 2.7 |
| Mexico | 2.8 | 3.1 | 3.2 | 3.0 | 3.0 | 2.8 |

*Source* : Author's calculations based on WDI, 2003.

## Table A7.2

*Per Capita GDP (at PPP) Growth Rate*

| *Country* | *Average Growth Rate (%)* | | | *Projected Growth Rate (%)* | | |
|---|---|---|---|---|---|---|
| | *(1980-2002)* | *(1990-2002)* | *(1998-2002)* | *(2003-2015)* | *(2016-2025)* | *(2026-2035)* |
| China | 8.2 | 8.2 | 6.8 | 6.9 | 6.2 | 5.7 |
| USA | 1.8 | 1.8 | 1.9 | 2.0 | 2.0 | 2.2 |
| India | 3.6 | 3.6 | 3.6 | 5.2 | 6.0 | 5.9 |
| Japan | 2.0 | 1.1 | -0.1 | 2.6 | 2.9 | 3.0 |
| Germany | 1.6 | 1.3 | 1.4 | 1.5 | 2.3 | 2.6 |
| France | 1.6 | 1.4 | 2.2 | 1.8 | 2.1 | 2.4 |
| UK | 2.0 | 1.8 | 2.0 | 2.0 | 1.9 | 2.0 |
| Russia | | -2.1 | 4.2 | 4.9 | 4.5 | 4.1 |
| Italy | 1.8 | 1.4 | 1.7 | 2.0 | 2.2 | 2.2 |
| Brazil | 0.7 | 0.5 | 0.3 | 0.7 | 1.5 | 1.5 |
| Korea, S. | 5.7 | 5.3 | 3.9 | 4.3 | 4.1 | 3.9 |
| Canada | 1.6 | 1.5 | 2.9 | 2.4 | 2.1 | 2.3 |
| Mexico | 0.8 | 1.4 | 1.6 | 1.8 | 2.1 | 2.3 |

*Source* : Author's calculations based on WDI, 2003.

## Table A7.3

*World Share of GDP at Purchasing Power Parity*

| *Economy* | *Current: Unipolar 2002* | | | *Projected (2002 Prices)* | | | | | |
|---|---|---|---|---|---|---|---|---|---|
| | | | | *2015:Bipolar* | | *2025* | | *2035:Tripolar* | |
| | *(Int.$bi.)* | *Share* | *Rank* | *Share* | *Rank* | *Share* | *Rank* | *Share* | *Rank* |
| China | 5861 | 12.1% | 2 | 19.5% | 1 | 25.2% | 1 | 30.0% | 1 |
| USA | 10308 | 21.3% | 1 | 19.5% | 2 | 17.8% | 2 | 16.0% | 2 |
| India | 2800 | 5.8% | 4 | 8.2% | 3 | 11.2% | 3 | 14.3% | 3 |
| Japan | 3425 | 7.1% | 3 | 6.2% | 4 | 5.5% | 4 | 4.8% | 4 |
| Germany | 2236 | 4.6% | 5 | 3.5% | 5 | 3.0% | 5 | 2.6% | 5 |
| France | 1601 | 3.3% | 6 | 2.7% | 6 | 2.4% | 7 | 2.1% | 8 |
| UK | 1549 | 3.2% | 7 | 2.7% | 7 | 2.3% | 8 | 2.0% | 9 |
| Russia | 1186 | 2.4% | 10 | 2.6% | 8 | 2.6% | 6 | 2.5% | 6 |
| Italy | 1525 | 3.1% | 8 | 2.5% | 9 | 2.0% | 9 | 1.6% | 11 |
| Brazil | 1355 | 2.8% | 9 | 2.2% | 10 | 1.9% | 12 | 1.6% | 12 |

## Table A7.4

*GDP at 2002 Exchange Rate Relative to USA*

| *Country* | *Actual* | | *Projected* | | | | | |
|---|---|---|---|---|---|---|---|---|
| | *2002* | | *2015* | | *2025* | | *2035* | |
| | *Ratio* | *Rank* | *Ratio* | *Rank* | *Ratio* | *Rank* | *Ratio* | *Rank* |
| USA | 1.00 | 1 | 1.00 | 1 | 1.00 | 1 | 1.00 | 1 |
| China | 0.12 | 6 | 0.27 | 3 | 0.45 | 2 | 0.68 | 2 |
| Japan | 0.38 | 2 | 0.38 | 2 | 0.38 | 3 | 0.39 | 3 |
| India | 0.05 | 11 | 0.09 | 8 | 0.15 | 4 | 0.25 | 4 |
| Germany | 0.19 | 3 | 0.16 | 4 | 0.15 | 5 | 0.15 | 5 |
| UK | 0.15 | 4 | 0.14 | 5 | 0.13 | 6 | 0.12 | 6 |
| France | 0.14 | 5 | 0.12 | 6 | 0.12 | 7 | 0.12 | 7 |
| Italy | 0.11 | 7 | 0.10 | 7 | 0.09 | 8 | 0.08 | 9 |
| Korea, S. | 0.05 | 12 | 0.06 | 11 | 0.08 | 9 | 0.09 | 8 |
| Spain | 0.06 | 9 | 0.07 | 10 | 0.07 | 10 | 0.07 | 10 |
| Canada | 0.07 | 8 | 0.07 | 9 | 0.07 | 11 | 0.07 | 11 |
| Mexico | 0.06 | 10 | 0.06 | 12 | 0.06 | 12 | 0.06 | 12 |

# 8

## A Tripolar Century

*USA, China and India*

### 1. INTRODUCTION

The fast growth of Japan till the mid-eighties, gave birth to several books on the 'Pacific century' (Gibert, 1988; McCord, 1991; Gibney, 1992) and the Asia-Pacific century (Sutter, 1992; Cronin, 1992). This talk gradually disappeared after the bursting of the Japanese bubble. The talk revived with the phenomenal growth of the Tigers (Manning and Stern, 1994; Lingle, 1995; Mahbubani, 1997) but was soon overcome by the Asian Crisis (Emerson, 1998). Virmani (1999 b, c) showed that India (the elephant) was among the ten fastest growing economies of the world since 1980 and projected that in the next decade its growth rate would accelerate above that of the Tigers and reach the top three. It also asserted that though China's past growth had been overestimated by about 2 per cent it (the dragon) would remain the fastest growing economy in the world during the first decade of the 21st century.

Krauthammer (1990-91) had heralded the arrival of "The Unipolar Moment" and set off a debate on its many ramifications. The reality of the unipolar world returned to centre-stage after the Asian crisis even though some questioned whether the unipolar moment had passed (Nye, 1999; Huntington, 1999). Since 9/11 the USA has asserted its primacy and the unipolar nature of the world has been re-asserted. There is, however, a variety of views on how long the unipolar world will last.[1] Bergsten (2004) and Virmani (2004e) have written about the possibility of the unipolar world order of the past half century converting into a bipolar or tripolar one.

My thanks to K. Subrahmaniam and Vice Admiral (retd.) Prem vir Das and Admiral (retd.) Gulab Hirnandani for detailed comments and to Dr. Bimal Jalan, Shri Lalit Mansingh, Shashank, T.C.A. Srinivasa Raghavan, Satish Nambiar, Prof. Paul Evans and Ambassador Frank Wisner for their comments.

1. See for instance Mediros and Fravel (2003), Albright (2003), Nye (2003).

State power is the "extent that [one] affects others more than they affect [one]"(Waltz, 1979). It is, therefore, a "combination of its capacity to resist the unwelcome influence of others and conversely, to influence others to behave as it wants them to." With increasing globalisation, democratisation and inter-dependence, the form in which such power is expressed will likely change over this century. However, history is unlikely to end (Fukoyama, 1989) and old ways of using power may not fade away that quickly. The powerful will also find new ways to express their power.

The current chapter argues that the global economy is evolving in a direction that will result in a tripolar world by the middle of the 21st century. Thus, the 21st century will be a 'Tripolar Century' with two of the poles in Asia and one on the other side of the Pacific. So ironically, it could end up as partly a Pacific, partly an Asia-Pacific and partly an Asian century. This is based largely on an economic view of power *a la* Kennedy (1988). The next two sections outline this approach and present the index of power potential that we have defined earlier, the $VIP^2$, from another perspective. Section 4 shows how this index captures the current unipolar world. Section 5 outlines the evolution of global power first into bipolar and then into a tripolar world based on our economic projections. Section 6 presents the rationale for the growth assumptions about China and India that underlie these results. Section 7 discuss the reasons why the European Union (EU) may not become a fourth pole. Section 8 concludes the chapter with some policy suggestions.

## 2. ECONOMICS OF GLOBAL POWER

The globalised world of the 21st century will be driven by economic growth. The relative power of nation states will depend on the relative size of national economies. The size of a country's economy is measured by GDP at purchasing power parity (PPP), which is the product of its population (N) and its per capita GDP at PPP (PCgdp). This, in turn, means that within the set of 'emerging economies', the rate of catch-up growth and relative population, indicate the shape of the likely future.

Developed economies with relatively high per capita income are at the frontiers of technology (knowledge) and grow relatively slowly. Growth varies among them based largely on technological change and invention. Low and middle-income countries lie well within the technology frontier and their growth rate depends on the transfer of technology (knowledge) from the developed countries, and its adaptation, application and diffusion. Such knowledge flows take place through multiple channels, such as machinery import and investment, FDI, foreign trade, internet, media and travel. The globalisation of the world economy during the 20th century has removed many of the constraints on such movement and reduced the cost of such flows. The low and middle-income economies can, in principle, grow much faster than the advanced economies as long as their income is well below that of the advanced countries. There is, however, a much greater variance in growth rates among them, with many growing even slower than the developed countries. The Asian tigers were the first to take full advantage of the benefits of globalisation through appropriate policies. Other Asian countries have followed in their footsteps. Between 1980 and 2003, eight of the ten fastest growing economies in the world, in terms of average per capita GDP (the measure of catch-up growth), were in Asia.[2]

If catch-up growth is sustained over several decades, as it has been in Singapore, Hong Kong, Taiwan (China) and S. Korea, the economy will eventually reach the technology/income frontier.[3] The growth rate of an economy is likely to slow as it comes closer to the frontier and the scope for catch-up growth is exhausted and more of the growth must come from its own technological innovation.[4] With per capita incomes/GDP almost identical, the relative size of the population is the primary determinant of relative economic size. Thus, over the medium-long term relative population is an important determinant of size. The economic size, and therefore, the relative power of large relatively fast growing economies will, therefore, rise over time. The two most heavily populated countries in the world are China and India. They are among the ten fastest growing economies in the world and are projected to be among the five fastest growing economies. Their relative power will, therefore, inevitably rise. The question is only about the speed with which this will happen and the level that will be reached.

2. Table 3 in Virmani (2004e).
3. Defined as within 10-15 per cent of the income of the richest country.
4. "Bell curve of catch-up growth," Virmani (1999 b, c). Singapore was able to overcome this constraint for a while because of increasing female labour participation rates.

# 3. POWER POTENTIAL: $VIP^2$

We defined an index of relative power potential $VIP^2$ in chapter 6 that is parameterised by a weighting factor '$\alpha$' that can range from 0 to 1. It was also shown that when $\alpha = 0$, the power potential is captured by ($VIP^2$ is equal to) the relative size of GDP measured at PPP and when $\alpha = 0.5$, the power potential is approximately equal to ($VIP^2$ is equal to) the relative size of the economy at current market exchange rate. The Virmani index of power potential for country j ($VIP^2_j$) is calculated as:

$$VIP^2_j = (N / N_{usa}) * (PCgdp_j / PCgdp_{usa})^{\beta} = (GDP_j / GDP_{usa}) * (PCgdp_j / PCgdp_{usa})^{\alpha}$$

Where N, GDP and PCgdp are the population, GDP at PPP and per capita GDP at PPP respectively. The sub-scripts j and usa denote country j and the USA respectively. As shown in previous chapters, the last term in $VIP^2$ represents a technology factor that is applied to economic size.

The weighting factor '$\alpha$' gives extra weight to a country's inherent technological capability. The reasoning is as follows. As a result of globalisation knowledge/technology, capital and human skills can flow freely across countries given appropriate policies. If all technological flows were unconstrained by national restrictions then all technology can be freely purchased. Each country's ability to produce goods and services is measured by the GDP at PPP and is a summary measure of its resource endowments (technology, capital and human resources) and includes its ability to buy technology. In this case $\alpha=0$ would be the best parameter.

The flow of defence, strategic and 'dual Use Technologies' are, however, constrained by national polices and technology denial regimes. They cannot be commercially and freely purchased on the global market. In this situation, inherent technological capability constrains access to such technologies. Such inherent technological capability is most simply and effectively captured by per capita GDP measured at PPP. The parameter $\alpha > 0$ is the extra weight on this (technology) variable. In our view $VIP^2$ with $\alpha = 0.5$ captures the power potential of nations adequately and will be the focus of our analysis.

For those who think that military power and consequently strategic technological capability, play a greater role than economic power, a could be set at 0.75 or 1. The main difference is that the USA's predominance over other countries is heightened if the technology weight is increased. In addition, the relative position of the poorer countries worsens much more than that of the richer ones (details in Section 4).

There is also a contrasting view that, even if military power was important in the past, its importance will diminish to the point at which soft power becomes more important than military power.[5] There are a number of reasons for an increase in the role of economic power *vis-à-vis* military power. (a) Increased economic interdependence means that the disruptions of war have a negative economic effect on oneself. This increases the costs of military action and reduces the probability. (b) Conventional war against a nuclear capable state will be highly risky, reducing its probability as well as its usefulness. (c) The ability of non-state actors to inflict enormous damage with little military power, reduces the power of conventional military threats. If this view is correct, the EU would play a much greater role than in our mean scenario and the relative power of India would be enhanced *vis-à-vis* China.

## 4. ACTUAL POWER

Actual power can, however vary from the level indicated by the power potential index $VIP^2$ because of, (a) Differing national objectives (the will to power). For instance, the will to power of post-war Japan was very low, while that of the USSR, and of China since 1980 is, very high. (b) Different allocation of national revenues to military and strategic R & D and equipment relative to that on other public goods and services (e.g. environment). Thus, Russia continues to benefit from the high investment of the USSR in strategic technology.[6] (c) Alliances that transfer restricted technology and equipment and thus, effectively supplement national technological resources. For instance, in the past, China used its alliance with the

5. For instance K. Subrahmaniam. For soft power see Keohane and Nye (1977), Nye (1990) and Held *et al.*, (1999).
6. At that time the E. European countries were part of the Soviet empire and, thus, contributed their economic weight to its technological development and power.

USSR to develop its strategic technology and also benefited from its informal partnership with the USA.[7] Many countries including Israel have benefited from their formal or informal alliance with the USA.

Sophisticated models of global power, such as those of Tellis *et al.*, (2000) have incorporated both economic and strategic technology dimensions of national power. The Index of Power Potential VIP² is designed to capture most of the economic factors analysed in such sophisticated models, in the simplest possible way (*a la* the principle of Ocam's Razor).

## 5. SOARING EAGLE: UNIPOLAR MOMENT

The USA has been the sole super power since the collapse of the USSR and remains so today, even in terms of the VIP². Thus, for instance, Japan, the second ranked power, has less than 30 per cent of the power potential of the USA today (column headed $\alpha = 0.5$ in Table 8.1). China and Germany, the third and fourth ranked powers, have about 1/5th the power potential of the USA. France, UK and Italy occupy the next three positions with a power potential of about 13 per cent of the USA. Canada, India and Spain occupy the last three positions among the top ten with about 7 per cent of the USA's power.

The USA's predominance over all these countries is however, heightened if we use $\alpha = 0.75$ or $\alpha = 1$. In addition, the relative position of the poorer countries such as Indonesia, India and China worsens much more than that of the richer ones. Currently, China is a lower-middle income country while India is a low-income country. The position of Russia, which is ranked 12th with $\alpha = 0$, also worsens though at $\alpha = 1$ it moves just above India.[8] Looking at this Table, one might easily conclude that the unipolar world will continue well into the 21st century, that China will not be a global competitor of the USA and India will remain a regional power. This conclusion is, however, very misleading.

---

7. It is only about five years ago that President Clinton called China a strategic partner.
8. Only if $\alpha=0.8$, can the current power potential of Russia, Brazil and S. Korea be taken as greater than that of India. This suggests that a reasonable upper value for $\alpha$ is 0.6.

## Table 8.1

*Power Potential of the Largest Countries in 2002*

| | $VIP^2$: $\alpha = 0$ | | $VIP^2$ $\alpha = 0.5$ | | $VIP^2$ $\alpha = 0.75$ | | $VIP^2$ $\alpha = 1$ | |
|---|---|---|---|---|---|---|---|---|
| | *Rank* | *Index* | *Rank* | *Index* | *Rank* | *Index* | *Rank* | *Index* |
| USA | 1 | 1.00 | 1 | 1.00 | 1 | 1.00 | 1 | 1.00 |
| China | 2 | 0.57 | 3 | 0.20 | 5 | 0.12 | 8 | 0.07 |
| Japan | 3 | 0.33 | 2 | 0.29 | 2 | 0.27 | 2 | 0.25 |
| India | 4 | 0.27 | 9 | 0.07 | 14 | 0.04 | 16 | 0.02 |
| Germany | 5 | 0.22 | 4 | 0.19 | 3 | 0.18 | 3 | 0.17 |
| France | 6 | 0.16 | 5 | 0.13 | 4 | 0.13 | 4 | 0.12 |
| UK | 7 | 0.15 | 6 | 0.13 | 6 | 0.12 | 5 | 0.11 |
| Italy | 8 | 0.15 | 7 | 0.13 | 7 | 0.12 | 6 | 0.11 |
| Brazil | 9 | 0.13 | 11 | 0.06 | 12 | 0.04 | 13 | 0.03 |
| Russia | 10 | 0.12 | 12 | 0.05 | 15 | 0.04 | 15 | 0.03 |
| Canada | 11 | 0.09 | 8 | 0.08 | 8 | 0.08 | 7 | 0.07 |
| Mexico | 12 | 0.09 | 15 | 0.04 | 17 | 0.03 | | 0.02 |
| Spain | 13 | 0.09 | 10 | 0.07 | 9 | 0.06 | 9 | 0.05 |
| Korea, S. | 14 | 0.08 | 13 | 0.05 | 11 | 0.05 | 12 | 0.04 |
| Indonesia | 15 | 0.07 | | 0.02 | | 0.01 | | 0.01 |
| Australia | 16 | 0.05 | 14 | 0.05 | 10 | 0.05 | 10 | 0.04 |
| Netherlands | 17 | 0.05 | 16 | 0.04 | 13 | 0.04 | 11 | 0.04 |

There are many foreign policy experts who question the importance of economic factors in national power by citing the cases of Japan and Germany.[9] According to the Power Potential Index $VIP^2$ their relative power was about 34 per cent and 25.5 per cent of the USA's respectively at its peak in the early-1980s. In 1975, the relative power of Japan was about 30 per cent. Germany was divided so its (W. Germany's) power was fragmented. This was not sufficient for either of them to have challenged US power even if they wanted to, given the fear and resentment that it would have aroused in their neighbours. It can also be argued that the victors of World War II the USA, France and UK ensured that the losers, Japan and Germany did not develop great power ambitions, by imposing a pacifist constitution and tying them into the EU/NATO and US-Japan alliances.

The case of Russia contrasts with that of Japan and Germany. Many observers continue to talk about Russia as a future great power. Russia's actual power appears to be much greater than its power

9. Krauthammer (1990).

potential. Its power potential as per the VIP$^2$ is currently about 5 per cent of that of the USA. It was, however, as high as 17 per cent in the early-1980s but has declined steadily since then. The economy of the Soviet empire (including former USSR and E. European satellite states), which constituted a unified 'virtual State' ruled from the Kremlin/Moscow, was much larger than the Russia of 1982. Therefore, the power potential of the USSR (whose data is not available), was much higher than the 17 per cent of Russia in early-1980s and its VIP$^2$ was probably even higher in the 1970s. This allowed the USSR to devote much more resources to the development of strategic technology and equipment, a legacy from which the much smaller current day Russia benefits greatly.

## 5.1 A Tripolar Century

How long will this "Unipolar Moment" *a la* Krauthammer last? For at least a quarter century (i.e. 1990 to 2015). The world is likely to become bipolar by the end of the first quarter of this century and become tripolar by the middle of the 21st century. These conclusions are based on our projection of growth of per capita income and the population projections of the United Nations (summarised in Appendix Tables A8.1 and A8.2).[10] The precise numbers and years emerging from them are not sacrosanct, but the trends are clear and show us the nature of the world that will emerge over the next 50 years.

## 5.2 Towards A Tripolar World

The Dragon has emerged from the dungeons of Maoist communism to grab the benefits of globalisation (FDI, exports, education and skills) without singeing it with its fiery breath. It has successfully combined communist party ownership and control with elements of a globalised market economy. The vegetarian Elephant has similarly emerged from the Indian version of socialism to experiment with market reforms in its usual slow and steady but plodding democratic way.[11] Though, both started the transition in 1980, the Dragon has attained a lead over the Elephant that may take a century to be 'completely' eliminated.

---

10. Source: *http://esa.un.org/unpp/p2k0data.asp (2004)*.
11. Both countries' reforms started in 1980. Curiously India's economic reforms followed its own temporary regression from democracy, the 'declaration of emergency' in 1976, as part of which civil rights were suspended.

During the first half of this century, India's population will increase from 3.6 times to 3.75 times that of the USA, while China's population will decline from 4.5 to 3.4 times that of the USA. Population growth is 'not' therefore, the primary driver of the change from a unipolar to a tripolar world. The population trends in other countries relative to these three do, however, bear on whether the world will become multipolar. Russia's (Japan's) population will halve from about 50 per cent (45 per cent) of US today to about 25 per cent (27 per cent) of US by 2050. Similarly, the total population of the EU6 would fall from 110 per cent of US to about 75 per cent of US. Thus, the world is unlikely to become multipolar, in terms of nation states, during this century. The question of the role and importance of an association of states such as the EU is analysed separately (Section 7).

The primary driver of the evolution of a unipolar world into a tripolar one is income covergence between India, China and the USA and other rich countries. Over the next 50 years, both China and India will become high-income countries, with India lagging China by about a dozen years in reaching this level/category. China's per capita GDP at PPP will increase from 11 per cent of the USA's to 57 per cent. India's per capita GDP (PPP) will increase from 7 per cent to 36 per cent of US per capita GDP (by 2050). The global economy and polity will be transformed by this convergence of incomes, as the two most populous countries of the world will, after centuries, close the income gap that resulted from the industrial revolution.

Figure 8.1 shows the evolution of power potential of the biggest countries as measured by $VIP^2$ with $\alpha = 0$, which is equivalent to the relative size of the economy measured at PPP. China's GDP at PPP will equal that of the USA in about 10 years (Figure 8.1).[12] China will have become an upper-middle income country by then.[13] India's GDP at PPP will exceed that of Japan within 5 years and will exceed that of the US by 2040.[14] By then, India will be a high-income country.

12. 2017 in the current projection.
13. The ratio of its GDP at PPP to India's will have peaked prior to this.
14. 2039 in the current projection.

## FIGURE 8.1

*GDP at Purchasing Power Parity Relative to US (VIP$^2$ $\alpha = 0$)*

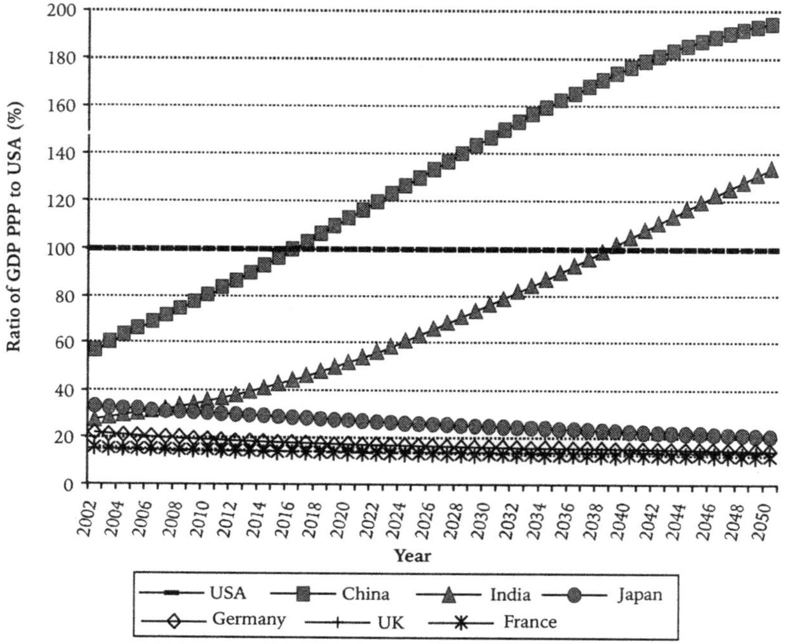


Figure 8.2 show the evolution of the power potential of the biggest countries as measured by VIP$^2$ with $\alpha = 0.5$ and can be taken as the mean scenario in terms of power potential. The curve also approximates the trend in relative GDP in US $ (measured at 2002 exchange rates and prices), though the current deviations from the regression line are compounded over time (e.g. for China and India). In principle, it can indicate the overall impact of each economy on the world economy (relative to that of the US). This impact is a composite of international trade, financial flows and movement of technology and skills.

According to our mean scenario, China's and India's power potential will equal that of USA during the second quarter and third quarters of the 21st century, respectively. This does not mean that income levels of the former will be equal to that of the USA. The remaining gap in income level will be offset by larger population size.

Around 2035, China's per capita GDP at PPP will only be about 43 per cent of the USA, but its power potential $VIP^2$ will equal that of the USA (Figure 8.2) because its population will be about 3.8 times that of the US. Before the end of the first quarter of the century India's power potential $VIP^2$ will exceed that of Japan. India's power potential will also reach that of the USA during the third quarter of the 21st century, about 25 years after China. At this point India's per capita GDP at PPP will be around 40 per cent of the US and its population about 3.9 times.

## FIGURE 8.2

*Projected Power Potential of the Major Powers ($VIP^2$ $\alpha$ = 0.5)*

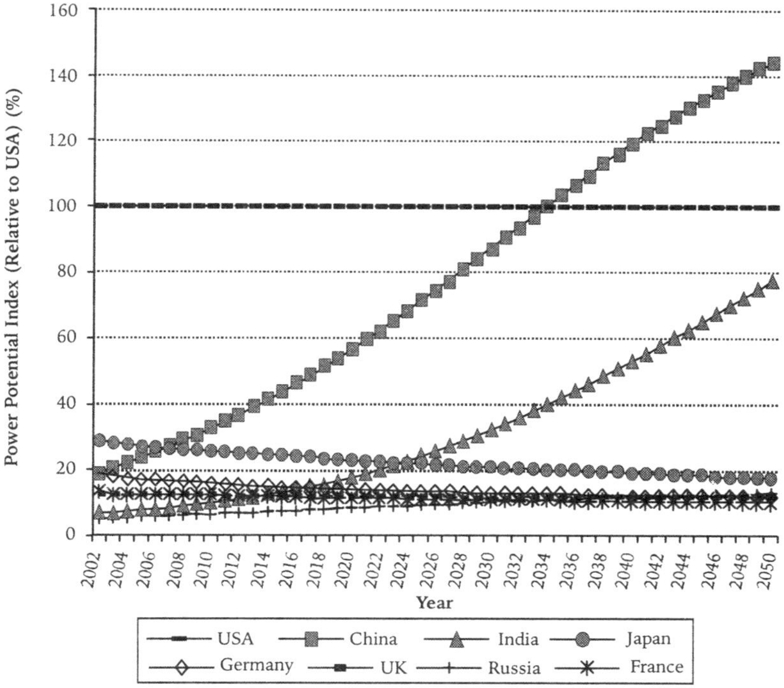


As bipolarity or tripolarity does not require that each pole be exactly equal, the world is likely to become bipolar by the end of the first quarter of this century and become tripolar by the end of the second quarter of the century.[15] As half the century will be tripolar it could be called a Tripolar Century. It follows from this emerging tripolarity that the nature and quality of relations between India, China and the USA will have an important bearing on peace and stability in Asia and on economic prosperity generally.

## 5.3 The Eagle and the Dragon

With China's economy equalling that of the USA in size in about ten years and equalling it in power potential $VIP^2$ in about 30 years, the balance of power in Asia will tilt towards China within the first quarter of this century. China will almost certainly challenge USA's economic power in Asia and across the globe and likely be much more unabashed in asserting its economic claims in the South China Sea and its economic interests in Asia, Africa and Latin America. The law recently passed by China authorising the use of force against Taiwan (China) is perhaps a pointer to this emerging reality. There are also signs that earlier US complacency about the relative military and technological power of the USA *vis-à-vis* China is giving way to heightened concern. This is reflected for instance in US, efforts to stop the EU from lifting its arms embargo on China.

## 5.4 The Dragon And The Elephant

Sino-Indian relations will play a critical role in ensuring peace and stability in Asia during the second quarter of this century. Figure 8.3 shows the evolution of India's GDP at PPP and its power potential relative to China's. India's GDP has fallen from more than that of China's in 1980 to half of it in 2000. It will reach a relative trough of 44 per cent around 2012, before starting to rise and close the gap. By 2025, the ratio of India's to China's GDP and power will be 50 per cent and 35 per cent respectively. By 2050, the ratio of GDP and power potential will have risen to 70 per cent and 55 per cent respectively. We project both gaps to be completely eliminated by the end of the century, thus restoring the position that prevailed in the early 1980s.[16]

---

15. This is analysed further in Table 8.2.
16. A US-India partnership could help eliminate the gaps decades earlier.

## FIGURE 8.3

*India's GDP at Purchasing Power Parity and Power Potential Relative to China's*

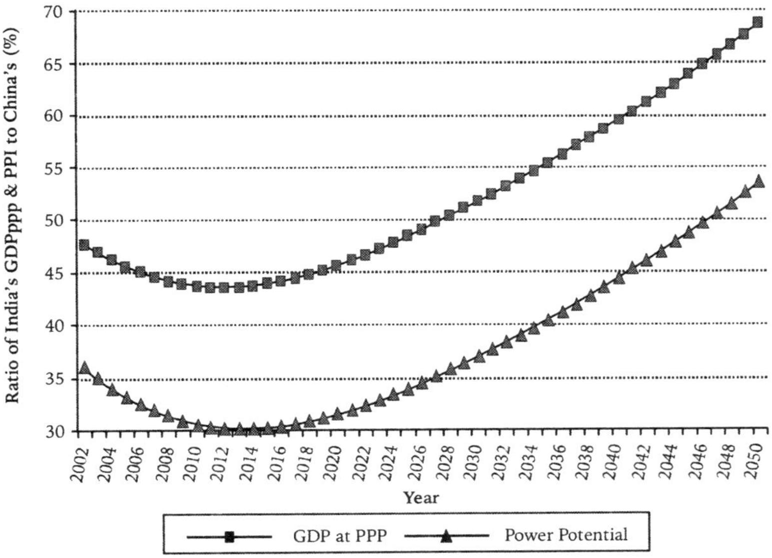


It is, therefore, imperative for China and India to normalise their bilateral relations based on mutual respect and recognition of each other's role in Asia and across the world. As China is the stronger power, its attitude to relations with India will be an important driver of the India-China relationship. There are three key issues that need to be addressed. First, a settlement of the India-China border. China's willingness to accept a settlement that is 'no worse' for India than the one proposed in the sixties by Premier Chou en Lai, would be a positive indication. Second, a credible policy regarding nuclear proliferation to countries ill disposed towards India.[17] Third, a willingness to build new inclusive regional economic organisations, which give India and other Asian countries their due share in economic power. A border settlement and removal of restrictions and

17. Routine denial of internationally recognised proliferation activities does not enhance credibility.

barriers to trade in goods and services could form the foundation for good relations.

Based on the lessons of European history and the EU, India and China must develop inclusive and co-operative structures in Asia that will ensure the peaceful development of all countries. China, India and other Asian oil importers could jointly bargain with the oil supply cartel that has been charging them an (unjustified) Asian Premium. This co-operation could be developed into an Asian oil community, patterned on the European steel community. India could also take the initiative in developing an Asian Economic Community patterned on the European Economic Community with India, China, Japan, Indonesia and other ASEAN countries at its core.

## 5.5 The Elephant and the Eagle

The point at which the world becomes tripolar, China would be the strongest pole and India the weakest. The combined size of the US and Indian economy will be larger than China's, as would their combined power potential. This relative position is likely to prevail through the second half of the century and has important implications for economic and technological co-operation between the USA and India. As India and the USA share fundamental human, social, institutional and democratic values, it will be in the interest of the USA to ensure that the economic and technological gap between India and China is closed as rapidly as possible so that India can act as a stronger pole in Asia.[18] This will also help expand the freedom of action of other countries in West Asia, Central Asia and of the members of ASEAN.

One element of Indo-US partnership would be a comprehensive economic co-operation agreement (CECA) between India and the USA covering goods, services, FDI and temporary movement of skilled and semi-skilled persons. Another element would be for the USA to lead the abandonment of the nuclear apartheid imposed by the West on India after its nuclear explosion in 1974.[19] This requires changes in

---

18. Classical realist theory is consistent with this proposition.
19. India was the only major country not to sign the NPT in 1972. China became a nuclear power in 1968 and as a member of the NPT has had much freer access to Western technology since 1980.

laws, rules and bureaucratic procedures. The third element would be a strategic partnership that deepens and widens India's access to defence, space and nuclear technology. Will the US, at the peak of unipolarity, have the far sightedness and wisdom to treat India (currently less than a tenth of its power) as an equal? The recent announcement by the US State department about co-operation in the field of nuclear power and defence production in India and introduction of India into the G8 suggests that it might!

Though, USA will remain the repository for the most advanced strategic technology for half a century, Japan, the EU6 and Russia will continue to have a competitive supply of some of these technologies. The traditional Indo-Russian co-operation will therefore remain important for closing India's technology gap, for at least a decade.[20] The interest of France and others in a multipolar world could also spur enhanced technology transfers to India. If the democratic governing institutions in the USA and India move at their usual speed, the development of a true (genuine, balanced) partnership between the USA and India could take a decade. With US interests currently focussed on terrorism and West Asia (Middle East), the USA appears to be overly-dependent on the Pakistan government.[21] Given that strategic technology has strong elements of monopoly, India will have to continue tapping multiple sources so as to obtain the most cost effective technology.

## 5.5 Regional Powers

At mid-century, China's economy will be almost the same size as the aggregate of the economies of India, Japan, Russia, Indonesia, S. Korea and Australia.[22] Its power potential will thus be equal to (or greater than) the combined power potential of the six largest democratic economies in Asia. It would, therefore, be in the interest of these democracies to greatly enhance their economic and

---

20. The emerging India-Israel relationship can also play a critical role in closing the technology gap.
21. Giving rise to, the US's willingness to overlook Pakistan's acquisition of bomb designs (from China), its illegal purchase of equipment and materials from the West, its proliferation of nuclear technology through the nuclear black market, its role as a progenitor and supporter of the Taliban and the home of Osama Bin Laden.
22. The position will be even more asymmetric if Hong Kong and Taiwan are incorporated in China.

technological co-operation during the next two decades. It should also act as a spur to development of a comprehensive co-operation agreement between India and ASEAN based on the framework agreement for an India-ASEAN FTA that has been signed in 2004.

Figure 8.2 shows that Japan has passed the peak of its potential power $VIP^2$ and will be on a declining trend over this century. Its power potential has already fallen below that of China and will fall below that of India within the next 20 years. The gap between Japan and the European powers of the 20th century, will close steadily over this century. It will, however, remain a significant power during the first quarter of this century, if it changes its pacifist approach and develops a more muscular foreign and national security policy. Japan has been shaken out of its complacency by the N. Korean missile test over its territory and the development of nuclear weapons by the latter.[23] Recent statements of the Japanese Prime minister and joint statements with the USA in the context of the US-Japan security treaty give a hint of this change. If Japan indeed becomes a 'normal nation' it can play a critical role in securing peace in Asia in co-operation with other democratic countries of Asia during the first quarter of this century.[24] It is in the interests of an aging Japan to increase its economic and technological co-operation with India.[25] It could go further and partner India in promoting democracy, securing the sea-lanes from W. Asia to E. Asia and strengthen ASEAN independence (freedom of action). The process of change in Japan's policy may, however, be too slow and incremental (given the strong resistance and the nature of consensual decision making).

According to our mean forecast, the power potential $VIP^2$ of Russia will rise slowly to exceed that of Germany by mid-century. It will, however, remain less than that of Japan, reaching about 3/4th of that of Japan by mid-century. If these scenarios turn out to be correct, both Japan and Russia would be classed as regional powers at that point. However, in the interim period, they can play a critical role in closing

---

23. Is China involved in this proliferation to larger/smaller extent than in Pakistan? Was the objective the same, namely, to undermine potentially powerful neighbours i.e. Japan and India respectively?
24. One sign of non-normality was the contrast between Japan-China and Japan-India relations during the 1980s and 1990s.
25. First to a level that it has had with China.

the India-China economic and technology gap (respectively) and, thus, help ensure a stable balance of power in Asia.

## 5.7 Timing of Tripolarity

Will it matter if the most appropriate technology parameter for measuring power is 1 rather than 0.5? Not really, as the only effect would be to increase the time it would take for the world to become bipolar and tripolar! It is not necessary for a country's power to exactly equal that of the strongest power to emerge as a second pole. A power of 50 per cent ($VIP^2$ with $\alpha = 1$) would make a country an alternative pole. China will clearly emerge as the second pole by the beginning of the second quarter of the century as its power potential will be over 50 per cent of the USA by 2030 and equal it by 2045 (Table 8.2). China will, therefore, be in a position to challenge the US power in Asia by the end of the first quarter of this century. Whether and how it chooses to do so will depend on many factors including the balance of power in Asia and its level of strategic technology.

**Table 8.2**

*Variation in Power Potential with α*

| | *2000* | *2010* | *2020* | *2030* | *2040* | *2050* |
|---|---|---|---|---|---|---|
| China | | | | | | |
| $\alpha = 0$ | 0.50 | 0.81 | 1.13 | 1.47 | 1.76 | 1.94 |
| $\alpha = 0.5$ | 0.16 | 0.34 | 0.58 | 0.89 | 1.21 | 1.45 |
| $\alpha = 0.75$ | 0.10 | 0.23 | 0.43 | 0.70 | 1.02 | 1.28 |
| $\alpha = 1$ | 0.06 | 0.15 | 0.31 | 0.55 | 0.85 | 1.11 |
| India | | | | | | |
| $\alpha = 0$ | 0.25 | 0.35 | 0.52 | 0.76 | 1.05 | 1.34 |
| $\alpha = 0.5$ | 0.06 | 0.10 | 0.18 | 0.33 | 0.54 | 0.79 |
| $\alpha = 0.75$ | 0.03 | 0.06 | 0.12 | 0.23 | 0.40 | 0.62 |
| $\alpha = 1$ | 0.02 | 0.03 | 0.07 | 0.15 | 0.29 | 0.48 |
| Japan | | | | | | |
| $\alpha = 0$ | 0.34 | 0.30 | 0.27 | 0.25 | 0.22 | 0.20 |
| $\alpha = 0.5$ | 0.29 | 0.26 | 0.23 | 0.21 | 0.19 | 0.18 |
| $\alpha = 0.75$ | 0.27 | 0.24 | 0.22 | 0.20 | 0.18 | 0.17 |
| $\alpha = 1$ | 0.25 | 0.23 | 0.20 | 0.18 | 0.17 | 0.15 |

Similarly, in the case of India, even with a technology parameter of 1, India's power potential will exceed that of Japan by 2035. By the middle of the century it will be about 50 per cent of that of the USA. Thus, it will emerge as a third pole in a tripolar world. By way of comparison, second ranked Japan's power potential ($\alpha=1$) at the height of its potential power in the early-1980s was less than one third of the USA. It has declined to one-fourth of the US by 2000. France, Russia and other countries had a fraction of this power potential and were, therefore, in no position to challenge the USA. In the case of the rich countries, the power potential does not vary much with the technology parameter.

## 6. DYNAMICS OF ASIAN GROWTH

Few observers have taken the possibility of India's emergence as a global power seriously or have acknowledged that China could challenge US power within the first quarter of this century. As our projections for India and China differ significantly from those by earlier authors, it is necessary to provide a rationale.

### 6.1 China

Collins and Bosworth (1996), later corroborated by the World Bank and IMF, have shown that China's growth from 1980 to end-nineties was over-estimated by 1 per cent to 2 per cent. Young (2000) has asserted that China's growth is over-estimated by as much as 3 per cent. If we make an adjustment of 2 per cent, China has demonstrated its ability to sustain growth at about 7.5 per cent per annum over 25 years. Most observers have, however, been forecasting a slowdown in this growth rate and a few have even predicted a dramatic slowdown.[26]

The IMF (2004) has shown that China's growth so far is on a trajectory similar to that of Japan and the Newly Industrialising Economies (NIEs) in a similar period of their development, though it is faster than that of the ASEAN-4. The 1990s were a period of above average international trade growth and the current decade could see

26. See IMF, World Bank and ADB reports on China and Chang (2001). See also Virmani (1999 b, c).

a slower growth in goods trade. As China's share of the world's goods exports rises to US levels, its export growth will slow. The rise of its per capita income (and wages) to upper-middle income levels and then to high-income levels will contribute to this slowdown. Other factors (discussed below) will also contribute to the slowdown. In our mean forecast we have, therefore, assumed that China's growth rate will fall gradually to more normal levels (Table A8.1).

A stylised model of China's 'socialist market economy' is needed to understand its strengths and weaknesses.[27] China is a corporate state with a clear vision of national power through economic growth and technological catch-up. The Communist party of China (CPC) forms a command and control network that is a mix of centralisation and de-centralisation. The CPC/State translates this vision into reality at multiple levels (large firm, city, province, nation) that are broadly coherent but far from perfect (not devoid of contradictions). A very large fraction of assets are still owned and controlled by the State/CPC network which appoints the top management in listed companies, co-operatives, T & V enterprises and state owned enterprises. The State, therefore, has a high share of national profits and consequently, the ability to have both low tax rates and very high investment rates (including in infrastructure). These high investment rates are one element of the growth strategy.

We know from the USSR experience that this can lead to unsaleable inventory stock, falling capacity utilisation and collapse. China has successfully dealt with this problem by liberalising output/product markets and orienting its system to push exports. The promotion of export-oriented FDI is a vital means for achieving the latter. The parallel push to attract technology oriented FDI helps avoid the other failing of the USSR, stagnant or negative technical change in the civil economy (i.e. all non-strategic areas). The primary 'market' economy is in products (goods and non-infrastructure services) where even CPC controlled enterprises compete to maximise growth, as in a private corporate economy. The socialist planning system still operates, however, in factor markets (land, labour, capital) and

27. In the late-1930s Oskar Lange put forward the idea of "Market Socialism," an economy in which assets (means of production) were owned socially (party), but which mimicked the supply-demand price adjustment of the competitive market economy.

infrastructure and the pricing of these inputs is used to provide (hidden) subsidies to foreign investors and domestic exporters.[28]

The key driver of economic growth since 1985 has been FDI and exports.[29] Adoption of an FDI-export led growth strategy converted China from an autarchy into an essential link in the global production chain developed by the NIEs and ASEAN 4 between 1965 and 1985. China created conditions (suspension of normal labour rights, capital subsidies to counter every negative) for a wholesale shift of labour intensive (LI) production by Chinese entrepreneurs from Hong Kong, Taiwan and other countries in S. E. Asia to the Special Export Zones (SEZs) and regions. These labour intensive (LI) export goods are now highly competitive.

The conventional wisdom is that China's phenomenal success in LI exports is due to the superior productivity of Chinese workers.[30] In reality the per-hour worker productivity is not much different from that in any other country, at a similar level of income (perhaps lower). The output per man-month is, however, much higher because hours worked per week/month are 50 per cent to 100 per cent higher than in equivalent democratic market economies, being unconstrained by labour laws.[31] China does, however, have an unassailable comparative advantage in mass scale organised manufacturing and construction.

Non-labour intensive exports (even those produced by FDI) are not necessarily globally competitive. The banking system, provides loans to state enterprises producing capital goods, intermediate goods and infrastructure services at zero effective capital cost. 'Non-performing assets' (NPA) is a misnomer as it is known in advance that many loans will not be repaid.[32] These implicit subsidies are then

28. Cities/provinces can and do price land to any buyer at any price. The labour responsibility system determines where a person can work legally and where he/she cannot. The banking system is like a government department where loans are decided by the concerned CPC boss on the basis of provincial/national objectives and the ability to repay is irrelevant (zero cost of capital). Infrastructure pricing and supply (particularly to foreign invested enterprises) is similarly decided on the basis of national/provincial/city objectives and can vary with enterprise.

29. Like Thailand and Indonesia.

30. To this, a second point has been added in the last five years—the first class infrastructure in and around the FDI-export hubs. It is forgotten that poor infrastructure in Jakarta/Indonesia and Bangkok/Thailand did not prevent these two countries from growing fast for decades.

31. Reports suggest that 10 hours a day 7 days a week is not uncommon in labour intensive units producing for export. This ironically results in a reduction in per hour productivity below what it would be, if working hours were the same as in state owned enterprises.

32. A Mckinsey journal volume on China (2004) gives just a hint of this.

transformed through below cost prices, into explicit subsidies to the FDI-export complex and to hi-tech industry.[33] This is a significant factor in attracting hi-tech FDI and capital intensive exports.

The FDI-export drive is critically dependent on building and sustaining optimistic expectations about the economy and the Asian crises demonstrated the vulnerability of this model. The obverse of high social ownership of domestic assets and consequent high investment rates, is a low share of private consumption in GDP. The rate of capacity build up is much faster than the growth of private consumption, leaving exports as the only means for balancing supply and demand. China's membership of WTO and rising job fears in OECD countries will result in increased scrutiny of and resistance to subsidised exports. Given the continuing generation of NPAs, China is somewhat more vulnerable on this count.[34] Its income distribution is also worse than in other successful Asian economies. On the other hand China's large economy has domestic strengths and bargaining power that were absent in the smaller Asian countries. These will result in a slowing of growth and not a sudden collapse if the CPC/Government continues to adapt its policy to the changing circumstances and imperatives as it has repeatedly done since 1980.

There are political arguments for a sharp slowdown in economic growth. The distribution of income has worsened dramatically since 1979. Part of this deterioration is the reversal of unsustainable levels of equality reached during the Maoist years. The rest of the deterioration was a conscious decision to accelerate growth by focussing subsidies and infrastructure development into the FDI-export areas in the coastal regions during 1985 to 2000. Given the restrictions on internal movement of workers (the labour responsibility system), this translated into growing income inequality. Further, the retreat of the state from provision of social goods has also translated into greater inequality in the receipt of public and quasi-public goods. Out of a total of 127 countries, China ranks 91 in terms of the Gini co-efficient of inequality, and 94th in terms of the

33. The prices of intermediate goods in China are reportedly less than their price on the high seas outside India—i.e. before taxes, delays or red tape.

34. Which have resulted in a (disguised) national debt of 50 per cent to 100 per cent of GDP.

consumption share of the poorest 20 per cent of the population. Rising inequality has a potential for socio-political upheaval and counter repression that could disrupt growth.

Some have gone further to argue that there is an inherent contradiction between the market economy whose success requires competition and plurality and the centralised political system that suppresses independent democratic thinking and impulses.[35] If the contradiction cannot be managed, it has within it the seeds of a socio-political explosion that will bring growth to a halt for a substantial period of time (after which it could resume at a much slower rate). This contradiction is much more than it was in S. Korea (say) and the latter eventually succumbed to the democratic impulse. The counter argument is that dictators can and have maintained highly repressive regime for decades after upheaval. Whether growth rate can be maintained along with repression, depends on the response of the rest of the world. The probability of such an economic collapse is, in our view, less than 15 per cent.

If the above contradiction can be successfully managed, we would have a third scenario in which China becomes even more powerful than is anticipated in the mean scenario. In this Communist China, the ultimate corporate state (mammoth version of Singapore), is able to maintain inordinately high growth for half a century to become the sole super-power by mid-century. This seems to us the least likely scenario with a probability of less than 10 per cent.

In both these scenarios (with probability less than 25 per cent) the danger to peace and security in Asia would be heightened. In the first case, because oligarchies are more likely to use nationalist jingoism and create external threats to divert the attention of the dis-affected. In the second case, because "power corrupts and absolute power corrupts absolutely." In both these scenarios, there would be a greater need for all democratic countries in Asia to co-operate much more closely with each other and provide mutual support. Similarly, the logic of an Indo-US partnership for peace would be even stronger.

---

35. K. Subrahmaniam *et al.*, (1995).

## 6.2 India

In contrast to China, we assume a steady rise in the underlying growth rate of the Indian economy over the next 10 years. According to India's National Accounts data the GDP and per capita GDP have grown at an average of 5.8 per cent per annum and 3.7 per cent per annum, respectively, during the last 24 years (1980-81 to 2003-04).[36] The comprehensive reforms instituted in the 1990s have increased competitive pressures on the Indian economy while at the same time enhancing its ability to compete globally. The growth rate has, however, increased by only about 0.6 per cent point.[37] The opening of the economy to international trade seems to produce a J-curve effect. The direct negative effects of competition appear immediately as capacity utilisation falls in un-competitive product lines. With capital immobile, reduction in capital stock is limited by the rate of depreciation. The positive effects of competition on productivity appear gradually. New technology is first adopted by the pioneers and effected through new investment. It diffuses gradually to other firms in the industry.[38] Improvements in productivity will, therefore, appear at the aggregate level only after a lag. We, therefore, expect the underlying trend rate of growth in India to move up to around 6.5 per cent over the next few years.

The growth rate is assumed to rise further to 7 per cent thereafter on the assumption that reforms will continue at the average pace seen since 1991 (Virmani, 2004a).[39] Three specific (modern services, FDI and demographic transition) and three general factors make this increased growth feasible and sustainable. First, the one area in which the improved competitiveness of the Indian economy is clearly visible, is in the double-digit (20 per cent to 30 per cent per year) growth of

36. The WDI data underestimate the GDP growth rate substantially though the per capita GDP growth rate is almost the same.

37. From 5.5 per cent per annum during 1980-81 to 1991-92 to 6.1 per cent during 1992-93 to 2003-04.

38. There are numerous cases of firms that have transformed their systems and shown large increases in productivity. The effects of these are not, however, available in the sector data.

39. This book summarises the reforms proposed in a series of internal papers done in the Ministry of Finance (Department of Economic Affairs), Govt. of India, from 1995 onwards. The underlying theme of these suggestions is to increase competition in every market and sector by removing the distortions introduced by the Indian version of socialism and to focus government effort on the supply of public and quasi-public goods and services.

information technology (IT) and IT enabled services (ITES) export. Though, such non-traditional (i.e. excluding transport and tourism) service exports are already a significant share of India's total exports, they constituted a very small part of the economy. Therefore, the impact on GDP growth was limited. With the continuing high growth of non-traditional service export, they are now becoming large enough to have a measurable impact on GDP and contribution to GDP growth could rise from 0.5 per cent to 1.5 per cent points over a decade.[40] India is likely to become one of the largest suppliers of non–traditional services to the world over the next few decades (including R & D, financial, medical, educational and social services).[41]

The second factor is the un-exploited potential of foreign direct investment (FDI). India is already an attractive location for skill-intensive manufacturing because of the high quality and availability of middle management/technical skills and knowledge workers. Several areas of competitiveness related to such skills are already visible, namely biotechnology, auto engineering (parts) and specialised chemicals.[42] (Ch. 7)

With China's per capita income more than twice that of India's its hourly wage will eventually attain the same ratio. Membership of the WTO and scrutiny by global NGOs will make it increasingly difficult for foreign invested firms in China to make people work 100 hours a week. India will, therefore, become a more attractive location for low and medium scale labour-intensive manufactured exports *vis-à-vis* China. The new SEZ law can reduce red tape/bureaucracy, introduce much needed flexibility in labour laws, rules and procedures and accelerate the development of high quality infrastructure, thus expediting this process. FDI can play a critical role in integrating India into the global supply chain for a host of products. If domestic hurdles to global operation are removed, FDI could add at least a point to growth.

The third important factor is the demographic transition that is taking place across the world. The high growth of E. and S.E. Asian

40. Starting at the lower end and going up to the higher end of the range.
41. OECD aging citizens will benefit greatly from the universalisation of services that their lower cost will make possible.
42. With the introduction of a product patent regime from this year, the protection of the legal system will now be available to drug developers.

countries was to a substantial degree due to the demographic transition (Bloom *et al.*, 2001). China is nearing the end of its demographic transition while India has entered its most positive phase. We estimate that this could add between 0.5 per cent to 0.8 per cent points to the growth of the Indian economy.

In addition, the population of Europe and Japan is aging rapidly and there will be a great demand from these economies for 'youth-intensive' goods and services. Over the next half century India will have the youngest labour force in the world. India is therefore likely to become the largest exporter of such items.[43]

There are also several general factors that will sustain growth. One is the existence of a large 'under-utilised' pool (20 million to 100 million) of free thinking, autonomous working, high IQ people.[44] The second is the high quality and diversity of India's institutions and the social capital built over centuries.[45] The democratic system, including the relatively new non-governmental institutions and free and vibrant media, is a great source of long-term strength.[46] The third is the experience of working with citizens of very diverse backgrounds (religious, ethnic, language, sub-culture) and the facility with English. This pluralism and language facility is a unique advantage in the globalised 21st century. India is also ideally placed to partner OECD countries in the emerging global knowledge economy of the 21st century. These specific and general factors are sufficient to overcome

---

43. As China's population will age much earlier than that of India it is not in a position to exploit this opportunity.

44. The normal distribution of IQ in a population, means that two per cent of the population has very high IQ and 10 per cent has high IQ. Applying this to India we get 20 million and 100 million people respectively. Bad economic policies till 1980 resulted in gross under-utilisation of this resource.

45. Infirmities in its political system have led over the last four decades, to a deterioration in the quality and quantity of public goods (roads, policing and legal system.) and quasi-public goods supplied. The high fiscal deficit is merely a symptom of this deterioration in governance. This down trend in governance must and will be reversed. China had similarly high levels of social capital but much of this was destroyed during the Communist Revolution and the Cultural Revolution.

46. Rodrik and Subramanian (2004) estimate that India's (China's) income level is 15 per cent lower (higher) than that predicted by the quality of its institutions. India's income will, therefore, rise to the predicted level with the correction of wrong policies, while China will not be able to sustain the same growth at higher income levels where these institutions are critical.

any negative growth factors, to raise growth to a sustainable 7 per cent or so.[47]

There are some questions raised by India-sceptics about poverty and inequality in India, which have to be viewed in the light of the following facts. India is a low-income country, so the proportion of poor is still high (about 23 per cent).[48] The absolute number of poor is, thus, larger than the total population of all but two countries (USA and China). It is democratic so the poor are free to live and work anywhere and are therefore visible everywhere. India's income distribution is, however, among the top quarter of the 127 countries for which the Gini co-efficient is available.[49] It does very well for the poorest 10 per cent whose consumption share is the 6th highest among these 127 countries.[50] India is one of a handful of high growth countries whose income distribution has not worsened significantly during the high growth period (Cornea and Court, 2001). By 2010, when India becomes a lower-middle income country, the poverty rate will be reduced to about 15 per cent.[51] Poverty is likely to be completely eliminated by the time it becomes an upper-middle income country around 2025.[52]

What about the down side? The greatest long-term weakness is on the political side. Infirmities in the political system have led to a gradual deterioration in the quality and quantity of public goods (policing, legal system) and quasi-public goods supplied. The governments' lack of success in suppressing Maoist and other insurgencies in the interiors of the country is a reflection of this failure.[53] Political/governmental reforms are necessary over the next decade to ensure that the system remains on even keel.[54] Though,

47. A more optimistic scenario is also possible in which growth reaches the 7.5 per cent-8 per cent range and remains there for a decade or so. The probability of this is 10-15 per cent in our view. Surjit Bhalla (2000) has been asserting for the last 3 years that India's growth rate will soon exceed 8 per cent.

48. The poverty rate or head count ratio is 29th out of 87 countries for which data is reported.

49. 32nd to be precise.

50. 14th for consumption share of bottom 20 per cent and 25th for bottom 40 per cent of the population.

51. Based on official rate in 1999-2000 (26 per cent) adjusted for survey changes (*i.e* 28 per cent-29 per cent). We assume a decline of 1 per cent point per year based on the average decline since 1980.

52. Before that, the national poverty line will probably be raised.

53. The high fiscal deficit is (merely) a symptom of this deterioration in governance.

54. See Virmani (2004a) for the new development paradigm needed for high growth in India.

Indian democracy responds slowly to such intangible threats, it has always been able to deal with them in a democratic and non-disruptive manner. The mean scenario assumes that the Indian economy will not grow above 7 per cent because of this weakness despite other strengths. I would put the probability of a more serious governance failure that reduces aggregate growth significantly, at less than 10 per cent.

Will India's power potential be translated into actual power as (implicitly) assumed? Historically, Indian forays into the outside world have been driven by commerce and culture. Even the culturally Indian kingdoms that came to be established in S.E. Asia had no connection with India—they were neither colonies controlled from India nor paid tribute or bore allegiance to any ruler in India. India therefore lacks a tradition of strategic thought and experience, Tanham (1992). There are some who feel that there is an 'intrinsic timidity in the Indian character' that results in a lack of geopolitical will. If true, this could open a gap between its power potential and actual power. Consequently, the gap between the actual power of China and India could be even larger than the gap in power potential.[55] This would increase the risks to global peace and make it even more important for OECD democracies like the USA, Japan, UK, Germany and France to help and support India in acquiring a global role.

## 6.3 Japan and Russia

Our assumption for Japan is perhaps more optimistic than justified by its growth over the last 25 years. The growth projection could, therefore, be viewed as an upper bound. If Japan's growth is slower than assumed and India's growth does not match up to the forecast, balance of power will be even more unbalanced in Asia than in our base scenario.

Russia's growth is also assumed to be much higher than it has been in the past. Even though the oil price rise has led to an acceleration of growth, this push will end after oil prices have stabilised. Russia has the advantage of a relatively educated/skilled workforce and vast natural resources. The growth rate will depend on policies that ensure their effective utilisation.

---

55. There is little doubt about China's determination to become a 'Great Power'.

Similarly our projections for Brazil are more pessimistic than that of others. We have assumed that Brazil's economic growth will pick up gradually above the average that has prevailed since 1980, but will not exceed three times this average. This is very modest compared to the performance of Asian economies at similar income levels. In other words, the assumption is that Brazil's growth will not get anywhere close to its growth performance during the high growth period of the sixties and seventies.

## 7. THE EUROPEAN UNION: MULTIPOLARITY?

Whether or not the EU can emerge as another pole in a multipolar world depends on its evolution into a 'virtual state'. A 'virtual state' is a super-national body with elements of a nation state, such as the power to tax and to use the tax revenues for security (defence and offence). As the primary focus of the EU has been on economic union, let us first analyse this aspect. The economy of Europe and Central Asia is projected to decline from a little over 125 per cent of the US economy to about 90 per cent to 100 per cent of the US economy.[56] The EU constitution, if and when passed, will certainly make the EU administration another player on the global scene. It is also within the realm of possibility that over the next few decades the EU government will take over all the functions of member states with respect to external economic policy. This would imply a one point EU/EC interaction on economic matters with other countries, regions, the IMF, World Bank and other economic bodies of the United Nation and surrender of their individual seats on the latter by member states. Such a unified EU could, therefore, have an economic clout equal to that of the USA.

Let us turn to the traditional attributes of national power in terms of national security and diplomacy. Conceptually, the EU's global power could be the aggregate of its member countries if they all surrendered it to a single unitary EU presidency. If they surrender half their power, while retaining half of it, the EU virtual state's power would be approximately half that of the aggregate power of members, that is about 45 per cent to 50 per cent of the USA's power potential ($VIP^2$ $\alpha = 0$). This could make the EC a major player on the global

56. This can be taken as approximating the future EU.

scene. The other side of the coin, however, is that this would reduce the EU4 to minor global players in their own right. The EU4 (Germany, UK, France, Italy) whose aggregate power would still be about 48 per cent of the USA in 2050 are unlikely, to surrender so much of their diplomatic and military power to the EU and become minor powers.

A surrender of mere 1/4th of each member's power to the EU will mean that the latter has about 20-25 per cent of US power in 2050. An alternative scenario is one in which all the smaller powers of the EU surrender most if not all of their global power to the EC, while the EU4 retain most of their independent national power. This could result in the EC having about 1/3rd the power of the USA. This would put the EC in a position similar to that of Japan at its peak power.

Would the EC have the will to emerge as the fourth pole if this means an eclipse of the individual power of the EU4. In other words, would Germany, UK, France and Italy permit their individual global power to be completely eclipsed by that of the EC? According to current indications this amount of power accumulation by EU (surrender by member states) is unlikely. This is reflected in: (a) the increased resistance to the surrender of financial power by UK and others to the EU, (b) the strong push by Germany to become a permanent member of the Security Council, and (c) the move to include 'Asian' Turkey into the EU so as to strengthen multiculturalism and diversity in the EU. Its current direction, therefore, appears to be towards an umbrella organisation with increasing soft power and not a powerful virtual state in the traditional mold. If soft power counts more than military power in the 21st century then the EU could be the fourth pole in a quadripolar world.

## 8. A PARTNERSHIP FOR PEACE

Within a decade, China's economy will become larger than the US economy and may be almost twice as large by the middle of the century (in terms of GDP at purchasing power parity). Its power potential $VIP^2$ will therefore equal that of the USA sometime during the second quarter of this century. The world will become bipolar much before that happens, probably at the end of the first quarter. In parallel, India's economy will overtake Japan's within five years to become the third largest in the world (GDP ppp). India will become a global growth engine in about 15 years, with its impact on the world economy larger than that of Japan. The Indian economy will equal the US economy in size by 2040 (GDP ppp). The world will, therefore, become tripolar by the middle of the century. The size and power of China relative to India is projected to peak within a decade (at around 2.3 times and 3.5 times respectively). The gap will close steadily, thereafter, and be eliminated during the fourth quarter of the century. India will consequently be the weakest pole for most of this century, and China's attitude towards India will have a vital bearing on peace in Asia. Good relations between India and China based on mutual respect and equality will be critical to peace in Asia.

As peace and stability in Asia will be of vital economic interest to the rest of the world, the advanced democratic countries (EU, Japan, US) must consider how to ensure a stable balance in Asia. The USA and India share fundamental human and democratic values. It will be in their mutual interest to develop a strong partnership for peace in Asia. India's then Prime Minister, Mr. Atal Behari Vajpayee stated on a visit to the USA that, India and USA are "natural allies." The USA, as the predominant power today, should strengthen India's economic and technological capabilities so as to benefit in future from its young labour force and large potential supply of knowledge workers. One element of this partnership should, thus, be a comprehensive economic co-operation agreement. The USA must also recognise the critical strategic role that a democratic India will play in the 21st century and change its laws, rules and procedures to help close the latter's technology gap with China. In parallel, India must recognise the critical role that current sole super-power USA can play in sustaining peace in Asia during the first half of this century and co-operate confidently with it for mutual benefit.[57]

For the next decade or so, US foreign policy will be driven by its traumatic experience of 9/11 and its desire to protect the US

57. The pre-independence generation must jettison its post-colonial dread of economic and political exploitation by the West and the post-independence establishment must abandon its cold war, bipolar, non-aligned approach to national security. The Indian government and people will also have to learn that national security is not and cannot be based merely on fellow feeling, bonhomie, grand words and charity; it requires hard headed evaluation of gains and losses from each partnership.

homeland and citizens from terrorist attack.[58] This factor is, therefore, likely to be a major driving force in its policy towards Islamic countries particularly those situated between India and Europe. A radical change in the US policy towards India appears less likely than a gradual evolution, though recent statements by the US Secretary of State, Condelezza Rice, suggests that the former cannot be ruled out. India's traditional technology partnership with Russia and evolving ones with UK, Germany, France and Japan will likely continue to play a role in narrowing critical gaps in India's strategic technology.

The role of Russia, Japan and the EU in the tripolar world that will emerge three decades from now is uncertain. It is unclear whether Russia will focus on the opportunities and threats in Europe, Central Asia or East Asia. Japan's dependence on the Japan-US security treaty is likely to increase over time. This is, however, not inconsistent with a more assertive Japanese role in Asia. It is not clear, however, how long it would take for Japan to develop a new social consensus to acquire all the characteristics of a 'normal nation'. The EU can play a role similar to the US in Asia if it has the will to do so.[59]

India must take the initiative in developing co-operative and inclusive economic structures in Asia, based on the lessons of European history and the EU with support from the EU. A vital stabilising role could be played by an Asian Economic Community that includes all the major powers of Asia (China, India, Japan) as well as S. Korea and the ASEAN countries.[60] The Indian Prime Minister, Dr. Manmohan Singh has endorsed this concept at an ASEAN summit at which an India-ASEAN FTA (framework) agreement was signed. By analogy with the European Coal and Steel Community the Asian Energy or (petroleum) Oil Community proposed by India's Minister (PNG), Mr. Mani Shankar Aiyar, could act as a precursor to the Asian Economic Community. The EU should support the formation of an Asian Economic Community in the interest of peace and stability in Asia.

---

58. While preserving its traditional role of Israel's protector.
59. The EU and its member countries have only recently started re-evaluating their approach to India *vis-à-vis* China. How quickly the ground situation will change is unclear.
60. The possible inclusion of West Asian and Central Asian countries and Russia can also be considered at some stage.

## Appendix A8.1

*Assumptions and Projections*

The assumptions regarding the future growth rates in per capita GDP at PPP are summarised in Table A8.1. This gives the evolution of per capita GDP at PPP. These are used along with the UN's population projections to derive the index of power projection. The evolution of the VIP$^2$ ($\alpha = 0.5$) is summarised in Table A8.2.

**Table A8.1**

*Growth Rate of Per Capita GDP at PPP*

*(Per Cent)*

| *Country* | *(1980 to 2002)* | *(2003 to 2015)* | *(2016 to 2025)* | *(2026 to 2035)* | *(2036 to 2050)* |
|---|---|---|---|---|---|
| USA | 1.8 | 2.0 | 2.0 | 2.0 | 2.0 |
| China | 8.2 | 6.6 | 5.6 | 4.9 | 4.0 |
| Japan | 2.0 | 1.8 | 2.0 | 2.1 | 2.0 |
| India | 3.6 | 5.2 | 6.0 | 5.7 | 4.8 |
| Germany | 1.6 | 1.4 | 2.0 | 2.1 | 2.2 |
| France | 1.6 | 1.8 | 2.0 | 2.1 | 2.3 |
| UK | 2.0 | 2.2 | 2.2 | 2.2 | 2.4 |
| Italy | 1.8 | 1.6 | 1.9 | 2.0 | 2.0 |
| Brazil | 0.7 | 0.7 | 1.5 | 1.5 | 2.2 |
| Russia | | 4.9 | 4.5 | 4.1 | 3.6 |
| Canada | 1.6 | 2.5 | 2.3 | 2.2 | 2.2 |
| Mexico | 0.8 | 1.8 | 2.1 | 2.3 | 2.3 |
| Spain | 2.3 | 3.0 | 2.8 | 2.6 | 2.2 |
| Korea, S. | 5.7 | 4.3 | 4.0 | 3.7 | 2.6 |
| Indonesia | 3.7 | 3.3 | 3.7 | 3.6 | 3.5 |
| Australia | 2.0 | 2.5 | 2.4 | 2.1 | 2.2 |

*Source*: *http://esa.un.org/unpp/p2kodata.asp(2004).*

## Table A8.2

*Index of Power Potential $VIP^2$ ($\alpha = 0.5$)*

| *Country* | *Actual* | | *Projected* | | | | |
|---|---|---|---|---|---|---|---|
| | *1980* | *2000* | *2010* | *2020* | *2030* | *2040* | *2050* |
| USA | 1.00 | 1.00 | 1.00 | 1.00 | 1.00 | 1.00 | 1.00 |
| China | 0.03 | 0.16 | 0.34 | 0.58 | 0.89 | 1.21 | 1.45 |
| India | 0.03 | 0.06 | 0.10 | 0.18 | 0.33 | 0.54 | 0.79 |
| Japan | 0.31 | 0.29 | 0.26 | 0.23 | 0.21 | 0.19 | 0.18 |
| Germany | 0.25 | 0.19 | 0.16 | 0.14 | 0.13 | 0.13 | 0.12 |
| UK | 0.14 | 0.13 | 0.12 | 0.12 | 0.12 | 0.12 | 0.12 |
| France | 0.17 | 0.13 | 0.13 | 0.12 | 0.11 | 0.11 | 0.11 |
| Korea, S. | 0.01 | 0.05 | 0.07 | 0.09 | 0.11 | 0.12 | 0.11 |
| Russia | 0.15 | 0.05 | 0.07 | 0.09 | 0.11 | 0.12 | 0.13 |
| Canada | 0.09 | 0.08 | 0.09 | 0.09 | 0.09 | 0.09 | 0.09 |
| Italy | 0.17 | 0.13 | 0.11 | 0.09 | 0.08 | 0.07 | 0.06 |
| Spain | 0.07 | 0.06 | 0.07 | 0.07 | 0.07 | 0.07 | 0.07 |
| Australia | 0.05 | 0.05 | 0.05 | 0.05 | 0.05 | 0.05 | 0.05 |
| Mexico | 0.06 | 0.05 | 0.04 | 0.04 | 0.04 | 0.04 | 0.05 |
| Brazil | 0.08 | 0.06 | 0.05 | 0.05 | 0.04 | 0.04 | 0.04 |
| Indonesia | 0.01 | 0.02 | 0.02 | 0.03 | 0.04 | 0.04 | 0.05 |

*Source*: *http://esa.un.org/unpp/p2kodata.asp(2004)*.

# 9

# East Asian Regionalism and its Impact

## 1. INTRODUCTION

Regional economic integration in E. Asia is essentially a response of the ASEAN group of nations to the imperatives of economic recovery in the post-crisis period. In its search for relevance and its pre-crisis dynamism ASEAN has been working towards deepening the process of integration in the region. ASEAN is aware that regional economic integration will not only strengthen the economies and make them more efficient but also enable them to effectively meet the challenges and competition posed by globalisation and emergence of preferential trading arrangements (PTAs) in the rest of the world.

PTAs have been growing in number and importance in recent years. By their nature, PTAs favour trade among nations and discriminate against non-members. Trade among members grows at the expense of the rest of the world. With the emergence of powerful trading blocs like the European Union (EU) and North American Free Trade Association (NAFTA) about 60 per cent of world trade is conducted on a preferential basis rather than on most favoured nation (MFN) basis. The consequent diversion of trade and increasing intra-regional trade has an adverse affect on the growth process in the regions that are not a part of these trading blocs. Asian countries that have followed multi-lateralism rather faithfully find that their products are discriminated against in the world markets. Also, the extent of complementarities at the level of the existing sub-regional groupings in Asia like SAARC and ASEAN, are limited. Trade creation on account of the formation of these blocs has not been significant (DeRosa, 1995; Ikemoto and Elliott, 2003). In fact, intra-ASEAN trade is only about 1/10 the level of total ASEAN trade.

---

Co-authored with Dr. Amita Batra.

The Asian Crisis has further diminished growth prospects of the ASEAN nations at a time when global trade growth was slowing. Growth in the region is subject to increased volatility and the region is perceived to be more susceptible to financial boom and bust cycles. There is a need, therefore, for ASEAN to look for growth impulses outside the ASEAN countries and to diversify its engines of growth further from the traditional ones like the US and Japan towards other Asian economies and its trading partners like Korea, China and India. China and India constitute the new growth poles in Asia.

ASEAN should actively engage India and China along with Korea and Japan to provide the region with the necessary diversity in resources, productive structures and wider economic opportunities, both actual and potential. India, in particular, with its complementary economic structure, can provide opportunities for economic cooperation and mutual benefit to the ASEAN member nations. The economic opportunities, existing and potential, thus, provide the rationale for ASEAN, SAARC, China, Korea and Japan to think of a singular economic entity in Asia rather than to treat each other as distinct and divided by race and ideology. A common Asian economic identity that extends ASEAN to include India along with China, Korea and Japan is the subject of this chapter.

The chapter is organised as follows. In the next section, the rationale of a singular economic Asian identity is explained. Section 3 presents the case for the extension of ASEAN plus three westwards to include India. The section also highlights the deepening ASEAN-India institutional and economic relations. A brief review of the bilateral and sub-regional cooperation initiatives that India is currently involved in, and that complement the efforts at regionalism, in Asia, is given in Section 4. Section 5 concludes the chapter.

## 2. RATIONALE FOR A REGIONAL GROUPING IN ASIA

The concept of Asian unity or Asian Economic Community (AEC) was first conceived by India's first Prime Minister Jawahar Lal Nehru and revived recently, in October 2003 at the Bali ASEAN summit by the then Indian Prime Minister. While the improved growth performance and the direction and pace of economic reforms in S. Asia make the divide between South and East/South East Asia much less meaningful, there are also several other factors that contribute to the idea of the AEC. These are discussed below.

## 2.1 Economic Factors

### *2.1.1 Financial Resources, Size and Diversity of the Market*

The region comprising the 14 nations (ASEAN 10 plus China, Korea, Japan and India) has a sufficiently large market and financial resources to support and sustain rapid development of the region's economies. The region's population at 3 billion is about half the world's population. China and India, the region's largest and fastest growing economies in the world, can together provide a large market. The GNP of all the economies in the region adds to over US $ 7.2 trillion and is comparable to EUs in 2000 (US $ 8.2 trillion). In terms of purchasing power parity (PPP), ASEAN 14's national income is US $ 15 trillion, which is more than that of NAFTA (US $ 12 trillion) or EU (US $ 11 trillion). The combined total reserves of this region are over $ 1 trillion, which are much larger than that of EU. The proposed 14 country singular economic entity has a 19 per cent share in total world trade, which is comparable to the 21 per cent share that NAFTA has in world trade.

**Table 9.1**

*Comparison of ASEAN with Regional Blocks*

| | ASEAN | NAFTA | EU |
|---|---|---|---|
| National Income (Trillion US $) | 15 | 12 | 11 |
| Population (Billion) | 3.03 | 0.42 | 0.45 |
| Total Reserves (Trillion US $) | 1.2 | 0.25 | 0.52 |
| Share of World Trade (%) | 19.22 | 20.97 | 38.8 |

*Source*: World Development Indicators, World Bank.

In addition, the level and diversity of economic development in the proposed regional grouping is such as to provide for requisite economies of scale and scope. While for smaller countries, access to larger markets will enhance their growth, the accumulated wealth of Japan and the Republic of Korea and the huge markets of China and India will create new opportunities for trade driven growth in the region.

### *2.1.2 Magnitude of Intra-regional Trade*

Intra-regional trade for the proposed Asian grouping is significantly larger than intra-SAARC or intra-ASEAN trade. Intra-SAARC trade is a paltry US $ 3 billion while intra-ASEAN trade at US $ 74 billion is also less than the intra-AEC trade figure of US $ 404 billion. Intra-SAARC trade constitutes about 2 per cent of total SAARC trade and intra-ASEAN about 12 per cent of total ASEAN trade. Considerable scope, therefore, exists for expansion of trade for the two sub-regional groupings with their own member countries and with each other.

The AEC therefore, implies mutually beneficial linkages across all member countries. In fact, as shown in Table 9.1, the economic prospects of other existing economic communities pale in comparison to the potential held by the combined market of about half of the world's population in some of the fastest growing economies i.e. India and China in the world. India, in particular, with its complementary economic structure, stable and sustainable growth pattern provides the basis for its participation in the proposed broader regional economic grouping.

## 3. ASIAN ECONOMIC COMMUNITY—WHY INDIA?

With the end of Cold War and the creation of a new world order, India, recognising the economics of neighbourhood, has emerged as a willing partner in the process of regional economic integration. The convergence in economic policies in Asia has also led to a rethinking on the earlier strategic assumptions that influenced the emergence of particular regional groupings in Asia. The new world order, thus, provides scope for redefining the territorial compass of the groupings of the future. These developments are buttressed by India's conscious attempt to engage E. Asia through what has come to be known as India's Look East Policy.[1]

Further, over the last decade and a half India has attained the identity of a dynamic economy in pursuit of a high rate of economic growth through the process of liberalisation and economic reform.

1. India's Look East Policy is a product of both the force of liberalisation and the desire to emulate the East Asian growth miracle.

ASEAN, in its post-1997-98 crisis scenario, could use the fresh infusion of the stable and sustainable economic dynamism of India. The Indian economy has grown at an average rate of 5.8 per cent during the 1980s and at 6 per cent during the 1990s. India recorded the second highest average growth rate of 6.06 per cent per annum during 1992-2001 after China. The growth process in India has been accompanied by macroeconomic stability. The CV (Table 9.2) in the rate of growth of GDP in India was only 0.24 during 1992-2001 in comparison with the other ASEAN member countries like Indonesia (CV = 1.58), Philippines (CV = 0.61), Thailand, etc. The exchange rate in India has also moved within a narrow range. Stability in exchange rate is evident from the CV that was 0.33 in the pre-reform period and has since fallen to 0.18 in the post-reform period. Even in the turbulent period of the East Asian crisis, the Indian rupee did not undergo any wild fluctuations, as was the case in many of the E. Asian and South E. Asian economies. Further, the inflationary forces in India have been under control and in fact, inflation has been maintained at single digit levels almost throughout the period of reform. The stability in the pattern of growth observed in India over the last decade, is in contrast with the growth fluctuations experienced by E. Asia and S. East Asia. Table 9.2 provides evidence in favour of this.

**Table 9.2**

*Coefficient of Variation (CV)*

| Country | *Exchange Rate* | | | *Growth Rate* | | |
|---|---|---|---|---|---|---|
| | *(1980-1991)* | *(1992-2000)* | *(1995-2000)* | *(1980-1991)* | *(1992-2001)* | *(1995-2000)* |
| India | 0.33 | 0.18 | 0.13 | 0.40 | 0.24 | 0.26 |
| Indonesia | 0.40 | 0.74 | 0.62 | 0.37 | 1.58 | 3.59 |
| Japan | 0.26 | 0.10 | 0.11 | 0.33 | 1.20 | 1.14 |
| Korea | 0.11 | 0.24 | 0.23 | 0.46 | 0.82 | 1.12 |
| Malaysia | 0.08 | 0.21 | 0.21 | 0.52 | 0.88 | 1.15 |
| Philippines | 0.40 | 0.24 | 0.24 | 2.50 | 0.61 | 0.60 |
| Singapore | 0.07 | 0.07 | 0.09 | 0.49 | 0.75 | 0.57 |
| Thailand | 0.08 | 0.23 | 0.22 | 0.40 | 1.41 | 3.40 |
| Vietnam | - | - | - | 0.32 | 0.20 | 0.26 |

*Source*: International Financial Statistics, IMF and World Development Indicators, World Bank.

Further, India's growth process is regarded as more sustainable relative to other emerging economies of the region. Growth in India is an outcome of a protracted process of liberalisation and economic reform. Domestic private consumption has been the primary driving force for the growth process. As such, therefore, the fear of over-heating, as is the case of export-led growth processes adopted in many other countries of the region, does not hold for India.

Growth in India has also been accompanied by a steady structural transformation of the economy. The services sector is emerging as the leading sector in the Indian economy. The average contribution of the services sector to GDP in India in the post-reforms period is 46 per cent. This share has increased from a pre-reform share of around 40 per cent. The share of the agricultural sector in GDP has, over the same period, experienced a decline while that of the industry has remained almost constant. Figure 9.1 depicts the movement in sectoral shares in GDP in India over the period 1980 to 2002. The period has been divided into two phases—the pre-reform phase between 1980-1991 and the post-reform phase of 1992-2002. The year 1991-92 has been separately marked as the year of balance of payment crisis in India.

## FIGURE 9.1

*Sectoral Shares in GDP in India*

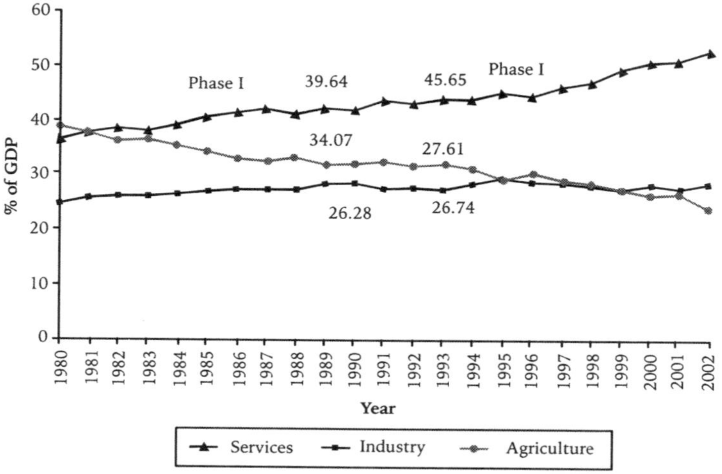

Increasing importance of the services sector in India complements the economic structure of East/South East Asia that is dominated by the manufacturing sector. S.E. Asia and E. Asia have a pre- eminent position in the world as a leading centre for production. India is emerging as a service provider for the global community. India has managed to corner a lion's share of the world's business processing outsourcing (BPO) needs while simultaneously acquiring the status of the largest player in the global software market. Complementarities in the economic structure of ASEAN, China, Japan, Korea and India are, therefore, evident. The AEC will provide the necessary platform to harness the complementarities.

Alongside the Indian economy acquiring a complementary structure to the manufacturing sector dominated E. Asian economies, it has also become a more open economy. The trade to GDP ratio has increased from an average of less than 15 per cent in the period prior to reforms to, 24 per cent in the post reforms period. The ratio has been increasing on a consistent basis in the post reform period and attained the maximum of 31 per cent in 2002. (Figure 9.2)

## FIGURE 9.2

*Trade Performance of India*

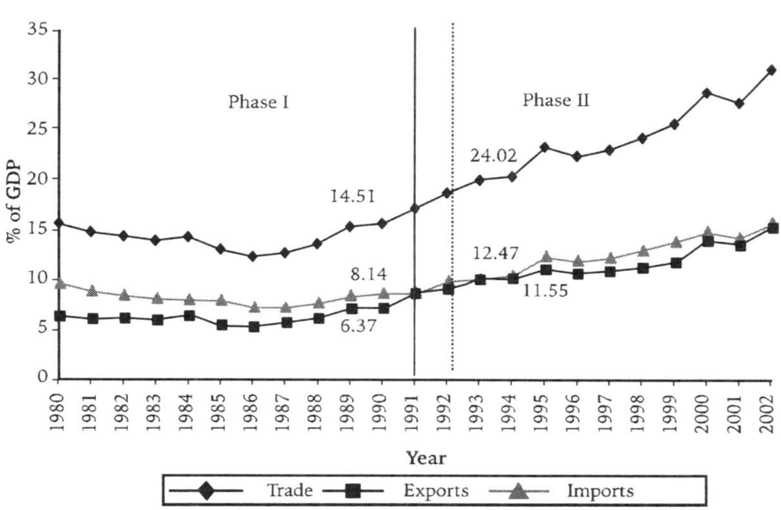

In the post-East Asian crisis period, the rate of growth in total trade in India has been comparable to and sometimes greater than that recorded by many of the South East/East Asian economies. India registered an average annual rate of growth of 13 per cent in total trade second after China (18 per cent) in the region during 1998-2002 (Table 9.3).

**Table 9.3**

*Growth Rate in Total Trade: 1998-2002*

*(Per Cent)*

| *Country* | *Average Rate of Growth in Total* |
|---|---|
| China | 18.1 |
| India | 12.9 |
| S. Korea | 10.5 |
| Thailand | 6.5 |
| Malaysia | 3.9 |
| Philippines | -.06 |
| Indonesia | -1.4 |

*Source*: World Bank, WDI, 2004.

Even while India is in the process of becoming a more outward oriented, services dominated economy that will complement the ASEAN member nations' manufacturing dominated economic structure, the density of India-ASEAN association has steadily increased. The relationship is more broad-based than it was a decade ago and ASEAN-India relations today encompass not just the institutional aspects but also a broad-based economic relationship.

## 3.1 ASEAN-India Association

### *3.1.1 Institutional Aspects*

ASEAN-India relations have progressed from sectoral dialogue partnership to annual summit-level meetings. India became a sectoral dialogue partner of ASEAN in 1992. The sectors were trade, investment, tourism and science and technology. The relationship was upgraded to full dialogue partnership in December 1995 at the fifth ASEAN summit in Bangkok. India became a member of the ASEAN Regional Forum in 1996. The ASEAN-India relationship was upgraded to summit level in 2002. India is now an ASEAN summit partner along with Japan, China and South Korea. The first ASEAN-India summit was held in November 2002 in Phnom Penh, Cambodia. This is an important milestone in the ASEAN-India association.

### *3.1.2 ASEAN-India Economic Relations*

The overall trend of ASEAN-India economic relations has been upwards, except during the East Asian crisis period of 1997-98. After the East Asian crisis and between 1999-2000 to 2002-03 total trade between ASEAN and India has grown by 42 per cent. Merchandise exports have increased by 106 per cent and ASEAN's share in India's total exports increased from 6 to 9 per cent, surpassing thereby the pre-crisis peak. In 2002-03 India-ASEAN trade was US $10 billion. Table 9.4 presents a detailed picture of the trends in ASEAN-India trade between 1998-2004.

**Table 9.4**

*Trends in India-ASEAN Trade*

| | (1998-99) | (1999-2000) | (2000-01) | (2001-02) | (2002-03) | (2003-04) |
|---|---|---|---|---|---|---|
| Exports | 1.6 | 2.2 | 2.9 | 3.5 | 4.6 | 5.8 |
| *% share* | 4.3 | 6.1 | 6.5 | 7.9 | 8.8 | |
| *% change* | -33.9 | 37.3 | 30.2 | 18.6 | 33.6 | |
| Imports | 4.3 | 4.6 | 4.1 | 4.4 | 5.2 | 7.4 |
| *% share* | 10.2 | 9.3 | 8.2 | 8.5 | 8.4 | |
| *% change* | 27.1 | 7.2 | -10.4 | 5.8 | 17.4 | |
| Total trade | 5.9 | 6.9 | 7.1 | 7.8 | 9.8 | 13.2 |
| *% share* | 7.9 | 7.9 | 7.4 | 8.2 | 8.6 | 9.3 |
| *% change* | 141.3 | 15.5 | 2.8 | 11.1 | 24.5 | 35.7 |

*Source*: Directorate General of Foreign Trade, India.

The share of all ASEAN member nations in India's exports rose during 1991-2003. Singapore has continued to remain the largest market for Indian exports followed by Indonesia, Malaysia, Thailand and the Philippines. The share of Vietnam, in Indian exports to ASEAN has experienced a six-fold increase in the same period.

Notwithstanding the positive trends in the ASEAN-India trade, the share of ASEAN in total trade for India is only 8 per cent and ASEAN-India trade constitutes less than 2 per cent of ASEAN's total trade. There is, therefore, potential for deeper economic integration. This is further reinforced by the fact that ASEAN and India share common land border[2] and historical and cultural backgrounds. Geographical proximity and common civilisational links open vast opportunities for trade for the economies of ASEAN and India. As the economic outlook of ASEAN and India converges, there appears to be enough common ground between ASEAN and India to forge ahead in cultivating the environment for expanding and deepening trade, investments and capital flows.

A growing body of research is suggestive of the complementary economic structure of India and ASEAN. As earlier stated, India is emerging as a largely service oriented economy while the ASEAN economies are known for specialising in manufactured commodities. There is scope for collaboration and cooperation with implications of mutual benefit for both ASEAN and India in areas like pharmaceuticals and healthcare, agricultural research, agro-processing and biotechnology, mineral exploration and processing, metal scraps, leather goods, textiles, machinery and electronic components and gems and jewellery. The IT sector offers vast opportunities for cooperation. India excels in software capabilities while ASEAN plus three member nations have expertise in the hardware industry. ICT services trade is another area where opportunities are in abundance. Another sector that offers substantial opportunities for ASEAN-India cooperation is the energy sector.

### 3.1.3 *ASEAN-India-Trade Expansion: Facilitating Factors*

Several factors facilitate trade expansion between ASEAN and India. India is pursuing a policy of speedy alignment of its tariff levels with the ASEAN countries. In 2000, average tariff rate in India was about 29 per cent compared to an average of 10-12 per cent for ASEAN. In February 2004, India announced wide-ranging reduction in tariffs, with peak tariff rate falling to 20 per cent for all manufactures. The gap between applied tariff rates in India and the ASEAN countries has, therefore, been reduced to a large extent. Recommendations for a further reduction and greater alignment of the peak tariff rates in India with ASEAN have also been made. Virmani (2002) recommends that with some exceptions, the peak tariff rate

2. With the westward expansion of ASEAN to include Myanmar, India and ASEAN are no longer just maritime neighbours but share a land boundary of 1600 kilometres.

should be brought down to 10 per cent for all imports by the end of the Tenth Plan and to 5 per cent by the end of the Eleventh Plan. In the light of the efficiency improvement induced by earlier tariff reform[3] and the accrual of foreign exchange reserves since then, it is recommend that peak tariff rate in India be reduced to 5 per cent by 2008-09.

A clear institutional framework for operationalising economic cooperation between India and ASEAN is already laid out. The framework agreement (FA) was signed during the second India-ASEAN summit held in Bali in October 2003. The FA covers free trade agreement (FTA) in goods, services and areas of economic cooperation. The negotiations on the FTA in goods are expected to be concluded by June 2005. The tariff reductions will start from January 1, 2006. The FA aims at increasing bilateral merchandise trade to US$ 15 billion by 2005 and to US$ 30 billion by 2007. The FA also provides for an Early Harvest Programme that specifies the areas for economic cooperation and a common list of items for exchange of tariff concessions. The exchange of tariff concessions on these products will start from November 1, 2004 and tariffs will be eliminated in three years. Discussions on the Rules of Origin and modalities for tariff reductions are to be finalised soon. A trade negotiating committee has been set up to carry out the programme of negotiations as spelt out in the FA.

The widening arena for economic cooperation made possible by the AEC will also have important spillover benefits for all the member nations. These benefits relate to strategic and developmental initiatives in the region.

## 3.2 India and the Initiative for ASEAN Integration (IAI)

India can play a role in the ASEAN initiative for ASEAN integration (IAI) aimed at helping the lesser-developed countries like Cambodia, Laos, Myanmar and Vietnam to catch up with the rest of the grouping. ASEAN is a two-tiered structure with more developed member countries like Singapore, Malaysia, Thailand and new entrants like Vietnam alongside the least developed economies in the region like Cambodia, Laos and Myanmar. It is, therefore, a challenge for

3. "Impact of Tariff Reforms on Indian Industry: Impact based on a Multi-Sector Model", *ICRIER Working Paper* 135, 2004.

partner countries in the regional bloc to learn to deal cooperatively with different approaches for different levels. India is already involved in development initiatives in these countries to bridge the intra-ASEAN developmental gap in different areas such as defence, combating drugs and illegal trafficking. India provides a line of assistance to the least developed S.E. Asian economies to enhance trade and investment as well as project assistance besides offering technical and technological cooperation.

### 3.3 Regional Security

India and ASEAN share common concerns over cross-border international terrorism. A common ASEAN umbrella will provide a forum to address issues of mutual concern including international terrorism and business interests. India, given its size, and strategic location in the Indian Ocean and its military strength, can play a positive role in this regard. India's accession to the Treaty of Amity and Cooperation (TAC) with South East Asia has reassured the members of ASEAN who had been alarmed at India's nuclear tests in 1998. India has also signed the agreement on combating terrorism and there are joint efforts to protect the sea-lanes to ensure energy supply lines. The vital commercial sea-lanes between W. Asia and S. E. Asia straddle the Indian mainland and its island territories. India has been a member of the ASEAN Regional forum (ARF) since 1996. The forum comprises Australia, Canada, China, EU, Japan, New Zealand, Papua New Guinea, Russia, South Korea, US, ASEAN 10 and India. It is a valuable initiative to promote a stable relationship between the major powers and also serves as a useful complement to the bilateral alliances and dialogues, which are at the heart of the region's security architecture.

While association with India will benefit ASEAN given the complementary economic structure and strategic positioning of India, the association holds significant gains for India as well.

### 3.4 Asian Economic Community: Gains for India

ASEAN plus three (China, Japan and Korea) provides a large market and wider investment opportunities for India given the economic potential of countries like Malaysia, Thailand and Singapore. Further, ASEAN plus three countries can serve as forward posts for

India's trade and investment initiatives towards N.E. Asia and Southwest Pacific. Given ASEAN's strategic importance in the Asia-Pacific region, India's current linkages with ASEAN and ARF can be used as a springboard to the Asia Pacific region, NAFTA and other important world trade groupings.

Realising the potential for gains of the AEC, India has actively pursued its relationship with the ASEAN plus three nations by way of involvement in cooperative frameworks both at the sub-regional and bilateral level. India's bilateral and sub-regional cooperation attempts, in fact, provide another dimension to the efforts at regionalism in Asia, which were hitherto being restricted to East Asia.

## 4. BILATERAL AND SUB-REGIONAL COOPERATION

India has actively supported the creation of bilateral and sub-regional groupings. Bilateral and sub-regional cooperation frameworks complement the larger goal of enhancing ASEAN-India ties. At present, India has ongoing bilateral initiatives in the form of a free trade agreement with Thailand and Comprehensive Economic cooperation Agreement (CECA) with Singapore. India-China relations have entered a phase where economics is taking precedence over all other issues. A Joint Study Group (JSG) has been set up to explore the possibilities for economic cooperation between the two countries. At the sub-regional, level, BIMSTEC and Mekong Ganga Cooperation (MGC) are the two important cooperative frameworks that India is involved in, in the South East Asian neighbourhood.

### 4.1 Bilateral Cooperation

India-Thailand, FTA: A framework agreement for the creation of a FTA with Thailand was signed in October 2003. A list of 82 items for which tariff reduction will be effective in three years has been specified. A zero duty regime will emerge by 2010. This agreement could help India's connectivity with ASEAN. Thailand is the only country that has (FTAs) with the two biggest markets—China and India. The India–Thailand FTA, thus, offers Indian investors access to the large Chinese market, besides that of ASEAN.

India-Singapore, CECA: India has a CECA with Singapore. Singapore is an important facilitator to India-ASEAN ties. It also acts as a bridge between India and China.

India-China, JSG: Economic engagement between India-China has been enhanced in recent years. Both countries are speeding up the efforts to facilitate bilateral trade and the tripling of trade in coming years seems to be a realistic target. The JSG was set up in 2004 to explore opportunities for economic cooperation in trade and investment. The two economies are already members of the Bangkok Agreement.

India and East Asia: India has had longstanding relations with countries of East Asia. India and Korea cooperate under the Bangkok Agreement. India and Japan have had longstanding economic and political cooperation. Japan is a major investor and a bilateral donor in India.

## 4.2 Sub-Regional Cooperation

At the sub-regional level, India is a member of BIMSTEC comprising Bangladesh, India, Myanmar, Sri Lanka, Thailand, Bhutan and Nepal. This initiative includes countries from both SAARC and ASEAN and, in fact, acts as a bridge between the two. In the ministerial meeting held in February 2004, members have evolved a framework agreement for establishing regional trade and investment among themselves. The first ever summit-level meeting for BIMSTEC was held in July 2004 when it acquired its new incarnation—as a Bay of Bengal Community. BIMSTEC is now SAARC minus Pakistan plus Thailand and Myanmar. In its new incarnation, it is known as the Bay of Bengal Initiative for Multi-Sectoral Technical and Economic Cooperation. The identified areas of cooperation are trade, investment, technology, transport, communication, energy, tourism and fisheries. This Bay of Bengal initiative is more dynamic and offers the prospect of widening the network for outward oriented growth in this part of Asia. It can emerge as a bridge between the more inward oriented South Asia, India in particular and the more outward oriented S. E. and E. Asia. Through this route India can reach out to the S. E. Asian region and beyond to the Asia-Pacific community. Also as the ASEAN component, Thailand can help speed up the pace of trade liberalisation and regional economic cooperation. It is important for India and Thailand to take some bold steps to widen the scope and relevance of this sub-regional arrangement. The Bay Bengal Community could also contribute to a better understanding of security concerns in the region.

MGC Group is the other sub-regional cooperative framework that India is involved in. Besides India, MGC involves Cambodia, Laos, Myanmar, Vietnam, and Thailand. The initiative, thus, spans many of the newer ASEAN member countries. The grouping aims at broadening and intensification of joint efforts at economic cooperation between ASEAN and India in the Mekong Basin. One major goal of this is enhancing the transport links that span India, Myanmar, Thailand, Cambodia and Vietnam. A major vision of this programme is to establish a Delhi-Hanoi road and railway link in the near future. These are important initiatives as the development of transport and infrastructure links ease the cross-border movement of goods and services across these nations and in the process, will facilitate the operation of the ASEAN-India FTA.

## 5. CONCLUSIONS

The AEC would, therefore, operationalise the bolder vision of Asian unity. Together, the 14 member nations can make this an Asian century and the region can emerge as not just the manufacturing hub but also the principal market of the future and global provider of services. The formation of a trading arrangement in this region will also help the region to play a more effective role in shaping the emerging world trade and financial system that is more responsive to its needs. The new challenges of globalisation including the risk of contagion in times of financial and economic crisis makes closer cooperation an imperative. The proposed AEC would not just act as an useful counterbalance to the NAFTA and the EU in world trade, but would also strengthen regionalism as an important instrument of trade policy across Asian economies.

To achieve integration, larger and stronger countries must take lead. This calls for involvement of India and China as the main gravitational forces in this region and also the richer countries like Japan, Republic of Korea and Singapore to play a proactive role.

The proposed economic grouping is already active in the form of ASEAN-India and ASEAN plus three. Currently, ASEAN holds two annual summits. The first is called 'ASEAN plus three' (China, Japan and South Korea) summit. The second is called ASEAN plus One (India) summit. It would be useful to explore ways to combine the two separate summits into a single forum. This would then represent all the major Asian economies and, in the process, signal Asia's ability and willingness to cooperate and pursue economic cooperation. Economic cooperation in the form of a financial arrangement—the Chiang Mai Initiative—a bilateral swap arrangement between ASEAN-China, Japan and Korea that links the international reserves of these countries, the Asian Cooperation Dialogue (ACD) and the Asian Bond Fund (ABF) are already functional. The latter two initiatives are at Thailand's initiative and India is an active participant in these initiatives. India is committed to contribute US $ 1 billion to the ABF.

India is already engaged in cooperative frameworks with countries of ASEAN individually, ASEAN itself through a FTA and with countries of East Asia such as Korea, China and Japan. The ASEAN-India FTA, the CECA with Singapore and the FTA with Thailand have deepened India's relations with S.E. and E. Asia. With ongoing efforts to form an E. Asia wide FTA under the ASEAN plus three framework, ASEAN could serve as a link between India and East Asian economies. The complementary economic structure and combined financial strength of the proposed Asian entity will provide the necessary impetus to the process of economic integration. The AEC would also enable both north and S.E. Asia to interact more effectively with India, that is already being recognised as being one of the future growth poles of Asia. The increased economic engagement could be a forerunner to an ASEAN plus four framework.

A combined AEC is, therefore, not difficult to envision and can be seen to evolve along the areas of complementarity discussed earlier in the chapter. However, economic integration in Asia will have to proceed in a phased manner resolving, on the way, the challenges of heterogeneity of ASEAN itself. The E. Asian region is one of vast diversity—culturally, politically and economically. Differences in value systems, political systems and stages of economic development are an undeniable reality. The challenges of heterogeneity have to be managed in a judicious manner so as to progress with the prospects of regional economic cooperation.

# 10

## India-China Economic Relations

The debate on India China economic ties has been catapulted to the centre stage of policy and academic enquiry across, international fora owing to the spectacular rise in bilateral trade observed in the last three years. In 2003-04, Sino-Indian bilateral trade touched a high of US $ 7 billion, up 47 per cent over 2002-03, the year in which the bilateral trade also rose by 60 per cent. In 2004-05 the two-way trade reached 9 billion, almost 10 times that of the figure a decade ago. Bilateral trade relations between India and China have, thus, witnessed a transformation in the last decade. India has emerged as the largest among China's trading partners in South Asia and among the top 20 trading partners of China otherwise. China is India's third largest trading partner. However, while this economic engagement is being taken forward with great vigour, definite contours of this engagement have yet to take shape. As the evolution of this economic relationship, within the larger socio-political context, is likely to have implications for the profile of regional economic integration in Asia and possible reverberations globally, a discussion of some issues that arise in this context is appropriate. In this chapter, after a review of the recent trends in bilateral trade, we analyse the available options for furthering bilateral trade and economic relations between India and China.

### 1. A REVIEW OF THE RECENT TRENDS IN BILATERAL TRADE

A review of the recent trends in trade between India and China is revealing. Trade between India and China has increased dramatically, both, in terms of volume and percentage growth. Total bilateral trade between India and China in 2003-2004 was US $ 7.0 billion, having registered an increase of 47 per cent over the 2002-2003 value of US

Co-authored with Dr. Amita Batra.

$ 4.7 billion. Indian exports to China in 2003-2004 amounted to US $ 3.0 billion, while imports from China in the same year were US $ 4.0 billion. Imports from China and exports to China have been increasing on a consistent basis between 1999-2000 and 2003-2004, leading to an increasing share of both, exports to and imports from China, in India's total exports and imports. Indian exports to China constituted a little over one per cent of India's total exports in 1998-99. This share increased to about 5 per cent in 2003-2004. The share of Indian imports from China in India's total imports has also registered a similar increase, from around 3 per cent in 1998-99 to a little over 5 per cent in 2003-2004.

The trade balance between India and China has, however, historically been in favour of China. In 2003-2004, India registered a trade deficit of over US$ 1 billion with China. In 2002-2003 India registered a trade deficit of US$ 817 million with China. The trade deficit was smaller in 2002-2003, in comparison with the deficit in 2001-2002, largely on account of a 107 per cent increase in India's exports to China. Imports from China, during this period grew by 37 per cent.

Some changes are evident even in the composition of the basket of goods traded. India's export basket, traditionally dominated by primary and resource based products, is now showing signs of diversification. Exports of auto components, pharmaceuticals and machinery items have been increasing over the last few years even though products like iron ore and iron and steel continue to dominate the export basket. In 2004-05, exports of iron ore registered a growth of almost 200 per cent. Along with iron ore and primary and semi-finished iron and steel, India's top ten exports to China now also comprise commodities like machinery and instruments, plastic and linoleum products, processed minerals, drugs and pharmaceuticals and inorganic/organic chemicals. In fact, commodity categories—primary and semi-finished iron and steel and marine products have registered negative growth in the last one year. Both these categories have also experienced a fall in their share in total exports from India to China. There is, therefore, a movement away from primary commodities and towards manufactured commodities in India's export basket to China.

Chinese exports to India, on the other hand, are fairly diversified and include resource based, manufactured items, as also low and medium technology products. Electronic goods, coal, coke and briquettes and organic chemicals constitute a major proportion of China's exports to India. Items like machinery and coal, coke and briquette have registered a growth of over 100 per cent. Items such as silk yarn and fabrics and other textile yarn, fabrics and made up articles have registered an increase in growth by over 50 per cent. There has been consistent positive growth in all items of India's top 10 imports from China in 2003-2004 and 2004-2005.

The increase in the quantum and changes in the structure of bilateral trade are conducive to a further expansion of bilateral trade. So that even though trade between India and China has undergone a dramatic transformation, there is yet, potential for more.

## 2. POTENTIAL FOR EXPANSION OF BILATERAL TRADE

ICRIER Working Paper 151 (Batra, 2004) has shown that the potential trade between India and China can be about 2.5 times the actual bilateral trade. The estimates are based on the analysis of international trade flows using the gravity model for a sample of 145 reporter countries for the year 2000. Indicators of economic size and, hence, proximity in demand and tastes (e.g. GNP in terms of purchasing power parity (PPP) and current international dollar values, population, per capita incomes, bilateral distance, geographical and cultural proximity like landlockedness, common borders, common language, common historical/colonial past and common membership in regional trading arrangements (RTA), have been included as explanatory variables in the model. The natural links between India and China and their geographical proximity open vast opportunities for bilateral trade. The economic dynamism displayed by India and China in the last decade also contributes to increased trade possibilities. India and China are among the fastest growing economies of the world and the high rate of economic growth has been accompanied by an increasing share of trade in GDP in both the countries. India and China are the two countries in the world with over one billion population each. The size of the market and trade possibilities are further enhanced owing to common membership of the Bangkok Agreement. The Bangkok Agreement is the largest preferential trade agreement (PTA) in terms of market potential. The size of the market and proximity of the two economies are, thus, indicative of a huge and as yet unexploited potential for trade between India and China.

Several other factors are also indicative of this potential for expansion of trade between India and China.

Share of bilateral trade in total trade of India and China, respectively, is small. Trade between India and China accounted for 5 per cent of India's total trade in 2003-2004. In the same year, India's exports to were US$ 3 billion, while imports from China were US$ 4 billion. However, exports to China account for only about 5 per cent of India's total exports and less than 1 per cent of China's total imports while Chinese exports account for 5 per cent of India's total imports and less than one per cent of China's total export volume. The fact that bilateral trade between India and China is increasing and trade shares are rather small clearly implies that there is a huge potential for enhancement of bilateral trade between the two countries.

This is further reinforced by the increasing trend in total external trade for both the countries, in recent years. China's total trade aggregated to US$ 851.21 billion at the end of 2003, representing an increase of 37.1 per cent over 2002. In the same period, exports registered an increase of 34.6 per cent and imports increased by 39.9 per cent. Between 2002-2003 and 2003-2004, India registered a growth of 22.3 per cent in total trade. In this period, imports grew by 25.8 per cent and exports by 18.2 per cent. In the last two years with industrial recovery in process and existence of current account surplus, Indian total imports have been growing fast (21.2 per cent) indicating a potential for higher total import growth. In 2003-2004, India's total imports were US $ 75.4 billion and China's exports US$ 437.9 billion in 2003. Hence, India and China can mutually gain through expanded bilateral trade.

The momentum for increased bilateral trade is also reflected in the higher and more broad-based propensity for consumption that is an inherent feature of sustained high economic growth. India and China have revealed significant economic dynamism in the 1990s. China is the global economic powerhouse and its contribution to the world economy was highest in 2003. The average GDP growth of China between 1990 and 2003 was as high as 9.3 per cent, and the annual GDP growth rate of India was 6.2 per cent between 1994 and 2002. In the foreseeable future, the Indian and Chinese economies are expected to maintain the rapid pace of economic growth, and the consequent increase in domestic demands will undoubtedly spur the development of bilateral trade. Also, with sustained high economic growth, as the number of consuming households and consequently the demand for consumer goods constantly increases in India, there is an increasing potential for export of Chinese goods in areas where they appear to be particularly competitive like durable consumer goods, electronic components, plastics etc.

There are also economic complementarities between India and China and that augurs well for trade and economic cooperation. The usual example given is that, while China is strong in hardware, India has the world-class basis for software, and there is therefore, opportunity for India and China to work together in embedded technology. It should, however, be remembered that Japan, South Korea and Taiwan are even stronger in hardware. A combination of India's software skills and any of these countries' hardware expertise can trigger a shift in the global technological landscape. China's keenness to harness this opportunity was reflected in the importance given to the Bangalore leg of the Chinese Premier's recent visit to India

As India and China enjoy a surplus of low cost labour and exports of labour-intensive products from both countries are growing rapidly, the two countries are bound to be seen as competitors in such products in global markets. An analysis of the relative comparative advantage for both countries in the global market, however, indicates the magnitude of competition in manufactured commodities to be almost non-existent. Possibilities for intra industry trade do, however, exist.

The process of globalisation has led to production chains being extended beyond national boundaries. So, even though both India and China have comparative advantage in similar sectors, such as chemicals, processed metals and alloys, machinery and equipment and textiles, within each sector they have comparative advantage in different sub-sectors and products. There is, thus, a possibility of developing intra industry trade between the two economies. India and

China can use their respective comparative advantages and build on different aspects of the value chain in similar products.

It is also true that, countries with similar economic structures and factor endowments can have large-scale trade with each other. Similar countries in terms of per capita income have intensive horizontal intra industry bilateral trade. It is a well-known fact that almost 60 per cent of US and EU trade is intra industry trade. The growing levels of per capita incomes of India and China give us a reason to expect the extent of intra industry trade to grow between India and China.

Scaling up of trade between the two countries is, therefore, highly desirable and perhaps even necessary. Economic cooperation between India and China can imply economic development and improvement in the standard of living, both being common goals of the governments of the two economies. The nature of economic cooperation/future economic relationship, however, is a topic worthy of discussion/debate. Considering the huge potential and recent trend of regional economic integration we may ask if a Free Trade Agreement (FTA) is the logical next step in taking the bilateral trade and economic ties between India and China to a new and higher level.

## 3. FTA-THE NEXT LOGICAL STEP?

Both China and India have, of late, emphasised regional economic integration as a complement to multilateralism. India and China are negotiating FTAs/CECA/PTAs with several countries/regions. India has actively supported the creation of regional and sub-regional groupings. At present, India has ongoing bilateral initiatives in the form of a free trade agreement with Thailand, Sri Lanka and Comprehensive Economic Cooperation Agreement (CECA) with Singapore. China has signed the Closer Economic Partnership Arrangement (CEPA) with Hong Kong and Macao and is negotiating FTAs with Chile, Australia and New Zealand. Against the background of India-China relations having entered a new phase, where economics is taking precedence over other issues, a Joint Study Group (JSG) was set up in 2004 to explore the possibilities for economic cooperation between the two countries. It is estimated that China-India regional trade agreement (RTA) would create an aggregate market of 2.3 billion consumers with a combined GDP of US $ 1.8 trillion. On the face of it, any such cooperation would help exploit the existing complementarities between India and China. China could learn from India in development of services and India could learn from China in promoting industrialisation.

However, the economic benefits of a bilateral FTA between India and any other country are not so apparent. Till two years ago, India had the highest non-agricultural tariffs in the world. Even though the peak rate has been reduced and is now close to the top 1/5th or 1/4th, tariffs on agricultural goods continue to remain high. As an FTA ultimately aims at reducing all tariffs to zero, any FTA would imply substantial trade diversion and welfare loss. So that, as long as India's tariff rates are high, the *a priori* assumption would be that an FTA with any country with lower tariffs is more likely to result in economic losses. The average applied tariff rate in China is 12 per cent in comparison with India's average tariff level of 29 per cent. Chinese tariff on agricultural goods is 19 per cent whereas in India, for many agricultural goods, the tariff rate continues to be about 100 per cent. For non-agricultural goods, India's tariff average is about 28 per cent as against the Chinese tariff rate of about 11 per cent. It remains to be explored however, whether an FTA between the two countries, will be equally beneficial to the two countries.

There are other reasons for scepticism towards establishment of an FTA between India and China in the immediate future. As stated above, the trade volumes between the two countries account for only 5 per cent of India's foreign trade and less than one per cent of China's total external trade. Given these very small shares in each other's total external trade, whether priority can be given to the FTA negotiations between China and India remains questionable at a time when regional trade blocs are rapidly gaining momentum amidst changing perceptions of the multilateral trading system. An FTA between India and China may, therefore, be hard to achieve in the short-term, even though its significance in forming a multi-country regional free trade system is more apparent given the extent of complementarities between and economic size of the union (*China Business Weekly*, 2004).

Another challenge to the forging of a free trade agreement on an immediate basis, between the two countries, is the reservation expressed by the Indian industry. Even though Indian manufacturing has now come of age and is exporting and investing internationally, there exists a certain amount of resistance to a surge in imports of inexpensive goods from China. That the opinion of the Indian industry should be considered as an input into the design of the FTA and a level playing field ensured for the indigenous industry, is borne out by the experience of the India-Thailand FTA. Substantial preparatory work must, therefore, be undertaken both at the policy and industry level prior to the FTA.

There is also a more basic objection to the India-China FTA. An FTA, by definition, does not include services, FDI or the movement of people—all issues that are of vital interest to India and those that may be covered under a CECA. An FTA may benefit China more than India considering the nature and composition of trade. Trade balance continues to remain in favour of China and India has not yet been able to make inroads in the Chinese market for high value-added manufactured goods. In the context of any FTA with China, a key issue that, therefore, would need to be addressed is the inclusion of the services sector. Can we achieve a balance by better access for our service exporters? Many in fact, would be tempted to answer in the affirmative, arguing that given the strength that India has developed in the service sector, any meaningful FTA with China must include this sector.

While this may be a possibility, it is unlikely during the next three years. Service trade is heavily dependent on domestic rules, regulations and procedures. Partly because of the language barrier and partly because China is still a Socialist nation run on the principle of the 'dictatorship of the proletariat', such rules and regulations can be extremely non-transparent to Indian exporters and subject to individualistic application and change. It would be a serious mistake to assume that if we reduce our goods tariffs to zero (the essence of a Free Trade Agreement), China will allow India free access to its service exports and the associated movement of skilled personnel. This will require a clear understanding of our national interest, hard bargaining, clear and explicit agreements and forceful implementation. In the next five years, China will open its economy to service exports in line with its accession agreement with WTO. This will open opportunities for Indian service exports and will also indicate how open China's service market will truly be. During the same period, the gap between India's and China's general tariff rates will be narrowed perhaps even eliminated. The scope for a mutually beneficial bilateral agreement will be much greater and we can and should revisit the issue in about three years.

A RTA with India may, nonetheless, benefit China in many ways. China needs to accelerate its process of regionalisation. The process of negotiation of the China-ASEAN, FTA has been slow after the initial agreement was signed in November 2002. Some of the more developed ASEAN countries like Singapore, Malaysia and Thailand have since launched separate FTA talks with Japan, Australia, US and also India. Further, China's efforts at regional economic integration cannot solely rest upon E. Asia as progress in this direction is severely constrained by the economic and political conditions in N. E. Asia. For China, therefore, talks with India are worthwhile and take the process of regional economic integration further. In fact, they may enable China, ultimately, to make its economic presence felt in Asia.

So while benefits to China may be more obvious and China's eagerness to open Indian markets to industrial exports from China through an FTA rather evident, it is pertinent to ask, how easy is it for India to respond. It is also important to explore the benefits that India may attain now or in the future, through an intensification of the economic relationship with China.

A possible benefit for India could be that in the light of growing Chinese proximity to India, others in Asia may also want to build closer ties with India to counter the Chinese strength. This may eventually accelerate the process of India's integration with ASEAN which has for long been opposed by China. Eventually, of course, a broader and deeper trade and economic relationship between India and China will not only serve the two economies but also accelerate the process of regional economic integration in Asia and maybe even the evolution of the Asian Economic Community.

As for India's response, it may be true that better trade relations are not necessarily contingent on and hostage to the building of trust. The essence of modern markets is impersonality. The systems of laws and rules that constitute the market as an institution allow strangers to trade with each other. If we only traded with our friends and relatives, the modern industrial economy could not exist. Impersonal trade can however, lead to greater information flows and knowledge and, therefore, help remove misperceptions. But, if trade is good then is more trade, engineered through a FTA, even better? This is false logic: More trade based on removal of distortions (e.g. a general reduction of our very high tariffs) is good for the Indian public; more trade based on creation of new distortions (e.g. selective reduction in tariffs for China) is bad both for the industry and the public.

Again, it may be true that today, there is, between India and China, a newfound enthusiasm and initiative to use improved economic relations as a tool for resolving long standing political problems. But can larger trade volumes act as a substitute for rebuilding trust where it has been destroyed? Between India and China, the basic source of mistrust is the undefined border and the supply of nuclear technology (e.g. atomic bomb designs, in violation of NPT) and material to countries/regimes hostile to us. Other issues impinging on 'trust' include: (a) Opposition to the entry of India into pan-Asian economic organisations such as East Asian economic organisation and ASEAN+3. (b) Implicit (through Pakistan) opposition to permanent membership of India in the UN Security Council. The fact that India supported replacement of Taiwan, China by China, PRC in the Security Council decades ago is merely proof of India's soft and sentimental approach in contrast to China's hard realistic approach. Trust can only be re-established by addressing these issues. The willingness, after a long time, of China's leadership to realistically address the border issue gives hope. On the other hand, the supply of nuclear and strategic technology to hostile countries/ regimes is not conducive to building trust. Trust is critically important in a broader 'partnership' in economic, technological or strategic areas. Trust cannot be compartmentalised. It can only be rebuilt by addressing the broad range of issues in a sustained way.

What then are the options before us to forge a closer economic partnership?

## 4. OPTIONS FOR CLOSER ECONOMIC PARTNERSHIP

A deeper understanding of the Chinese economy is revealing in this context. The ICRIER Working Paper 160 (Virmani, 2005a) has given a stylised model of the Chinese economy. Based on the analysis in the paper on China's growth strategy and the four pillars thereof: FDI-export policy, social ownership of capital assets, normal markets for most goods and services and control over banks and capital markets—it may not be inappropriate to suggest that the arguments for an FTA with China and according it, the market economy status are very weak. The price mechanism in China lacks transparency. In the wake of this argument Virmani (2005c) suggests that concerning India-China relations, it would be best to focus on normalisation of economic relations, settlement of the border issue and collaboration in areas where there are clear identity of interests (e.g. oil purchases) rather than jump from one extreme to another. A normal, realistic and well rounded relationship would augur well for the rest of Asia and last through the 21st century. Let us not, therefore, get euphoric over words like 'strategic partnership'.

Taking this line of argument further, the immediate task would be to identify and implement concrete measures so as to diversify India's export basket. Today, the Chinese economy has an immense need for materials. Its consistent growth in GDP and galloping exports has made it the world's biggest consumer of materials. China accounts for half of the world's consumption of cement, 30 per cent of coal and 36 per cent of steel. Its demand for metals impacted the global metal prices. All this has given great scope to countries such as India to boost their exports to China. India has taken some advantage already. This is reflected in the increasing exports of iron ore and iron and steel from India to China. The large share of iron and steel in the export basket is owing to the current high demand for steel in China owing to the construction boom. But this is likely to last only for the next few years. The eventual slackening of demand could hurt India's interests quite considerably over the long run. A proper assessment of the areas in which India has a distinct comparative advantage in the Chinese market would, thus, go a long way in creating a sustainable basis for taking the India-China economic relationship into the future.

The ICRIER study has identified the sectors that have the potential for achieving both these objectives. Other than agriculture and allied products—edible fruits, nuts etc., oilseeds, animal and vegetable fats and oils and marine products where India has traditionally enjoyed comparative advantage, there are other sectors that have potential for expansion of exports to China. These include material based manufactures like cotton; manmade staple fibres and filaments; plastics; organic and inorganic chemicals; machinery and equipment, etc. These sectors have many constituent commodities where India's export potential remains as yet unexploited in the Chinese market. A time bound plan to further exports in these categories can be drawn up by the respective authorities.

At the same time, the two countries should, jointly identify the constraints and barriers to bilateral trade and take measures to eliminate these. At present, constraints exist in the form of rules and procedures and their application, transparency, flow of information and language barrier. Trade facilitation, therefore, needs to be actively promoted. Uniform system of customs valuation, procedures and supervision should be evolved while simultaneously aiming at removal of all non-tariff barriers. The India-China study group has identified constraints and barriers that impede the attainment of this objective and recommended solutions. If these are sincerely and speedily implemented, there will be a mutually beneficial increase in trade, and the gap between potential and reality in respect of bilateral trade between India and China can be closed.

# Section III

## Political Economy: Social Welfare and Voting

# 11

# Economic Growth, Governance and Voting Behaviour

## *An Application to Indian Elections*

## 1. INTRODUCTION

Human actions, such as voting in a democratic election, are extremely complex phenomenon and depend on a host of economic and social factors (etc. caste, feudalism, coercion/fear), as well as political alliances. Though, economics plays an important role in many human decisions, it is not the sole determinant. The focus of this chapter is on the potential economic factors underlying voter behaviour in a democracy. It develops a simplified model based on economic theory (welfare and conditional probabilities) and governance problems prevalent in developing countries and emerging economies. The formal model does, however, include non-economic factors. The motivation for the chapter came from the General Election in India in 2004. Many fascinating economic explanations were advanced for the surprising result in which the incumbent party was defeated despite a universal forecast to the contrary. Even the best forecast, one by NDTV-Indian Express, did not predict the surprising upset. Most of the analysis so far bears little relationship to publicly available data. We use available economic data and the results of the General Election in 2004 as well as the state elections in the previous two years to check its consistency with publicly available data.[1]

Economic factors play a role in voting behaviour in two ways. An improvement/worsening of economic conditions can increase/decrease the probability of voting for the party perceived to be responsible for the change. Further, the independent or floating voter is more likely

1. That is, we validate (not test) the model in the spirit of validation of general equilibrium models.

to be affected by economic conditions than voters committed to a particular party for social, caste, religious and cultural reasons. As we know, small swings in vote share of a party can play a significant role in the number of seats won by different parties (along with alliances) and, therefore, this set of voters play an important role in electoral 'swings'.

Section 2 outlines a simplified model relating growth performance and economic governance to voting behaviour. Those who are interested only in practical implications (or are uncomfortable with algebra), can see the model results in sub-section 2.2 and go directly to Section 3. Section 3 examines the growth data and links it to voting patterns in the General Election of 2004 and the state elections that preceded it by less than 6 months. Though, our discussion is in terms of GDP growth rates (Table A11.1), per capita GDP growth rates reveal the same picture (Table A11.2). These per capita GDP growth rates reflect the growth of individual income and capture the rate of growth of the average person's income. The average person is acutely aware of the growth of his/her income even if he/she does not know the statistics of national or state GDP growth or per capita GDP growth.

Section 4 presents a qualitative analysis of the role of governance and the supply of public goods and services and shows how this is linked to the 'anti-incumbency factor'. Section 5 explores some complexities that arise in general elections when the incumbents are different at the Centre and state levels and when the period of incumbency is not coterminous. Section 6 summarises the conclusions.

## 2. MODEL

### 2.1 Simplified Economics

The welfare of the average citizen can be represented by a function containing his/her consumption of private goods and services Q and public goods and services X,[2] or:

$$U = U(Q, X) \quad (1)$$

2. Strictly all these are vectors.

X can be viewed as the quality adjusted quantity of public goods and services supplied. Private goods purchased are limited by the real disposable income Y and the quality adjusted price p of goods. That is:

$$p\,Q = Y,\ Y = (1\text{-}T)Y',\ T = Tx - Tr \qquad (2)$$

Y' is earned income, Tx is the tax rate and Tr is transfers received from the government per unit of Y'. The change in welfare of the average person/voter over a given period t (dU) can be represented as:

$$dU = U_1\, dQ + U_2\, dX \qquad (3)$$

$U_1$ and $U_2$ are the marginal utility of consumption of private and public goods respectively, dQ is the change in the value of private goods and services purchased and dX is the change in the supply of public goods and services by the government. We can replace private consumption by income to get:

$$dU = U_1\ (1\text{-}m)\ \{(1\text{-}T)\ [dY - (Y/p)\ dp] - Ydt\}/p + U_2\ dX\ ,\ \text{or}$$

$$dU = A'\ dY + B'\ dX - C'\ dp - D'dT,$$

$$A' = (1\text{-}T)(1\text{-}m)U_1\ /p,\ B' = U_2,\ C' = (1\text{-}T)(1\text{-}m)U_1Y/\ p^2\ ,\ D' = U_1\ Y(1\text{-}m)/p. \qquad (4)$$

m is the marginal propensity to save. For simplicity, savings are assumed either to be a fixed proportion of income or absent. The first term in (4) represents the effect of income (net of taxes and transfers) received by the average voter. Thus, the negative effect of increased taxes and the positive effect of increased transfers on the average voter can, in principle, be captured in this model. The last term represents the change in the price and quality of private goods available to the public. Thus, if policy reform and increased competition reduce prices or increase the variety and quality of consumer durable goods available to the average voter, such reform would have a positive effect.

$$dU_t = A'\ dY_t + B'\ dX_t - C'\ dp_t - D'\ dT \qquad (5)$$

We hypothesise that the average voter looks at the improvement in his/her welfare during the term of the incumbent party or coalition as represented by the Equation 5 and compares it to some benchmark $U^b$ (H1).[3] We further hypothesise (H2) that the benchmark is the

3. In India a full term is of five years. A government can fall because of loss of majority or it may call for mid-term election, which can be anytime between few months and five years.

welfare improvement during the previous government's term ($dU_{t-1}$) adjusted for the expectations aroused by the current government's promises and election slogans.[4]

The median voter model, which assumes a two party system and 100 per cent voting, provides a theoretical under-pinning for focussing on the marginal or swing voter. In our context of a multiparty system we modify this as follows: The probability of voting for the incumbent Pr is hypothesised (H3) to be a function F of the difference between a Utility benchmark $U^b$ and the actual Utility, and non-economic factors Z.

$$Pr = F(U_t - U^b, Z\text{-}Z^b) = F(U_t - U^b, Z) \quad (6)$$

Though, in general, the public service benchmark $Z^b$ may be non-negative, we assume for the empirical analysis of this chapter that it is zero. On differentiating Equation 6, substituting $U_{t-1}$ for $U^b$ and using Equation 5, we get,

$$dPr = F_1(U_t - U^b, Z)(dU_t - dU^b) + F_2(U_t - U^b, Z)\, dZ \quad (7)$$

The change in voting probability is related to the difference between the increase in welfare during the rule of the incumbent compared to the increase in welfare expected i.e. the benchmark ($dU^b = dU_{t-1}$) and the effect of change in non-economic factors (dZ). Substituting $U_{t-1}$ for $U^b$ and using (5) we get,

$$dPr = A(dY_t - dY_{t-1}) + B(dX_t - dX_{t-1}) - C'(dp_t - dp_{t-1}) - D(dT_t - dT_{t-1}) + E\, dZ,$$

$$A = F_1 A', B = F_1 B', C = C' F_1, E = F_2, \text{ where } A, B, C, E > 0. \quad (8)$$

$$dPr/dT = -(1-m)\, Y\, U_1\, F_1 < 0 \quad (9)$$

## 2.2 Implications

The following propositions follow from Equation 8 and Equation 9 along with earlier equations:

P1: The Probability of voting for the incumbent increases (decreases) with an acceleration (deceleration) in the rate of growth of income and an improvement (deterioration) in the supply of public goods.

4. The term of the incumbent may be different from that of the previous government (more or less).

P2: An increase (decrease) in the taxes paid or transfers received by the average voter will reduce (increase) the probability of voting for the incumbent.

As income taxes and transfers received by the average voter is generally a very small faction of earned income, its effect will usually be swamped by the growth factor. In cases where there is little or no change in income growth, they could, however, play a role, but still be dominated by the governance effects. In the empirical analysis, we approximate the growth of income of the average voter by the growth of GDP per capita. The change in supply of public services (quantity and quality) is analysed qualitatively and related to the quality of governance.

## 2.3 Complication: Divided Responsibilities

The model outlined in Section 2.1 assumes a single level of government for which voting is taking place. It is, therefore, appropriate for state (Provincial) elections and for general (Central/ Federal) elections in which the same party or coalition is ruling at the centre and the state. With multiple levels of government the ruling party can be different at the two levels. It therefore, needs to be refined further for a Central/Federal election in which the ruling party in the state/province is different from that at the Central/Federal level.

Before doing this we simplify the model along two dimensions. Measurement of the effect of quality changes (hedonic price indices) is beyond the scope of this chapter. We, therefore, simplify Equation 4 by assuming that dp=0 and also ignore tax changes by setting dt=0. As the focus of the chapter is on economic factors we can also simplify Equation 8 (further) by dropping the non-economic factors Z from the equation to obtain the simpler one:

$$dPr = A\ (dY_t - dY_{t-1}) + B\ (dX_t - dX_{t-1}) \qquad (10)$$

The average voter directly experiences performance at the state level. The question is how much of this (s)he attributes to the state government (S party) and how much to the central government (C party). We, therefore, get two probabilities as follows:

$$dPr(S) = a\ A\ (dY_t - dY_{t-1}) + b\ B\ (dX_t - dX_{t-1}), \quad a < b \leq 1 \qquad (11)$$

where a is the proportion of growth performance attributed to the party in power in the state and b is the proportion of the public goods performance attributed to it.

$$dPr(C) = (1\text{-}a)\ A\ (dY_t - dY_{t-1}) + (1\text{-}b)\ B\ (dX_t - dX_{t-1}),\ a < b \leq 1 \qquad (12)$$

In this situation, we would need to go deeper into the voting percentage of each party to see whether the reduction (increase) in each party leaves the relative position unchanged or inverts it.

A simplifying hypothesis is that b = 1. In this case, Equation 11 and Equation 12 simplify to,

$$dPr(S) = a\ A\ (dY_t - dY_{t-1}) + B\ (dX_t - dX_{t-1}) \qquad (13)$$

$$dPr(C) = (1\text{-}a)\ A\ (dY_t - dY_{t-1}) \qquad (14)$$

We expect that a would generally be quite close to 1, in which case Equation 13 would determine the outcome. Only in exceptional circumstances would the incumbent S party be able to pass the blame for poor performance of the state on to the Centre or the central party be able to claim the credit for good performance of the state.

Equation 11 to Equation 14 assume that the tenure of central and state parties/coalitions is identical. Adjustments have also to be made if the period of incumbency is different, as for instance, if the general election is taking place after the full five-year term but the S party has been in power in the state for only 2-3 years. First, the period represented by the t in Equation 11 (Equation 13) will be different from that in Equation 12 (Equation 14). Second, the a will be much lower if the C party was in power in the state earlier (i.e. before the 2-3 years that the S party has been in power). Third, the benchmark may be a hybrid.

## 2.4 State Monopoly of Private Good

In India, many sectors were exclusively reserved for investment by the public sector. Through this process of state monopoly, private goods were removed from the market. Some of these (e.g. electricity, railway) are still public monopolies and have below-market prices and supply rationing. Equation 2 and subsequent equations therefore, need to be modified to reflect this. The main changes are given below.

$$p' Q' = Y - p_1 Q_1,\ Y = (1\text{-}T)Y',\ T = Tx - Tr. \qquad (15)$$

Where $Q_1$ represents the rationed (private) goods supplied by the public monopoly, and Q' represents all other private goods. $p_1$ is the below market price charged by the public monopolist. As a result, Equation 5 and Equation 10 are modified to:

$$dU_t = A' \, dY_t + H' \, dQ_{1t} + B' \, dX_t - C' \, dp_t - D' \, dT \quad (16)$$

$$dPr = A \, (dY_t - dY_{t-1}) + B \, (dX_t - dX_{t-1}) + H \, (dQ_{1t} - dQ_{1t-1}) \quad (17)$$

This means that the average person is concerned not only about his/her income and supply of public goods, but also the supply of private goods (such as electricity and railway services) for which the government is a monopoly supplier. As in the case of public goods, the quality of supply of private goods produced by public monopolies has deteriorated over time. This is partly because these organisations are bankrupted by under-pricing and partly because of increasing X-inefficiency. Some of them have also been infected by the general deterioration of governance. Thus, in addition to the supply of public goods and services, the supply of private goods that the government has chosen to monopolise, also affects the voting behaviour of the average voter in India. Lack of electricity or availability of train seats, train robbery and rail accidents will effect voters (who use electricity or rail travel) over and above any effect they may have on income growth as long as they are monopolised by the government.

One implication is that privatisation of electricity distribution and passenger railway services will tend to free governments from direct responsibility and, thus, make it less likely to directly blame the incumbent governing party for any deterioration (as Equation 10 would become applicable).[5]

# 3. GDP GROWTH MATTERS

## 3.1 National Expectations and Reality

In a set of papers done at ICRIER, we have analysed the linkages between policy, reforms and economic growth. This analysis has brought out two sets of facts that are relevant to the issue. First the

5. In a transitional period, till such time as an efficient regulatory system is instituted by the government, they may continue to hold the party responsible for medium-long term trends.

facts about economic growth: India has indeed been 'shining' for the last 24 years relative to the previous 30 years. From 1980-81 to 2003-04 the Indian economy grew at an average rate of 5.8 per cent per year, the eighth highest in the world. This compares with the 3.5 per cent growth rate of the previous 30 years from 1950-51 to 1979-80, which placed us at the bottom of the global growth rankings during that period.

Thus, the benchmark that citizens use in gauging the performance of the government with respect to economic development and growth of their personal income has gradually risen over the last two decades. This is especially true of younger citizens who have become adults during the past two decades.

In any election, the voters are more concerned about the recent past than the more distant one. If one had asked any member of our substantial educated middle class about the growth rate of the economy before the election, they would have given a figure in the range of 6 to 8 per cent with a mean around 7 per cent (many are giving this number even now). The buzz in the media was about 8 per cent growth rates, a take-off of the Indian economy and India growing faster than China over the decade. The facts are quite different. The Indian economy grew at a rate of 5.7 per cent per annum during the past five years (term of incumbent), a rate, which is not only below the benchmark rate (the average for 24 years) but much less than the 6.1 per cent per year average during 1992-93 to 2003-04. Thus, the reality experienced by the average citizen was a GDP growth rate of 5.7 per cent during 1999-2000 to 2003-04 compared to an average growth rate of 6.7 per cent per year in the previous five years, 1994-95 to 1998-99 (Table 11.1). Per capita GDP growth correspondingly declined from 4.7 per cent per annum to 3.8 per cent per annum over the two periods (Table 11.2).

Campaign slogans tended to raise the benchmark towards the 7-8 per cent range. The educated elite may have convinced themselves of the boom in (/take-off of) the Indian economy, but the reality that the 'average voter' knew from personal experience was a significant 'slowdown' in the growth of the Indian economy since 1996-97. He/she could clearly see the big gap between the 'verbal' and the actual growth rate and would be more inclined (i.e. other things being equal) to vote against the party in power during these five years (in the Centre or the state). Further, political economy studies in the US suggest, that the economic performance that matters is not that of the six months preceding the election. Thus, the high growth rate of the last two quarters of 2003-04 (even taken at face value) may not have affected even Indian voters, contrary to what was assumed by neutral observers/analysts.

## 3.2 Reforms: Verbal and Actual

Incidentally, the slower growth rate does not represent the failure of reform. The 'verbal reforms' during the five years have been far in excess of the actual reforms. The main areas of actual reforms have been in telecom (price reduction and market growth), insurance (26 per cent FDI), highways (institutional reform but not policy reform) and the Electricity Act, 2003. The first three have been successful sector reforms, while the last is too recent to judge its effect. Though, half a dozen companies were privatised (for the first time), the programme came to a halt about two years before the election. In other areas new 'verbal reform' initiatives have not been followed up by 'actual reform'. The question of success or failure of the reforms, therefore, does not arise in their case.

## 3.3 State Results: Madhya Pradesh, Rajasthan and Bihar

The election results from Rajasthan and Madhya Pradesh, including the state elections that preceded the General Election, are consistent with our hypothesis. Economic growth in Madhya Pradesh declined from a simple average of 5.4 per cent per annum during 1994-95 to 1998-99 to an estimated 60 per cent of this level during 1999-2000 to 2003-04 (Table A11.1).[6] Per capita GDP growth correspondingly decelerated from 3.1 per cent per year to 0.5 per cent per year (Table A11.2). Economic growth in Rajasthan had decelerated even more sharply from 9.4 per cent per year to an estimated 45 per cent of this rate during the tenure of the incumbent party (Congress). Per capita GDP growth, therefore, collapsed from 6.7 per cent per year to 0.5 per cent per year (Table 11.2). The average voter in each state was, therefore, more likely to vote against the Congress party in these

6. State data is available at best till 2002-03. Data for Chhattisgarh is however available only till 2001-02, so, accurate estimates of growth are not possible.

states both in the state and the General Elections (held within 6 months of the former). Neither the global reputation of the Madhya Pradesh's CM as social sector innovator and leader in decentralisation, nor last year efforts of the Rajasthan's CM to project good governance could counter the impact of the sharp slowdown in growth.

The conventional wisdom on Bihar's growth performance under Shri Lalu Yadav is, that it has been performing very poorly. Recall the joke about Mr. Yadav responding to a comment about turning Bihar into a Japan in three years by asserting that he could transform Japan into a Bihar in three days. So, how come he confounded expectations by winning hands down in the general election? Surprise, Surprise! The average rate of growth of Bihar's GDP during the last five years (1999-2000 to 2003-04) is about 60 per cent higher than it was in the previous five years (4.8 per cent per annum). The rate of growth of per capita GDP correspondingly accelerated from 1.9 per cent per year to about 5.4 per cent per year (Table A11.2). The average Bihar (registered) voter would, therefore, be more likely to vote for the ruling/incumbent state party in election 2004 than in the previous general election.[7] That is why contrary to all forecasts the RJD improved its performance.

## 3.4 Growth Complexities: Delhi

The 'simple' economic analysis fails for Delhi because the incumbent won despite a reduction in the (per capita) GDP growth rate from 9.6 per cent (5.5 per cent) per year during 1994-95 to 1998-99, to (an estimated) 7.8 per cent (4.2 per cent) per year during the past five years (Table A11.1 and Table A11.2). A more 'complicated' analysis has to account for the fact that the growth rate was still among the highest in India and comparable to the best in the world. The relatively better educated/informed electorate in Delhi was also convinced that the incumbent was sincerely trying to improve governance i.e. the supply of public goods and services in Delhi (including through privatisation of electricity distribution) and would do a better job than the challenger. The governance factor is analysed further below.

---

7. Unregistered voters, those without voter ID cards or those who temporarily resided outside the state do not count in this arithmetic.

## 3.5 Benchmarks and Expectations: Andhra Pradesh and Orissa

What about Andhra Pradesh and Orissa? The international and national media, the stock markets and industry knew that Andhra had been shining under Shri Chandra Babu Naidu while Mr. Naveen Patnaik had botched the electricity privatisation! In both these states, the rate of economic growth during the past five years is estimated to be approximately the same as that in the previous five years. In Orissa the past five years the GDP growth was marginally higher than the 4.3 per cent (2.7 per cent) GDP (per capita) growth in 1994-95 to 1998-99, while in Andhra Pradesh it was marginally lower than (the same as) the earlier 5.7 per cent (4.3 per cent). Yet, one incumbent won and the other lost. The explanation seems to lie in the expectations aroused. The high profile Mr. Naidu raised the benchmark against which Andhra voters judged him, while the low key (non-Oriya speaking) Mr. Patnaik lowered the benchmark against which Orissa voters judged him. Another difference was that Mr. Naidu had served two terms as CM while Mr. Patnaik had served only one. The anti-incumbency/governance factor (see below) was stronger in the former than in the latter. Other factors, such as the association of Mr. Naidu with a party that in Gujarat aided violation of citizens' fundamental right to life and security (till the Supreme court intervened), may also have affected voters. As a consequence, the former was found by the average/marginal voter to be under-performing while the latter was perceived to be performing at an acceptable level.

## 3.6 Agriculture Growth and Rural Vote

These results have little to do with the rich-poor divide or the India-Bharat divide. There is no data to determine (a) whether the 'change' in poor citizens voting behaviour was different from the 'change' in middle class voter behaviour, and (b) that any group (poor, middle-class, rural, urban) voted for or against reforms.

Available data does, however, allow us to delve a little deeper into a sector on which rural voters are relatively more (but not solely) dependent, the agricultural sector. We find that the average rate of growth of agriculture has declined even more sharply from an average of 3.5 per cent per annum during 1994-95 to 1998-99 to an average of 2.1 per cent per annum during 1999-2000 to 2003-04. Thus, the average person/voter dependent primarily on agricultural income is likely to have concluded that his/her progress has slowed, rather than accelerated (as per the campaign slogans), during the last five years, relative to the benchmark of the previous five years. He/she would, therefore, be more likely, *ipso facto* (i.e. other things being the same) to vote against the party in power at the state level, responsible for the poorer agricultural growth performance.

This is, however, the average national situation and rainfall variations have a strong regional dimension. States such as Karnataka and Andhra Pradesh have been particularly affected by poor rainfall and drought conditions in the last 3-5 years.[8] In Andhra Pradesh, agricultural growth during 1999-2000 to 2003-04 is estimated to be 20-25 per cent lower than during 1994-95 to 1998-99. Thus, following the earlier logic, the average rural voter in Andhra Pradesh was more likely to vote against the ruling party. The ruling party of such states would, therefore, be more vulnerable (than is implied by the national average) to the attribution of poor agricultural performance to their lack of concern or competence. In Bihar's case the compound growth rate of GDP from agriculture in the last five years was similarly about *50* per cent 'higher' than the average of the previous five years even though the simple average growth was almost the same. This reinforces the earlier analysis of Andhra Pradesh and Bihar.

What about the 9.1 per cent growth in agriculture and allied sector during 2003-04, which as per arguments advanced, then would have endeared the voter to the ruling party? Well, this was preceded by a 5.2 per cent decline in agriculture and allied output during 2002-03 and all that the 9.1 per cent growth did was to bring output in 2003-04 back to where it would have been at a steady 2.3 per cent growth. Unlike the media watcher, the person dependent on agriculture would not likely have forgotten that the fall in agriculture output was earlier explained, as solely due to the weather, so the rise should symmetrically be attributed to the weather. Those directly affected knew quite well that the government had nothing to do with the short term fluctuations, but would remember how the government performed with respect to drought relief measures in 2002-03. The average agriculture dependent voter would consequently be even more

8. It is difficult to make accurate estimates of growth for Karnataka and West Bengal, as the data is available till 2001-02 only.

likely (i.e. higher probability) to vote against a state government that did not provide adequate relief during the drought of 2002-03.

## 4. GOVERNANCE AND PUBLIC SERVICES

The second important explanatory factor is the widening gap between individual income and the private goods and services purchased with this income (e.g. food, clothing durable goods) and the public and quasi-public goods and services provided by the government. While the former has increased/improved in line with the GDP, this is not necessarily true of the latter (police protection, roads, drinking water, sanitation and sewerage, public health, primary education services, agriculture R&D and extension). The ICRIER working papers have shown that there has been a slow but steady decline (over the past four decades) in the quality and efficiency of government institutions. The quality and average quantity of public services provided by the government to its citizens has, therefore, deteriorated. Deterioration in the quality of private goods supplied by government monopolies such as electricity boards has accentuated the citizens' negative experience of government performance (as private purchase from a competitor is not allowed).

### 4.1 Anti-incumbency Factor

This deterioration in governance is an important economic factor underlying the so-called 'anti-incumbency' vote observed by political analysts over the last three and a half decades. It has also been argued that the deterioration in governance has 'reduced the ability of the government to do good relative to its ability to do harm to the economy/its citizens' (Virmani, 2002b). Unless an incumbent government takes an active interest in improving the supply of public services, benign neglect will inevitably lead to a gradual deterioration. Thus, the anti-incumbency factor is closely linked to the slow and steady deterioration of governance systems. As long as the deterioration in governance is not halted and reversed, increasing the expenditure on public and quasi-public goods will not overcome the anti-incumbency factor. On the other hand, introducing competition into the supply of private goods and services such as electricity can not only help improve the supply of such goods, but also distance the government to some extent from the negative political fall-out of temporary shortcomings (but not permanent ones).

## 4.2 Beating Anti-incumbency

Though, we do not have detailed information on the quality and quantity of public goods and services provided by states, there is wide agreement among analysts that the Shiela Dixit government in Delhi has beaten the anti-incumbency factor through better governance and sincerity of purpose. Mr. Naidu and Mr. Digvijay Singh seem to have also done so in their first re-election bid 4-5 years ago but could not sustain it in the second re-election bid in 2003/2004. Mr. Naveen Patnaik has also managed it in his first re-election bid. The voters are perhaps more willing to give credit for good intentions and sincere effort in the first re-election bid, than they are in the second and subsequent re-election bids (when they judge by actual improvement). The credibility of the challenger is clearly important when the voters' judgement is based not on actual performance but on potential.

Only Mr. Yadav in Bihar and the Left Front in W. Bengal have beaten the anti-incumbency/governance factor the second time to win a third consecutive term. Migration from Bihar to other states and the flow of remittances from these migrants seem to have played a role in accelerating the growth of the Bihar economy (particularly services). Such migrants may also incidentally have voted with their feet (because of caste/party bias in terms of jobs, personal safety etc.) and therefore reduce the anti-incumbency vote. Another factor could be, a withering away of red tape and bureaucratic controls along with the state governance apparatus, an eastern version of 'Wild West Capitalism' (US West in the 17th century). The negative effect of such withering is perhaps reflected in activities such as extortion, kidnapping for ransom and contract murder. The deterioration in personal safety and security can in principle be managed to ensure that it is largely directed at castes and groups who do not vote for the ruling party. If controlled and moderated, most of the rents can be extracted from such opponent groups and can be channelled to supporting groups to ensure re-election (as against self-aggrandisement). Thus, any deterioration in opposition voters' economic well-being has no effect on the ruling party vote. Shekhar Gupta has written that the use of coercion and fear (in W. Bengal and

Bihar) also helps keep the ruling party vote bank intact during elections. This is a possible explanation for W. Bengal successfully beating the anti-incumbency factor in the second and subsequent re-election bid.[9]

# 5. COMPLEX CONDITIONS

## 5.1 Different Incumbents: Punjab

Punjab is another interesting/complicated case. At the time of the state elections, the economic growth rate under the incumbent (Akali) government had declined to 4 per cent per annum (1993-94 to 1997-98) compared to 4.4 per cent per annum during 1998-99 to 2002-03 (the benchmark). This combined with the governance factor, the deteriorating supply of public services, would have turned the average voter against the incumbent. The victory of the Congress Party in the state elections is, therefore, consistent with our model. But why did the Congress lose Punjab in the General Elections 2004? Within a year the electorate seems to have concluded that the governance of the new incumbent was perhaps even worse than that of the previous governing party. Because there was a Congress government in the state for only one year, the importance that the voters attached to growth performance during this very short period is not clear. Non-economic factors such as the perception of personal vendetta against the former Chief Minister seems, however, to have played a role in the voting outcome.

## 5.2 Non-economic Factors: Gujarat

There is widespread agreement that the BJP won the Gujarat elections in 2002-03 because of the post-Godhra riots. The results of our analysis support this conclusion. GDP growth during the five years 1998-99 to 2002-03 is estimated to have fallen to 3.1 per cent per annum about 40 per cent of the 7.4 per cent per annum growth during the previous five-year period 1993-94 to 1997-98. Thus, the average voter would have been a lot less inclined to vote for the incumbent than before. If we add to this the governance factor, the Congress party would have been very likely to win the state election

9. Bihar's growth performance seems sufficient to explain the general election success.

in 2002-03, as most people expected before the riots. Non-economic factors such as the post-Godhra riots, therefore, seem to have played an important role in the re-election of the Modi government in the state elections of 2002-03. Further, it seems that these non-economic factors were diluted over 2003-04, as people realised the full import of what had happened including the negative effect on investment and growth that the failure to punish murderers, was having. Thus, in the General Elections, the growth factor seems to have re-asserted itself as the original non-economic/emotional factors have waned.

### 5.3 Alliance Arithmetic: Tamil Nadu

In Tamil Nadu alliances clearly played a critical role by raising the potential vote for the alliance to an unbeatable 58 per cent, thus, virtually guaranteeing a victory. In this situation, even a large 8 per cent swing in favour of the incumbent would have no affect on the outcome, and even an unprecedented 20 per cent swing would have had a small effect. Thus, non-economic factors such as misuse of POTA against political opponents or dismissal of state government employees were irrelevant to the seats lost by the incumbent, and re-instatement of the employees and free power to farmers will not change the outcome of the next state election. Though, economic performance (higher growth and better governance) will increase the vote count of the incumbent, this will also not change the outcome as long as the opposition coalition is not undermined in some way. It will, however, raise the benchmark for the new state government and, thus, make a return to power more likely after a spell in the opposition.

Alliances may also have changed the seat count in a few other states.

## 6. CONCLUSIONS

Contrary to the conventional wisdom, economic growth, in general and agricultural growth, in particular, was much lower during the five year tenure (1999-2000 to 2003-04) of the NDA government, than that in the previous five years (1994-95 to 1998-99). Thus, on the margin, the average voter was more likely to vote against the ruling party in the general election of 2004. The benchmark against which economic performance is judged has also risen during the last two decades because of consistently higher growth during the past 24 years relative to the growth rate prior to that. Rhetorical excess during the six months prior to the election raised the benchmark even higher. It was, therefore, easy for even the un-educated and information deprived to understand that there was large gap between the professed and the actual.

Added to this is the slow but steady deterioration in governance over the past four decades, that has resulted in a deterioration in the quality and quantity of public services provided by the state. This factor is, in our view, closely linked to the anti-incumbency factor observed in the voting behaviour during the past three decades and also operated against incumbent ruling parties and representatives during the 2004 Election. In India, where the government monopolises even the production of private goods/services like electricity and railways, the deterioration in these services is also attributable to governance failure and adds to the anti-incumbency factor. Parties that have made a sincere effort to improve governance (i.e. the quality and quantity of public goods and services supplied to citizens), have been able to beat the anti-incumbency factor once. More radical changes in governance and policy seem to be necessary for a law-abiding party to beat the anti-incumbency factor more than once in a row.

Non-economic factors such as the Gujarat riots clearly play a role in voter behaviour. They also appear to play a greater role in the relatively few cases in which a(n) party or alliance has been able to beat the anti-incumbency factor more than once in a row.

---

An abbreviated version of this chapter appeared as "Election 2004: A Different Explanation", *Economic and Political Weekly* (EPW), Vol. XXXIX, No. 25, June 19-25, 2004 and an even shorter version as "The Real Story of E-2004" in *India Today*, June 28, 2004. My thanks to Surjit S. Bhalla for his questions and criticism of the earliest version of this chapter and to Vijay Kelkar for his suggestions. Available at: *http://www.icrier.org/*avnotes and *http://www.icrier.res.in/*avnotes.

## Appendix A11.1

*Growth of GDP at 1993-94 Prices*

| | Incumbent | *Simple Average Growth Rate (%)* (1994-95 1998-99) 5 Yrs. | (1999-00 2003-04) 5 Yrs. | (1999-00 2002-03) | (2003-04) Estimate (%) |
|---|---|---|---|---|---|
| India | lost | 6.7 | 5.7 | 5.0 | 8.2 |
| *States* | | | | | |
| Andhra Pradesh | lost | 5.7 | 5.5 | 4.6 | 9.1 |
| Bihar | won | 4.9 | 7.7 | 8.4 | 4.6 |
| Delhi | won | 9.6 | 7.7 | 7.6 | 8.0 |
| Madhya Pradesh | lost | 5.4 | 3.1 | 1.4 | 9.7 |
| Orissa | won | 4.3 | 4.4 | 3.3 | 8.8 |
| Rajasthan | lost | 9.4 | 3.2 | 1.1 | 11.3 |
| Agriculture | | | | | |
| India | | 3.5 | 2.1 | | 9.1 |

*Source* : (1) State data: NAS for 1993-94 to 2002-03, and author's estimate for 2003-04.
(2) All India: NAS CD ROM and web site.

*Note* : 2002-03 data not available for Karnataka and certain other states.

## Appendix A11.2

*Per Capita GDP Growth Rate*

| | Incumbent | *Simple Average Growth Rate (%)* (1994-95 1998-99) | (1999-00 2003-04) | (1999-00 2002-03) | (2003-04) Estimate (%) |
|---|---|---|---|---|---|
| India | lost | 4.7 | 3.8 | 3.2 | 6.4 |
| *States* | | | | | |
| Andhra Pradesh | lost | 4.3 | 4.3 | 3.4 | 4.1 |
| Bihar | won | 1.9 | 5.4 | 5.9 | 3.4 |
| Delhi | won | 5.5 | 4.2 | 4.0 | 3.7 |
| Madhya Pradesh | lost | 3.1 | 0.5 | -0.6 | 1.4 |
| Orissa | won | 2.7 | 3.1 | 2.0 | 3.4 |
| Rajasthan | lost | 6.7 | 0.5 | -1.5 | 1.3 |

*Source* : National Account Statistic–Stated Domestic Product.

# References


Acharya, Shankar (2001). "India's Macroeconomic Management in the Nineties", *Occasional Paper*, Indian Council for International Economic Relations, October.

———. (2002). "India's Medium-Term Growth Prospects", *Economic and Political Weekly*, July 13.

Ahluwalia, Isher Judge (1985). *Industrial Growth in India: Stagnation since the Mid-Sixties*, Oxford University Press, Delhi.

———. (1991). *Productivity and Growth in Indian Manufacturing*, Oxford University Press, Oxford & New York.

———. (1995). "New Economic Policies, Enterprises and Privatisation in India", in *India: The Future of Economic Reform*, Robert Cassen and Vijay Joshi (eds.), Oxford University Press.

Ahluwalia, Isher and Lan. M. Little (1998) (eds.) *India's Economic Reforms & Development: Essays for Manmohan Singh*, Oxford University Press, Delhi, June.

Barro, Robert J. and J.W. Lee (1994). "Sources of Economic Growth", *Carnegie-Rochester Conference Series on Public Policy.*

Batra, Amita (2004). "India's Global Trade Potential: The Gravity Model Approach", *ICRIER Working Paper* 151, December.

Bergston, C. Fred (2004). "Foreign Economic Policy for The Next President", *Foreign Affairs*, March-April.

Bhagwati, Jagdish N. and Sukhamoy Chakravarty (1969). "Contributions to Indian Economic Analysis", *American Economic Review*, Vol. 59, Issue 4, Supplement, Surveys of National Economic Policy Issues and Policy Research: 1–73.

Bhagwati, J.N. and P. Desai (1970). *India: Planning for Industrialisation*, Oxford University Press, Delhi.

Bhagwati, J.N. and T.N. Srinivasan (1974). *Foreign Trade Regimes and Economic Development: India*, Columbia University Press.

———. (1984). "Indian Development Strategy: Some Comments", *Economic and Political Weekly*, November 24.

———. (1993). *India in Transition: Freeing the Economy*, Clarendon Press, Oxford.

———. (1998). "The Design of Indian Development", in *India's Economic Reforms and Development: Essays for Manmohan Singh*, Isher Judge Ahluwalia and IMD Little (eds.), Oxford University Press.

Bhalla, S. (2000). "Financial Sector Policies in India – Apne Pttir Pe Apni Kuilhadi", *Mimeo*, Oxus Fund Management, New Delhi.

Bhargava, Sandeep and Vijay Joshi (1990). "Increase in India's Growth Rate: Facts and a Tentative Explanation", *Economic and Political Weekly*, December 1.

Bloom, David E., David Canning and Jaypee Sevilla (2001). "Economic Growth and the Demographic Transition", *NBER Working Paper* No. 8685, December.

Brahmananda, P.R. (1982). "Productivity in the Indian Economy: Rising Inputs for Falling Outputs", Himalaya Publishing House, Mumbai.

Chakravarty, S. (1984). "Aspects of India's Development Strategy for the 1980s", *Economic and Political Weekly*, May 19–26.

———. (1987). *Development Planning; The Indian Experience*, Clarendon Press, Oxford.

Chang, Gordon G. (2001). *The Coming Collapse of China*, Random House, New York.

Chopra, Ajai, Charles Collyns, Richard Hemming, Karen Parker, Woosik Chu, Oliver Fratzsher, (1995). "India: Economic Reform and Growth", *Occasional Paper* 134, International Monetary Fund.

Collins, Susan and Barry Bosworth (1996). "Economic Growth in East Asia: Accumulation Versus Assimilation", *Brookings Papers on Economic Activity*, 2: 135-203.

Cornea, Giovanni A. and Julius Court (2001). "Inequality, Growth and Poverty in an Era of Liberalisation and Globalisation", *Policy Brief No. 4*, UN University, WIDER.

Dandekar, V.M. (1992). *Forty Years after Independence, in The Indian Economy: Problems and Prospects*, Bimal Jalan (ed.), Viking: Penguin, India.

Das, D.K. (2003). "Quantifying Trade Barriers: Has Protection Declined Substantially in Indian Manufacturing?" *Working Paper* No. 105, Indian Council for Research on International Economic Relations, New Delhi.

DeLong, J. Bradford and Lawrence Summers (1991). "Equipment Investment and Economic Growth", *Quarterly Journal of Economics*, 106, (May): 445-502.

———. (1992). "Equipment Investment and Economic Growth, How Strong is the Nexus", *Brooking Papers in Economic Activity*, 2: 157-99.

———. (1993). "Macroeconomic Policy and Long-Run Growth", *Federal Reserve Bank of Kansas City Quarterly Review.*

DeLong, J. Bradford (2001). "India Since Independence: An Analytic Growth Narrative", *<www.ksghome.harvard.edu/~.drodrik.academic.ksggrowthprogram. html>*

———. (2003). "India Since Independence: An Analytic Growth Narrative", in Dani Rodrik (ed.), *in Search of Prosperity: Analytic Narratives on Economic Growth*, Princeton University Press, Princeton, July.

DeRosa, Dean (1995). "Regional Trading Arrangements among Developing Countries: The ASEAN Example", Research Report 103, International Food Policy Research Institute, Washington.

Dhar, P.N. (1988). "The Indian Economy: Past Performance and Current Issues", in *The Indian Economy: Recent Development and Future Prospects*, Robert EB Lucas and Gustav F Papanek (eds.), Oxford University Press.

———. (1990). "Constraints on Growth: Reflections on the Indian Experience", fourth VT Krishnanmachari Memorial Lecture, 1989, delivered at the Institute of Economic Growth, Oxford University Press.

Emerson, Donald K. (1998). "Americanising Asia", *Foreign Affairs*, May/June.

Fukuyama, Francis (1989). "The End of History", The *National Interest*, 16, Summer 1989: 4-18.

———. (1992). *The End of History and the Last Man*, Penguin Books, London.

Garten, Jeffrey (1997). *The Big Ten: Big Emerging Markets and How They will Change Our Lives*, Basic Books.

Gibert, Stephen P. (1988). "Security in NorthEast Asia: Approaching The Pacific Century", Westview Press, Boulder Colorado.

Gibney, Frank (1992). *The Pacific Century: America and Asia in a Changing World*, Charles Scribner and Sons, New York.

Goldar, B. and Arup Mitra (2002). "Total Factor Productivity Growth in Indian Manufacturing Industries in the 1990s", in *National Accounts and Data Systems*, B.S. Minhas (ed.), Oxford University Press, New Delhi.

Goldar, B. and Anita Kumari (2003). "Import Liberalisation and Productivity Growth in Indian Manufacturing Industries in the 1990s", *The Developing Economies*, XLI (4), December.

Gordon, Jim and Poonam Gupta (2003). "Understanding India's Service Revolution", *mimeo* November.

Guha-Khasnobis, Basudeb and Faisal Bari (2003). "Sources of Growth in South Asian Countries", in *The South Asian Experience with Growth*, Isher Judge Ahluwalia and John Williamson (eds.), Oxford University Press, New Delhi.

Held, David, Anthony McGrew, David Goldblatt and Jonathan Perraton (1999). *Global Transformations, Politics, Economics and Culture*, Polity Press, Cambridge.

Hendricks, Lutz (2000). "Equipment Investment and Growth in Developing Countries", *Journal of Development Economics*, 61: 335-364.

Huang, Yasheng (2003). *Selling China: Foreign Direct Investment During the Reform Era*, Cambridge University Press, Cambridge.

Hulten, Charles R. (1992). "Growth Accounting When Technical Change is Embodied in Capital", *American Economic Review*, 82(4), September: 964-80.

Huntington, Samuel P. (1993). "The Clash of Civilisations", *Foreign Affairs*, May/June.

———. (1996). *The Clash of Civilisations and The Remaking of World Order*, Simon & Schuster, New York.

Ikemoto, K. and R.J.R. Elliott (2003). "AFTA and the Asian Crisis: Help or Hindrance to ASEAN Intra–Regional Trade", The School of Economics *Discussion Paper Series* 0311, School of Economics, The University of Manchester.

International Labour Organisation (2002). *Yearbook of Labour Statistics*, ILO.

International Monetary Fund (2004). "Advancing Structural Reform", *World Economic Outlook*, April.

———. (various years). "World Economic Outlook", IMF, Washington, DC, USA.

Joshi, Vijay and Ian M.D. Little (1996). *India's Economic Reforms 1991-2001*, Clarendon Press, Oxford.

Kennedy, Paul (1988). *The Rise and Fall of the Great Powers: Economic Change and Military Conflict from 1500 to 2000*, Random House, USA.

Keohane, Robert O. and Joseph S. Nye (1977). *Power and Interdependence*, Little Brown & Co., Boston.

King, R.G. and Ross Levine (1993). "Finance, Enterpreneurship and Growth: Theory and Evidence", *Journal of Monetary Economics*, 32: 513-542. Carnegie-Rochester Conference Series on Public Policy. June.

———. (1994). "Capital Fundamentalism, Economic Development and Economic Growth", Carnegie-Rochester Conference Series on Public Policy.

Kissinger, Henry A. (1994). *Diplomacy*, Simon & Schuster, New York.

Krauthammer, Charles (1990). "The Unipolar Moment", *Foreign Affairs*, America and The World, 1990/91.

Krishna, K.L. (2002). "Industrial Growth and Diversification", in Uma Kapila (ed.), *Indian Economy Since Independence*, 14th edition, Academic Foundation, New Delhi.

Krishna, P. and D. Mitra (1998). "Trade Liberalisation, Market Discipline and Productivity Growth: New Evidence from India", *Journal of Development Economics*, 56: 447-62.

Krishnamurthy, J. (1970). "Industrial Distribution of the Working Force in India, 1901-1961: A Study of Selected Aspects", PhD Thesis, Delhi School of Economics, Dept. of Economics.

Lange, Oscar (1971), "On The Economic Theory of Socialism," in Goldman, M. I. (ed.) Comparative Economic Systems, New York.

Lardy, Nicholas R. (1992). *Foreign Trade and Economic Reform in China*, 1978-1990, Cambridge University Press, Cambridge.

———. (1998). *China's Unfinished Economic Revolution*, Brookings, Washington DC.

———. (1999). "The Macro-economic Context: The Challenge of Bank Restructuring in China", *Strengthening the Banking System in China: Issues and Experience, BIS Policy Papers* No. 7, October.

Levy, Jack (1983). *War in the Modern Great Power System, 1945-1975*, University Press of Kentucky, Lexington.

Lingle, Christopher (1995). "The Propoganda Way", *Foreign Affairs*, May/June.

Mahbubani, Kishore (1995). "The Pacific Way", *Foreign Affairs*, 74 Jan./Feb.: 100-103.

———. (1997). "An Asia-Pacific Consensus", *Foreign Affairs*, September/October.

Manning, Robert A. and Paula Stern (1994). "The Myth of Pacific Community", *Foreign Affairs*, November/December.

McCord, William (1991). *The Dawn of The Pacific Century: Implications for Three Worlds of Development*, Transaction, New Brunswick, NJ.

Mearshiemer, John (2001). *The Tragedy of Great Power Politics*, W.W. Norton & Co., New York.

Nagaraj, R. (1990). "Growth Rate of India's GDP, 1950-51 to 1987-88: Examination of Alternative Hypotheses", *Economic and Political Weekly*, June 30.

Nehru, V. and A. Dhareshwar (1993). "A New Database on Physical Capital Stock: Sources, Methodology and Results", *Revista de Analisis Economiico*, Vol. 8: 3–59 [cited in Guha-Khasnobis and Bari (2003)].

Nye, Joseph S. (1990). "Soft Power", *Foreign Policy*, No. 80, Fall.

Parthasarathy, B., A.A. Munot, and D.R. Kothawale (1995). *Monthly and Seasonal Rainfall Series for All-India*, Homogeneous Regions and Meteorological Subdivisions: 1871-1994, *Research Report No RR-065*, Indian Institute of Tropical Meteorology, Pune.

Parthasarathi, Shome (1997). *Value-Added Tax in India: A Progress Report* Centax Publications, New Delhi.

Patel, I.G. (2002). *Glimpses of Indian Economic Policy: An Insiders View*, Oxford University Press, New Delhi.

Patnaik, Prabhat (1987). "Recent Growth Experience of the Indian Economy", *Economic and Political Weekly*, Annual Number, May, 1990.

Perkins, Dwight (1988). "Reforming China's Economic System", *Journal of Economic Literature*, Vol. 26, No. 2, June: 601-645.

———. (1994). "Completing China's Move to Market", *Journal of Economic Perspectives*, Vol. 8, No. 2, Spring: 23-46.

Pritchet, Lant (1997). "Divergence, Big Time", *Journal of Economic Perspectives* 11: 3-17.

Raj, K.N. (1962). "The Marginal Rate of Savings in the Indian Economy", *Oxford Economic Papers*, 14(1).

———. (1984). "Some Observations on Economic Growth in India over the Period 1952-53 to 1982-83", *Economic and Political Weekly*, October 13.

Reserve Bank of India (2003). *Handbook of Statistics on the Indian Economy 2002-03*, CD-ROM.

Rodrik, Dani and Arvind Subramanian (2004a). "Why India Can Grow at 7 Per cent a Year or More: Projections and Reflections", International Monetary Fund, *Working Paper No. 04/118*, July.

Segal, Gerald (1999). "Does China Matter?" *Foreign Affairs*, Vol. 78, No. 5, September-October.

Senhadji, Abdelhak (1999). "Sources of Economic Growth: An Extensive Growth Accounting Exercise", *International Monetary Fund Working Paper No. WP/99/77*, IMF Institute, June.

Singer, Bremer and Stuckey (1972). "Capability Distribution, Uncertainty, and Major Power War", in Bruce M Russet, *Peace, War and Numbers*, Sage Publications, Beverly Hills.

Sivasubramonian, S. (2000). "The National Income of India in the Twentieth Century", Oxford University Press, New Delhi.

Srinivasan, T.N. (2000). *Eight Lectures on India's Economic Reforms*, Oxford University Press, New Delhi.

Srinivasan, T.N. and N.S.S. Narayana (1977). "Economic Performance Since The Third Plan and Its Implications for Policy", *Economic and Political Weekly*, Vol. XII, Nos. 6, 7 and 8, February.

Subrahmaniam, K., M. Granger Morgan, K. Sunderji and Robert M. White (1995). "India and The United States", *Washington Quarterly*.

Sung, Yun-Wang (1991). *The China-Hong Kong Connection: The Key to China's Open Door Policy*, Cambridge University Press, Cambridge.

Sutter, Robert G. (1992). *East Asia and The Pacific: Challenges for US Policy*, Westview Press, Boulder.

Tellis, Ashley J., Janice Bially, Christopher Layne, Melissa Mcpherson (2000). *Measuring National Power in the Post Industrial Age: Analysis Handbook*, Rand, Santa Monica.

Tseng, Wanda and Harm Zebergs (2002). "Foreign Direct Investment in China: Some Lessons for Other Countries", International Monetary Fund Policy *Discussion Paper*, February.

UNCTAD (2004). Press release, Jan 12.

United Nations (2003). "World Population Prospects: The 2002 Revision", Population Division of the Department of Economic and Social Affairs of the United Nations Secretariat. *<http://esa.un.org/unpp>*

Virmani, Arvind (1989a). "Growth, Capital and Employment: Performance in Perspective", *Economic Research Paper* No. 3, February, Planning Commission (processed).

———. (1996). "Policy Framework for Power", August, *Chintan Policy Paper* No. 20. [*http://finance.nic.in/avirmani*.

———. (1997b). "India: Crises, Reform and Growth", *Economic and Political Weekly*, August 9.

———. (1997c). "Economic Development and Transition: India", presented at the *Tokyo Dialogue on Alternatives to the World Bank–IMF Approach to Reforms and Growth*, organised by the Economic Planning Agency, December 7, Tokyo, Japan.

———. (1999b). "Star Performers of the 20th (21st) Century: Asian Tigers, Dragons or Elephants", *Occasional Paper, Chintan*, September. *www.icrier.org/avpapers.html*.

———. (1999c). "Potential Growth Stars of the 21st Century: India, China and The Asian Century", *Occasional Paper, Chintan*, October, *www.icrier.org/avpapers.html*.

———. (2001b). "India's 1990-91 Crisis: Reforms, Myths and Paradoxes", *Planning Commission Working Paper* No. 4/2001-PC, December. *www.planningcommission.nic.in/reports/wrkpapers/rpwpf.htm*

———. (2002b). "A New Development Paradigm: Employment, Entitlement and Empowerment", *Economic and Political Weekly*, Vol. XXXVII No. 22, June 1-7: 2145-2154.

———. (2002b). "A New Development Paradigm: Employment, Entitlement and Empowerment", *Global Business Review*, International Management Institute, Vol. 3, No. 2, July-December: 222-45.

———. (2002c). *Bharatiya Rate of Growth: The Role of Services*, September. (*www.planningcommission.nic.in/artf.html* and *http://www.icrier.org/avnotes*).

———. and P.V. Rajeev (2002). "Excess Food Stocks, PDS, and Procurement Policy", *Planning Commission Working Paper* No. 5/2002-PC, Planning Commission, January. (*http://www.planningcommission.nic.in/reports/wrkpapers/rpwpf.htm*).

———. (2003). "India's External Reforms: Modest Globalisation Significant Gains", *Economic and Political Weekly*, Vol. XXXVII No. 32, August 9-15: 3373-3390.

———. (2004a). "Accelerating Growth and Poverty Reduction–A Policy Framework for India's Development", Academic Foundation, New Delhi.

———. (2004b). "Economic Reforms: Policy and Institutions, Some Lessons from Indian Reforms", *Working Paper* No. 121, Indian Council for Research on International Economic Relations, January, *http://www.icrier.org or http://www.icrier.res.in*.

———. (2004c). "India's Economic Growth: From Socialist Rate of Growth to Bharatiya Rate of Growth", *ICRIER Working Paper* No. 122, February. *www.icrier.org/wp122.pdf*.

———. (2004e). "Economic Performance, Power Potential and Global Governance: Towards a New International Order", *ICRIER Working Paper* No. 150, December. *www.icrier.org/wp150.pdf*.

———. (1989a). Growth, Capital and Employment: Performance in Perspective, *Economic Research Paper No. 3*, Planning Commission (processed), February.

Virmani, Arvind and Amita Batra (2005a). "A Tripolar Century: USA, China and India", *ICRIER Working Paper* No. 160, March. *www.icrier.org/wp160.pdf*.

———. (2005b). "China's Socialist Market Economy: Lessons of Success", *ICRIER Occasional Policy Paper*, April. *http://www.icrier.org/China05_policy7.pdf*.

———. (2005c). "A Tripolar World: India, China and USA", *ICRIER Public Lecture*, May. *www.icrier.org/public/TripolarWrld_IHC4c.pdf*.

Visaria, Praveen (2002). "Workforce and Employment in India, 1961-94", in B.S. Minhas (ed.), *National Income Accounts and Data Systems*, OUP.

Wallack, Jessica S. (2003). "Structural Breaks in Indian Macroeconomic Data", *Economic and Political Weekly*, October 11.

Waltz, Kenneth (1979). *Theory of International Politics*, Addison-Wesley, Reading.

Williamson, John and Roberto Zagha (2002). "From the Hindu Rate of Growth to the Hindu Rate of Reform", *Working Paper* No. 144, Centre for Research on Economic Development and Policy Reform, Stanford University, USA, July.

World Bank (2003). *World Development Indicators*, CD-ROM, (Ref. pg 246) Chapter 7, Table 7.3.

———. (2004). *World Development Indicators*, CD ROM.

Young, Alwyn (2000). "Gold into Base Metals: Productivity Growth in The People's Republic of China During the Reform Period", *NBER Working Paper* No. 7856, August.

# Bibliography


Acemoglu, Daron, Simon Johnson and James A. Robinson (2001). "The Collonial Origins of Comparative Development: An Emperical Investigation", *The American Economic Review* 91, 5 December: 139-1401.

Acemoglu, Daron (2003). "Root Causes: A Historical Approach to Assessing the Role of Institutions in Economic Development", *Finance and Development*, June.

Acemoglu, Daron and Simon Johnson (2003). "Unbundling Institutions", *NBER Working Paper No. 9934*, September.

Acharya, Shankar (2001). "India's Macroeconomic Management in the Nineties", *Occasional Paper*, Indian Council for International Economic Relations, October.

———. (2002). "India's Medium-Term Growth Prospects", *Economic and Political Weekly*, July 13.

Ahluwalia, Isher Judge (1985). *Industrial Growth in India: Stagnation Since the Mid-Sixties*, Oxford University Press, Delhi.

———. (1991). *Productivity and Growth in Indian Manufacturing*, Oxford University Press, Oxford & New York.

———. (1995). "New Economic Policies, Enterprises, and Privatisation in India", in *India: The Future of Economic Reform*, Robert Cassen and Vijay Joshi (eds.), Oxford University Press.

Ahluwalia, Isher and Lan. M. Little (1998) (eds.) *India's Economic Reforms & Development: Essays for Manmohan Singh*, Oxford University Press, June.

Ahluwalia, Montek S. (1988). "India's Economic Performance, Policies, and Prospects", in Robert E.B. Lucas and Gustav F. Papanek (eds.), *The Indian Economy: Recent Development and Future Prospects*, Oxford University Press.

Aitken, B. and A. Harrison (1997). "Do Domestic Firms Benefit from FDI? Evidence from Venezuela", *American Economic Review* 89 (3): 605-618.

Alatas, Ali (2001). "ASEAN Plus Three - Equals Peace Plus Prosperity", ISEAS, Singapore.

Antkiewicz, Agata and John Whalley (2004). "China's New Regional Trading Agreements", CATPRN *Working Paper* 2004-1. *http://www.catrade.org*.

Aron, Janine (2000). "Growth and Institutions: A Review of the Evidence", *The World Bank Research Observer*, Vol. 15, No. 1, (Feb. 2001): 99-135.

Arrow, Kenneth (2000). "Economic Transition, Speed and Scope", *Journal of Institutional and Theoretical Economics*, 156 (March): 9-18.

Asher, Mukul G. and Sadhna Srivastava (2003). "India and the Asian Economic Community", *Discussion Paper No.* 51, RIS.

Athukorala, P. and S. Chand (2000). "Trade Orientation and Productivity Gains from International Production: A Study of Overseas Operations of United States TNCs", Transnational Corporations, 9(2): 1-27.

Bagchi, Amiya Kumar (1990). "An Economic Policy for the New Government", *Economic and Political Weekly*, Vol XXV, No. 6, February 10.

Baillie, R.T. and T. Bollerslev (2000). "The Forward Premium Anomaly is Not as Bad as You Think", *Journal of International Money and Finance*, Vol.19 (4) August: 471-88.

Bajpai, N. and Sachs Jeffery (1996). "Fiscal Policy in India's Economic Reforms", *Paper* presented at the *Harvard Conference on India's Reforms*, Boston.

Balakrishnan, P., K. Pushpangadan and M. Suresh Babu (2000). "Trade Liberalisation and Productivity Growth in Manufacturing: Evidence from Firm Level Panel Data", *Economic and Political Weekly*, 7 October: 3679-3682.

Balasubramanyam, V.N., M.A. Salisu and D. Sapsford (1996). "Foreign Direct Investment and Growth in EP and IS Countries", *Economic Journal*, 106 (434): 92-105.

Banga, R. (2003a). "Do Productivity Spillovers Differ?" R. Jha (ed.), *Indian Economic Reforms*, Palgrave Macmillan.

———. (2003b). "Impact of Japanese and U.S. Foreign Direct Investments on Productivity Growth: A Firm Level Analysis", *Economic and Political Weekly*, Vol XXXIX, No. 5, January 31.

———. (2003c). "The Differential Impact of Japanese and U.S. Foreign Direct Investments on Exports of Indian Manufacturing", presented in *Fourth Annual Global Development Conference (GDN)*, World Bank, Cairo, Egypt on 18-22 January.

———. (2003d). "The Export-Diversifying Impact of Japanese and U.S. Foreign Direct Investments in Indian Manufacturing Sector", *ICRIER Working Paper* No. 110: September.

———. (2003e). "Impact of Government Policies and Investment Agreements on FDI Inflows"*ICRIER Working Paper* No. 116, November.

———. (2004). "Technology Up-Gradation Strategies and Level of Technology Adoption in Japanese and U.S. Firms in Indian Manufacturing", in H. Kehal (ed.), *FDI in India and China*, Palgrave Macmillan.

Banks, J. and S. Smith (2000). "UK Household Portfolios", *Working Paper* No. 14, Institute for Fiscal Studies, April.

Bansal, R. and M. Dahquist (2000). "The Forward Premium Puzzle: Different Tales from Developed and Emerging Markets", *Journal of International Economics*, Vol.51 (1) : 115-44.

Barik and Pradhan (1999). "Total Factor Productivity Growth in Developing Economies: A Study of Selected Industries in India", *Economic and Political Weekly*, July 31.

Barnhart, S.W., R. McNown and M.S. Wallace (1999). "Non-informative Tests of the Unbiased Forward Exchange Rate", *Journal of Financial and Quantitative Analysis*, Vol.34 (2) June: 265-91.

Baru, Sanjay (2001). India and ASEAN: "The Emerging Economic Relationship towards A Bay of Bengal Community", *ICRIER Working Paper* No. 61.

Barro, Robert J. and J.W. Lee (1994). "Sources of Economic Growth", *Carnegie-Rochester Conference Series on Public Policy.*

Batra, Amita (2004). "India's Global Trade Potential: The Gravity Model Approach", *ICRIER Working Paper* 151, December.

Bergston, C. Fred (2004). "Foreign Economic Policy for The Next President", *Foreign Affairs*, March-April.

Besley, Timothy and Robin Burgess (2002). "Can Labour Regulation Hinder Economic Performance? Evidence from India", London School of Economics, DEDPS 33, February.

Bhagwati, J.N. (1978). *Anatomy and Consequences of Exchange Control Regimes*, Balinger Publishing, New York.

Bhagwati, Jagdish N. and Sukhamoy Chakravarty (1969). "Contributions to Indian Economic Analysis", *American Economic Review*, Vol. 59, Issue 4, Supplement, Surveys of National Economic Policy Issues and Policy Research: 1–73.

Bhagwati, J.N. and P. Desai (1970). *India: Planning for Industrialisation*, Oxford University Press, Delhi.

Bhagwati, J.N. and T.N. Srinivasan (1974). *Foreign Trade Regimes and Economic Development: India*, Columbia University Press.

———. (1984). "Indian Development Strategy: Some Comments", *Economic and Political Weekly*, November 24.

———. (1993). *India in Transition: Freeing the Economy*, Clarendon Press.

———. (1998). "The Design of Indian Development", in Isher Judge Ahluwalia and IMD Little (eds.), *India's Economic Reforms and Development: Essays for Manmohan Singh*, Oxford University Press.

———. (1975). *Foreign Trade Regimes and Economic Development: India*, National Bureau of Economic Research, New York.

Bhalla, G.S., Peter Hazell and John Kerr (1999). "Prospects for India's Cereal Supply and Demand to 2020", *Discussion Paper* 29, IFPRI Food, Agriculture and the Environment.

Bhalla, S. (2000). "Financial Sector Policies in India – Apne Pttir Pe Apni Kuilhadi", *mimeo*, Oxus Fund Management, New Delhi.

Bhargava, Sandeep and Vijay Joshi (1990). "Increase in India's Growth Rate: Facts and a Tentative Explanation", *Economic and Political Weekly*, December 1.

Bhattacharya, B.B. (1985). "Role of Interest Rates As an Incentive for Household Savings in India, 1960-61 to 1980-81", *mimeo*, Institute of Economic Growth, Delhi.

Bhole, L.M. (1985). "Administered Interest Rates in India", *Economic and Political Weekly*, Vol. XX, Nos. 25 and 26, June 22-29: 1089-1104.

———. (1988). "The Structure of Interest Rates in Theory and Practice", *Indian Journal of Economics*, Vol. LXIX, Part II, No 273, 119-134.

Blomstrom, M. and E. Wolf (1994). "Multinational Corporations and Productivity Convergence in Mexico", in W. Bahmol, R. Nelson and E. Wolff (eds.), *Convergence of Productivity: Cross National Studies and Historical Evidence*: 243-259 Oxford University Press, New York.

Blomstrom and Kokko (1998). "Multinational Corporations and Spillovers", *Journal of Economic Surveys*, 12 (2): 1-31.

Bloom, David E., David Canning and Jaypee Sevilla (2001). "Economic Growth and the Demographic Transition", *NBER Working Paper* No. 8685, December.

Bonaglia, Federico, Jorge Braga de Macedo and Maurizio Bussolo (2001). "How Globalisation Improves Governance", OECD Development Centre, *Technical Papers* No. 181, November.

Brahmananda, P.R. (1982). "Productivity in the Indian Economy: Rising Inputs for Falling Outputs", Himalaya Publishing House.

Brainard, W.C. and J. Tobin (1969). "Pitfalls in Financial Model Building", *American Economic Review*, papers and proceedings.

Buchanan, James M. and Gordon Tullock (1962). *The Calculus of Consent: Logical Foundations of Constitutional Democracy*, University of Michigan Press, Ann Arbor.

Bureau of Industrial Costs and Prices (1991). "Report on the Operations of the Food Corporation of India".

Caballero, R.J. and M.L. Hammour (2000). "Creative Destruction and Development: Institutions, Crises and Restructuring", *NBER Working Paper* No. 7849.

Caves, Richard E. (1974). "Multinational Corporations, Competition and Productivity in Host Country Markets", *Economica*, 41: 176-193.

———. (1996). *Multinational Enterprise and Economic Analysis*, Cambridge University Press, Cambridge.

CENVAT, (2001). "Central Value Added Tax: CENVAT", *Economic and Political Weekly*, Vol. XXXVI No. 8, February 24-March 2: 630-632.

Cerra, Valarie and Sweta C. Saxena (2000). "What Caused the 1991 Currency Crisis in India?" *International Monetary Fund Working Paper*, WP/00/157, October.

Chadha, R., S. Pohit, A.V. Deardorff and R.M. Stern (1998). *The Impact of Trade and Domestic Policy Reforms in India: A CGE Modeling Approach*, The University of Michigan Press, Ann Arbor.

Chakravarty, Sukhamoy (1973). "Reflections on the growth Process in the Indian Economy", Foundation Day Lecture at the administrative Staff College of India, Hyderabad, December.

———. (1984). "Aspects of India's Development Strategy for the 1980s", *Economic and Political Weekly*, May 19–26.

———. (1987). *Development Planning; The Indian Experience*, Clarendon Press.

Chandhok, H.L. (1991). *India Database: The Economy*, Living Media India Ltd., New Delhi.

Chang, Gordon G. (2001). *The Coming Collapse of China*, Random House, New York.

Chase, S.B. Jr. (1969). "Household Demand for Savings Deposits, 1921-1965", *The Journal of Finance*, Vol.24, No. 4: 643-658.

Chaudhuri, S. (2002). "Economic Reforms and Industrial Structure in India", *Economic and Political Weekly*, January 12, 37: 155-168.

Chopra, Ajai, Charles Collyns, Richard Hemming, Karen Parker, Woosik Chu, Oliver Fratzsher, (1995). "India: Economic Reform and Growth", *Occasional Paper* 134, International Monetary Fund.

Christensen, M. (2000). "Uncovered Interest Parity and Policy Behavior: New Evidence", *Economics Letters*, Vol.69 (1) October: 81-87.

Collins, Ann and R. Harris (1999). "Ownership and Productive Efficiency in the UK Motor Vehicles industry", University of Portsmouth.

Collins, Susan and Barry Bosworth (1996). "Economic Growth in East Asia: Accumulation Versus Assimilation", *Brookings Papers on Economic Activity*, 2:135-203.

———. (1996). "Total Factor Productivity", *Brookings Papers on Economic Activity*, 1996: 2.

Connolly, Michelle (2003). "The Dual Nature of Trade: Measuring its Impact on Imitation and Growth", *Journal of Development Economics*, 72, 31-55.

Contributions from Indian Institute of Tropical Meteorolgy (1995). *Research Report RR-065*, August, Pune.

Conyon, M.J., S. Girma, S. Thompson and P.W. Wright (2002). "The Productivity and Wage Effects of Foreign Acquisition in the United Kingdom", *Journal of Industrial Economics*, 50: 85-102.

Cornea, Giovanni A. and Julius Court (2001). "Inequality, Growth and Poverty in an Era of Liberalisation and Globalisation", *Policy Brief No. 4*, UN University, WIDER.

Cornell, B. (1989). "The Impact of Data Errors on Measurement of the Foreign Exchange Risk Premium", *Journal of International Money and Finance*, Vol.8: 147-57.

Cronin, Richard P. (1992). *Japan, the U.S. and Prospects for the Asia-Pacific Century: Three Scenarios*, St. Martins Press, New York.

Dandekar, V.M. (1992). *Forty Years after Independence, in The Indian Economy: Problems and Prospects*, Bimal Jalan (ed.), Viking: Penguin, India.

Das, D.K. (2003). "Quantifying Trade Barriers: Has Protection Declined Substantially in Indian Manufacturing?" *Working Paper No. 105*, Indian Council for Research on International Economic Relations, New Delhi.

———. (2003). "Manufacturing Productivity under Varying Trade Regimes: India in the 1980s and 1990s", *ICRIER Working Paper* No. 107, August. (*www.icrier.org*).

David Held, Anthony McGrew, David Goldblatt and Jonathan Perraton (1999). *Global Transformations, Politics, Economics and Culture*, Cambridge Polity.

Davies, K.E., M.J. Treblicock (2001). "Legal Reforms and Development", *Third World Quarterly*, 22 (1): 21-36.

de Melo, Luiz R. Jr. (1997). "Foreign Direct Investment in Developing Countries and Growth: A Selective Survey", *Journal of Development Studies*, Vol 34, No. 1, October: 1-34.

———. (1999). "Foreign Direct Investment-led Growth: Evidence from Time Series", *Oxford Economic Papers*, Vol 51: 133-151.

Deaton, A.S. (1981). "Theoretical and Empirical Approaches to Consumer Demand under Rationing", in Angus Deaton (ed.), *Essays in the Theory and Measurement of Consumer Behaviour*, Cambridge University Press: 55-72.

DeLong, J. Bradford and Lawrence Summers (1991). "Equipment Investment and Economic Growth", *Quarterly Journal of Economics*, 106, (May): 445-502.

———. (1992). "Equipment Investment and Economic Growth, How Strong is the Nexus", *Brooking Papers in Economic Activity*, 2: 157-99.

———. (1993). "Macroeconomic Policy and Long-Run Growth", *Federal Reserve Bank of Kansas City Quarterly Review*.

DeLong, J. Bradford (2001). "India since Independence: An Analytic Growth Narrative". *www.ksghome.harvard.edu/~.drodrik.academic.ksggrowthprogram. html*

———. (2003). "India Since Independence: An Analytic Growth Narrative", in Dani Rodrik (ed.), *in Search of Prosperity: Analytic Narratives on Economic Growth*, Princeton University Press, July.

Demsetz, Harold (1969). "Information and Efficiency: Another Viewpoint", *Journal of Law and Economics*, 12 (April): 1-22.

DeRosa, Dean (1995). *Regional Trading Arrangements Among Developing Countries: The ASEAN Example. Research Report 103*, International Food Policy Research Institute, Washington.

Dewatripont, Mathais and Gerard Roland (1995). "The Design of Reform Packages Under Uncertainty", *American Economic Review*, 85(5): 1207-23.

Dhar, P.N. (1988). "The Indian Economy: Past Performance and Current Issues", in *The Indian Economy: Recent Development and Future Prospects*, Robert EB Lucas and Gustav F Papanek (eds.), Oxford University Press.

———. (1990). "Constraints on Growth: Reflections on the Indian Experience", Fourth VT Krishnanmachari Memorial Lecture, 1989, delivered at the Institute of Economic Growth, Oxford University Press.

Dhar, Biswajeet (2005). "Does an FTA with China Make Sense?" *Times of India*, April 12.

Dixit, Avinash (1996). *The Making of Economic Policy: A Transaction Cost Politics Perspective*, MIT Press, Cambridge, MA.

Djankov, S., and B. Hoekman (2000). "Foreign Investment and Productivity Growth in Czech Enterprises", The *World Bank Economic Review*, Vol.14, (1): 49-64.

Dooley, Michael, David Folkerts-Landau, Shunming Zhang (2004). "Inequality Change in China and (Hokou) Labour Mobility Restrictions", *NBER Working Paper* No. W10649, July.

Downs, Anthony (1967). *Inside the Bureaucracy*, Little Brown and Company, Boston.

Dunning, J.H. (1993). *Multinational Enterprise and the Global Economy*, Addison Wesley Wokingham, England and Reading, Mass.

Dunning, John. H., Chang Su Kim and Jyh-Der Lin (2001). "Incorporating Trade into the Investment Development Path: A Case Study of Korea and Taiwan", *Development Studies*, 29(2): 145-54, Oxford.

Dutta, Bhaskar and Bharat Ramaswami (2001). "Targeting and Efficiency in the Public Distribution System – Case of Andhra Pradesh and Maharashtra", *Economic and Political Weekly*, May 5.

Dyson, Tim and Amresh Hanchate (2000). "India's Demographic and Food Prospects: State Level Analysis", *Economic and Political Weekly*, November 11.

Easterly, William and Ross Levine (2002). "Tropics, Germs and Crops: How Endowments Influence Economic Development", *mimeo*, Center for Global Development and Institute for International Economics.

Economic Advisory Council to the Prime Minister (Head Prof. Sukhamoy Chakravarty) (1989). "Report on the Current Economic Situation and Priority Areas for Action", Govt. of India, Ministry of Finance, December.

Edwards, Sebastian (1997). "Openness, Productivity And Growth: What Do We Really Know", *NBER Working Paper* 5978, March.

Eichengreen, Barry, Yeongseop Rhee, Hui Tong (2004). "The Impact of China on The Exports of Other Asian Countries", *NBER Working Paper* No. W10727, September.

Emerson, Donald K. (1998). "Americanising Asia", *Foreign Affairs*, May/June.

Encanacion D.J. and L.T. Wells (1986). "Evaluating Foreign Investment", in T.H. Moran *et al*, *Investing in Development: New Roles for Private Capital*, Transaction Books, New Brunswick: 61-86.

Engel, C. (1996). "The Forward Discount Anomaly and the Risk Premium: A Survey of the Recent Evidence", *Journal of Empirical Finance*, Vol.3 (2): 123-92.

Engerman, Stanley L. and Kenneth L. Sokoloff (1994). *NBER Historical Working Paper* No. 066.

Epstein, Gerald, Ilene Grabel and K.S. Jomo (2003). "Capital Management Techniques In Developing Countries: An Assessment of Experiences from the 1990's and Lessons For the Future", *Working Paper* No. 56, Political Economy Research Institute, University of Massachusetts, Amherst.

Fagerberg, Jan (1994). "Technology and International Differences in Growth Rates", *Journal of Economic Literature*, 32: 1147-1175.

Fama, E.F. (1984). "Forward and Spot Exchange Rates", *Journal of Monetary Economics*, Vol.14 (3) November: 319-38.

Feige, E. (1964). "The Demand for Liquid Assets: A Temporal Cross – Section Analysis", Prentice-Hall, Englewood Cliffs.

———. (1997). "Underground Activity And Institutional Change: Productive, Protective and Predatory Behavior in Transition Economies", in *Transforming Post-Communist Political Economies* Nelson, Tilly and Walker (eds.), National Academy Press, Washington, DC.

Feldstein, M.S. (1976). "Personal Taxation and Portfolio Composition: An Econometric Analysis", *Econometrica*, 44: 631-649.

FICCI (2001). "The Experience of Foreign Investors in India", April.

Flood, R.P. and A.K. Rose (1996). "Fixes: of the Forward Discount Puzzle", *Review of Economics and Statistics*, Vol.78 (4) November: 748-52.

———. (2002). "Uncovered Interest Parity in Crisis", *Staff Papers*, International Monetary Fund, Vol. 49 (2): 252-66.

Fogel, Robert W. (1999). "Economic Growth, Population Theory and Physiology: The Bearing of Long-Term Processes on the Making of Economic Policy", *The American Economic Review*, Vol. 84, No. 3 (June 1994): 369-95.

Frankel, J.A. and K.A. Froot (1990). "Exchange Rate Forecasting Techniques, Survey Data, and Implications for the Foreign Exchange Market", *NBER Working Paper* No. 3470.

Frankel, Jeffrey and David Romer (1999). "Does Trade Cause Growth?" *American Economic Review*, June 1999 Vol. 89, No. 3: 379-99.

Friedman, M. (1957). *A Theory of Consumption Function*, Princeton University Press: 143-145.

———. (1959). "The Demand for Money: Some Theoretical and Empirical Results", *Journal of Political Economy*, 67: 327-351.

Froot, K.A. and J.A. Frankel (1989). "Forward Discount Bias: Is it an Exchange Risk Premium?" *Quarterly Journal of Economics*, Vol.104 (1) February: 139-61.

Froot, K.A. and R.H. Thaler (1990). "Anomalies: Foreign Exchange", *Journal of Economic Perspectives*, Vol.4 (3): 179-92.

Fukuyama, Francis (1989). "The End of History", The *National Interest*, 16, Summer 1989: 4-18.

———. (1992). *The End of History and the Last Man*, Penguin Books, London.

Garten, Jeffrey (1997). *The Big Ten: Big Emerging Markets and How They will Change Our lives*, Basic Books.

Gaur, Seema (2003). "ASEAN-India Ties Entering a New Phase", Institute of South East Asian Studies.

Gelb, Alan and William Byrd (1990). "Township, Village, and Private Industry in China's Economic Reform", *Policy Research Working Paper*, World Bank, April.

Ghosh, Arun (1991). "Eighth Plan: Challenges and Possibilities-IV, Balance of Payments", *Economic and Political Weekly*, Vol. XXVI, No. 6, February 9.

Ghosh, Jayati (1990). "Exchange Rates and Trade Balance: Some Aspects of Recent Indian Experience", *Economic and Political Weekly*, Vol. XXV, No. 9, March 3.

Gibert, Stephen P. (1988). "Security in NorthEast Asia: Approaching The Pacific Century", Westview Press, Boulder Colorado.

Gibney, Frank (1992). *The Pacific Century: America and Asia in a Changing World*, Charles Scribner and Sons, New York.

Girma, S., D. Greenaway and K. Wakelin (1999). "Wages, Productivity and Foreign Ownership in UK Manufacturing", *Research Paper* No. 99/14, Center for Research on Globalisation and Labour Markets, School of Economics, University of Nottingham.

Globerman, S. (1979). "Foreign Direct Investment and Spillover Efficiency Benefits in Canadian Manufacturing Industries", *Canadian Journal of Economics*, 12: 42-56.

Goldar, B.N. and H.N. Saleem (1992). "India's Tariff Structure: Effective Rates of Protection of Indian Industries", *Studies in Industrial Development*, Paper No. 5, Ministry of Industry, Government of India, October.

Goldar, B. and Arup Mitra (2002). "Total Factor Productivity Growth in Indian Manufacturing Industries in the 1990s", in *National Accounts and Data Systems*, B.S. Minhas (ed.), Oxford University Press, New Delhi.

Goldar, Biswanath (2002). "TFP Growth in Indian Manufacturing in 1980s", *Economic and Political Weekly*, December 7: 4966-4968.

Goldar, B. and Anita Kumari (2003). "Import Liberalisation and Productivity Growth in Indian Manufacturing Industries in the 1990s", *The Developing Economies*, XLI (4), December.

Goldar B.N., R. Renganathan and R. Banga (2003). "Ownership and Efficiency in Engineering Firms in India, 1990-91 to 1999-2000", *Economic and Political Weekly*, Vol XXXIX, No. 5, January 31, 2004.

Goldsmith, D. (1976). "Transaction Costs and the Theory of Portfolio Selection", *The Journal of Finance*, Vol. 31, No. 4: 1127-1139.

Good D.H., M.I. Nadiri and R.C. Sickles (1996). "Index Number and Factor Demand Approaches to the Estimation of Productivity", *NBER Working Paper* No. 5790, October.

Gordon, Jim and Poonam Gupta (2003). "Understanding India's Service Revolution", *mimeo* November.

Government of Andhra Pradesh (2001). "Note on Public Distribution System", (Prepared for the Planning Commission).

Grare, Frederic and Amitabh Mattoo (eds.) (2003). *Beyond the Rhetoric – the Economics of India's Look East Policy*, Centre de Sciences Humaines, A publication of the French Research Institutes in India.

Greenwood, J., Zvi Hercowitz and Per Krusell (1997). "Long Run Implications of Investment Specific Technological Change", *Americal Economic Review*, 87 (3): 342-362.

Gruijters, A.P.D. (1991). "De efficientie van valutamarkten: een overzicht", *Maandschrift Economie*, Vol.55 (4): 244-67.

Guha-Khasnobis, Basudeb and Faisal Bari (2003). "Sources of Growth in South Asian Countries", in *The South Asian Experience with Growth*, Isher Judge Ahluwalia and John Williamson (eds.), Oxford University Press, New Delhi.

Gulati, A. and G. Purcell (1995). "Trade Policy, Incentives and Resource Allocation in Indian Agriculture", World Bank, Washington, D.C.

Gylfason, Thorvaldur and Gylfi Zoega (2001). "Natural Resources and Economic Growth: The Role of Investment", *EPRU Working Paper* No. 2001-02, Institute of Economics, University of Copenhagen.

Haass, Richard (1997). *The Reluctant Sheriff*, Council on Foreign Relations; 148 pages.

Haddad, M., J. Demelo and B. Horton (1996). "Morocco, 1984-89: Trade Liberalisation, Exports and Industrial Performance", in Roberts, Mark J. and Tybout, James R, (eds.) *Industrial Evolution in Developing Countries*, Oxford University Press, Oxford: 285-313.

Hall, Robert and Chad I. Jones (1999). "Why Do Some Countries Produce So Much More Output per Worker Than Others?" *Quarterly Journal of Economics*, 114, 1, February: 83-116.

Hamburger, M.L. (1968). "Household Demand for Financial Assets", *Econometrica*, Vol.36, No. 1: 97-118.

Held, David, Anthony McGrew, David Goldblatt and Jonathan Perraton (1999). *Global Transformations, Politics, Economics and Culture*, Polity Press, Cambridge.

Hendricks, Lutz (2000). "Equipment Investment and Growth in Developing Countries", *Journal of Development Economics*, 61, (2000): 335-364.

Hennipman, Pieter (1995). *Welfare Economics and the Theory of Economic Policy*, Brookfield, VT: Edward Elgar.

Hepeng, Jia (2004). "Likely Sino-Indian FTA Conducive to Nation", *China Daily*, April.

Hinds, Manuel (1990). "Issues in the Introduction of Market Forces in Eastern European Socialist Economies", The World Bank, *Report* No. IDP-0057.

Hodrick, R. (1987). *The Empirical Evidence on the Efficiency of Forward and Futures Foreign Exchange Markets*, Harwood.

Hong, Mark (2003). "India-Singapore Relations- A Brief Overview", Institute of South East Asian Studies.

Huang, Yasheng (2003). *Selling China: Foreign Direct Investment During the Reform Era*, Cambridge University Press.

Hulten, Charles R. (1992). "Growth Accounting When Technical Change is Embodied in Capital", *American Economic Review*, 82(4), September: 964-80.

Huntington, Samuel P. (1993). "The Clash of Civilisations", *Foreign Affairs*, May/June.

———. (1996). *The Clash of Civilisations and The Remaking of World Order*, Simon & Schuster, New York.

———. (1999). "The Lonely Superpower", *Foreign Affairs*, March/April.

ICRIER papers on web sites; *http://www.icrier.org* and *http://www.icrier.res.in*.

Ikemoto, K. and R.J.R. Elliott (2003). "AFTA and the Asian Crisis: Help or Hindrance to ASEAN Intra-Regional Trade", The School of Economics *Discussion Paper Series* 0311, School of Economics, The University of Manchester.

Indirect Tax Evasion and Production Efficiency, *Journal of Public Economics*, Vol. 39 (1989): 223-237.

International Labour Organisation (2002). *Yearbook of Labour Statistics*, ILO.

International Monetary Fund (2004). "Advancing Structural Reform", *World Economic Outlook*, April.

———. (various years). "World Economic Outlook", IMF, Washington, DC, USA.

Jenkins, R.O. (1991). "The Impact of Foreign Investment on Less Developing Countries: Cross Section Analysis Versus Industry Study", in P.J. Buckley and J. Clegg, (eds.) *Multinational Enterprises in Less Developed Countries*, Macmillan, Basingstoke.

Jha, R. and I. Longjam (2003). "A Divisia Type Saving Aggregate for India", *Working Paper*, ASARC, Division of Economics, RSPAS, Australian National University.

———. (2003). "Structure of Financial Savings during Indian Economic Reforms", *Working Paper*, ASARC, Division of Economics, RSPAS, Australian National University.

Jha, Shikha and P.V. Srinivasan (2001). "Taking the PDS to the Poor: Directions for Further Reform", *Economic and Political Weekly*, September 29.

Jia, Kang and Zhao Quan-hou (2001). "The Size of China's National Debt", *World Economy and China. http://www.iwep.org.en/wec/english/article/2001_01/jiakang.htm.*

Joshi, Vijay and Ian M.D. Little (1994). *India: Macroeconomics and Political Economy*, World Bank, Washington and Oxford University Press, New Delhi.

———. (1996). *India's Economic Reforms 1991-2001*, Clarendon Press, Oxford.

Kathuria, V. (2001). "Foreign Firms, Technology Transfer and Knowledge Spillovers to Indian Manufacturing firms: A Stochastic Frontier Analysis", *Applied Economics*, 33: 625-642.

Kaufmann, D., A. Kraay and P. Zoido-Lobaton (2002). "Governance Matters II – Updated Indicators for 2000/01", World Bank Policy Research Department, *Working Paper* No. 2772, Washington D.C.

Kearney, A.T., Global Business Policy Council (2001). "FDI Confidence Audit: India".

Keefer, Philip and Mary Shirley (2000). "Formal Versus Informal Institutions in Economic Development", in Claude Menard (ed.) Institutions, Contracts, Organisations: Perspectives from *The New Institutional Economics*, Edward Elgar, Williston VT.

Kennedy, Paul (1988). *The Rise and Fall of the Great Powers: Economic Change and Military Conflict from 1500 to 2000*, Random House, USA.

Keohane, Robert O. and Joseph S. Nye (1977). *Power and Interdependence*, Little Brown & Co, Boston.

Kesavapany, K. (2003). "ASEAN's Contribution to the Building of an Asian Economic Community", *Discussion Paper* No. 50, RIS.

Khanna, T. and Y Huang (2003). "Can India Overtake China", *Foreign Policy*, July/August.

King, M.A. and J.I. Leape (1987). "Asset Accumulation, Information and the Life Cycle", *NBER Working Paper* No. 2392.

King, R.G. and Ross Levine (1993). "Finance, Enterpreneurship and Growth: Theory and Evidence", *Journal of Monetary Economics*, 32: 513-542. Carnegie-Rochester Conference Series on Public Policy. June.

———. (1994). "Capital Fundamentalism, Economic Development and Economic Growth", Carnegie-Rochester Conference Series on Public Policy.

Kissinger, Henry A. (1994). *Diplomacy*, Simon & Schuster, New York.

Kokko, A., R. Tansini and M.C. Zejan (1996). "Local Technological Capability and Productivity Spillovers from FDI in the Uruguayan Manufacturing Sector", *Journal of Development Studies* 32 (4), April: 602-1.

Krauthammer, Charles (1990). "The Unipolar Moment", *Foreign Affairs*, America and The World, 1990/91.

Krishna, K.L. (2002). "Industrial Growth and Diversification", in Uma Kapila (ed.), *Indian Economy Since Independence*, 14th edition, Academic Foundation, New Delhi.

Krishna, P. and D. Mitra (1998). "Trade Liberalisation, Market Discipline and Productivity Growth: New Evidence from India", *Journal of Development Economics*, 56: 447-62.

Krishnamurthy, J. (1970). "Industrial Distribution of the Working Force in India, 1901-1961: A Study of Selected Aspects", PhD Thesis, Delhi School of Economics, Dept of Economics.

Kumar, N. and N.S. Siddharthan (1997). *Technology, Market Structure and Internationalisation*, Routledge New York and London.

Kumar, N. (1998). "Multinational Enterprises, Regional Economic Integration, and Export-Platform Production in the Host Countries: An Empirical Analysis for the US and Japanese Corporations", *Weltwirtschaftliches Archiv*, 134 (3): 450-83.

Kumar, Praduman (1998). "Food Demand and Supply Projections for India", *Agricultural Economics Policy Paper* 98-01, (IARI), New Delhi.

Kumar, Nagesh (2002). "Towards an Asian Economic Community-Vision of Closer Economic Cooperation in Asia: An Overview".

———. (2002). "Towards an Asian Economic Community: The Relevance of India", *Discussion Paper* No. 34, RIS.

Kuppuswamy, C.S. (2000). "India's Policy-looking Eastward", *Paper* No. 176, South Asia Analysis Group.

———. (2003). "India's Look East Policy: Gaining Momentum with the Prime Minister's Visit", *Paper* No. 819, South Asia Analysis Group.

Lall, S. and P. Streeten (1977). "Foreign Investment, Transnationals and Developing Countries", MacMillan, London.

Lall, S. and S. Mohammad (1983). "Multinationals in Indian Big Business: Industrial Characteristics of Foreign Investments in a Heavily Regulated Economy", *Journal of Developing Economics*, 13: 143-57.

Lange, Oscar (1971). "On The Economic Theory of Socialism", in Goldman, M.I. (ed.) *Comparative Economic Systems*, New York.

Lardy, Nicholas R. (1992). *Foreign Trade and Economic Reform in China*, 1978-1990, Cambridge University Press, Cambridge.

———. (1998). *China's Unfinished Economic Revolution*, Brookings, Washington DC.

———. (1999). "The Macro-economic Context: The Challenge of Bank Restructuring in China", Strengthening the Banking System in China: Issues and Experience, *BIS Policy Papers* No. 7, October.

Lau, Lawrence, J., Yingyi Qian and Gerard Roland (2000). "Reform Without Losers: An Interpretation of China's Dual-Track Approach to Transition", *The Journal of Political Economy*, Vol 108, No. 1, February: 120-143.

Lee, J.W. (1995). "Capital Goods Imports and Long Run Growth", *Journal of Development Economics*, 48(1): 91-110.

Lee, T.H. (1964). "Income, Wealth, and the Demand for Money: Some Evidence from Cross - Section Data", *American Statistical Association Journal*, September: 746-762.

———. (1966). "Substitutability of Non-bank Intermediary Liabilities for Money: The Empirical Evidence", *The Journal of Finance*, Vol. 21, No. 3: 441-457.

Lerner, Abba, P. (1934). "Economic Theory and Socialist Economy", *Review of Economic Studies*, (Rejoinder in RES 1935).

Levy, Brian and Pablo Spiller (1994). "The Institutional Foundations of Regulatory Commitment: A Comparative Analysis of Telecom Regulation", *Journal of Law, Economics and Organisation*, 10, No. 1 (October): 201-246.

Levy, Jack (1983). *War in the Modern Great Power System, 1945-1975*, University Press of Kentucky, Lexington.

Lewis, K.K. (1995). "Puzzles in International Financial Markets", in G. Grossman, K. Rogoff (eds.) *Handbook of International Economics*, Vol.3. Elsevier: 1913-71.

Lingle, Christopher (1995). "The Propoganda Way", *Foreign Affairs*, May/June.

Lucas, R.E.B. (1989). "Liberalising of Indian Trade and Industrial Licensing: A Disaggregated Econometric Model with Simulations", *Journal of Development Economics*.

Lydall, H.F. (1958). "Income, Assets and the Demand for Money", *Review of Economics and Statistics*, 40: 1-14.

Macintyre, Andrew (2003). "Institutions and Political Economy of Corruption in Developing Countries", *Working Paper*, Workshop on Corruption, Stanford University, Jan-Feb.

Mahbubani, Kishore (1995). "The Pacific Way", *Foreign Affairs*, 74 Jan./Feb.: 100-103.

———. (1997). "An Asia-Pacific Conscensus", *Foreign Affairs*, September/October.

Manning, Robert A. and Paula Stern (1994). "The Myth of Pacific Community", *Foreign Affairs*, November/December.

Martin, Dufwenberg and Guth Werner (1999). "Indirect Evolution Versus Strategic Delegation: A Comparison of Two Approaches to Explaining Economic Institutions", *European Journal of Political Economy*: 281-95.

Mayfield, E.S. and R.G. Murphy (1992). "Interest Rate Parity and the Exchange Risk Premium: Evidence from Panel Data", *Economics Letters*, Vol.40 (3) November: 319-24.

Mayshar, J. (1981). "Transaction Costs and the Pricing of Assets", *The Journal of Finance*, Vol. 36, No. 3: 583-597.

Mazumdar, J. (1996). "Do Static Gains from Trade Lead to Medium Run Growth?" *Journal of Political Economy*, 104(6): 1328-37.

McCallum, B.T. (1994). "A Reconsideration of the Uncovered Interest Parity Relationship", *Journal of Monetary Economics*, Vol.33 (1) February: 105-32.

McCord, William (1991). *The Dawn of The Pacific Century: Implications For Three Worlds of Development*, Transaction, New Brunswick, NJ.

McDougall, Walter, Promised Land, Crusader State: The American Encounter with the World Since 1776, Houghton Mifflin.

McFarland, J.W., P.C. McMahon and Y. Ngama (1994). "Forward Exchange Rates and Expectations during the 1920s: A Re-examination of the Evidence", *Journal of International Finance*, Vol.13 (6) December: 627-36.

Mearshiemer, John (2001). *The Tragedy of Great Power Politics*, W.W. Norton & Co., New York.

Meenakshi, J.V. (2001). "The Public Distribution System in the Context of Changing Food Consumption Trends: A review of the Evidence", (Prepared for the Planning Commission).

Mehta, Rajesh (2002). "Establishment of Free Trade Arrangement Among BIMST-EC Countries: Some Issues", *Discussion Paper* No. 23, RIS.

———. (2002). "Potential of India's Bilateral Free Trade Arrangements: A Case Study of India and Thailand", *Discussion Paper* No. 24, RIS.

Ministry of Consumer Affairs and Public Distribution (2000). "National Policy on Handling, Storage and Transportation of Foodgrains", Government of India.

Ministry of Finance, Department of Revenue, (1991). *Tax Reforms Committee: Interim Report*, New Delhi, December.

———. (1992). "Tax Reforms Committee Final Report Part I", GoI, New Delhi, August.

———. (1993). "Tax Reform Committee: Final Report Part II", GoI, New Delhi.

———. (1993). Report of the Committee on, "Extension of MODVAT to Textiles", GoI, June-July.

———. (2000). "Report of The Expenditure Reforms Commission on Food Subsidy", Government of India.

———. (2001). Report of the Inter-Ministerial Working Group on, "Customs Tariff Reform", GoI, New Delhi, November.

———. *Economic Survey*, Government of India, various issues.

Ministry of Finance & Company Affairs (2002). "Task Force on Indirect Taxes: Consultation", *Paper*, GoI, New Delhi, October.

Mohanty, S.K. (2003). "Possibility of Close Economic Cooperation between India and Singapore", *Discussion Paper* No. 45, RIS.

Muhleisen, M. (1997). "Improving India's Saving Performance", *Finance & Development*, June: 38-41.

Mujumdar, N.A., T.R. Venkatachalam and M.V. Raghavachari (1980). "The High Saving Phase of the Indian Economy: 1976-79 - An Exploratory Interpretation", *RBI Occasional Papers*, Vol. 1, No 1, June: 1-32.

Mundell, Robert A. (1968). *International Economics*, Macmillan Co., New York.

Nadiri, M.I. (1991). "U.S. Direct Investment and the Production Structure of the Manufacturing Sector in France, Germany, Japan and U.K.", *mimeo*, New York University and NBER, December.

Nagai, Fumio (2002). "Thailand's Trade Policy: WTO Plus FTA?" *Working Paper Series* 01/02 APEC Study Center Institute of Developing Economies.

Nagaraj, R. (1990). "Growth Rate of India's GDP, 1950-51 to 1987-88: Examination of Alternative Hypotheses", *Economic and Political Weekly*, June 30.

Naik, Gopal (2001). "Agricultural Support Programme for Farm Income Protection". (Prepared for Ministry of Agriculture).

Nakagawa, S. and S. Tomoko (1999). "Portfolio Selection of Financial Assets by Japan's Households", *Bank of Japan Monthly Bulletin*, November.

Nambiar, R.G., B.L. Mumgekar and G.A. Tadas (1999). "Is Import Liberalisation Hurting Domestic Industry and Employment?" *Economic and Political Weekly*, February 13, 34: 417-424.

National Accounts Statistics (2004). *Supply New Series*, Floppy disc containing current and constant price (1993-94 prices) data by State.

Nayyar, Deepak (1976). *India's Exports and Export Policies in the Sixties*, Cambridge Universtiy Press, Cambridge.

Nayyar, D. (1983). "International Relocation of Production and Industrialisation in LDCs", *Economic and Political Weekly*, 18: PE 13-26.

NCAER (2000). *Protection in Indian Industry*, National Council of Applied Economic Research, New Delhi.

Nehru, V. and A. Dhareshwar (1993). "A New Database on Physical Capital Stock: Sources, Methodology and Results", *Revista de Analisis Economiico*, Vol. 8: 3-59 [cited in Guha-Khasnobis and Bari (2003)].

Newbery, David M.G. and Joseph E. Stiglitz (1981). *The Theory of Commodity Price Stabilisation*, Clarendon Press, Oxford.

Nicita, A. and M. Olarreaga (2001). "Trade and Production, 1976-1999", *Working Paper* No.: 2701, Development Research Group, World Bank.

Niskanen, W.A. (1973). *Bureaucracy: Servant or Master?* Institute of Economic Affairs, London.

North, Douglass C. (1990). "Institutions, Institutional Change and Economic Performance", Cambridge University Press, New York.

———. (1994). "Economic Performance through Time", *The American Economic Review*, Vol. 84, No. 3 (June): 359-68.

Nouroz, H. (2001). *Protection in Indian Manufacturing: An Empirical Study*, MacMillan India Ltd., New Delhi.

Nye, Joseph S. (1990). "Soft Power", *Foreign Policy*, No. 80, Fall.

———. (1999). "Redefining The National Interest", *Foreign Affairs*, July/August.

———. (2003). "U.S. Power and Strategy After Iraq", *Foreign Affairs*, July/August.

Panchmukhi, V.R. and Rehman Sobhan (eds.) (1995). *Towards An Asian Economic Area*, Macmillan India Limited.

Parikh, Kirit (1999). "Food Security: Individual and National", Indira Gandhi Institute of Development Research, Mumbai.

Parthasarathy, B., A.A. Munot, and D.R. Kothawale (1995). *Monthly and Seasonal Rainfall series for All-India*, Homogeneous Regions and Meteorological Subdivisions: 1871-1994, Research Report No. RR - 65, Indian Institute of Tropical Meteorology, Pune.

Parthasarathi, Shome (1997). *Value-Added Tax in India: A Progress Report* Centax Publications, New Delhi.

Patel, I.G. (2002). *Glimpses of Indian Economic Policy: An Insiders View*, Oxford University Press.

Patibandla, Murali (1999). "Internal Policy Reforms and Market Structure in an Emerging Economy: The Case of India", *Working Paper* No. 7-1999, Department of Economics and Management, Copenhagen Business School.

Patnaik, Prabhat (1987). "Recent Growth Experience of the Indian Economy", *Economic and Political Weekly*, Annual Number, May, 1990.

Paxson, C. (1990). "Borrowing Constraints and Portfolio Choice", *Quarterly Journal of Economics*, 105: 535-543.

Perkins, Dwight (1988). "Reforming China's Economic System", *Journal of Economic Literature*, Vol. 26, No. 2, June: 601-645.

———. (1994). "Completing China's Move to Market", *Journal of Economic Perspectives*, Vol. 8, No. 2, Spring: 23-46.

Perkovich, George (2003). "The Measure of India: What MakesGreatness", 2003 Annual Fellows Lecture, Center for the Advanced Study of India, University of Pennsylvania, April.

Pesek, B.P. (1963). "Determinants of the Demand for Money", *Review of Economics and Statistics*, 45: 419-424.

Phillips, P.C.B., J.W. McFarland and P.C. McMahon (1996). "Robust Tests of Forward Exchange Market Efficiency with Empirical Evidence from the 1920s", *Journal of Applied Econometrics*, Vol.11 (1) Jan-Feb: 1-22.

Planning Commission (2000). "Mid-Term Appraisal of the Ninth Five Year Plan".

———. (2001). "India's 1990-91 Crisis: Reforms, Myths and Paradoxes", *Working Paper* No. 4/2001-PC, Planning Commission, December.

———. (2001). "Report of the Working Group on Public Distribution System and Food Security for the Tenth Five Year Plan".

Pradhan, B.K., M.R. Saluja, P.K. Roy, S.L. Shetty (2003). "Household Savings and Investment Behaviour in India", *Economic and Political Weekly,* Research Foundation.

Prasad, Eswar and Shang-Jin Wei (2005). "The Chinese Approach to Capital Inflows: Patterns and Possible Explanations", *NBER Working Paper* No. 11306, April.

Pritchet, Lant (1997). "Divergence, Big Time", *Journal of Economic Perspectives* 11: 3-17.

Raj, K.N. (1962). "The Marginal Rate of Savings in the Indian Economy", *Oxford Economic Papers,* 14(1).

———. (1984). "Some Observations on Economic Growth in India over the Period 1952-53 to 1982-83", *Economic and Political Weekly,* October 13.

———. (1986). "New Economic Policy", Second V.T. Krishnanmachari Memorial Lecture, 1985, delivered at the Institute of Economic Growth, Oxford University Press.

Rajakumar, J.D. (2000). "Financing Patterns and Investment: A Study of the Private Corporate Sector in India", unpublished Ph.D Thesis submitted to the Jawaharlal Nehru University, New Delhi, Centre for Development Studies, Trivandrum.

Rajeev, P.V. (1997). "Poverty and Food Security in India", *Southern Economist,* January 15.

Rao, C.H. Hanumantha (2000). "Declining Demand for Foodgrains in Rural India – Causes and Implications", *Economic and Political Weekly,* January 22.

Rao, V.K.R.V. (1980). "Savings, Capital formation and National Income", *Economic and Political Weekly,* 15, 22.

Reserve Bank of India (1998). "Flow of Funds Accounts of the Indian Economy: 1990-91 to 1993-94", *RBI Bulletin,* January.

———. Annual reports, various issues.

———. (2000). *Handbook of Statistics on the Indian Economy,* (CD ROM).

———. (2002). *Report on Currency and Finance – 2001-02.*

———. (2003). *Handbook of Statistics on the Indian Economy 2002-03,* CD-ROM.

———. (various years). *Reserve Bank of India Bulletin,* RBI.

Rodriguez, Francisco and Dani Rodrik (1999). "Trade Policy and Economic Growth: A Sceptics Guide to Cross-National Evidence", *NBER Working Paper* No. w 7081, April.

Rodrik, Dani (2000). "Institutions for High Quality Growth: What they are and how to acquire them," Studies in *Comparative International Development,* Vol. 35, No. 3, Fall.

———. (2003a). "Growth Strategies", *NBER Working Paper* No. 10050, October.

———. (2003b). "Institution, Integration and Geography: In Search of The Deep Determinants of Economic Growth", in Rodrik (ed.), *In Search of Prosperity: Analytic Country Studies on Growth,* Princeton University Press, Princeton, NJ.

———. (2003c). "Introduction", in Dani Rodrik (ed.), *In Search of Prosperity: Analytic Narratives on Economic Growth,* Princeton University Press, Princeton.

Rodrik, Dani and Arvind Subramanian (2004a). "Why India Can Grow at 7 Per cent a Year or More: Projections and Reflections", International Monetary Fund, *Working Paper No. 04/118,* July.

———. (2004b). "From 'Hindu Growth' Rate To Productivity Surge: The Mystery of The Indian Growth Transition", *NBER Working Paper* No. 10376, March.

Rodrik, Dani, Arvind Subramanian and Francesco Trebbi (2002). "Institutions Rule: The Primacy of Institutions over Geography and Integration in Economic Development".

Rybezynski, T.M. (1986). "The Internationalisation of the Financial System and the Developing Countries: The Evolving Relationship", *World Bank Staff Working Paper* No. 788.

Sebastian, Morris (2001). "Societal Change, States and Governance: Insights from History and other Societies", *IIMA Working Paper* No. 2001-10-02, Research and Publication Department, Indian Institute of Management, Ahmedabad.

———. (2001). "The Challenge of Governance of India Today", *IIMA Working Paper* No. 2001-10-01, Research and Publication Department, Indian Institute of Management, Ahmedabad.

Segal, Gerald (1999). "Does China Matter?" *Foreign Affairs*, Vol. 78, No. 5, September-October.

Sen, Rahul, Mukul G. Asher and Ramkishen S. Rajan (2004). "ASEAN-India Economic Relations: Current Status and Future Prospects", *Discussion Paper* No. 73, RIS.

Senhadji, Abdelhak (1999). "Sources of Economic Growth: An Extensive Growth Accounting Exercise", *International Monetary Fund Working Paper* No. WP/99/77, IMF Institute, June.

Shah, Ajay (1999). "Institutional Change in India's Capital Market", *Economic and Political Weekly*, January 16-23.

Shah, Ajay, and Susan Thomas (2002). "Evolution of the Securities Markets in India in the 1990s", *Working Paper* No. 91, Indian Council of Research on International Economic Relations (ICRIER), New Delhi, December. (*www.icrier.org*).

Sharma, A.N. (1997). "Trends in Structure and Pattern of Employment and Unemployment in India", *Institute of Economic Growth Working Paper* No. E/188/97.

Sharma, Anil (2001). "Minimum Support Prices and the Excessive Stocks of Wheat and Rice", National Council of Applied Economic Research.

Sheng-Jin Wei (2005). "Pitfalls of a State Dominated Financial System: The Case of China", *NBER Working Paper* No. W11181, March.

Shetty, S.L. (1990). "Saving Behaviour in India In the 1980s", *Economic and Political Weekly*, March 17: 555-560.

Shleifer, A. and M. Vishney (1993). "Corruption", *Quarterly Journal of Economics*, Vol 108, No. 3: 599-617.

Shorrocks, A. (1982). "The Portfolio Composition of Asset Holdings in the United Kingdom", *The Economic Journal*, Vol. 92, No. 366: 268-284.

Siddharthan, N.S. (2001). "Technology Transfer, WTO, and Emerging Issues", *mimeo*, Institute of Economic Growth.

Simon, Herbert A. (1962). "The Architecture of Complexity", Proceedings of the American Philosophical Society, 10 (December): 467-482.

Singer, Bremer and Stuckey (1972). "Capability Distribution, Uncertainty, and Major Power War", in Bruce M Russet, *Peace, War and Numbers*, Sage Publications, Beverly Hills.

Singh, Swaran (2005). "China India Economic Engagement – Building Mutual Confidence", *Occasional Paper* No.10, *Centre de Sciences Humaines*.

Singh, Manmohan (1964). "India's Export Trends and The Prospects for Self-sustained Growth", Clarendon Press, Oxford.

Sivasubramonian, S. (2000). "The National Income of India in the Twentieth Century", Oxford University Press, New Delhi.

Srinivasan, T.N. (1996). "Trade Orientation, Trade Liberalisation and Economic Growth", Yale University, New Haven, Connecticut.

———. (1998). "India's Export Performance: A Comparative Analysis", in I.J. Ahluwalia and I.M.D. Little (eds.), *India's Economic Reforms and Development: Essays for Manmohan Singh*, Oxford University Press, Delhi.

———. (2000). *Eight Lectures on India's Economic Reforms*, Oxford University Press.

———. (2002). "China and India: Economic Performance, Competition and Cooperation - An Update", paper presented at a seminar on *WTO Accession, Policy Reform and Poverty* sponsored by the World Trade Organisation in Beijing.

Srinivasan, T.N. and N.S.S. Narayana (1977). "Economic Performance Since The Third Plan and Its Implications for Policy", *Economic and Political Weekly*, Vol. XII, Nos. 6, 7 and 8, February.

Srivastava, V. (1996). "Liberalisation, Productivity and Competition: A Panel Study of Indian Manufacturing", Oxford University Press, Delhi.

———. (2000). "The Impact of India's Economic Reforms on Industrial Productivity, Efficiency and Competitiveness", report of a project sponsored by the Industrial Development Bank of India and NCAER, New Delhi.

Srivastava, Sadhana and Ramkishen S. Rajan (2003). "Implications of the Economic Rise of the PRC for ASEAN and India: Trade and Foreign Direct Investment", *IPS Working Paper* No. 14.

Subrahmaniam, G. and S.B. Swami (1995). "A Direct Translog Model of India's Household Sector Financial Portfolios", *Indian Economic Review*, 30, 2: 265-274.

Subrahmaniam, K., M. Granger Morgan, K. Sunderji and Robert M. White (1995). "India and The United States", *Washington Quarterly*.

Sundaram, K. (2001). "Employment and Poverty in the 1990's Furthur Results from NSS 55th Round Employment-Unemployment Survey 1999-2000", *Economic and Political Weekly*, Special Article, August.

Sung, Yun-Wang (1991). *The China-Hong Kong Connection: The Key to China's Open Door Policy*, Cambridge University Press, Cambridge.

Sutter, Robert G. (1992). *East Asia and The Pacific: Challenges for US Policy*, Westview Press, Boulder.

Tanham, George (1992). "Indian Strategic Culture," *Washington Quarterly*, Vol. 15, No. 1, Winter.

Tellis, Ashley J., Janice Bially, Christopher Layne, Melissa Mcpherson (2000). *Measuring National Power in the Post industrial Age: Analysis Handbook*, Rand, Santa Monica.

(1983). "The Microeconomics of a Corrupt Tax Bureaucracy", *DRD Discussion Paper* No. 54, World Bank, May.

Topalova, Petia (2003). "Trade Liberalisation and Firm Productivity: The Case of India", Yale University.

Tseng, Wanda and Harm Zebergs (2002). "Foreign Direct Investment in China: Some Lessons for Other Countries", International Monetary Fund Policy *Discussion Paper*, February.

Tsou, M.W. and J.T. Liu (1998). "The Spillover Effect from FDI: Empirical Evidence from Taiwan Manufacturing Industries", *Taiwan Economic Review*, 6: 155-81. *www.econ.yale.edu/seminars/NEUDC03/topalova1.pdf.*

Uhler, R.S. and J.G. Cragg (1971). "The Structure of the Asset Portfolios of Households", *The Review of Economic Studies*, Vol. 38, No. 3: 341-357.

UNCTAD (2004). Press release, Jan 12.

———. (various issues). World Investment Reports.

———. (2002b). "Handbook of Statistics 2002", UNCTAD.

———. [Online (b)]. "Handbook of Statistics Online", UNCTAD. *http://stats.unctad.org/restricted/eng/ReportFolders/Rfview/Explorerp.asp*

Unel, Bulent (2003). "Productivity Trends in India's Manufacturing Sectors in the Last Two Decades", *IMF Working Paper* No. 03/02.

United Nations (2003). "World Population Prospects: The 2002 Revision", Population Division of the Department of Economic and Social Affairs of the United Nations Secretariat, <*http://esa.un.org/unpp*>

Varma, J.R. (1997). "Indian Money Market: Market Structure, Covered Parity and Term Structure", *The ICFAI Journal of Applied Finance*, 3(2): 1-10.

Veeramani, Choorikhad (2003). "Liberalisation, Industry-specific Factors and Intra-Industry Trade in India", *ICRIER Working Paper* No. 97, March.

———. (2004). "Trade Liberalisation, Multinational Involvement And Intra-Industry Trade in Manufacturing", *ICRIER Working Paper* No. 143, September.

Virmani, Arvind (1982). "The Nature of Credit Markets in Developing Countries", *World Bank Staff Working Paper* No. 525, World Bank.

———. (1986a). "Implications for a VAT in India: The Deductibility System", *DRD Discussion Paper* No. 165, World Bank.

———. (1986b). "Measuring Income Tax Incentives Under Evasion: Effective Average and Marginal Rate Schedules", *DRD Discussion Paper* No. 187, World Bank, September.

———. (1987). "Tax Evasion, Corruption and Administration: Monitoring Tax Auditors Under Symmetric Dishonesty", paper presented at the *Conference on Political Economy: Theory and Policy Implications*, Washington, June.

———. (1988). "Tax Reform in Developing Countries: Issues, Policies and Information Gaps", *Public Finance* Vol. 43, No. 1: 19-37.

———. (1989a). "Growth, Capital and Employment: Performance in Perspective", *Economic Research Paper* No. 3, February, Planning Commission (processed).

———. (1989b). "Credit Markets in Developing Countries: Myth and Reality", *Greek Economic Review*, Vol. 11, No. 1 (June).

———. (1989c). "Indirect Tax Evasion and Production Effeciency", *Journal of Public Economics*, Vol. 39: 223-237.

———. (1990a). "Saving Performance and Prospects: A Historical Perspective", in Roy Choudhury and Bagchi (eds.) *Domestic Savings in India: Trends and Issues.*

———. (1990b). "International Trade and Balance of Payments", in *Eighth Plan Perspectives*, M.S. Adiseshiah (ed.), Lancer International, Delhi.

———. (1990c). "Size and Role of Government: Quality vs. Quantity of Intervention", *Indian Economic Journal*, Vol. 37, No. 4, April-June.

———. (1991). "Demand and Supply Factors in India's Trade", *Economic and Political Weekly*, Vol. XXVI, No. 6, February 9.

———. (1992a). "Trends in Current Account Deficit and the Balance of Trade: Separating Facts From Prejudices", *Journal of Foreign Exchange and International Finance*, Vol. VI, No. 1, April-June: 72-78.

———. (1992b). "Partial Convertibility of the Rupee (PCR) Implications for Exporters", *RBI Bulletin*, August: 1300-2.

———. (1996). "Policy Framework for Power", August, *Chintan Policy Paper* No. 20. *http://finance.nic.in/avirmani.*

———. (1997a). "An Agenda for Tax Reform", *Chintan Policy Paper* No. 2, May.

———. (1997b). "India: Crises, Reform and Growth", *Economic and Political Weekly*, August 9.

———. (1997c). "Economic Development and Transition: India", presented at the *Tokyo Dialogue on Alternatives to the World Bank–IMF Approach to Reforms and Growth*, organised by the Economic Planning Agency, December 7, in Tokyo, Japan.

———. (1997d). "A New Foreign Exchange Act (FEA)", *Chintan Policy Paper* No. 3, June.

———. (1997e). "Exchange Rate Management", *Chintan Policy Paper* No. 5, December.

———. (1998). "Macro-management of Economic Growth with Underemployed Labour and Technological Inertia", ADB-World Bank Senior Policy Seminar on *Managing Global Financial Integration in Asia*, Manila, Philippines: 10-12, March.

———. (1999a). "From Poverty To Middle Income: Reforms for Accelerating Growth in the 21st Century," *Chintan Monograph*, April. *http://www.icrier.org/avpapers*

———. (1999b). "Star Performers of the 20th (21st) Century: Asian Tigers, Dragons or Elephants", *Occasional Paper, Chintan*, September. *www.icrier.org/avpapers.html*.

———. (1999c). "Potential Growth Stars of the 21st Century: India, China and The Asian Century", *Occasional Paper, Chintan*, October. *www.icrier.org/avpapers.html*

———. (1999d). "Agenda for Reforms: Fiscal", *Chintan Policy Paper* No. 12, October.

———. (1999e). "Urban Infrastructure, Real Estate & Housing Policy: Eliminating Slums and generating Employment", *Chintan Policy Paper* No. 8, May.

———. (1999f). "Agenda for Reform: External", *Chintan Policy Paper* No. 14, December.

———. (1999g). "Capital Account Convertibility: Timing and Phasing", *Chintan Policy Paper* No. 16, December.

———. (2000a). "A Communication Policy for the 21st Century", *Economic and Political Weekly*, Volume XXXV, No. 23, June 3-9: 1907-1910.

———. (2000b). "Policy for Investment Revival", *Chintan Policy Paper* No. 21, October. *http://www.icrier.org/avpapers*,

———. (2001a). "Central Value Added Tax: CENVAT", *Economic and Political Weekly*, Vol. XXXVI No. 8, February 24-March 2: 630-632.

———. (2001b). "India's 1990-91 Crisis: Reforms, Myths and Paradoxes", *Planning Commission Working Paper* No. 4/2001-PC, December. *www.planningcommission.nic.in/reports/wrkpapers/rpwpf.htm*

———. (2002a). "Towards a Competitive Economy: VAT and Customs Duty Reform," *Planning Commission Working Paper* No. 4/2002-PC, April). *http://planningcommission.nic.in/reports/wrkpapers/rpwpf.htm*.

———. (2002b). "A New Development Paradigm: Employment, Entitlement and Empowerment", *Economic and Political Weekly*, Vol. XXXVII No. 22, June 1-7: 2145-2154.

———. (2002b). "A New Development Paradigm: Employment, Entitlement and Empowerment", *Global Business Review*, International Management Institute, Vol. 3, No. 2, July-December: 222-45.

———. (2002c). *Bharatiya Rate of Growth: The Role of Services*, September. *www.planningcommission.nic.in/artf.html* and *http://www.icrier.org/avnotes*

———. (2002d). "India's BoP Crisis and External Reforms: Myths and Paradoxes", *ICRIER Public Policy Workshop Paper*, December. *http://www.icrier.org/avpapers*

———. and P.V. Rajeev (2002). "Excess Food Stocks, PDS, and Procurement Policy", *Planning Commission Working Paper* No. 5/2002-PC, Planning Commission, January. *http://www.planningcommission.nic.in/reports/wrkpapers/rpwpf.htm*

———. (2003). "India's External Reforms: Modest Globalisation Significant Gains", *Economic and Political Weekly*, Vol. XXXVII No. 32, August 9-15: 3373-3390.

———. (2004a). "Accelerating Growth and Poverty Reduction – A Policy Framework for India's Development", Academic Foundation, New Delhi.

———. (2004b). "Economic Reforms: Policy and Institutions, Some Lessons from Indian Reforms", *Working Paper* No. 121, Indian Council for Research on International Economic Relations, January. *http://www.icrier.org or http://www.icrier.res.in.*

———. (2004c). "India's Economic Growth: From Socialist Rate of Growth to Bharatiya Rate of Growth", *ICRIER Working Paper* No. 122, February. *www.icrier.org/wp122.pdf.*

———. (2004d). "Sources of India's Economic Growth: Trends in Total Factor Productivity", *ICRIER Working Paper* No. 131, May. *www.icrier.org/wp131.pdf.*

———. (2004e). "Economic Performance, Power Potential and Global Governance: Towards a New International Order", *ICRIER Working Paper* No. 150, December. *www.icrier.org/wp150.pdf.*

Virmani, Arvind and Bishwanath Goldar, Choorikkad Veeramani and Vipul Bhatt (2004). "Impact of Tariff Reforms on Indian Industry: Assessment Based on A Multi-Sector Econometric Model", *ICRIER Working Paper* No. 135, June.

Virmani, Arvind and Amita Batra (2004). "Response to East Asian Regionalism and its Impact – The Indian View", paper presented at the conference on *East Asian Regionalism and its Impact*, IAPS, CASS, Beijing, October 21-22.

———. (2005a). "A Tripolar Century: USA, China and India", *ICRIER Working Paper* No. 160, March. *www.icrier.org/wp160.pdf.*

———. (2005b). "China's Socialist Market Economy: Lessons of Success", *ICRIER Occasional Policy Paper*, April. *http://www.icrier.org/China05_policy7.pdf.*

———. (2005c). "A Tripolar World: India, China and USA", *ICRIER Public Lecture*, May. *www.icrier.org/public/TripolarWrld_IHC4c.pdf.*

Visaria, Praveen (2002). "Workforce and Employment in India, 1961-94", in B.S. Minhas (ed.), *National Income Accounts and Data Systems*, OUP.

Wadhva, Charan (1990). "Economic Advisory Council's Report on the Economy: An Appraisal", *Economic and Political Weekly*, Vol. XXV, No. 9, March 3.

Wallack, Jessica S. (2003). "Structural Breaks in Indian Macroeconomic Data", *Economic and Political Weekly*, October 11.

Waltz, Kenneth (1979). *Theory of International Politics*, Addison-Wesley, Reading.

Wei, Shang-Jin (1997). "Gradualism *Versus* Big Bang: Speed and Sustainability of Reforms", *Canadian Journal of Economics*, 30 (4B): 1234-47.

———. (1999). "Can China and India Double Their Inward Foreign Direct Investment?" NBER/NCAER Conference.

Williamson, John and Roberto Zagha (2002). "From the Hindu Rate of Growth to the Hindu Rate of Reform", *Working Paper* No. 144, Centre for Research on Economic Development and Policy Reform, Stanford University, USA, July.

Williamson, Oliver E. (2000). "The New Institutional Economics: Taking Stock, Looking Ahead", *Journal of Economic Literature*, 38: 595-613.

———. (2002). "The Lens of Contract: Applications To Economic Development and Reform", April, USAID-IRIS Forum series on the *Role of Institutions in Promoting Growth*.

Willmore, Larry (1992). "Transnationals and Foreign Trade: Evidence from Brazil", *Journal of Development Studies*, 28 (2): 314-335.

Wilson, Dominic and Roopa Purushothaman (2003). "Dreaming with BRICs: The Path to 2050", *Global Economics Paper* No. 99, Goldman Sachs.

World Bank (2001). *Finance for Growth*, Oxford University Press.

———. (2001). *World Development Indicators*, (CD ROM).

———. (2001). "India: Improving Household Food and Nutrition Security", Rural Development Sector Unit, South Asia Region.

———. (2002). *World Development Indicators*, CD-ROM, Washington D.C., The World Bank Group.

———. (2004). *World Development Indicators*, CD ROM.

World Trade Organisation (2001). *World Merchandise Trade by Regions and Categories*, Selected Years, WTO Website.

Young, Alwyn (2000). "Gold into Base Metals: Productivity Growth in The People's Republic of China during the Reform Period", *NBER Working Paper* No. 7856, August.

Zabel, E. (1973). "Consumer Choice, Portfolio Decisions and Transaction Costs", *Econometrica*, Vol.41, No.2: 321-335.

# Index

## B



## C

## D

# F

## L



## M

## N

# O

# P

## Q



## R

## T

# U

## X



## Y



## Z